Schizophrenia Research and Care—Advancements and Challenges

Schizophrenia Research and Care—Advancements and Challenges

Editor

Armida Mucci

MDPI

Basel • Beijing • Wuhan • Barcelona • Belgrade • Novi Sad • Cluj • Manchester

Editor
Armida Mucci
University of Campania
"Luigi Vanvitelli"
Naples
Italy

Editorial Office
MDPI
St. Alban-Anlage 66
4052 Basel, Switzerland

This is a reprint of articles from the Special Issue published online in the open access journal *Journal of Clinical Medicine* (ISSN 2077-0383) (available at: https://www.mdpi.com/journal/jcm/special_issues/Schizophrenia_Care?authAll=true).

For citation purposes, cite each article independently as indicated on the article page online and as indicated below:

Lastname, A.A.; Lastname, B.B. Article Title. *Journal Name* **Year**, *Volume Number*, Page Range.

ISBN 978-3-0365-9816-1 (Hbk)
ISBN 978-3-0365-9817-8 (PDF)
doi.org/10.3390/books978-3-0365-9817-8

Contents

About the Editor

Armida Mucci

Armida Mucci, MD, PhD in Neuroscience. The Guest Editor of this Special Issue is a Full Professor of Psychiatry at the University of Campania Luigi Vanvitelli, as well as the Director of the School of Specialization in Psychiatry and the Rector Delegate for the Ph.D. programs at the same university. Her research interests lie in the fields of pharmaco-EEG, event-related potentials, brain electrical activity mapping, on factors associated with real-life functioning in schizophrenia, cognitive and brain imaging correlates of negative symptoms and cognitive remediation approaches. She is the Co-Chair of the European College of Neuropsychopharmacology (ECNP) Schizophrenia Network and the Chair of the Italian Society of Psychosocial Rehabilitation. She has actively participated in many international and national workshops and congresses as a speaker, a member of the scientific committee or as the chairperson. She has published approximately 277 papers in scientific journals and in national and international books. Her publication track record is as follows: Scopus H-index, 43; Google Scholar H-index, 51; total number of Scopus citations, 5656.

Journal of
Clinical Medicine

MDPI

Viewpoint

Schizophrenia: A Narrative Review of Etiopathogenetic, Diagnostic and Treatment Aspects

Laura Orsolini, Simone Pompili and Umberto Volpe *

Unit of Clinical Psychiatry, Department of Clinical Neurosciences/Department of Experimental and Clinical Medicine (DIMSC), Polytechnic University of Marche, 60126 Ancona, Italy
* Correspondence: u.volpe@staff.univpm.it; Tel.: +39-71-5963301; Fax: +39-71-5963540

Abstract: Although schizophrenia is currently conceptualized as being characterized as a syndrome that includes a collection of signs and symptoms, there is strong evidence of heterogeneous and complex underpinned etiological, etiopathogenetic, and psychopathological mechanisms, which are still under investigation. Therefore, the present viewpoint review is aimed at providing some insights into the recently investigated schizophrenia research fields in order to discuss the potential future research directions in schizophrenia research. The traditional schizophrenia construct and diagnosis were progressively revised and revisited, based on the recently emerging neurobiological, genetic, and epidemiological research. Moreover, innovative diagnostic and therapeutic approaches are pointed to build a new construct, allowing the development of better clinical and treatment outcomes and characterization for schizophrenic individuals, considering a more patient-centered, personalized, and tailored-based dimensional approach. Further translational studies are needed in order to integrate neurobiological, genetic, and environmental studies into clinical practice and to help clinicians and researchers to understand how to redesign a new schizophrenia construct.

Keywords: construct; schizophrenia; schizophrenia spectrum; renaming; rethinking; revising

Citation: Orsolini, L.; Pompili, S.; Volpe, U. Schizophrenia: A Narrative Review of Etiopathogenetic, Diagnostic and Treatment Aspects. *J. Clin. Med.* **2022**, *11*, 5040. https://doi.org/10.3390/jcm11175040

Academic Editor: Armida Mucci

Received: 16 July 2022
Accepted: 24 August 2022
Published: 27 August 2022

1. Introduction

Schizophrenia is a severe mental illness (SMI) affecting more than 21 million people worldwide that frequently leads to a persistent disability and impaired cognitive, social, and emotional functioning [1]. Schizophrenia is currently conceptualized as being characterized by at least positive symptoms (such as delusions and hallucinations), negative symptoms (including anhedonia, alogia, avolition, and social withdrawal), and cognitive symptoms (such as deficits in attention, processing speed, verbal learning, visuospatial learning, problem solving, working memory, and cognitive flexibility) [2–5]. Moreover, social cognition (including emotional intelligence, facial emotion recognition, emotion evaluation, and social inference) impairment may significantly impact the functional recovery in schizophrenia patients, due to the negative effects on interpersonal relationships, community adjustment, and vocational functioning [6,7]. Schizophrenia patients may also experience higher rates of co-occurring medical and/or mental illnesses, such as substance use disorders (mainly alcohol and cannabis), with prevalence rates up to 41% [8]. Due to a disordered lifestyle, an unhealthy diet, a lack of exercise, smoking, the adverse effects of antipsychotic treatment, a limited access to medical care, and the psychiatric illness itself [9–11], patients with schizophrenia are more likely to have a metabolic syndrome, a cardiovascular disease, diabetes, other endocrinopathies, an immune disease, and pulmonary illness, in particular, chronic obstructive pulmonary disease [10–14]. The concomitant comorbidity with other mental disorders determines the higher rates in symptomatology relapse, hospitalizations, suicidality, and family and social issues (such as higher rates of incarceration due to mental disorder relapse, treatment discontinuation, higher impulsivity and violent behaviors, and so forth), as well as a higher risk of negative outcomes in the short-term, including higher mortality rates [15,16]. A very recent meta-analysis showed that all causes of mortality were increased in people with schizophrenia, compared to the control group [17]. The specific causes of mortality included suicide, injury, poisoning, pulmonary diseases, endocrine diseases, respiratory diseases, urogenital diseases, diabetes, cancer, and cardio-cerebrovascular causes [17]. Moreover, it has also been found that treatment with an antipsychotic (AP) drug, in particular with second-generation long-acting injectable antipsychotics (SGA-LAIs), seems to be protective against all causes of mortality [17].

However, schizophrenia is a syndrome including a collection of signs and symptoms with heterogeneous etiology, etiopathogenesis, and psychopathological mechanisms that are potentially implicated, with many research directions and pathways currently under investigation [18–20]. Nowadays, there are several emerging neurobiological research directions that are suggested to be implicated in the pathogenesis of schizophrenia that could also be helpful in the clinical characterization of the disease, such as the following: (a) genetic factors (e.g., copy number variants [CNV], de novo nonsense genetic mutation, risk genes, polymorphisms in a gene, single nucleotide polymorphisms [SNPs], and so forth) that are implicated in the disrupted development at various stages of fetal life, which program the brain to manifest pre-psychotic features in the prepubertal or puberal age; (b) the neurodevelopmental model of schizophrenia, which considers several non-genetic factors, including perinatal complications, immigration status, and childhood maltreatment and neglect, which could mediate epigenetic changes, potentially determining structural and functional neurodevelopmental aberrations; (c) pathological alterations in multiple brain regions, including the frontal, temporal, parietal, cingulate, and glia components, as well as an excessive synaptic pruning and/or a disruption of neuroplasticity, and so forth; (d) the hypothesis of immune dysfunction and the neuroinflammatory model; (e) many others research pathways, including the emergence of the transdiagnostic model across multiple psychiatric disorders and the different abnormalities that are in the implicated neurotransmitters, such as the dopaminergic and glutammatergic pathways [21–23]. Indeed, there is an increased need for a better clinical characterization of individuals who are affected by schizophrenia, considering a more patient-centered, personalized, and tailored-based dimensional approach, which could consider all of the above-mentioned heterogeneous clinical manifestations and endophenotypes of the disease, including the investigation of all of the underpinned genetic and environmental factors [24,25]. Accordingly, the management of schizophrenic individuals should require better data integration towards the personalization of diagnosis and treatment [24,26,27]. Within this context, there have also been recently developed artificial intelligence (AI)- and machine learning (ML)-based approaches, which promise an interesting implementation of statistical tools to build more accurate and precise predictive models of schizophrenia onset, illness course, and potential therapeutic outcomes [28]. These can also identify candidate variables that are putative to be characteristics of schizophrenia spectrum disorders, by allowing a personalized diagnosis, such as a set of resting-state electroencephalographic (EEG) quantitative features, and magnetic resonance imaging of structural and functional anomalies, and so forth [29–31].

Therefore, due to the growing knowledge in schizophrenia research and the underpinned mechanisms, we aimed to provide some insights into and a viewpoint on the recently investigated schizophrenia research fields in order to discuss the potential future research directions in schizophrenia research, including the overview of recently developed new constructs and implemented classificatory systems.

2. Definitions and Concepts on Schizophrenia

While the cluster of symptoms that clinically define the schizophrenia concept has been noted historically before the 1990s, schizophrenia scientific research was mainly developed following the studies that were carried out by the German psychiatrist Emil Kraeplin (1856–1926) who identified a set of symptoms related to the schizophrenia disease in his

Psychiatrie manual, which provided a descriptive classification of mental disorders that were based on his clinical observations and experience [32]. In his essay, he identified a set of mental disorders, which he named *'processes of psychic degeneration'*, that were characterized by a rapid development of a mental deterioration (later named *'dementia praecox'*) [33]. 'Dementia praecox' included catatonic syndrome (characterized by a tensive voluntary motor activity), the hebephrenic syndrome (characterized by a distinctive deteriorative course, based on the importance of silliness and minimal positive psychotic symptoms), and the paranoid dementia (characterized by the presence of hallucinations and delusions). Kraeplin [34] mainly focused on the illness course and the chronicity of the disease, rather than on a set of diagnostic criteria, in describing the concept of the 'dementia praecox'. Kraeplin [34] defined those individuals as distinct from the insanity of tertiary syphilis or the cyclic, non-deteriorating psychosis of a manic-depressive illness. Accordingly, the dementia praecox diagnosis still contained the illness prognosis [33].

Indeed, Kraepelin's system of mental diseases substantially contributed to the foundation of the modern psychiatric diagnosis in the Diagnostic and Statistical System of Mental Disorders (DSM) and the International Classification of Diseases (ICD). However, since the schizophrenia construct that was developed by Emil Kraeplin [33], several schizophrenia definitions and concepts have changed considerably over the past century, with an increasing disagreement about the core features of schizophrenia [35,36]. In fact, the originally developed Kraeplenian concept was subsequently revised by the Swiss psychiatrist Eugen Bleuler, who mainly focused, during his lecture at a meeting of the German Psychiatric Association in Berlin on 24 April 1908, on the dissociative symptomatology that is related to the illness [37]. At that meeting, Bleuler indeed argued that dementia praecox was associated with neither dementia nor precociousness and emphasized that the splitting of psychic functioning represented the essential schizophrenia feature [38]. Accordingly, Bleuler mainly described schizophrenia originally as a disorder in which "*emotionally charged ideas or drives attain a certain degree of autonomy so that the personality falls into pieces. These fragments can then exist side by side and alternately dominate the main part of the personality, the conscious part of the patient*" [37]. Accordingly, he coined the term "*schizophrenia*" (which was derived from the Greek verb 'schizein', indicating splitting, and 'phren' denoting the 'soul, spirit, mind'). Bleuler also stated that schizophrenia was primarily represented by a thought and feeling disorder, comprising the '4 As' (alogia, autistic isolation, ambivalence, and affect blunting) [37,38].

Indeed, the Bleulerian concept of schizophrenia, with the heterogeneity of prognosis and outcomes, indirectly paved the way for later subdivisions of the schizophrenia concept [39]. Consequently, the German psychiatrist Kurt Schneider (1887–1967) proposed a set of fundamental symptoms, named Schneider's first-rank symptoms (FRS), of which the presence in the subject could be strongly suggestive of a schizophrenia diagnosis [40]. The FRS include the following: (a) auditory hallucinations; (b) thought withdrawal, insertion, and interruption; (c) thought broadcasting; (d) somatic hallucinations; (e) delusional perception; (f) feelings or actions that are made or are influenced by external agents [40]. The FRS are the so-called positive symptoms (i.e., the symptoms that are not usually experienced by people without schizophrenia), and they are usually given priority over other symptoms. In addition, second-rank symptoms include other perceptual disorders, delusional intuition, mood changes, affective flattening, perplexity, and other negative symptoms that represent the deficits of emotional responses and other thought processes [40]. The Schneiderian FRS, which were initially retained in the fourth edition of the Diagnostic and Statistical Manual of Mental Disorders (DSM) [41] and were included in a special schizophrenia diagnostic status in the 10th edition of the International Classification of Diseases (ICD-10) [42], were later dropped in the DSM-5 [43], the DSM-5-TR [44], and in the ICD-11 [45].

The "Neo-Kraepelinian" movement of the 1960s and 1970s argued for the empirical psychometric validation of psychiatric syndromes and posed the basis for the proposal of schizophrenia diagnostic criteria, which was subsequently integrated into both the DSM and ICD versions. Within this context, John Feighner and his colleagues, Eli Robins, Samuel

Guze, and George Winokur, at Washington University in St. Louis, Missouri, proposed the Feighner criteria, i.e., a set of influential psychiatric diagnostic criteria that was also developed for schizophrenia diagnosis [46]. In particular, Feighner et al. [46] required as essential criteria for a schizophrenia diagnosis the persistence of a limited set of symptoms (i.e., delusions, hallucinations, or thought disorders) for at least six months, without the return to the premorbid level of psychosocial adjustment. The Feighner criteria were later further expanded with the development of a set of specific diagnostic criteria (namely, research diagnostic criteria (RDC)) [46], which constituted the basis for the DSM-III, as developed by the American Psychiatric Association [47]. The RDC were, indeed, widely used in order to study a variety of schizophrenia-related research issues, particularly those that were related to genetics, psychobiology, and treatment outcomes [48].

Crow [49] simplified the schizophrenia description in terms of a positive form (type I schizophrenia syndrome) and a negative form (type II schizophrenia syndrome, occurring in the absence of positive symptoms), despite the fact that many patients with the type I syndrome can later acquire the features of the type II syndrome, and some patients can have both from an early stage. Type II syndrome is usually associated with the worst prognosis, corresponding more closely to the classical Kraepelinian schizophrenia diagnosis [49]. In addition, Carpenter et al. [50] distinguished between primary and secondary negative symptoms by reviving the long-standing question concerning the primary core deficits. More recently, Andreasen [51] more deeply investigated the negative symptoms that were originally described by Kraepelin [34] and Bleuler [37] as schizophrenic core symptoms. Both Andreasen [51] and Carpenter et al. [50] further investigated the originally developed Bleulerian concept of "thought disorder" as the primary defining feature of schizophrenia, rather than the presence of signs and symptoms such as delusions and hallucinations. Accordingly, Andreasen [51] proposed a neo-Bleulerian unitary model for schizophrenia, defining it as a neurodevelopmentally derived "misconnection syndrome" involving connections between the cortical regions and the cerebellum that are mediated through the thalamus (the cortico–cerebellar–thalamic–cortical circuit).

Meehl [52] proposed a model of the causes and the pathogenesis of schizophrenia and its related states, which emphasized on the presence of a genetically determined aberration in neural transmission that could be potentially responsible of the emergence of schizophrenia and non-psychotic schizotypal states within the diathesis-stressor framework [53]. Gottesman et al. [54] introduced the concept of the 'epigenetic puzzle' in schizophrenia, by proposing an explanatory model comprising the different causes of schizophrenia for etiological and phenomenological heterogeneity in schizophrenia [55]. Crow [56] proposed the viral hypothesis of schizophrenia, as derived by a mutagenesis that is caused by viral integration or transposition in human genomic DNA. Following studies that were carried out on subgroups of the non-psychotic relatives of patients who were affected with schizophrenia who displayed defects or abnormalities in clinical, cognitive, biological, social, and other dimensions of functioning that were similar to those shown in schizophrenic individuals [57,58], the hypothesis of schizophrenia liability syndrome [59] was proposed. In fact, based on Paul Meehl's conceptualization of 'schizotaxia' [52], Stone et al. [59] reformulated the concept of liability syndrome based on observable, clinically meaningful symptoms involving the negative symptoms and neurocognitive deficits in non-psychotic relatives [60]. Furthermore, from a more phenomenological perspective, it has been hypothesized that, in schizophrenia spectrum disorders, a profound transformation of subjectivity antedating the onset of major symptoms is accompanied by micro-experiences of self-alienation (e.g., derealization, perplexity, depersonalization, reduced self-presence, and an alteration of the stream of thought) [61]. The self-experiences, indeed, represent fundamental and enduring (more a trait-like feature) distortions of subjectivity, which typically emerge in late childhood and early adolescence [61].

Finally, recent evidence supports the concept that schizophrenia represents a multifactorial disorder that results from a complex interplay between additive and interactive genetic and environmental determinants [62], displaying a highly variable and heterogeneous clinical presentation [63]. Therefore, due to the absence of clear boundaries and the multiplicity of implicated etiological factors, pathophysiological mechanisms, and hypotheses [64–66], the schizophrenia concept has been more recently broadened to a spectrum concept in the DSM-5 (and the recently released DSM-5-TR) [43,44] or as a primary psychosis in the ICD-11 [39,45].

3. The Heterogeneity and the New Nosological Schizophrenia Constructs

The heterogeneity of schizophrenia resides in the high variability of the phenotypic and clinical expression, with highly varying degrees of functionality, symptoms and personal recovery, and outcomes across individuals, together with a variable range of underlying neurobiological abnormalities, which are potentially implicated in its pathogenesis [67,68]. Indeed, the multifactorial nature of the etiological factors has worsened the difficulty in addressing the causal mechanisms in the disease pathophysiology of the illness [69,70]. However, Tandon et al. [36] exhorted that *"heterogeneity cannot just be an explanation for our failure, but is a problem to be explained"*. Indeed, Carpenter [71] first proposed that the schizophrenia construct should be reconstructed according to the following four major targets: (a) the identification of patient subgroups in order to enhance homogeneity; (b) deconstructing the traditional schizophrenia construct by identifying the specific core psychopathology domains; (c) deconstructing schizophrenia at the levels of neural circuits and behavioral constructs; (d) considering the different stages from the vulnerability of development to the illness onset and disease progression.

Indeed, the traditional schizophrenia construct has elicited a continual debate as the concept has fluctuated across the years, according to the different psychopathological perspectives and the emerging advances in multiple areas of schizophrenia research (e.g., genomics, neuroimaging, epidemiology, and cognitive science) [72]. One of the major obstacles of the traditional schizophrenia construct regards the fact that disorders continue to be defined almost exclusively by a set of symptoms and signs, despite the association between the specific diagnostic categories and biological or behavioral measures having been proven to be modest or inconsistent, therefore, not allowing a better understanding of schizophrenia or the development of more effective interventions for the illness [73]. In particular, the inconclusive findings coming from the neurobiological studies have demonstrated the inadequacy of the current schizophrenia diagnosis by underlining how the current nosological construct does not appear to be exhaustive in identifying all of the multiple and potentially different pathophysiological substrates that are implicated within schizophrenia spectrum disorder [74]. However, many experts in schizophrenia research have pointed to continuing to use the traditional schizophrenia construct because of its utility (at least clinically) and the absence of any current better alternative [20,36,39,66,74,75]. Carpenter [75] suggested replacing it with a broader construct of "primary psychosis", while Gur [63] suggested replacing it with the "psychosis spectrum disorder" construct. On the other hand, Murray and Quattrone [76], Van Os and Goluksuz [77], and Zick et al. [68] proposed to completely eliminate it. The alternative proposed schizophrenia constructs include dimensional-based schizophrenia constructs [78], the hierarchical psychopathological model by Kotov et al. [79], and the biotype architecture [67,68,80,81], which is illustrated below. Therefore, in order to address these issues, an overview of the different diagnostic classificatory systems, from the traditional DSM/ICD to the recently developed alternative/integrative models, has been provided below.

4. The Systems of Diagnostic Classification

Overall, the diagnostic classifications have been ad hoc designed in order to address the following purposes: (a) facilitating research into the causes and the treatment of the illnesses; (b) guiding clinical decision making; (c) helping clinicians in more shared communication [82]. However, the extremely variable and discontinuing phenotypic presentation, diagnostic characteristics, illness trajectory, and treatment response in schizophrenic individuals, together with the highest rates of comorbid disorders, limit the feasibility and applicability of the current diagnostic systems and classifications in the clinical decision making practice in regard to schizophrenia [82]. Therefore, although the latest versions of the DSM-5-TR [44] and ICD-11 [45] might effectively represent some apparently useful approaches facilitating the information exchange among clinicians, they definitely fail to properly capture the biological and pathophysiological nature of schizophrenic individuals, as well as their phenotypical and clinical heterogeneity; indeed, not allowing for a personalized diagnosis or treatment [36,82]. For instance, neurocognitive deficits, which are commonly a core feature of schizophrenia, are not included in the criterion-based definition in the ICD-11 [45] nor in the DSM-5-TR [36,44]. Furthermore, the ICD-11 [45] also differs from the DSM-5 [43] (and the current DSM-5-TR) [44] according to the minimum duration of symptomatology. The ICD-11 [45] requires a minimum duration period of one month or more, whereas, the DSM-5 (and current DSM-5-TR) [36,44] requires the presence of continuous signs of the disturbances that should persist for at least six months beyond the required additional five months of symptoms, which could include prodromal or residual symptoms [83]. Obviously, the shorter duration requirement that is suggested in the ICD-11 was intended to encourage an earlier treatment in order to improve the patient's outcome. Both the DSM-5-TR and the ICD-11 require at least two types of schizophrenia symptoms lasting at least one month, even though the ICD-11 also includes the presence of experiences of influence, passivity, or control as a separate core symptom in schizophrenia, which represent disturbances in the 'ego-world boundary', including passivity experiences, thought withdrawal, and thought broadcasting [83], which were previously included among Schneider's FRS [40]. Finally, social processing dysfunction is represented as an integral part of the schizophrenia diagnostic criteria only in the DSM-5 [43] and the current DSM-5-TR [44], but not in the ICD-11 [24,45]. Indeed, although both the DSM-5-TR and ICD-11 incorporate, to a greater or lesser extent, the traditional clinical features that were investigated by Kraepelin [34], Bleuler [37] and Schneider [40], the latest iterations of the DSM and the ICD provide clinicians with dimensional assessments based on the key symptom domains covering the positive, negative, affective, and cognitive symptoms of the schizophrenia. However, as one of the most dominant etiological models for schizophrenia postulated that the illness can represent the final state following abnormal neurodevelopmental processes, which may have started years before the illness onset [84], and that it is possible to identify a schizophrenia spectrum disorder, rather than only the presence or absence of the illness, the current diagnostic systems have a series of limitations [85]. In fact, while the original aim of the current diagnostic systems was to allow clinicians to have a shared and homogeneous information exchange, as well as for research purposes, the traditional diagnostic systems, which are mainly based on a set of symptoms and signs, are not able to incorporate any etiology-based components, neurodevelopmental markers, the genetic liability, the subthreshold schizophrenia vulnerability status (i.e., schizotaxia), or many other currently investigated aspects of the disease [75].

Therefore, beyond these classical/traditional diagnostic systems, the National Institute of Mental Health (NIMH) Research Domain Criteria (RDoC) initiative was first developed in 2009 with the aim to build a new classification system for a better understanding of underlying dimensional processes and the development of psychopathology, by using a dimensional approach [63,82]. The RDoC may effectively provide a bridge between the basic behavioral neuroscience research and clinical research by using a dimensional approach in which each function is quantitatively mapped onto specific brain circuits [63]. The RDoC was conceived as an experimental framework in order to support translational research in psychopathology organized around basic functional domains (e.g., cognition, motivation, and motor activity) [72,86]. The focus of the RDoC program is on the fundamental operations of adaptive behavioral/cognitive and brain functioning (e.g., working memory, fear, and behavior) and psychopathology, according to a perspective in terms of the dysregulation of these systems rather than starting with clinical syndromes and then trying to determine their source/causes. The RDoC investigates the entire dimensions of functioning (i.e., negative valence, positive valence, cognition, social processes, arousal/regulatory systems, and sensorimotor systems) from the normal range to increasingly abnormal extents, and no specific cut points for each disorder are specified in order to facilitate studies on the transitions from normality to the different degrees of pathology [72,86,87].

In addition, other research directions have been proposed to reconceptualize schizophrenia psychopathology as consisting of continuous dimensions of maladaptive behaviors, emotions, and cognitions, with some hierarchical taxonomies of phenotypic psychopathological dimensions proposed [88]. Within this context, the Hierarchical Taxonomy of Psychopathology (HiTOP) consortium aimed to integrate the evidence from studies on the organization of psychopathology in order to overcome the arbitrary boundaries between psychopathology and normality, the diagnostic instability, the frequent co-occurring disorders, the heterogeneity within the same diagnosis, and the lack ability to identify the subthreshold clinical cases [79,89–91]. HiTOP was built in order to define psychopathology according to a dimensional approach, which also investigates those individuals with subthreshold symptoms or unusual symptom profiles, with the aim to reduce the heterogeneity within those constructs by grouping related symptoms together, independently, by an established diagnosis [68,79]. According to HiTOP, schizophrenia, schizophreniform disorder, schizoaffective disorder, and schizotypal and paranoid personality disorders reflect elevations on both thought disorders and "detachment" spectra dimensions [89–91]. In particular, the "detachment" dimension can be considered as a vulnerability trait for negative symptoms and schizophrenia, also among the relatives of people who are affected with schizophrenia, compared to the relatives of healthy probands or probands with mood disorders [92]. Furthermore, the biotype-based architecture model was investigated with the aim to incorporate the biomarkers for differentiating individual cases by subtype [93]. The Bipolar-Schizophrenia Network for Intermediate Phenotypes (B-SNIP1) consortium sought to identify a broad range of biomarkers encompassing the neurocognitive and physiological correlations, with the aim to distinguish the three leading psychosis diagnoses (i.e., schizophrenia, schizoaffective disorder, and bipolar I disorder with psychosis) [67]. Identifying promising neurobiologically distinct subgroups of psychoses by using biomarkers could support genetic-based etiological investigations and may advance treatment developments [94,95]. Indeed, a biotype-based approach could significantly improve the development of new treatment targets, offering an opportunity to match interventions to pathophysiology and to implement more patient-centered, tailored, and personalized approaches to the disease towards a new precision, as well as personalized psychiatry in schizophrenia research and clinic.

5. Schizophrenia and Personalized Psychiatry

The concept of personalized medicine is based upon the hypothesis that each individual is unique, hence, diseases are heterogeneous regarding the specific contributing factors and also the specific treatment outcomes [96]. Personalized psychiatry aims to offer an individual and patient-centered approach, including an individualized clinical characterization (also using the tools of the precision psychiatry, including biomarkers, biotypes, endophenotypes, etc.), as well as tailored and personalized treatments for each individual real patient at the right time [97]. The topic of personalized psychiatry becomes more salient, particularly in the field of schizophrenia research, whereas a more concrete emphasis should be posed to the transdiagnostic conceptualization of psychopathology that is related to primary psychosis and schizophrenia, as already pointed out by Carpenter [98]. Furthermore, the investigation of specific biomarkers would be useful in early diagnosis, in clinical monitoring, and in treatment response [99].

According to the Biomarkers Definitions Working Group [100], a biomarker is "a characteristic that is objectively measured and evaluated as an indicator of normal biological processes, pathogenic processes, or pharmacological responses to a therapeutic intervention". Biomarkers can be molecular, histologic, derived from brain imaging, or physiologic in nature, being classified as diagnostic, prognostic, and theranostic [101]. Biomarkers are not represented by endophenotypes, which are heritable and are more specifically quantitative traits that are associated with disease liability, that instead explain the relationship between the genotype and the phenotype [102]. Indeed, biomarkers could be used as clinical predictors for schizophrenia, its illness course, and its phase, as well as for its treatment and intervention response [103]. A dimensional-based characterization along the RDoC domain [104,105] can help clinicians to identify the specific biomarkers for schizophrenia risk occurrence throughout the lifespan of the individual [63]. For example, dysregulated immunity and inflammatory processes were reported in schizophrenic individuals, despite the fact that the measurement and repeatability of these biomarkers display several challenges in terms of translating this approach in routine clinical practice [105–108]. Studies on those targeted on polygenic risk scores suggested better characterizing and identifying a specific subgroup of schizophrenic patients who had ongoing inflammation and immune dysfunction [107,108]. Therefore, blood-based biomarkers, including glucose and triglyceride levels, and pro-inflammatory markers (e.g., interleukin-6, tumor necrosis factor alpha, and so forth) have been investigated; however, their profile seems not to be specific to schizophrenia [79].

Further potential neurophysiological, immune, and endocrine biomarkers have been investigated through proteonomic gene expression (transcriptomic) and neuroimaging studies [63,99,109–111], even though these biomarkers have not yet been validated and, for this reason, they continue to be investigated in experimental settings rather than in clinical practice [100,112]. However, despite the fact that several biomarkers, including genetic biomarkers, have been identified or are currently under investigation, they have not yet been effectively implemented into routine clinical practice, mainly due to their inconclusive clinical reliability, with exception of a few pharmacogenetic-guided decision support tools [113]. In this regard, the pharmacogenetic research into antipsychotic drugs has examined a number of genetic variants and only a few polymorphisms have been found to be promising in explaining the therapeutic efficacy and side-effects of antipsychotic drugs in schizophrenia spectrum disorders, such as some polymorphisms in the brain-derived neurotrophic factor (BDNF), in some cytochrome CYP genes, and so forth [114,115]

6. Genomics

Genetic epidemiological studies have shown that schizophrenia is highly heritable, despite the fact that it has been better described as an underpinned multifactorial etiology with a complex polygenic genetic architecture [116]. Evidence has supported the role of both common and rare genetic variants that are implicated in the development of schizophrenia, as well as several environmental factors that may contribute to its etiology [63]. Indeed, few causal variants have been clearly identified and most of the genetic associations have not imparted any useful clinical implications [116]. For instance, many genome-wide associated variants (GWAV) have not been identified in genes, possibly indicating that they may have a regulatory role in modifying gene expression or they can represent the expression of quantitative trait loci [117]. Indeed, gene expression can be influenced by both genetic and environmental factors and the differences in gene expression can be a biomarker for the diagnosis, but also for a potential therapeutic target in schizophrenia [118–121]. However, although recent genome-wide association studies (GWAS) have identified more than 100 genetic risk loci in schizophrenia, they are overall responsible of a small effect on the schizophrenia risk [116]. The polygenic risk score (i.e., the measure of polygenic loading) [122] is able to address the polygenic architecture of schizophrenia and it can quantify the common risk allele burden that is carried by schizophrenia individuals [123,124]. Moreover, it has been suggested that the polygenic risk score may be useful in determining the association between schizophrenia and intermediate phenotypes, such as the brain structural alterations in schizophrenic individuals [125]. However, a recent systematic review by van der Merwe et al. [126] did not find any significant association between the polygenic risk score and the brain structural changes in schizophrenic individuals, suggesting the need for further research directions, particularly in the field of intermediate phenotypes other than altered brain structures.

Furthermore, according to a recent systematic review, copy number variant (CNV)-based studies have identified five schizophrenia-associated CNV regions containing genes that were found to be differentially expressed in schizophrenia (i.e., PPP1R2 in 3q29, HSPB1 in 7q11.23, INO80E and YPEL3 in 16p11.2, DHRS11 in 17q12, and SEPT5, RTN4R, and SLC2A11 in 22q11.2) [121]. However, the CNVs in these regions are also associated with neurodevelopmental delays, intellectual disabilities [127,128], and other neuropsychiatric phenotypes, including anxiety (3q29, 7q11.23, and 17q12), autism spectrum disorder (ASD; 3q29, 7q11.23, 16p11.2, 17q12, and 22q), attention-deficit/hyperactivity disorder (ADHD; 7q11.23 and 22q), and bipolar disorder (3q29, 7q11.23, and 17q12), as well as in immune system dysfunction, cardiac pathologies, and many other medical issues [119,120]. The most well-investigated CNV that is associated with an increased risk of schizophrenia is the 22q11.2 deletion syndrome, with it being related to a 25-fold increase in schizophrenia risk [129–132]. Furthermore, several neurotransmitters (i.e., dopamine, serotonin, and glutamate), acting through metabotropic G protein-coupled receptors (GPCRs), which mediate the intracellular signal transduction and the induction of gene expression in order to exert antipsychotic activity, have been genetically investigated in schizophrenia [133,134]. The genetic studies have identified associations between the SNPs in genes that are related to GPCRs and schizophrenia [135]; in particular, some metabotropic glutamate receptors (mGlu), subtype 3 ($mGlu_3$), 5-hydroxytryptamine 2A receptor ($5\text{-}HTA_{2A}$), and dopamine D_3 receptors (DRD_3). SNPs have been associated with schizophrenia, pathognomic measurable endophenotypes, and the treatment response to specific antipsychotics [136–140]. However, further studies are needed in order to investigate the role of GPCRs SNPs variants in schizophrenia and in the antipsychotic's treatment response [133,141].

However, beyond the genetic susceptibility, epigenetics (including all postnatal modifications of gene expression that are not associated with changes in DNA sequences, such as DNA methylation, chemical modification of histone proteins, non-coding RNA, and other mechanisms that are involved in epigenetic regulation) have demonstrated that not only genetic factors are implicated in schizophrenia, but more specifically epigenetic factors [142]. Epigenetic factors are derived from the interplay between genetic factors and various environmental factors occurring from the fetal period to the developmental period that may potentially influence and modify the psychopathological trajectory of the illness, as well as other post-developmental factors influencing the onset of schizophrenia through an epigenetic mechanism [143].

7. Neuroimaging

A set of specific brain structural abnormalities have been widely reported in schizophrenia spectrum disorders, which are mainly considered to be a brain development disorder [144–146]. A large-scale metanalysis has reported a smaller hippocampus volume, together with smaller amygdala, thalamus, nucleus accumbens, and intracranial volumes in patients with schizophrenia compared to controls [144]. Moreover, it has been found that a larger palladium and lateral ventricle volume also occurs, compared to healthy controls [144]. Individuals with schizophrenia have also been reported to have widespread cortical thinning and smaller cortical surface [145]. Cortical thickness reductions are larger in individuals under antipsychotic treatment and are negatively correlated with medication dose, symptoms severity, and duration of illness [145]. Limitations in the imaging studies on schizophrenia are represented by the issue that most of them mainly recruited chronic patients and individuals taking antipsychotic treatment, therefore making it difficult to identify the time of the brain changes and the effect of the treatment exposure [146,147]. Functional neuroimaging studies have shown alterations in the brain metabolism and the blood flow in the frontal, cingulate, parietal, putamen, and sensorimotor regions [148–151]. Dopamine dysfunction has also been observed in schizophrenic patients. Indeed, dopamine D_2 receptor density and the occupancy of D_2 receptors by dopamine has been shown to be increased in schizophrenic patients, along with an increased dopamine transmission [152,153]. For other neurotransmitters, the findings coming from neuroimaging studies are still inconsistent; however, some studies have reported a reduced 5-HT_1 receptor concentration in the midbrain and pons, reduced 5HT_2 receptors in the neocortex, and a hypofunction of N-methyl-D-aspartate (NDMA) [154,155]. The data that are currently available on the glutamatergic system are still unclear [156].

Neuroimaging data have been more recently extensively investigated with the aim to identify individuals who are at risk of psychosis at an early stage or a prodromal phase [146,157,158]. High-risk individuals who will subsequently develop psychosis or a schizophrenia spectrum disorder showed several structural and functional brain abnormalities compared to the healthy controls, such as grey matter changes in the frontal, temporal, and cingulate cortices, a reduced integrity of striatal and temporal white matter, subcortical volumes of the thalamus, amygdala, striatum, and cerebellum, and changes in the functional connectivity and network organization [159–163]. Further studies have also investigated, through neuroimaging, whether it is possible to identify some predictors of the response to pharmacological medication [146] by demonstrating that a greater striatal dopamine synthesis, an enlarged gray matter volume, and normal gyrification, as well as an increased brain activity in the fronto-parietal regions may act as potential predictors of a positive response to antipsychotic treatments [164–168].

8. Environmental Factors

A set of environmental factors, such as childhood adversity, substance use and misuse, minority and ethnicity status, birth season, urbanity, and pregnancy and/or perinatal complications, have been associated with differential clinical manifestations of schizophrenia spectrum disorders [169,170]. A recent systematic review and meta-analysis assessed the evidence for a gene–environment correlation (genes influencing the likelihood of environmental exposure) between schizophrenia polygenic risk score and childhood adversities, observing only a small effect; however, there are still inconsistent findings that do not allow us to draw definitive conclusions [170]. Meta-analyses have also shown that substance use, particularly continued use, was significantly associated with higher rates of positive psychotic symptoms and a higher likelihood of a history of violence and aggressive behaviors [171,172]. In addition, cannabis use, especially with higher potency cannabis, is associated with an increased risk for schizophrenia [173–176]. In addition, ethnic minority status is correlated with more severe reality distortion, disorganization, and the onset of negative symptomatology [177].

Moreover, the paradigm of the exposome was only recently investigated in the field of schizophrenia [63,178–180]. The exposome represents the entirety of the environmental vulnerability underlying the pathoetiology of schizophrenia spectrum disorders, to which an individual is exposed to throughout their life [178,180,181]. According to the exposome model, environmental factors are bi-directionally interlinked, such that cannabis use is associated with childhood adversity, the effects of urbanicity variables (such as population density, deprivation, etc.) can be modified or influenced by individual level factors, such as cannabis use, exclusion, discrimination, and social adversity [178,180]. Moreover, there is evidence to suggest a dose–response relationship between environmental load scores and the severity of the mental health status, as well as the outcomes [179,180,182,183].

9. Schizophrenia Treatment and Interventions

Despite several evidence- and consensus-based schizophrenia guidelines that have been generated over the last decades [184–188], the treatment interventions in schizophrenia research are far from being effective and many factors are involved in treatment response based on theoretical groundings, with some innovative fields of research yet to be implemented [21,185,189]. The current approach to schizophrenia in routine clinical practice worldwide is often stereotyped, being mostly prescribed a second-generation antipsychotic drug [190]. Indeed, antipsychotic treatments for schizophrenic individuals have been demonstrated to be effective in managing the core symptoms of schizophrenia, but also they has been reported to be associated with a decreased risk of all-cause, cardiovascular, and suicide mortality, also, in terms of cumulative antipsychotic exposure, particularly in those patients under clozapine treatment [191–193].

Furthermore, from a pharmacological perspective, despite the fact that the dopaminergic system has been hugely investigated in the pathophysiology of schizophrenia and has been guided in initially targeting antipsychotic treatments, there is clinical evidence that dopamine blockade is not effective in managing the negative and cognitive symptoms and, in some schizophrenic patients, it does not improve the positive symptoms either [194–196]. Therefore, researchers have recently directed their research interest towards new neurochemical targets, such as the glutamatergic system [194,197,198]. While, on the other hand, from a non-pharmacological perspective, despite the demonstrated evidence-based efficacy of cognitive–behavioral approach [199–202], its use is still poor in routine clinical practice for schizophrenic individuals [24,203]. In patients with treatment-resistant schizophrenia (TRS), researchers have explored the utility of brain stimulation procedures [204], such as electroconvulsive therapy (ECT), repetitive transcranial magnetic stimulation (rTMS), and deep brain stimulation (DBS). Despite the promising preliminary results [205,206], further studies are needed in order to better understand the potential role of these neuromodulatory techniques in the treatment of TRS patients [204]. Finally, psychosocial interventions and recovery-oriented rehabilitative interventions (e.g., cognitive remediation and metacognitive reflection and insight therapy (MERIT) etc.) have been rapidly developed in order to target cognitive and/or metacognitive deficits that can hamper the functional recovery of schizophrenic patients and in subjects at ultra-high risk of psychosis [203,207–210], even though they do not seem to be adequately integrated in the mental health services [24,203]. Similarly, family-based interventions and supported employment programs are seldom implemented in routine clinical practice [24,203,211]. In particular, there are also initiatives that are aimed at implementing and favoring social integration, regular employment, and reducing the social exclusion of all individuals who are affected by severe mental illnesses, including schizophrenia, such as the Individual Placement and Support (IPS) initiative [212,213]. The IPS became the standard of supported employment and the only evidence-based employment model for people with schizophrenia, indicating a moderate-to-large effect size [214,215], which has also been confirmed in long-term studies [216]. However, despite the recovery-oriented approach that is needed for the management of schizophrenic patients, a resilience-promoting environment (i.e., an environment that integrates interventions in order to increase a positive outcome, despite adversities, in order to implement wellbeing [217]) is often missing in many mental health services [24].

10. Discussion

Overall, schizophrenia could better represent an encompassing term referring to a group of related disorders, which have distinct etiologies and that require different treatment strategies [55]. Schizophrenia, indeed, describes a clinical syndrome, not a disease entity. A syndrome consists of co-emerging specific symptoms of unknown etiology and has no clear boundaries with other entities. Symptom dimensions explain more clinical characteristics than diagnostic categories and they are specifically associated with genetic and environmental risk factors that may operate across diagnostic categories [76,116–119,121,169,170,178,179]. However, the current conceptualization of schizophrenia only appears to be useful to establish evidence-based guidelines for diagnosis and treatment, and to provide valuable information on psychosocial outcomes [39]. In fact, if schizophrenia continues to be defined almost exclusively by a set of symptoms and signs, despite the modest and/or inconsistent association between the diagnostic categories and the biological and/or behavioral measures, the traditional construct of schizophrenia will not be able to clearly reach a comprehensive understanding of the disorder, its heterogeneous clinical presentation and treatment outcomes, or the development of more effective treatments [72]. In fact, it has been well documented that the real-life functioning of schizophrenic patients does not exclusively depend on their symptoms and/or signs, but is more strictly related to context-related factors rather than illness-related ones [218,219], by demonstrating an ability to be stable in their relationships after a four-year follow-up, as reported in the multicenter study that was carried out by the Italian Network for Research on Psychoses [220].

Therefore, the current concept and traditional constructs of schizophrenia appear to be not exhaustive enough in explaining the heterogeneity and the complexity, as well as the complex interplaying roles of additive factors (both genetic and environmental determinants) in the pathogenesis of schizophrenia spectrum disorders [67,68,72,81]. Moreover, the current and traditional schizophrenia constructs are not able to adequately provide a clinical characterization, nor a dimensional and personalized approach to the understanding of each individual who is affected by schizophrenia [24,25,63]. However, there is still no relatively easily applicable and precise biologically-based diagnostic technique for schizophrenia that has enough specificity and sensitivity to replace the traditional schizophrenia constructs [20,36]. The highest clinical utility for the diagnosis of severe brain diseases, such as schizophrenia, is still provided by another brain, the long-term trained brain of a psychiatrist [221]. However, it has been also proposed that a precise psychiatry-based approach could better clinicians to move from a categorical (i.e., ICD and DSM-based criteria) to a dimensional approach in order to better identify people who are at risk for schizophrenia onset, and better clinically and psychopathologically characterize individuals who are affected with schizophrenia spectrum disorder [63,72,86,87,98,99]. However, there is still an intense debate in the scientific community and, despite overcoming the categorical approach that could apparently represent the best way to implement knowledge about schizophrenia, the boundaries of the currently termed schizophrenia could be limited to a neurodevelopmental syndrome that is characterized by disorganization, negative and cognitive symptoms, with a significant presence of anomalous self-experiences that may be distinguishable from other forms of psychosis [222,223].

Our current knowledge and understanding of schizophrenia have been influenced by its multi-level and multi-causal etiology, and the advances in deepening our understanding of its underpinned neurobiology and genetics [63,94,95,99,109–111,224]. Therefore, transdiagnostic psychosis spectrum and multi-dimensional frameworks, or multiple functional domains whose combinations comprise significant biotypes that are associated with schizophrenia, have been proposed as replacements for the schizophrenia construct due to the many shared characteristics and the blurring of boundaries between schizophrenia and related entities [36,67,68,78–80,94].

Furthermore, advances in multiple areas of neurosciences, including genomics, neuroimaging, cognitive science, and epidemiology, have facilitated the emergence of new conceptions and constructs of schizophrenia, and have allowed us to bridge animal and human research in order to probe the underlying mechanisms of typical and abnormal behaviors in schizophrenia [63]. The genomic data provide increasing support for the concept of systematic transdiagnostic components of neurodevelopmental spectra in schizophrenia [130], although the high heritability has not been translated into satisfying evidence for genetic lesions. In fact, both GWAS- and CNV-based studies that were looking for common genetic variants that are associated with schizophrenia were disappointing, either because the early findings failed to replicate or the large-scale studies failed to detect genome-wide significance [68,94].

Finally, considering that schizophrenia is a severe mental illness that is most strongly associated with stereotyping, prejudice, and a stigmatizing attitude [63], recently several researchers have proposed renaming the word 'schizophrenia' (etymologically meaning '*split mind*') [63,68,225,226]. A recent systematic review has demonstrated that renaming schizophrenia could be associated with improvements in attitudes towards patients who are affected with the illness and may increase early diagnosis, mental health access, and reduce stigmatizing behaviors towards the disease and the patients who are affected [227]. Moreover, two recent large surveys of stakeholders demonstrated that approximately 75% of participants agreed to change the name, with the hope of reducing the stigma and the discrimination [228]. Accordingly, some authors have proposed to substitute it with the expression *'psychosis spectrum syndrome'* or *'psychosis spectrum illness (PSI)'*, which would be further characterized by key temporal features, such as the age of onset (i.e., childhood, adolescent, or adult), the symptom onset (i.e., acute/insidious), the illness course (i.e., single episode, intermittent, remitting/relapsing, or persistent), and the phase of the illness (i.e., clinical high risk, first episode, recent-onset/early phase, ongoing, or recovered), and so forth [68]. Furthermore, different names have been proposed to refer to schizophrenia in other countries [39]. For instance, the Taiwanese Society of Psychiatry introduced a new name for schizophrenia that means "disorder with dysfunction in thought and perception" in 2012 [229]. In 2022, the Japanese Society of Psychiatry and Neurology renamed the Japanese translation of schizophrenia from "seishin-bunretsu-byo" (meaning mind-split disease) to "togo-shitcho-sho" (meaning integration disorder) [230]. In addition, the Korean Neuropsychiatric Association changed the original Korean name for schizophrenia "jeongshin-bunyeol-byung" (meaning mind-split disorder) to "johyun-byung" (meaning attunement disorder) [231]. Several studies have demonstrated that renaming has significantly modified the attitude toward schizophrenia in health professionals and in the general population [217,231,232]. However, despite these pro-renaming movements, other authors have still declared themselves to be against changing the name for schizophrenia by supporting the idea that changing the name of the condition (or even abolishing the concept) will not affect the root cause of the stigma and will not provide clinicians with a more complete understanding of the causes and the pathophysiological mechanisms underlying schizophrenia [233–235].

Therefore, current emerging research supports the need to revise the schizophrenia concept, to implement and readapt the traditional and original schizophrenia constructs by developing new integrative, personalized approaches, to consider the unicity of each individual, the need to clinically characterize the illness onset, the clinical course, the clinical manifestation, the phenotypes, and to personalize the treatment interventions towards a better personalized and dimensional psychiatry. Furthermore, there is also the need to think about renaming, not only the schizophrenia concept, from a neurobiological perspective, but also renaming the term, in order to facilitate a changing mind of health professionals and of the general population.

Author Contributions: All authors equally contributed to the data collection and worked on the manuscript draft. All authors have read and agreed to the published version of the manuscript.

Funding: This research received no external funding.

Institutional Review Board Statement: Not applicable.

Informed Consent Statement: Not applicable.

Data Availability Statement: Not applicable.

Conflicts of Interest: The authors declare no conflict of interest.

References

1. WHO. *Key Factors and Publications Concerning Schizophrenia*; World Health Organization: Geneva, Switzerland, 2018.
2. McCutcheon, R.A.; Reis Marques, T.; Howes, O.D. Schizophrenia—An Overview. *JAMA Psychiatry* **2020**, *77*, 201–210. [CrossRef] [PubMed]
3. Menon, V. Brain Networks and Cognitive Impairment in Psychiatric Disorders. *World Psychiatry* **2020**, *19*, 309–310. [CrossRef] [PubMed]
4. Moritz, S.; Silverstein, S.M.; Dietrichkeit, M.; Gallinat, J. Neurocognitive Deficits in Schizophrenia Are Likely to Be Less Severe and Less Related to the Disorder than Previously Thought. *World Psychiatry* **2020**, *19*, 254–255. [CrossRef] [PubMed]
5. Moura, B.M.; Isvoranu, A.M.; Kovacs, V.; Van Rooijen, G.; Van Amelsvoort, T.; Simons, C.J.P.; Bartels-Velthuis, A.A.; Bakker, P.R.; Marcelis, M.; De Haan, L.; et al. The Puzzle of Functional Recovery in Schizophrenia-Spectrum Disorders—Replicating a Network Analysis Study. *Schizophr. Bull.* **2022**, *48*, 871–880. [CrossRef] [PubMed]
6. Alston, M.; Bennett, C.F.; Rochani, H. Treatment Adherence in Youth with First-Episode Psychosis: Impact of Family Support and Telehealth Delivery. *Issues Ment. Health Nurs.* **2019**, *40*, 951–956. [CrossRef]

7. Green, M.F.; Lee, J.; Wynn, J.K. Experimental Approaches to Social Disconnection in the General Community: Can We Learn from Schizophrenia Research? *World Psychiatry Off. J. World Psychiatr. Assoc. WPA* **2020**, *19*, 177–178. [CrossRef]
8. Hunt, G.E.; Large, M.M.; Cleary, M.; Lai, H.M.X.; Saunders, J.B. Prevalence of Comorbid Substance Use in Schizophrenia Spectrum Disorders in Community and Clinical Settings, 1990–2017: Systematic Review and Meta-Analysis. *Drug Alcohol. Depend.* **2018**, *191*, 234–258. [CrossRef]
9. Mamakou, V.; Thanopoulou, A.; Gonidakis, F.; Tentolouris, N.; Kontaxakis, V. Schizophrenia and Type 2 Diabetes Mellitus. *Psychiatr. Psychiatr.* **2018**, *29*, 64–73. [CrossRef]
10. Brink, M.; Green, A.; Bojesen, A.B.; Lamberti, J.S.; Conwell, Y.; Andersen, K. Excess Medical Comorbidity and Mortality across the Lifespan in Schizophrenia: A Nationwide Danish Register Study. *Schizophr. Res.* **2019**, *206*, 347–354. [CrossRef]
11. Nielsen, R.E.; Banner, J.; Jensen, S.E. Cardiovascular Disease in Patients with Severe Mental Illness. *Nat. Rev. Cardiol.* **2021**, *18*, 136–145. [CrossRef]
12. Pouget, J.G.; Han, B.; Wu, Y.; Mignot, E.; Ollila, H.M.; Barker, J.; Spain, S.; Dand, N.; Trembath, R.; Martin, J. Schizophrenia Working Group of the Psychiatric Genomics Consortium; Cross-Disorder Analysis of Schizophrenia and 19 Immune-Mediated Diseases Identifies Shared Genetic Risk. *Hum. Mol. Genet.* **2019**, *28*, 3498–3513. [CrossRef] [PubMed]
13. Melkersson, K. Schizophrenia- or Schizoaffective Disorder Diagnosis and the Risk for Subsequent Type 1- or Type 2 Diabetes Mellitus: A Swedish Nationwide Register-Based Cohort Study. *Neuro. Endocrinol. Lett.* **2020**, *41*, 245–254. [PubMed]
14. Misiak, B.; Stańczykiewicz, B.; Wiśniewski, M.; Bartoli, F.; Carra, G.; Cavaleri, D.; Samochowiec, J.; Jarosz, K.; Rosińczuk, J.; Frydecka, D. Thyroid Hormones in Persons with Schizophrenia: A Systematic Review and Meta-Analysis. *Prog. Neuropsychopharmacol. Biol. Psychiatry* **2021**, *111*, 110402. [CrossRef] [PubMed]
15. Drake, R.E.; Xie, H.; McHugo, G.J. A 16-year Follow-up of Patients with Serious Mental Illness and Co-occurring Substance Use Disorder. *World Psychiatry* **2020**, *19*, 397–398. [CrossRef]
16. Plana-Ripoll, O.; Musliner, K.L.; Dalsgaard, S.; Momen, N.C.; Weye, N.; Christensen, M.K.; Agerbo, E.; Iburg, K.M.; Laursen, T.M.; Mortensen, P.B.; et al. Nature and Prevalence of Combinations of Mental Disorders and Their Association with Excess Mortality in a Population-Based Cohort Study. *World Psychiatry Off. J. World Psychiatr. Assoc. WPA* **2020**, *19*, 339–349. [CrossRef] [PubMed]
17. Correll, C.U.; Solmi, M.; Croatto, G.; Schneider, L.K.; Rohani-Montez, S.C.; Fairley, L.; Smith, N.; Bitter, I.; Gorwood, P.; Taipale, H.; et al. Mortality in People with Schizophrenia: A Systematic Review and Meta-Analysis of Relative Risk and Aggravating or Attenuating Factors. *World Psychiatry* **2022**, *21*, 248–271. [CrossRef] [PubMed]
18. van Os, J.; Linscott, R.J.; Myin-Germeys, I.; Delespaul, P.; Krabbendam, L. A Systematic Review and Meta-Analysis of the Psychosis Continuum: Evidence for a Psychosis Proneness-Persistence-Impairment Model of Psychotic Disorder. *Psychol. Med.* **2009**, *39*, 179–195. [CrossRef] [PubMed]
19. Insel, T.R. Rethinking Schizophrenia. *Nature* **2010**, *468*, 187–193. [CrossRef]
20. Barch, D.M.; Karcher, N.; Moran, E. Reinventing Schizophrenia-Embracing Complexity and Complication. *Schizophr. Res.* **2022**, *242*, 7–11. [CrossRef]
21. Chekroud, A.M.; Bondar, J.; Delgadillo, J.; Doherty, G.; Wasil, A.; Fokkema, M.; Cohen, Z.; Belgrave, D.; DeRubeis, R.; Iniesta, R.; et al. The Promise of Machine Learning in Predicting Treatment Outcomes in Psychiatry. *World Psychiatry* **2021**, *20*, 154–170. [CrossRef]
22. DeLisi, L.E. Redefining Schizophrenia through Genetics: A Commentary on 50 Years Searching for Biological Causes. *Schizophr. Res.* **2022**, *242*, 22–24. [CrossRef] [PubMed]
23. Nasrallah, H.A. Re-Inventing the Schizophrenia Syndrome: The Elusive "Theory of Everything". *Schizophr. Res.* **2022**, *242*, 106–108. [CrossRef] [PubMed]
24. Maj, M.; van Os, J.; De Hert, M.; Gaebel, W.; Galderisi, S.; Green, M.F.; Guloksuz, S.; Harvey, P.D.; Jones, P.B.; Malaspina, D.; et al. The Clinical Characterization of the Patient with Primary Psychosis Aimed at Personalization of Management. *World Psychiatry Off. J. World Psychiatr. Assoc. WPA* **2021**, *20*, 4–33. [CrossRef]
25. Tortorella, A. We Should Improve Personalization of Management in Patients with a Diagnosis of Schizophrenia. *J. Clin. Med.* **2021**, *11*, 184. [CrossRef]
26. Owoeye, O.; Kingston, T.; Scully, P.J.; Baldwin, P.; Browne, D.; Kinsella, A.; Russell, V.; O'Callaghan, E.; Waddington, J.L. Epidemiological and Clinical Characterization Following a First Psychotic Episode in Major Depressive Disorder: Comparisons with Schizophrenia and Bipolar I Disorder in the Cavan-Monaghan First Episode Psychosis Study (CAMFEPS). *Schizophr. Bull.* **2013**, *39*, 756–765. [CrossRef]
27. Tamminga, C.A.; Ivleva, E.I.; Keshavan, M.S.; Pearlson, G.D.; Clementz, B.A.; Witte, B.; Morris, D.W.; Bishop, J.; Thaker, G.K.; Sweeney, J.A. Clinical Phenotypes of Psychosis in the Bipolar-Schizophrenia Network on Intermediate Phenotypes (B-SNIP). *Am. J. Psychiatry* **2013**, *170*, 1263–1274. [CrossRef] [PubMed]
28. Iniesta, R.; Stahl, D.; McGuffin, P. Machine Learning, Statistical Learning and the Future of Biological Research in Psychiatry. *Psychol. Med.* **2016**, *46*, 2455–2465. [CrossRef]
29. Tikka, S.K.; Singh, B.K.; Nizamie, S.H.; Garg, S.; Mandal, S.; Thakur, K.; Singh, L.K. Artificial Intelligence-Based Classification of Schizophrenia: A High Density Electroencephalographic and Support Vector Machine Study. *Indian J. Psychiatry* **2020**, *62*, 273–282. [CrossRef]
30. Lai, J.W.; Ang, C.K.E.; Acharya, U.R.; Cheong, K.H. Schizophrenia: A Survey of Artificial Intelligence Techniques Applied to Detection and Classification. *Int. J. Environ. Res. Public. Health* **2021**, *18*, 6099. [CrossRef]

31. Cortes-Briones, J.A.; Tapia-Rivas, N.I.; D'Souza, D.C.; Estevez, P.A. Going Deep into Schizophrenia with Artificial Intelligence. *Schizophr. Res.* **2022**, *245*, 122–140. [CrossRef]
32. Kraepelin, E. *Psychiatrie: Ein kurzes Lehrbuch für Studirende und Aerzte. Dritte, Vielfach Umgearbeitete Auflage*; Ambr. Abel: Leipzig, Germany, 1889.
33. Kraepelin, E. *Psychiatrie: Ein kurzes Lehrbuch für Studirende und Aerzte. Vierte, Vollstandig Umgerbeitete Auflage*; Ambr. Abel: Leipzig, Germany, 1893.
34. Kraepelin, E.; Robertson, G.M.; Barclay, R.M. *Dementia Praecox and Paraphrenia. Translated from the 8th German Edition of the Lehrbruch der Psychiatrie*; Chicago Medical Book Co.: Chicago, IL, USA, 1919; Volume iii.
35. Heckers, S.; Kendler, K.S. The Evolution of Kraepelin's Nosological Principles. *World Psychiatry Off. J. World Psychiatr. Assoc. WPA* **2020**, *19*, 381–388. [CrossRef] [PubMed]
36. Tandon, R. Agreement on the Contours of Schizophrenia: The First Order of Business. *Schizophr. Res.* **2022**, *242*, 135–137. [CrossRef] [PubMed]
37. Bleuler, E. *Dementia Praecox or the Group of Schizophrenias*; International Universities Press: New York, NY, USA, 1911.
38. Kuhn, R. Eugen Bleuler's Concepts of Psychopathology. *Hist. Psychiatry* **2004**, *15 Pt 3*, 361–366. [CrossRef]
39. Gaebel, W.; Salveridou-Hof, E. Reinventing Schizophrenia: Updating the Construct-Primary Schizophrenia 2021—The Road Ahead. *Schizophr. Res.* **2022**, *242*, 27–29. [CrossRef] [PubMed]
40. Schneider, K. *Clinical Psychopathology*; Grune & Stratton: New York, NY, USA, 1959.
41. APA. *Diagnostic and Statistical Manual of Mental Disorders*, 4th ed.; American Psychiatric Association: Washington, DC, USA, 2020.
42. WHO. *International Statistical Classification of Diseases and Related Health Problems*, 10th ed.; World Health Organization: Geneva, Switzerland, 1992.
43. APA. *Diagnostic and Statistical Manual of Mental Disorders*, 5th ed.; American Psychiatric Publishing, Inc.: Arlington, VA, USA, 2013.
44. APA. *Diagnostic and Statistical Manual of Mental Disorders*, 5th ed.; Text Revised; American Psychiatric Association: Arlington, VA, USA, 2022.
45. WHO. *International Statistical Classification of Diseases and Related Health Problems, 11th*; (ICD-11); World Health Organization: Geneva, Switzerland, 2019.
46. Feighner, J.P.; Robins, E.; Guze, S.B.; Woodruff, R.A.; Winokur, G.; Munoz, R. Diagnostic Criteria for Use in Psychiatric Research. *Arch. Gen. Psychiatry* **1972**, *26*, 57–63. [CrossRef]
47. APA. *Diagnostic and Statistical Manual of Mental Disorders*, 3rd ed.; American Psychiatric Publishing: Washington, DC, USA, 1980.
48. Spitzer, R.L.; Endicott, J.; Robins, E. Research Diagnostic Criteria: Rationale and Reliability. *Arch. Gen. Psychiatry* **1978**, *35*, 773–782. [CrossRef]
49. Crow, T.J. Molecular Pathology of Schizophrenia: More than One Disease Process? *Br. Med. J.* **1980**, *280*, 66–68. [CrossRef]
50. Carpenter, W.T.; Heinrichs, D.W.; Wagman, A.M. Deficit and Nondeficit Forms of Schizophrenia: The Concept. *Am. J. Psychiatry* **1988**, *145*, 578–583. [CrossRef]
51. Andreasen, N.C.A. Unitary Model of Schizophrenia: Bleuler's "Fragmented Phrene" as Schizencephaly. *Arch. Gen. Psychiatry* **1999**, *56*, 781–787. [CrossRef]
52. Meehl, P.E. Schizotaxia, Schizotypy, Schizophrenia. In *Schizophrenia: Seven Approaches*; Routledge: London, UK, 1969.
53. Lenzenweger, M.F. Schizotaxia, Schizotypy, and Schizophrenia: Paul E. Meehl's Blueprint for the Experimental Psychopathology and Genetics of Schizophrenia. *J. Abnorm. Psychol.* **2006**, *115*, 195–200. [CrossRef]
54. Roberts, D.F. Schizophrenia: The Epigenetic Puzzle. By I. I. Gottesman and J. Shields. Cambridge University Press: Cambridge. 1982. *Psychol. Med.* **1983**, *13*, 690–692. [CrossRef]
55. Schizophrenia Genesis: The Origins of Madness—Royal Holloway, University of London. Available online: https://librarysearch.royalholloway.ac.uk/primo-explore/fulldisplay/44ROY_ALMA_DS2128877520002671/44ROY_VU2 (accessed on 20 June 2022).
56. Crow, T.J.A. Re-Evaluation of the Viral Hypothesis: Is Psychosis the Result of Retroviral Integration at a Site Close to the Cerebral Dominance Gene? *Br. J. Psychiatry J. Ment. Sci.* **1984**, *145*, 243–253. [CrossRef] [PubMed]
57. Stone, W.S.; Faraone, S.V.; Seidman, L.J.; Olson, E.A.; Tsuang, M.T.; Consortium on the Genetics on Schizophrenia. Searching for the Liability to Schizophrenia: Concepts and Methods Underlying Genetic High-Risk Studies of Adolescents. *J. Child Adolesc. Psychopharmacol.* **2005**, *15*, 403–417. [CrossRef] [PubMed]
58. Keshavan, M.S.; Kulkarni, S.; Bhojraj, T.; Francis, A.; Diwadkar, V.; Montrose, D.M.; Seidman, L.J.; Sweeney, J. Premorbid Cognitive Deficits in Young Relatives of Schizophrenia Patients. *Front. Hum. Neurosci.* **2010**, *3*, 62. [CrossRef] [PubMed]
59. Stone, W.S.; Hsi, X.; Giuliano, A.J.; Tan, L.; Zhu, S.; Li, L.; Seidman, L.J.; Tsuang, M.T. Are Neurocognitive, Clinical and Social Dysfunctions in Schizotaxia Reversible Pharmacologically?: Results from the Changsha Study. *Asian J. Psychiatry* **2012**, *5*, 73–82. [CrossRef]
60. Tsuang, M.T.; Stone, W.S.; Faraone, S.V. Toward Reformulating the Diagnosis of Schizophrenia. *Am. J. Psychiatry* **2000**, *157*, 1041–1050. [CrossRef]
61. Raballo, A.; Poletti, M.; Preti, A.; Parnas, J. The Self in the Spectrum: A Meta-Analysis of the Evidence Linking Basic Self-Disorders and Schizophrenia. *Schizophr. Bull.* **2021**, *47*, 1007–1017. [CrossRef]
62. van Os, J.; Kenis, G.; Rutten, B.P.F. The Environment and Schizophrenia. *Nature* **2010**, *468*, 203–212. [CrossRef]
63. Gur, R.E. Considering Alternatives to the Schizophrenia Construct. *Schizophr. Res.* **2022**, *242*, 49–51. [CrossRef]

64. Tandon, R.; Gaebel, W.; Barch, D.M.; Bustillo, J.; Gur, R.E.; Heckers, S.; Malaspina, D.; Owen, M.J.; Schultz, S. Definition and Description of Schizophrenia in the DSM-5. *Schizophr. Res.* **2013**, *150*, 3–10. [CrossRef]
65. Taghia, J.; Cai, W.; Ryali, S.; Kochalka, J.; Nicholas, J.; Chen, T.; Menon, V. Uncovering Hidden Brain State Dynamics That Regulate Performance and Decision-Making during Cognition. *Nat. Commun.* **2018**, *9*, 2505. [CrossRef] [PubMed]
66. Cannon, T.D. Psychosis, Schizophrenia, and States vs. Traits. *Schizophr. Res.* **2022**, *242*, 12–14. [CrossRef] [PubMed]
67. Clementz, B.A.; Trotti, R.L.; Pearlson, G.D.; Keshavan, M.S.; Gershon, E.S.; Keedy, S.K.; Ivleva, E.I.; McDowell, J.E.; Tamminga, C.A. Testing Psychosis Phenotypes from Bipolar-Schizophrenia Network for Intermediate Phenotypes for Clinical Application: Biotype Characteristics and Targets. *Biol. Psychiatry Cogn. Neurosci. Neuroimag.* **2020**, *5*, 808–818. [CrossRef]
68. Zick, J.L.; Staglin, B.; Vinogradov, S. Eliminate Schizophrenia. *Schizophr. Res.* **2022**, *242*, 147–149. [CrossRef] [PubMed]
69. Namkung, H.; Kim, S.H.; Sawa, A. The Insula: An Underestimated Brain Area in Clinical Neuroscience, Psychiatry, and Neurology. *Trends Neurosci.* **2017**, *40*, 200–207. [CrossRef]
70. Sawa, A.; Yang, K.; Cascella, N.G. Paradigm Shift on the Concept of Schizophrenia That Matches with Both Academic and Clinical Needs. *Schizophr. Res.* **2022**, *242*, 123–125. [CrossRef] [PubMed]
71. Carpenter, W.T. How the Diagnosis of Schizophrenia Impeded the Advance of Knowledge (and What to Do About It). In *Schizophrenia: Evolution and Synthesis*; Silverstein, S.M., Moghaddam, B., Wykes, T., Eds.; MIT Press: Cambridge, MA, USA, 2013.
72. Cuthbert, B.N.; Morris, S.E. Evolving Concepts of the Schizophrenia Spectrum: A Research Domain Criteria Perspective. *Front. Psychiatry* **2021**, *12*, 641319. [CrossRef]
73. Kapur, S.; Phillips, A.G.; Insel, T.R. Why Has It Taken so Long for Biological Psychiatry to Develop Clinical Tests and What to Do about It? *Mol. Psychiatry* **2012**, *17*, 1174–1179. [CrossRef]
74. Dazzan, P. Is Our Mistake Trying to Identify a "Homogeneous" Schizophrenia Construct? *Schizophr. Res.* **2022**, *242*, 20–21. [CrossRef]
75. Carpenter, W.T. Schizophrenia: A View of Immediate Future. *Schizophr. Res.* **2022**, *242*, 15–16. [CrossRef]
76. Murray, R.M.; Quattrone, D. The Kraepelian Concept of Schizophrenia: Dying but Not yet Dead. *Schizophr. Res.* **2022**, *242*, 102–105. [CrossRef] [PubMed]
77. van Os, J.; Guloksuz, S. Schizophrenia as a Symptom of Psychiatry's Reluctance to Enter the Moral Era of Medicine. *Schizophr. Res.* **2022**, *242*, 138–140. [CrossRef] [PubMed]
78. Kendler, K.S.; Heckers, S. The Schizophrenia Concept. *Schizophr. Res.* **2022**, *242*, 67–69. [CrossRef] [PubMed]
79. Kotov, R.; Jonas, K.G.; Carpenter, W.T.; Dretsch, M.N.; Eaton, N.R.; Forbes, M.K.; Forbush, K.T.; Hobbs, K.; Reininghaus, U.; Slade, T.; et al. Validity and Utility of Hierarchical Taxonomy of Psychopathology (HiTOP): I. Psychosis Superspectrum. *World Psychiatry* **2020**, *19*, 151–172. [CrossRef]
80. Tamminga, C.A. Assessing Striatal Dopamine in Schizophrenia. *Biol. Psychiatry* **2022**, *91*, 170–172. [CrossRef]
81. Keshavan, M.S.; Nasrallah, H.A.; Tandon, R. Schizophrenia, "Just the Facts" 6. Moving Ahead with the Schizophrenia Concept: From the Elephant to the Mouse. *Schizophr. Res.* **2011**, *127*, 3–13. [CrossRef]
82. Gordon, J.A.; Morris, S.E.; Avenevoli, S.A. Framework for Integration of Dimensional and Diagnostic Approaches to the Diagnosis of Schizophrenia. *Schizophr. Res.* **2022**, *242*, 98–101. [CrossRef]
83. First, M.B.; Gaebel, W.; Maj, M.; Stein, D.J.; Kogan, C.S.; Saunders, J.B.; Poznyak, V.B.; Gureje, O.; Lewis-Fernández, R.; Maercker, A.; et al. An Organization- and Category-Level Comparison of Diagnostic Requirements for Mental Disorders in ICD-11 and DSM-5. *World Psychiatry Off. J. World Psychiatr. Assoc. WPA* **2021**, *20*, 34–51. [CrossRef]
84. Rapoport, J.; Giedd, J.; Gogtay, N. Neurodevelopmental Model of Schizophrenia: Update 2012. *Mol. Psychiatry* **2012**, *17*, 1228–1238. [CrossRef]
85. Reichenberg, A.; Akbarian, S. Towards DSM 10: A Bio-Classification of Developmental Schizophrenia? *Schizophr. Res.* **2022**, *242*, 4–6. [CrossRef]
86. Sanislow, C.A. RDoC at 10: Changing the Discourse for Psychopathology. *World Psychiatry* **2020**, *19*, 311–312. [CrossRef] [PubMed]
87. Ross, C.A.; Margolis, R.L. Research Domain Criteria: Strengths, Weaknesses, and Potential Alternatives for Future Psychiatric Research. *Mol. Neuropsychiatry* **2019**, *5*, 218–236. [CrossRef] [PubMed]
88. Lahey, B.B.; Moore, T.M.; Kaczkurkin, A.N.; Zald, D.H. Hierarchical Models of Psychopathology: Empirical Support, Implications, and Remaining Issues. *World Psychiatry* **2021**, *20*, 57–63. [CrossRef] [PubMed]
89. Kotov, R.; Krueger, R.F.; Watson, D.; Achenbach, T.M.; Althoff, R.R.; Bagby, R.M.; Brown, T.A.; Carpenter, W.T.; Caspi, A.; Clark, L.A.; et al. The Hierarchical Taxonomy of Psychopathology (HiTOP): A Dimensional Alternative to Traditional Nosologies. *J. Abnorm. Psychol.* **2017**, *126*, 454–477. [CrossRef]
90. Kotov, R.; Jonas, K.G.; Lian, W.; Docherty, A.R.; Carpenter, W.T. Reconceptualizing Schizophrenia in the Hierarchical Taxonomy of Psychopathology (HiTOP). *Schizophr. Res.* **2022**, *242*, 73–77. [CrossRef]
91. Krueger, R.F.; Hobbs, K.A.; Conway, C.C.; Dick, D.M.; Dretsch, M.N.; Eaton, N.R.; Forbes, M.K.; Forbush, K.T.; Keyes, K.M.; Latzman, R.D.; et al. HiTOP Utility Workgroup. Validity and Utility of Hierarchical Taxonomy of Psychopathology (HiTOP): II. Externalizing Superspectrum. *World Psychiatry Off. J. World Psychiatr. Assoc. WPA* **2021**, *20*, 171–193. [CrossRef]
92. Hjorthøj, C.; Albert, N.; Nordentoft, M. Association of Substance Use Disorders with Conversion From Schizotypal Disorder to Schizophrenia. *JAMA Psychiatry* **2018**, *75*, 733–739. [CrossRef]

93. Clementz, B.A.; Parker, D.A.; Trotti, R.L.; McDowell, J.E.; Keedy, S.K.; Keshavan, M.S.; Pearlson, G.D.; Gershon, E.S.; Ivleva, E.I.; Huang, L.Y.; et al. Psychosis Biotypes: Replication and Validation from the B-SNIP Consortium. *Schizophr. Bull.* **2022**, *48*, 56–68. [CrossRef]
94. Clementz, B.A.; Sweeney, J.A.; Hamm, J.P.; Ivleva, E.I.; Ethridge, L.E.; Pearlson, G.D.; Keshavan, M.S.; Tamminga, C.A. Identification of Distinct Psychosis Biotypes Using Brain-Based Biomarkers. *Am. J. Psychiatry* **2016**, *173*, 373–384. [CrossRef]
95. Hall, M.H.; Smoller, J.W.; Cook, N.R.; Schulze, K.; Hyoun Lee, P.; Taylor, G.; Bramon, E.; Coleman, M.J.; Murray, R.M.; Salisbury, D.F.; et al. Patterns of Deficits in Brain Function in Bipolar Disorder and Schizophrenia: A Cluster Analytic Study. *Psychiatry Res.* **2012**, *200*, 272–280. [CrossRef]
96. Ginsburg, G.S.; McCarthy, J.J. Personalized Medicine: Revolutionizing Drug Discovery and Patient Care. *Trends Biotechnol.* **2001**, *19*, 491–496. [CrossRef]
97. Roffman, J.L. Biomarkers and Personalized Psychiatry. *Harv. Rev. Psychiatry* **2011**, *19*, 99–101. [CrossRef] [PubMed]
98. Carpenter, W.T. Primary Psychosis: More to Know, Much More to Do. *World Psychiatry* **2021**, *20*, 1–2. [CrossRef]
99. Levchenko, A.; Nurgaliev, T.; Kanapin, A.; Samsonova, A.; Gainetdinov, R.R. Current Challenges and Possible Future Developments in Personalized Psychiatry with an Emphasis on Psychotic Disorders. *Heliyon* **2020**, *6*, e03990. [CrossRef]
100. FDA-NIH Biomarker Working Group. *BEST (Biomarkers, EndpointS, and Other Tools) Resource*; Food and Drug Administration: Silver Spring, MD, USA, 2016.
101. Weickert, C.S.; Weickert, T.W.; Pillai, A.; Buckley, P.F. Biomarkers in Schizophrenia: A Brief Conceptual Consideration. *Dis. Markers* **2013**, *35*, 3–9. [CrossRef] [PubMed]
102. Gottesman, I.I.; Gould, T.D. The Endophenotype Concept in Psychiatry: Etymology and Strategic Intentions. *Am. J. Psychiatry* **2003**, *160*, 636–645. [CrossRef]
103. Califf, R.M. Biomarker Definitions and Their Applications. *Exp. Biol. Med.* **2018**, *243*, 213–221. [CrossRef]
104. de Andrada Pereira, B.; Wangsawatwong, P.; Lehrman, J.N.; Sawa, A.G.U.; Lindsey, D.P.; Yerby, S.A.; Godzik, J.; Waguespack, A.M.; Uribe, J.; Kelly, B.P. Biomechanics of a Laterally Placed Sacroiliac Joint Fusion Device Supplemental to S2 Alar-Iliac Fixation in a Long-Segment Adult Spinal Deformity Construct: A Cadaveric Study of Stability and Strain Distribution. *J. Neurosurg. Spine* **2022**, *36*, 42–52. [CrossRef]
105. Kelly, D.L.; Buchanan, R.W. Can the Current Schizophrenia Construct Endure? *Schizophr. Res.* **2022**, *242*, 64–66. [CrossRef]
106. Khandaker, G.M.; Cousins, L.; Deakin, J.; Lennox, B.R.; Yolken, R.; Jones, P.B. Inflammation and Immunity in Schizophrenia: Implications for Pathophysiology and Treatment. *Lancet Psychiatry* **2015**, *2*, 258–270. [CrossRef]
107. Chen, J.; Mize, T.; Wu, J.S.; Hong, E.; Nimgaonkar, V.; Kendler, K.S.; Allen, D.; Oh, E.; Netski, A.; Chen, X. Polygenic Risk Scores for Subtyping of Schizophrenia. *Schizophr. Res. Treat.* **2020**, *2020*, 1638403. [CrossRef] [PubMed]
108. Maes, M.; Sirivichayakul, S.; Matsumoto, A.K.; Maes, A.; Michelin, A.P.; de Oliveira Semeão, L.; de Lima Pedrão, J.V.; Moreira, E.G.; Barbosa, D.S. Increased Levels of Plasma Tumor Necrosis Factor-α Mediate Schizophrenia Symptom Dimensions and Neurocognitive Impairments and Are Inversely Associated with Natural IgM Directed to Malondialdehyde and Paraoxonase 1 Activity. *Mol. Neurobiol.* **2020**, *57*, 2333–2345. [CrossRef] [PubMed]
109. Fabbri, C.; Hosak, L.; Mössner, R.; Giegling, I.; Mandelli, L.; Bellivier, F.; Claes, S.; Collier, D.A.; Corrales, A.; Delisi, L.E.; et al. Consensus Paper of the WFSBP Task Force on Genetics: Genetics, Epigenetics and Gene Expression Markers of Major Depressive Disorder and Antidepressant Response. *World J. Biol. Psychiatry Off. J. World Fed. Soc. Biol. Psychiatry* **2017**, *18*, 5–28. [CrossRef] [PubMed]
110. Gandal, M.J.; Haney, J.R.; Parikshak, N.N.; Leppa, V.; Ramaswami, G.; Hartl, C.; Schork, A.J.; Appadurai, V.; Buil, A. CommonMind Consortium; PsychENCODE Consortium; iPSYCH-BROAD Working Group. Shared Molecular Neuropathology across Major Psychiatric Disorders Parallels Polygenic Overlap. *Science* **2018**, *359*, 693–697. [CrossRef] [PubMed]
111. Schmitt, A.; Martins-de-Souza, D.; Akbarian, S.; Cassoli, J.S.; Ehrenreich, H.; Fischer, A.; Fonteh, A.; Gattaz, W.F.; Gawlik, M.; Gerlach, M.; et al. Members of the WFSBP Task Force on Biological Markers. Consensus Paper of the WFSBP Task Force on Biological Markers: Criteria for Biomarkers and Endophenotypes of Schizophrenia, Part III: Molecular Mechanisms. *World J. Biol. Psychiatry Off. J. World Fed. Soc. Biol. Psychiatry* **2017**, *18*, 330–356. [CrossRef]
112. Kalia, M.; Costa, E.; Silva, J. Biomarkers of Psychiatric Diseases: Current Status and Future Prospects. *Metabolism.* **2015**, *64* (Suppl. S1), S11–S15. [CrossRef]
113. Lydon-Staley, D.M.; Bassett, D.S. Network Neuroscience: A Framework for Developing Biomarkers in Psychiatry. *Curr. Top. Behav. Neurosci.* **2018**, *40*, 79–109. [CrossRef]
114. Yenilmez, E.D.; Tamam, L.; Karaytug, O.; Tuli, A. Characterization CYP1A2, CYP2C9, CYP2C19 and CYP2D6 Polymorphisms Using HRMA in Psychiatry Patients with Schizophrenia and Bipolar Disease for Personalized Medicine. *Comb. Chem. High Throughput Screen.* **2018**, *21*, 374–380. [CrossRef]
115. Han, M.; Deng, C. BDNF as a Pharmacogenetic Target for Antipsychotic Treatment of Schizophrenia. *Neurosci. Lett.* **2020**, *726*, 133870. [CrossRef]
116. Owen, M.J.; Sawa, A.; Mortensen, P.B. Schizophrenia. *Lancet Lond. Engl.* **2016**, *388*, 86–97. [CrossRef]
117. Schizophrenia Working Group of the Psychiatric Genomics Consortium. Biological Insights from 108 Schizophrenia-Associated Genetic Loci. *Nature* **2014**, *511*, 421–427. [CrossRef] [PubMed]
118. Darby, M.M.; Yolken, R.H.; Sabunciyan, S. Consistently Altered Expression of Gene Sets in Postmortem Brains of Individuals with Major Psychiatric Disorders. *Transl. Psychiatry* **2016**, *6*, e890. [CrossRef] [PubMed]

119. Charney, A.W.; Stahl, E.A.; Green, E.K.; Chen, C.Y.; Moran, J.L.; Chambert, K.; Belliveau, R.A.; Forty, L.; Gordon-Smith, K.; Lee, P.H.; et al. Contribution of Rare Copy Number Variants to Bipolar Disorder Risk Is Limited to Schizoaffective Cases. *Biol. Psychiatry* **2019**, *86*, 110–119. [CrossRef] [PubMed]
120. Hubbard, L.; Rees, E.; Morris, D.W.; Lynham, A.J.; Richards, A.L.; Pardiñas, A.F.; Legge, S.E.; Harold, D.; Zammit, S. Rare Copy Number Variants Are Associated with Poorer Cognition in Schizophrenia. *Biol. Psychiatry* **2021**, *90*, 28–34. [CrossRef]
121. Merikangas, A.K.; Shelly, M.; Knighton, A.; Kotler, N.; Tanenbaum, N.; Almasy, L. What Genes Are Differentially Expressed in Individuals with Schizophrenia? A Systematic Review. *Mol. Psychiatry* **2022**, *27*, 1373–1383. [CrossRef]
122. Murray, G.K.; Lin, T.; Austin, J.; McGrath, J.J.; Hickie, I.B.; Wray, N.R. Could Polygenic Risk Scores Be Useful in Psychiatry?: A Review. *JAMA Psychiatry* **2021**, *78*, 210–219. [CrossRef]
123. Mistry, S.; Harrison, J.R.; Smith, D.J.; Escott-Price, V.; Zammit, S. The Use of Polygenic Risk Scores to Identify Phenotypes Associated with Genetic Risk of Bipolar Disorder and Depression: A Systematic Review. *J. Affect. Disord.* **2018**, *234*, 148–155. [CrossRef]
124. Ronald, A.; Pain, O. A Systematic Review of Genome-Wide Research on Psychotic Experiences and Negative Symptom Traits: New Revelations and Implications for Psychiatry. *Hum. Mol. Genet.* **2018**, *27*, R136–R152. [CrossRef]
125. Kauppi, K.; Westlye, L.T.; Tesli, M.; Bettella, F.; Brandt, C.L.; Mattingsdal, M.; Ueland, T.; Espeseth, T.; Agartz, I.; Melle, I.; et al. Polygenic Risk for Schizophrenia Associated with Working Memory-Related Prefrontal Brain Activation in Patients with Schizophrenia and Healthy Controls. *Schizophr. Bull.* **2015**, *41*, 736–743. [CrossRef]
126. van der Merwe, C.; Passchier, R.; Mufford, M.; Ramesar, R.; Dalvie, S.; Stein, D.J. Polygenic Risk for Schizophrenia and Associated Brain Structural Changes: A Systematic Review. *Compr. Psychiatry* **2019**, *88*, 77–82. [CrossRef]
127. Richards, A.L.; Pardiñas, A.F.; Frizzati, A.; Tansey, K.E.; Lynham, A.J.; Holmans, P.; Legge, S.E.; Savage, J.E.; Agartz, I.; Andreassen, O.A.; et al. The Relationship Between Polygenic Risk Scores and Cognition in Schizophrenia. *Schizophr. Bull.* **2020**, *46*, 336–344. [CrossRef] [PubMed]
128. Legge, S.E.; Cardno, A.G.; Allardyce, J.; Dennison, C.; Hubbard, L.; Pardiñas, A.F.; Richards, A.; Rees, E.; Di Florio, A.; Escott-Price, V.; et al. Associations Between Schizophrenia Polygenic Liability, Symptom Dimensions, and Cognitive Ability in Schizophrenia. *JAMA Psychiatry* **2021**, *78*, 1143–1151. [CrossRef] [PubMed]
129. Costain, G.; Lionel, A.C.; Merico, D.; Forsythe, P.; Russell, K.; Lowther, C.; Yuen, T.; Husted, J.; Stavropoulos, D.J.; Speevak, M.; et al. Pathogenic Rare Copy Number Variants in Community-Based Schizophrenia Suggest a Potential Role for Clinical Microarrays. *Hum. Mol. Genet.* **2013**, *22*, 4485–4501. [CrossRef]
130. Owen, M.J.; O'Donovan, M.C. Schizophrenia and the Neurodevelopmental Continuum: Evidence from Genomics. *World Psychiatry Off. J. World Psychiatr. Assoc. WPA* **2017**, *16*, 227–235. [CrossRef]
131. Marshall, C.R.; Howrigan, D.P.; Merico, D.; Thiruvahindrapuram, B.; Wu, W.; Greer, D.S.; Antaki, D.; Shetty, A.; Holmans, P.A. CNV and Schizophrenia Working Groups of the Psychiatric Genomics Consortium. Contribution of Copy Number Variants to Schizophrenia from a Genome-Wide Study of 41,321 Subjects. *Nat. Genet.* **2017**, *49*, 27–35. [CrossRef]
132. Cleynen, I.; Engchuan, W.; Hestand, M.S.; Heung, T.; Holleman, A.M.; Johnston, H.R.; Monfeuga, T.; McDonald-McGinn, D.M.; Gur, R.E.; Morrow, B.E.; et al. International 22q11.2DS Brain and Behavior Consortium. Genetic Contributors to Risk of Schizophrenia in the Presence of a 22q11.2 Deletion. *Mol. Psychiatry* **2021**, *26*, 4496–4510. [CrossRef]
133. Komatsu, H.; Fukuchi, M.; Habata, Y. Potential utility of Biased GPCR signaling for treatment of psychiatric disorders. *Int. J. Mol. Sci.* **2019**, *20*, 3207. [CrossRef]
134. Boczek, T.; Mackiewicz, J.; Sobolczyk, M.; Wawrzyniak, J.; Lisek, M.; Ferenc, B.; Guo, F.; Zylinska, L. The role of G Protein-Coupled Receptors (GPCRs) and calcium signaling in schizophrenia. Focus on GPCRs activated by neurotransmitters and chemokines. *Cells* **2021**, *10*, 1228. [CrossRef]
135. Morozova, A.; Zorkina, T.; Pavlov, K.; Pavlova, O.; Storozheva, Z.; Zubkov, E.; Zakharova, N.; Karpenko, O.; Reznik, A.; Chekjonin, V.; et al. Association of rs4680 COMT, rs6280 DRD3, and rs7322347 5HT2A with clinical features of youth-onset schizophrenia. *Front. Psuchiatry* **2019**, *10*, 830. [CrossRef]
136. Maj, C.; Minelli, A.; Giacopuzzi, E.; Sacchetti, E.; Gennarelli, M. The role of metabotropic glutamate receptor genes in schizophrenia. *Curr. Neurophamacol.* **2016**, *14*, 540–550. [CrossRef]
137. Saini, S.M.; Mancuso, S.G.; Mostaid, M.S.; Liu, C.; Pantelis, C.; Everall, I.P.; Bousman, C.A. Meta-analysis support GWAS-implicated link between GRM3 and schizophrenia risk. *Transl. Psychiatry* **2017**, *7*, e1196. [CrossRef] [PubMed]
138. Kang, Y.; Zhang, W.; Lv, Y.; Cai, S.; Xu, H.; Wang, J.; Huang, L. Effects of the 5-HT2A and DRD3 genotypes on cortical morphology and functional connectivity density in drug-naïve first episode schizophrenia. *Schizophr. Res.* **2020**, *216*, 213–221. [CrossRef] [PubMed]
139. Zakharyan, R.; Ghazaryan, H.; Kocourkova, L.; Chavushyan, A.; Mkrtchyan, A.; Zizkova, V.; Arakelyan, A.; Martin, P. Association of genetic variations of dopamine and serotonin in schizophrenia. *Arch. Med. Res.* **2020**, *51*, 13–20. [CrossRef] [PubMed]
140. Zhao, M.; Ma, J.; Li, M.; Zhu, W.; Zhou, W.; Shen, L.; Wu, H.; Zhang, N.; Wu, S.; Fu, C.; et al. Different responses to risperidone treatment in schizophrenia: A multicenter genome-wide association and whole exome sequencing joint study. *Transl. Psychiatry* **2022**, *12*, 173. [CrossRef]
141. Rahman, M.M.; Mim, S.A.; Islam, M.R.; Sultana, N.; Ahmed, M.; Kamal, M.A. Role of G-proteins and GPCR-mediated signaling in neuropathophysiology. *CSN. Neurol. Disord. Drug. Targets* **2022**, preprint. [CrossRef]

142. Smigielski, L.; Jagannath, V.; Rössler, W.; Walitza, S.; Grünblatt, E. Epigenetic Mechanisms in Schizophrenia and Other Psychotic Disorders: A Systematic Review of Empirical Human Findings. *Mol. Psychiatry* **2020**, *25*, 1718–1748. [CrossRef]
143. Radua, J.; Ramella-Cravaro, V.; Ioannidis, J.P.A.; Reichenberg, A.; Phiphopthatsanee, N.; Amir, T.; Yenn Thoo, H.; Oliver, D.; Davies, C.; Morgan, C.; et al. What Causes Psychosis? An Umbrella Review of Risk and Protective Factors. *World Psychiatry* **2018**, *17*, 49–66. [CrossRef]
144. van Erp, T.G.M.; Hibar, D.P.; Rasmussen, J.M.; Glahn, D.C.; Pearlson, G.D.; Andreassen, O.A.; Agartz, I.; Westlye, L.T.; Haukvik, U.K.; Dale, A.M.; et al. Subcortical Brain Volume Abnormalities in 2028 Individuals with Schizophrenia and 2540 Healthy Controls via the ENIGMA Consortium. *Mol. Psychiatry* **2016**, *21*, 547–553. [CrossRef]
145. van Erp, T.G.M.; Walton, E.; Hibar, D.P.; Schmaal, L.; Jiang, W.; Glahn, D.C.; Pearlson, G.D.; Yao, N.; Fukunaga, M.; Hashimoto, R.; et al. Cortical Brain Abnormalities in 4474 Individuals with Schizophrenia and 5098 Control Subjects via the Enhancing Neuro Imaging Genetics Through Meta Analysis (ENIGMA) Consortium. *Biol. Psychiatry* **2018**, *84*. 644–654. [CrossRef]
146. Keshavan, M.S.; Collin, G.; Guimond, S.; Kelly, S.; Prasad, K.M.; Lizano, P. Neuroimaging in Schizophrenia. *Neuroimaging Clin. N. Am.* **2020**, *30*, 73–83. [CrossRef]
147. Wheeler, A.L.; Voineskos, A.N. A Review of Structural Neuroimaging in Schizophrenia: From Connectivity to Connectomics. *Front. Hum. Neurosci.* **2014**, *8*, 653. [CrossRef] [PubMed]
148. Hill, K.; Mann, L.; Laws, K.R.; Stephenson, C.M.E.; Nimmo-Smith, I.; McKenna, P.J. Hypofrontality in Schizophrenia: A Meta-Analysis of Functional Imaging Studies. *Acta Psychiatr. Scand.* **2004**, *110*, 243–256. [CrossRef] [PubMed]
149. Glahn, D.C.; Ragland, J.D.; Abramoff, A.; Barrett, J.; Laird, A.R.; Bearden, C.E.; Velligan, D.I. Beyond Hypofrontality: A Quantitative Meta-Analysis of Functional Neuroimaging Studies of Working Memory in Schizophrenia. *Hum. Brain Mapp.* **2005**, *25*, 60–69. [CrossRef]
150. Kühn, S.; Gallinat, J. Resting-State Brain Activity in Schizophrenia and Major Depression: A Quantitative Meta-Analysis. *Schizophr. Bull.* **2013**, *39*, 358–365. [CrossRef] [PubMed]
151. Guimarães, T.M.; Machado-de-Sousa, J.P.; Crippa, J.A.S.; Guimarães, M.R.C.; Hallak, J.E.C. Arterial Spin Labeling in Patients with Schizophrenia: A Systematic Review. *Arch. Clin. Psychiatry* **2016**, *43*, 151–156. [CrossRef]
152. Laruelle, M.; Abi-Dargham, A.; Gil, R.; Kegeles, L.; Innis, R. Increased Dopamine Transmission in Schizophrenia: Relationship to Illness Phases. *Biol. Psychiatry* **1999**, *46*, 56–72. [CrossRef]
153. Abi-Dargham, A.; Rodenhiser, J.; Printz, D.; Zea-Ponce, Y.; Gil, R.; Kegeles, L.S.; Weiss, R.; Cooper, T.B.; Mann, J.J.; Van Heertum, R.L.; et al. Increased Baseline Occupancy of D2 Receptors by Dopamine in Schizophrenia. *Proc. Natl. Acad. Sci. USA* **2000**, *97*, 8104–8109. [CrossRef]
154. Poels, E.M.P.; Kegeles, L.S.; Kantrowitz, J.T.; Slifstein, M.; Javitt, D.C.; Lieberman, J.A.; Abi-Dargham, A.; Girgis, R.R. Imaging Glutamate in Schizophrenia: Review of Findings and Implications for Drug Discovery. *Mol. Psychiatry* **2014**, *19*, 20–29. [CrossRef]
155. Nikolaus, S.; Müller, H.W.; Hautzel, H. Different Patterns of 5-HT Receptor and Transporter Dysfunction in Neuropsychiatric Disorders—A Comparative Analysis of in Vivo Imaging Findings. *Rev. Neurosci.* **2016**, *27*, 27–59. [CrossRef]
156. Egerton, A.; Modinos, G.; Ferrera, D.; McGuire, P. Neuroimaging Studies of GABA in Schizophrenia: A Systematic Review with Meta-Analysis. *Transl. Psychiatry* **2017**, *7*, e1147. [CrossRef]
157. Cannon, T.D.; Chung, Y.; He, G.; Sun, D.; Jacobson, A.; van Erp, T.G.M.; McEwen, S.; Addington, J.; Bearden, C.E.; Cadenhead, K.; et al. North American Prodrome Longitudinal Study Consortium. Progressive Reduction in Cortical Thickness as Psychosis Develops: A Multisite Longitudinal Neuroimaging Study of Youth at Elevated Clinical Risk. *Biol. Psychiatry* **2015**, *77*, 147–157. [CrossRef] [PubMed]
158. Fusar-Poli, P.; Cappucciati, M.; Rutigliano, G.; Schultze-Lutter, F.; Bonoldi, I.; Borgwardt, S.; Riecher-Rössler, A.; Addington, J.; Perkins, D.; Woods, S.W.; et al. At Risk or Not at Risk? A Meta-Analysis of the Prognostic Accuracy of Psychometric Interviews for Psychosis Prediction. *World Psychiatry Off. J. World Psychiatr. Assoc. WPA* **2015**, *14*, 322–332. [CrossRef] [PubMed]
159. Koutsouleris, N.; Meisenzahl, E.M.; Davatzikos, C.; Bottlender, R.; Frodl, T.; Scheuerecker, J.; Schmitt, G.; Zetzsche, T.; Decker, P.; Reiser, M.; et al. Use of Neuroanatomical Pattern Classification to Identify Subjects in At-Risk Mental States of Psychosis and Predict Disease Transition. *Arch. Gen. Psychiatry* **2009**, *66*, 700–712. [CrossRef]
160. Mechelli, A.; Riecher-Rössler, A.; Meisenzahl, E.M.; Tognin, S.; Wood, S.J.; Borgwardt, S.J.; Koutsouleris, N.; Yung, A.R.; Stone, J.M. Neuroanatomical Abnormalities That Predate the Onset of Psychosis: A Multicenter Study. *Arch. Gen. Psychiatry* **2011**, *68*, 489–495. [CrossRef] [PubMed]
161. Koutsouleris, N.; Riecher-Rössler, A.; Meisenzahl, E.M.; Smieskova, R.; Studerus, E.; Kambeitz-Ilankovic, L.; von Saldern, S.; Cabral, C.; Reiser, M.; Falkai, P.; et al. Detecting the Psychosis Prodrome across High-Risk Populations Using Neuroanatomical Biomarkers. *Schizophr. Bull.* **2015**, *41*, 471–482. [CrossRef]
162. Cao, H.; Chén, O.Y.; Chung, Y.; Forsyth, J.K.; McEwen, S.C.; Gee, D.G.; Bearden, C.E.; Addington, J.; Goodyear, B.; Cadenhead, K.S.; et al. Cerebello-Thalamo-Cortical Hyperconnectivity as a State-Independent Functional Neural Signature for Psychosis Prediction and Characterization. *Nat. Commun.* **2018**, *9*, 3836. [CrossRef]
163. Collin, G.; Seidman, L.J.; Keshavan, M.S.; Stone, W.S.; Qi, Z.; Zhang, T.; Tang, Y.; Li, H.; Anteraper, S.A.; Niznikiewicz, M.A.; et al. Functional Connectome Organization Predicts Conversion to Psychosis in Clinical High-Risk Youth from the SHARP Program. *Mol. Psychiatry* **2020**, *25*, 2431–2440. [CrossRef]
164. Demjaha, A.; Murray, R.M.; McGuire, P.K.; Kapur, S.; Howes, O.D. Dopamine Synthesis Capacity in Patients with Treatment-Resistant Schizophrenia. *Am. J. Psychiatry* **2012**, *169*, 1203–1210. [CrossRef]

165. Guimond, S.; Béland, S.; Lepage, M. Strategy for Semantic Association Memory (SESAME) Training: Effects on Brain Functioning in Schizophrenia. *Psychiatry Res. Neuroimag.* **2018**, *271*, 50–58. [CrossRef]
166. Cui, L.B.; Cai, M.; Wang, X.R.; Zhu, Y.Q.; Wang, L.X.; Xi, Y.B.; Wang, H.N.; Zhu, X.; Yin, H. Prediction of Early Response to Overall Treatment for Schizophrenia: A Functional Magnetic Resonance Imaging Study. *Brain Behav.* **2019**, *9*, e01211. [CrossRef]
167. Jauhar, S.; Veronese, M.; Nour, M.M.; Rogdaki, M.; Hathway, P.; Turkheimer, F.E.; Stone, J.; Egerton, A.; McGuire, P.; Kapur, S.; et al. Determinants of Treatment Response in First-Episode Psychosis: An 18F-DOPA PET Study. *Mol. Psychiatry* **2019**, *24*, 1502–1512. [CrossRef] [PubMed]
168. Tarcijonas, G.; Sarpal, D.K. Neuroimaging Markers of Antipsychotic Treatment Response in Schizophrenia: An Overview of Magnetic Resonance Imaging Studies. *Neurobiol. Dis.* **2019**, *131*, 104209. [CrossRef] [PubMed]
169. Pence, A.Y.; Pries, L.K.; Ferrara, M.; Rutten, B.P.F.; van Os, J.; Guloksuz, S. Gender Differences in the Association between Environment and Psychosis. *Schizophr. Res.* **2022**, *243*, 120–137. [CrossRef] [PubMed]
170. Woolway, G.E.; Smart, S.E.; Lynham, A.J.; Lloyd, J.L.; Owen, M.J.; Jones, I.R.; Walters, J.T.R.; Legge, S.E. Schizophrenia Polygenic Risk and Experiences of Childhood Adversity: A Systematic Review and Meta-Analysis. *Schizophr. Bull.* **2022**, *1*, sbac049. [CrossRef] [PubMed]
171. Large, M.; Mullin, K.; Gupta, P.; Harris, A.; Nielssen, O. Systematic Meta-Analysis of Outcomes Associated with Psychosis and Co-Morbid Substance Use. *Aust. N. Z. J. Psychiatry* **2014**, *48*, 418–432. [CrossRef]
172. Schoeler, T.; Petros, N.; Di Forti, M.; Pingault, J.B.; Klamerus, E.; Foglia, E.; Small, A.; Murray, R.; Bhattacharyya, S. Association Between Continued Cannabis Use and Risk of Relapse in First-Episode Psychosis: A Quasi-Experimental Investigation Within an Observational Study. *JAMA Psychiatry* **2016**, *73*, 1173–1179. [CrossRef]
173. Di Forti, M.; Marconi, A.; Carra, E.; Fraietta, S.; Trotta, A.; Bonomo, M.; Bianconi, F.; Gardner-Sood, P.; O'Connor, J.; Russo, M.; et al. Proportion of Patients in South London with First-Episode Psychosis Attributable to Use of High Potency Cannabis: A Case-Control Study. *Lancet Psychiatry* **2015**, *2*, 233–238. [CrossRef]
174. Di Forti, M.; Quattrone, D.; Freeman, T.P.; Tripoli, G.; Gayer-Anderson, C.; Quigley, H.; Rodriguez, V.; Jongsma, H.E.; Ferraro, L.; La Cascia, C.; et al. EU-GEI WP2 Group. The Contribution of Cannabis Use to Variation in the Incidence of Psychotic Disorder across Europe (EU-GEI): A Multicentre Case-Control Study. *Lancet Psychiatry* **2019**, *6*, 427–436. [CrossRef]
175. Ringen, P.A.; Nesvåg, R.; Helle, S.; Lagerberg, T.V.; Lange, E.H.; Løberg, E.M.; Agartz, I.; Andreassen, O.A.; Melle, I. Premorbid Cannabis Use Is Associated with More Symptoms and Poorer Functioning in Schizophrenia Spectrum Disorder. *Psychol. Med.* **2016**, *46*, 3127–3136. [CrossRef]
176. Seddon, J.L.; Birchwood, M.; Copello, A.; Everard, L.; Jones, P.B.; Fowler, D.; Amos, T.; Freemantle, N.; Sharma, V.; Marshall, M.; et al. Cannabis Use Is Associated with Increased Psychotic Symptoms and Poorer Psychosocial Functioning in First-Episode Psychosis: A Report From the UK National EDEN Study. *Schizophr. Bull.* **2016**, *42*, 619–625. [CrossRef]
177. Quattrone, D.; Di Forti, M.; Gayer-Anderson, C.; Ferraro, L.; Jongsma, H.E.; Tripoli, G.; La Cascia, C.; La Barbera, D.; Tarricone, I.; Berardi, D.; et al. Transdiagnostic Dimensions of Psychopathology at First Episode Psychosis: Findings from the Multinational EU-GEI Study. *Psychol. Med.* **2019**, *49*, 1378–1391. [CrossRef] [PubMed]
178. Guloksuz, S.; Rutten, B.P.F.; Pries, L.K.; Ten Have, M.; de Graaf, R.; van Dorsselaer, S.; Klingenberg, B.; van Os, J.; Ioannidis, J.P.A.; European Network of National Schizophrenia Networks Studying Gene-Environment Interactions Work Package 6 (EU-GEI WP6) Group. The Complexities of Evaluating the Exposome in Psychiatry: A Data-Driven Illustration of Challenges and Some Propositions for Amendments. *Schizophr. Bull.* **2018**, *44*, 1175–1179. [CrossRef] [PubMed]
179. Guloksuz, S.; van Os, J.; Rutten, B.P.F. The Exposome Paradigm and the Complexities of Environmental Research in Psychiatry. *JAMA Psychiatry* **2018**, *75*, 985–986. [CrossRef] [PubMed]
180. Pries, L.K.; Erzin, G.; Rutten, B.P.F.; van Os, J.; Guloksuz, S. Estimating Aggregate Environmental Risk Score in Psychiatry: The Exposome Score for Schizophrenia. *Front. Psychiatry* **2021**, *12*, 671334. [CrossRef]
181. Erzin, G.; Pries, L.K.; van Os, J.; Fusar-Poli, L.; Delespaul, P.; Kenis, G.; Luykx, J.J.; Lin, B.D.; Richards, A.L.; Akdede, B.; et al. Examining the Association between Exposome Score for Schizophrenia and Functioning in Schizophrenia, Siblings, and Healthy Controls: Results from the EUGEI Study. *Eur. Psychiatry J. Assoc. Eur. Psychiatr.* **2021**, *64*, e25. [CrossRef]
182. Pries, L.K.; Guloksuz, S.; Ten Have, M.; de Graaf, R.; van Dorsselaer, S.; Gunther, N.; Rauschenberg, C.; Reininghaus, U.; Radhakrishnan, R.; Bak, M.; et al. Evidence That Environmental and Familial Risks for Psychosis Additively Impact a Multidimensional Subthreshold Psychosis Syndrome. *Schizophr. Bull.* **2018**, *44*, 710–719. [CrossRef]
183. Barzilay, R.; Calkins, M.E.; Moore, T.M.; Wolf, D.H.; Satterthwaite, T.D.; Cobb Scott, J.; Jones, J.D.; Benton, T.D.; Gur, R.C.; Gur, R.E. Association between Traumatic Stress Load, Psychopathology, and Cognition in the Philadelphia Neurodevelopmental Cohort. *Psychol. Med.* **2019**, *49*, 325–334. [CrossRef]
184. Gaebel, W.; Falkai, P.; Hasan, A. The Revised German Evidence- and Consensus-Based Schizophrenia Guideline. *World Psychiatry Off. J. World Psychiatr. Assoc. WPA* **2020**, *19*, 117–119. [CrossRef]
185. Hasan, A.; Falkai, P.; Wobrock, T.; Lieberman, J.; Glenthoj, B.; Gattaz, W.F.; Thibaut, F.; Möller, H.J.; WFSBP Task force on Treatment Guidelines for Schizophrenia. World Federation of Societies of Biological Psychiatry (WFSBP) Guidelines for Biological Treatment of Schizophrenia, Part 2: Update 2012 on the Long-Term Treatment of Schizophrenia and Management of Antipsychotic-Induced Side Effects. *World J. Biol. Psychiatry Off. J. World Fed. Soc. Biol. Psychiatry* **2013**, *14*, 2–44. [CrossRef]
186. Remington, G.; Addington, D.; Honer, W.; Ismail, Z.; Raedler, T.; Teehan, M. Guidelines for the Pharmacotherapy of Schizophrenia in Adults. *Can. J. Psychiatry Rev. Can. Psychiatr.* **2017**, *62*, 604–616. [CrossRef]

187. Keepers, G.A.; Fochtmann, L.J.; Anzia, J.M.; Benjamin, S.; Lyness, J.M.; Mojtabai, R.; Servis, M.; Walaszek, A.; Buckley, P.; Lenzenweger, M.F.; et al. The American Psychiatric Association Practice Guideline for the Treatment of Patients with Schizophrenia. *Am. J. Psychiatry* **2020**, *177*, 868–872. [CrossRef]
188. National Institute for Health and Care Excellence: Guidelines. *Psychosis and Schizophrenia in Adults: Prevention and Management*; National Institute for Health and Care Excellence (NICE): London, UK, 2014.
189. Hasan, A.; Falkai, P.; Wobrock, T.; Lieberman, J.; Glenthoj, B.; Gattaz, W.F.; Thibaut, F.; Möller, H.J.; World Federation of Societies of Biological Psychiatry (WFSBP) Task Force on Treatment Guidelines for Schizophrenia. World Federation of Societies of Biological Psychiatry (WFSBP) Guidelines for Biological Treatment of Schizophrenia, Part 1: Update 2012 on the Acute Treatment of Schizophrenia and the Management of Treatment Resistance. *World J. Biol. Psychiatry Off. J. World Fed. Soc. Biol. Psychiatry* **2012**, *13*, 318–378. [CrossRef] [PubMed]
190. Verdoux, H.; Tournier, M.; Bégaud, B. Antipsychotic Prescribing Trends: A Review of Pharmaco-Epidemiological Studies. *Acta Psychiatr. Scand.* **2010**, *121*, 4–10. [CrossRef] [PubMed]
191. Taipale, H.; Tanskanen, A.; Mehtälä, J.; Vattulainen, P.; Correll, C.U.; Tiihonen, J. 20-Year Follow-up Study of Physical Morbidity and Mortality in Relationship to Antipsychotic Treatment in a Nationwide Cohort of 62,250 Patients with Schizophrenia (FIN20). *World Psychiatry Off. J. World Psychiatr. Assoc. WPA* **2020**, *19*, 61–68. [CrossRef] [PubMed]
192. Ostuzzi, G.; Vita, G.; Bertolini, F.; Tedeschi, F.; De Luca, B.; Gastaldon, C.; Nosé, M.; Papola, D.; Purgato, M.; Del Giovane, C.; et al. Continuing, Reducing, Switching, or Stopping Antipsychotics in Individuals with Schizophrenia-Spectrum Disorders Who Are Clinically Stable: A Systematic Review and Network Meta-Analysis. *Lancet Psychiatry* **2022**, *9*, 614–624. [CrossRef]
193. Huhn, M.; Arndt, T.; Schneider-Thoma, J.; Leucht, S. Effects of Antipsychotics on Heart Rate in Treatment of Schizophrenia: A Systematic Review and Meta-Analysis. *Ther. Adv. Psychopharmacol.* **2022**, *12*, 20451253221097260. [CrossRef]
194. McCutcheon, R.A.; Krystal, J.H.; Howes, O.D. Dopamine and Glutamate in Schizophrenia: Biology, Symptoms and Treatment. *World Psychiatry* **2020**, *19*, 15–33. [CrossRef]
195. Llorca, P.M.; Nuss, P.; Fakra, É.; Alamome, I.; Drapier, D.; El Hage, W.; Jardri, R.; Mouchabac, S.; Rabbani, M.; Simon, N.; et al. Place of the Partial Dopamine Receptor Agonist Aripiprazole in the Management of Schizophrenia in Adults: A Delphi Consensus Study. *BMC Psychiatry* **2022**, *22*, 364. [CrossRef]
196. Osugo, M.; Whitehurst, T.; Shatalina, E.; Townsend, L.; O'Brien, O.; Mak, T.L.A.; McCutcheon, R.; Howes, O. Dopamine Partial Agonists and Prodopaminergic Drugs for Schizophrenia: Systematic Review and Meta-Analysis of Randomized Controlled Trials. *Neurosci. Biobehav. Rev.* **2022**, *135*, 104568. [CrossRef]
197. Kumar, V.; Manchegowda, S.; Jacob, A.; Rao, N.P. Glutamate Metabolites in Treatment Resistant Schizophrenia: A Meta-Analysis and Systematic Review of 1H-MRS Studies. *Psychiatry Res. Neuroimag.* **2020**, *300*, 111080. [CrossRef]
198. Kiemes, A.; Davies, C.; Kempton, M.J.; Lukow, P.B.; Bennallick, C.; Stone, J.M.; Modinos, G. GABA, Glutamate and Neural Activity: A Systematic Review with Meta-Analysis of Multimodal 1H-MRS-FMRI Studies. *Front. Psychiatry* **2021**, *12*, 225. [CrossRef] [PubMed]
199. Bighelli, I.; Salanti, G.; Huhn, M.; Schneider-Thoma, J.; Krause, M.; Reitmeir, C.; Wallis, S.; Schwermann, F.; Pitschel-Walz, G.; Barbui, C.; et al. Psychological Interventions to Reduce Positive Symptoms in Schizophrenia: Systematic Review and Network Meta-Analysis. *World Psychiatry Off. J. World Psychiatr. Assoc. WPA* **2018**, *17*, 316–329. [CrossRef] [PubMed]
200. Barnicot, K.; Michael, C.; Trione, E.; Lang, S.; Saunders, T.; Sharp, M.; Crawford, M.J. Psychological Interventions for Acute Psychiatric Inpatients with Schizophrenia-Spectrum Disorders: A Systematic Review and Meta-Analysis. *Clin. Psychol. Rev.* **2020**, *82*, 101929. [CrossRef] [PubMed]
201. Todorovic, A.; Lal, S.; Dark, F.; De Monte, V.; Kisely, S.; Siskind, D. CBTp for People with Treatment Refractory Schizophrenia on Clozapine: A Systematic Review and Meta-Analysis. *J. Ment. Health Abingdon Engl.* **2020**, 1–8. [CrossRef] [PubMed]
202. Mc Glanaghy, E.; Turner, D.; Davis, G.A.; Sharpe, H.; Dougall, N.; Morris, P.; Prentice, W.; Hutton, P.A. Network Meta-Analysis of Psychological Interventions for Schizophrenia and Psychosis: Impact on Symptoms. *Schizophr. Res.* **2021**, *228*, 447–459. [CrossRef] [PubMed]
203. Gastaldon, C.; Mosler, F.; Toner, S.; Tedeschi, F.; Bird, V.J.; Barbui, C.; Priebe, S. Are Trials of Psychological and Psychosocial Interventions for Schizophrenia and Psychosis Included in the NICE Guidelines Pragmatic? A Systematic Review. *PLoS ONE* **2019**, *14*, e0222891. [CrossRef]
204. Nucifora, F.C.; Woznica, E.; Lee, B.J.; Cascella, N.; Sawa, A. Treatment Resistant Schizophrenia: Clinical, Biological, and Therapeutic Perspectives. *Neurobiol. Dis.* **2019**, *131*, 104257. [CrossRef]
205. Corripio, I.; Roldán, A.; Sarró, S.; McKenna, P.J.; Alonso-Solís, A.; Rabella, M.; Díaz, A.; Puigdemont, D.; Pérez-Solà, V.; Álvarez, E.; et al. Deep Brain Stimulation in Treatment Resistant Schizophrenia: A Pilot Randomized Cross-over Clinical Trial. *EBioMedicine* **2020**, *51*, 102568. [CrossRef]
206. Sciortino, D.; Pigoni, A.; Delvecchio, G.; Maggioni, E.; Schiena, G.; Brambilla, P. Role of RTMS in the Treatment of Cognitive Impairments in Bipolar Disorder and Schizophrenia: A Review of Randomized Controlled Trials. *J. Affect. Disord.* **2021**, *280 Pt A*, 148–155. [CrossRef]
207. Glenthøj, L.B.; Mariegaard, L.S.; Fagerlund, B.; Jepsen, J.R.M.; Kristensen, T.D.; Wenneberg, C.; Krakauer, K.; Medalia, A.; Roberts, D.L.; Hjorthøj, C.; et al. Effectiveness of Cognitive Remediation in the Ultra-High Risk State for Psychosis. *World Psychiatry Off. J. World Psychiatr. Assoc. WPA* **2020**, *19*, 401–402. [CrossRef]

208. Lysaker, P.H.; Hasson-Ohayon, I. Metacognition in Psychosis: A Renewed Path to Understanding of Core Disturbances and Recovery-oriented Treatment. *World Psychiatry* **2021**, *20*, 359–361. [CrossRef] [PubMed]
209. Phelan, S.; Sigala, N. The Effect of Treatment on Insight in Psychotic Disorders—A Systematic Review and Meta-Analysis. *Schizophr. Res.* **2022**, *244*, 126–133. [CrossRef] [PubMed]
210. Schroeder, A.H.; Bogie, B.J.M.; Rahman, T.T.; Thérond, A.; Matheson, H.; Guimond, S. Feasibility and Efficacy of Virtual Reality Interventions to Improve Psychosocial Functioning in Psychosis: Systematic Review. *JMIR Ment. Health* **2022**, *9*, e28502. [CrossRef]
211. Rodolico, A.; Bighelli, I.; Avanzato, C.; Concerto, C.; Cutrufelli, P.; Mineo, L.; Schneider-Thoma, J.; Siafis, S.; Signorelli, M.S.; Wu, H.; et al. Family Interventions for Relapse Prevention in Schizophrenia: A Systematic Review and Network Meta-Analysis. *Lancet Psychiatry* **2022**, *9*, 211–221. [CrossRef]
212. Bond, G.R.; Drake, R.E.; Becker, D.R. An Update on Individual Placement and Support. *World Psychiatry* **2020**, *19*, 390–391. [CrossRef]
213. Hellström, L.; Pedersen, P.; Christensen, T.N.; Wallstroem, I.G.; Bojesen, A.B.; Stenager, E.; Bejerholm, U.; van Busschbach, J.; Michon, H.; Mueser, K.T.; et al. Vocational Outcomes of the Individual Placement and Support Model in Subgroups of Diagnoses, Substance Abuse, and Forensic Conditions: A Systematic Review and Analysis of Pooled Original Data. *J. Occup. Rehabil.* **2021**, *31*, 699–710. [CrossRef] [PubMed]
214. Frederick, D.E.; VanderWeele, T.J. Supported Employment: Meta-Analysis and Review of Randomized Controlled Trials of Individual Placement and Support. *PLoS ONE* **2019**, *14*, e0212208. [CrossRef]
215. Brinchmann, B.; Widding-Havneraas, T.; Modini, M.; Rinaldi, M.; Moe, C.F.; McDaid, D.; Park, A.L.; Killackey, E.; Harvey, S.B.; Mykletun, A.A. Meta-Regression of the Impact of Policy on the Efficacy of Individual Placement and Support. *Acta Psychiatry Scand.* **2020**, *141*, 206–220. [CrossRef]
216. Baller, J.B.; Blyler, C.R.; Bronnikov, S.; Xie, H.; Bond, G.R.; Filion, K.; Hale, T. Long-Term Follow-Up of a Randomized Trial of Supported Employment for SSDI Beneficiaries with Mental Illness. *Psychiatry Serv.* **2020**, *71*, 243–249. [CrossRef]
217. Feldman, R. What Is Resilience: An Affiliative Neuroscience Approach. *World Psychiatry* **2020**, *19*, 132–150. [CrossRef]
218. Harvey, P.D.; Strassing, M. Predicting the Severity of Everyday Functional Disability in People with Schizophrenia: Cognitive Deficits, Functional Capacity, Symptoms, and Health Status. *World Psychiatry* **2012**, *11*, 73–79. [CrossRef] [PubMed]
219. Green, M.F.; Horan, W.P.; Lee, J. Nonsocial and Social Cognition in Schizophrenia: Current Evidence and Future Directions. *World Psychiatry Off. J. World Psychiatr. Assoc. WPA* **2019**, *18*, 146–161. [CrossRef] [PubMed]
220. Galderisi, S.; Rucci, P.; Mucci, A.; Rossi, A.; Rocca, P.; Bertolino, A.; Aguglia, E.; Amore, M.; Bellomo, A.; Bozzatello, P.; et al. Italian Network for Research on Psychoses. The Interplay among Psychopathology, Personal Resources, Context-Related Factors and Real-Life Functioning in Schizophrenia: Stability in Relationships after 4 Years and Differences in Network Structure between Recovered and Non-Recovered Patients. *World Psychiatry Off. J. World Psychiatr. Assoc. WPA* **2020**, *19*, 81–91. [CrossRef]
221. Jablensky, A. Psychiatric Classifications: Validity and Utility. *World Psychiatry* **2016**, *15*, 26–31. [CrossRef]
222. Kendler, K.S. The Nature of Psychiatric Disorders. *World Psychiatry Off. J. World Psychiatr. Assoc. WPA* **2016**, *15*, 5–12. [CrossRef]
223. Comparelli, A.; Raballo, A.; Pompili, M.; Galderisi, S. Beyond the Transnosographic Emphasis on Psychosis: Nosological Perspectives on Schizophrenia and Its Prevention. *Front. Psychiatry* **2019**, *10*, 666. [CrossRef]
224. Martínez-Alés, G.; Susser, E.S. A Useful Construct to Improve the Lives of People with Schizophrenia. *Schizophr. Res.* **2022**, *242*, 91–93. [CrossRef]
225. Maruta, T.; Volpe, U.; Gaebel, W.; Matsumoto, C.; Iimori, M. Should Schizophrenia Still Be Named So? *Schizophr. Res.* **2014**, *152*, 305–306. [CrossRef]
226. Nasrallah, H.A. To Change the Label of Schizophrenia, First Revise the Construct. *Schizophr. Res.* **2021**, *238*, 201–202. [CrossRef]
227. Yamaguchi, S.; Mizuno, M.; Ojio, Y.; Sawada, U.; Matsunaga, A.; Ando, S.; Koike, S. Associations between Renaming Schizophrenia and Stigma-Related Outcomes: A Systematic Review. *Psychiatry Clin. Neurosci.* **2017**, *71*, 347–362. [CrossRef]
228. Mesholam-Gately, R.I.; Varca, N.; Spitzer, C.; Parrish, E.M.; Hogan, V.; Behnke, S.H.; Larson, L.; Rosa-Baez, C.; Schwirian, N.; Stromeyer, C.; et al. Are We Ready for a Name Change for Schizophrenia? A Survey of Multiple Stakeholders. *Schizophr. Res.* **2021**, *238*, 152–160. [CrossRef]
229. Chiu, H.F.K.; Sato, M.; Kua, E.H.; Lee, M.S.; Yu, X.; Ouyang, W.C.; Yang, Y.K.; Sartorius, N. Renaming Dementia—An East Asian Perspective. *Int. Psychogeriatr.* **2014**, *26*, 885–887. [CrossRef] [PubMed]
230. Sato, M. Renaming Schizophrenia: A Japanese Perspective. *World Psychiatry Off. J. World Psychiatr. Assoc. WPA* **2006**, *5*, 53–55.
231. Cho, J.W.; Jang, E.Y.; Woo, H.J.; Park, Y.C.; Kim, S.H.; Hong, K.S.; Lee, Y.S.; Kwon, J.S. Effects of Renaming Schizophrenia in Korea: From "Split-Mind Disorder" to "Attunement Disorder". *Psychiatry Investig.* **2018**, *15*, 656–662. [CrossRef]
232. Koike, S.; Yamaguchi, S.; Ohta, K.; Ojio, Y.; Watanabe, K.I.; Ando, S. Mental-Health-Related Stigma among Japanese Children and Their Parents and Impact of Renaming of Schizophrenia. *Psychiatry Clin. Neurosci.* **2017**, *71*, 170–179. [CrossRef]
233. Lieberman, J.A.; First, M.B. Renaming Schizophrenia. *BMJ* **2007**, *334*, 108. [CrossRef] [PubMed]
234. Lasalvia, A.; Penta, E.; Sartorius, N.; Henderson, S. Should the Label "Schizophrenia" Be Abandoned? *Schizophr. Res.* **2015**, *162*, 276–284. [CrossRef] [PubMed]
235. Gaebel, W.; Kerst, A. The Debate about Renaming Schizophrenia: A New Name Would Not Resolve the Stigma. *Epidemiol. Psychiatry Sci.* **2018**, *28*, 258–261. [CrossRef]

Journal of
Clinical Medicine

MDPI

Opinion

We Should Improve Personalization of Management in Patients with a Diagnosis of Schizophrenia

Alfonso Tortorella

Department of Psychiatry, University of Perugia, 06132 Perugia, Italy; alfonso.tortorella@unipg.it

Abstract: The current management of patients with schizophrenia is marked by a lack of personalization. After the diagnosis is made, a second-generation antipsychotic is usually prescribed based on the current clinician's preferences, sometimes accompanied by a psychosocial intervention which is typically not evidence-based and not targeted to the specific needs of the individual patient. In this opinion paper, some steps are outlined that could be taken in order to address this lack of personalization. A special emphasis is laid on the clinical characterization of the patient who has received a diagnosis of schizophrenia. Considerations are put forward concerning the assessment of the negative dimension in ordinary clinical practice, which is often neglected; the evaluation of cognitive functioning using a simple test battery which requires limited professional training and takes no more than 15 min to administer; the evaluation of social functioning using a validated instrument focusing on personal care skills, interpersonal relationships, social acceptability, activities, and work skills; and the assessment of the unmet needs of the person (including practical, social, and emotional needs, and existential or personal recovery). The implications of the assessment of these domains for the formulation of the management plan are discussed.

Keywords: schizophrenia; diagnosis; negative symptoms; cognitive function; social skills training; physical comorbidities; childhood abuse; internalized stigma

Citation: Tortorella, A. We Should Improve Personalization of Management in Patients with a Diagnosis of Schizophrenia. *J. Clin. Med.* **2022**, *11*, 184. https://doi.org/10.3390/jcm11010184

Academic Editors: Armida Mucci and Domenico De Berardis

Received: 3 December 2021
Accepted: 29 December 2021
Published: 30 December 2021

The opinion I put forward in this paper is that the current management of patients with schizophrenia is marked, in several clinical contexts worldwide, by a considerable lack of personalization, and that much can be done to address this situation.

After a diagnosis of schizophrenia is made, often without referring to formal diagnostic systems [1,2], the management is often stereotyped, with the prescription of a second-generation antipsychotic based on the current preferences of the clinician [3] and sometimes the addition of a psychosocial intervention which may not be evidence-based and not targeted to the specific needs of the individual patient [4]. A psychotherapeutic intervention is rarely considered, despite currently available evidence [5–7]. Here I will briefly outline some steps that could be taken in order to address this lack of personalization. The paper is intended for clinicians worldwide, although it is understood that there are several contexts in which significant advances have been already made in the personalization of management of patients with schizophrenia, e.g., [8], and others in which the available resources will allow the implementation of only part of the steps indicated.

The first level to be considered is that of diagnosis. The term "schizophrenia" is often misused to refer to any primary psychosis (i.e., any psychosis which is not due to the effects of a substance or a medication and not secondary to another medical condition or mood disorder) or even to any psychosis. Conversely, there are clinical contexts in which the term "schizophrenia" is avoided, mostly due to the stigmatizing connotation that it has assumed [9], and the generic term "psychosis" is used as a synonym for "schizophrenia". These practices are of course incorrect and are currently obscuring the clinically crucial problem of differential diagnosis with respect to psychoses. The diagnosis of schizophrenia should be based on the current conceptualization of the syndrome, as it emerges from official diagnostic systems.

The second level to be considered is that of clinical characterization. The diagnosis of schizophrenia, as any other diagnosis in psychiatry, is not sufficient in itself to guide the formulation of the management plan [10]. It has to be complemented by a more detailed clinical characterization of the individual case on the basis of a series of domains that have been recently listed and described by a group of experts [11].

The first domain is that of psychopathological dimensions [12–14]. The negative dimension is particularly neglected in ordinary clinical practice, although some of its elements (in particular, poor emotional expression and avolition) have been reported to be strong predictors of several outcome measures, including socialization, participation in family life, behaviour in emergency situations, social contacts, and need for treatment [15].

Clinicians should become familiar with the actual contents of this dimension: affective blunting (i.e., a reduction in the expression of emotion and in reactivity to events); alogia (i.e., a reduction in the quantity of spoken words and the amount of information spontaneously given when answering a question); asociality (i.e., a reduction in social interactions and initiative), anhedonia (i.e., a reduction either in the experience or in the anticipation of pleasure), and avolition (i.e., a poor engagement in any activity due to lack of interest and motivation) [16–20].

There are now several rating scales for negative symptoms. One could argue that almost all of them are too detailed, take too much time to administer, and require too much training such that they are not suitable for use in ordinary clinical practice. However, there is at least one exception: the Brief Negative Symptom Scale (BNSS) [21], which is a very simple validated rating scale consisting of just 13 items which can be used in ordinary practice without much training and takes about 20 min to administer.

After the negative dimension has been characterized in the individual patient, it is first of all important to clarify whether negative symptoms are secondary or primary. In fact, in many cases, negative symptoms are secondary to other illness dimensions, such as positive symptoms, depression, extrapyramidal symptoms, sedation, environmental deprivation, or substance use. So, these elements should be considered in the individual patient, and if one of them emerges prominently as a likely explanation for the negative symptoms, then we should address this element in the management plan and it can be expected that negative symptoms will consequently improve.

We have today several non-pharmacological interventions validated for use in negative symptoms, including social skills training, cognitive behavioural therapy (CBT), and cognitive training, although their impact on primary negative symptoms remains to be tested in controlled trials [22–25]. These non-pharmacological interventions are implemented in several contexts worldwide, including rehabilitation day centers.

On the pharmacological side, there is just one antipsychotic which has been proved to be superior to another antipsychotic in treating primary negative symptoms. This is cariprazine in comparison with risperidone; however, there is just one study of it and no independent replication is available [26–28]. There are several studies concerning the impact of various antipsychotics on negative symptoms but they do not concern specifically primary negative symptoms.

A second domain which should be considered in the patient with schizophrenia is that of cognitive impairment [29–33]. In fact, according to currently available evidence, neurocognition is the strongest predictor of real-life social functioning in the future in psychotic patients. In the follow-up phase of the multicenter study of the Italian Network for Research on Psychoses, neurocognition at baseline was the most powerful predictor of everyday life skills at follow-up, a significant predictor of work skills at follow-up, and—mostly through social cognition—a strong predictor of interpersonal relationships at follow-up [34].

The neurocognitive processes that are most likely to be impaired in patients with schizophrenia are: speed of processing (i.e., the speed with which simple perceptual and motor tasks can be performed); verbal learning and memory (i.e., encoding, recognition, and recall of information involving language); visuospatial learning and memory (i.e., encoding, recognition, and recall of visuospatial information); working memory (i.e., temporary maintenance and manipulation of information in consciousness); attention/vigilance (i.e., ability to sustain a focus on relevant information over a prolonged period of time); reasoning and problem solving (i.e., strategic and logical thinking, planning, formation and maintenance of goals, and the coordination of these processes flexibly over time) [29,35–38].

The assessment of neurocognition in patients with schizophrenia in ordinary clinical practice remains today an open issue. In the Diagnostic and Statistical Manual of Mental Disorders (DSM-5), if we look at the chapter on psychotic disorders, it seems that the assessment of neurocognitive processes can simply be a part of the clinical interview, whereas if we look at Section 3 of the manual it seems that the use of a neuropsychological test battery is advised but no specific neuropsychological test battery is mentioned.

Indeed, there are many neuropsychological test batteries validated for use in psychotic patients [39–45]. One could argue that most of them require too much professional training and take too much time to administer, thus not being suitable for use in ordinary clinical practice.

However, there are now some tools which require limited professional training, usually available online, and which take 10–15 min to administer. Two of them are interview-based, so they are closer to the style to which the clinician is accustomed. They are the Brief Cognitive Assessment Tool for Schizophrenia [46], which takes about 10 min to administer; the Cognitive Assessment Interview [47], which is interview-based and takes about 15 min to administer; and the Schizophrenia Cognition Rating Scale [48], which is interview-based and takes about 15 min to administer.

We have now two validated interventions targeting neurocognitive impairment in schizophrenia. They are cognitive remediation, aerobic exercise, and their combination. There are several approaches to cognitive remediation, whose core features include using cognitive training techniques, usually computerized; therapist-guided refinement of problem-solving strategies; and facilitation of the transfer of cognitive strategies to daily life. Effect sizes have been reliably demonstrated to be medium for cognitive improvements [49]. It is very important to emphasize that both these interventions can be personalized, i.e., they can be tailored to the needs of the individual patient. They should be personalized on the basis of the profile of neurocognitive impairment emerging from the characterization that we have just mentioned [36,49–57].

I will now focus on two further related areas, that of social functioning and that of the patient's unmet needs. According once again to the results of the multicenter study of the Italian Network for Research on Psychoses [34], everyday life skills and functional capacity are at the core of the schizophrenia network, being the two nodes that are most central and most interconnected, whereas, for instance, positive symptoms represent a node which is more remote and less interconnected. Furthermore, according to the only study available using a machine learning approach to predict both short-term and medium-term treatment outcomes in patients with first-episode psychosis, the strongest predictors of both end points were all psychosocial in nature, including unemployment, poor education, functional deficits, and unmet psychosocial needs [58].

Social functioning can be assessed in patients with schizophrenia in ordinary clinical practice using a very well validated instrument, the Specific Level of Functioning Scale (SLOF), which takes just 30–40 min to administer and can be used without very extensive training. This tool is very simple, with five main subscales focusing on personal care skills, interpersonal relationships, social acceptability, activities, and work skills [59].

We have several validated social skills training interventions available for patients with schizophrenia but they are often used in a way that is stereotyped. The same protocol is applied to all patients, whereas the intervention can be personalized, it can be tailored on the basis of the profile of social dysfunction emerging from the abovementioned characterization of the individual patient [60].

Furthermore, if from that characterization it emerges that a lack of motivation is a prominent aspect in that individual patient, then you cannot expect social skills training to be effective [61]. In these cases, my advice is to use PRIME, a mobile app intervention validated for use in order to improve motivation, and only when the lack of motivation is at least in part corrected is social skills training to be applied [62].

We will focus now on the related area of patient's unmet needs. Every clinician will acknowledge that patients' unmet needs, in particular the unmet needs of psychotic patients, are important. However, this aspect is not commonly addressed systematically in ordinary clinical practice in order to guide the formulation of the management plan. The unmet needs of persons with schizophrenia can be actually subdivided into two categories: practical, social, and emotional needs; and the so-called existential or personal recovery [63,64].

The first category includes unmet needs, such as housing, food, cleaning, self-care, daytime activities, information on illness and treatment, social relationships, sexual life, education, security, financial tasks, employment, and social benefits. The expression existential recovery encompasses such aspects as the restoration of the sense of oneself or one's identity, of one's autonomy, of a perspective for the future, the feeling that life is meaningful and worth living [65].

For the systematic assessment of patients' practical, emotional and social needs, we have an instrument which has been translated into many languages and used for many years, which is the Camberwell Assessment of Need (CAN) [66–68], whereas for the evaluation of existential or personal recovery my advice is to use the Recovery Assessment Scale [69]. The systematic characterization of the practical, emotional, and social needs of the individual patient with a diagnosis of schizophrenia will have important implications for the formulation of the management plan, of course in collaboration with the patient. For instance, if unemployment emerges as a prominent unmet need, then the Individual Placement and Support (IPS) model is an intervention which has been validated in many countries and cultural contexts [70–72].

It is more complex to address the area of personal or existential recovery. There is the need for a more in-depth and intense shared decision making process with the patient, and, in addition to this, there is often the need to reconsider and readjust the characteristics of the therapeutic environment. In fact, while most clinicians will probably argue that their mental health service is recovery-oriented, this is not what emerges from the evaluation by patients themselves in ordinary clinical practice [65].

We will consider now an area whose importance most clinicians will acknowledge but which is often not concretely taken into account in the clinical characterization of the patient with a diagnosis of schizophrenia and in the formulation of the relevant management plan in ordinary clinical practice. This is the domain of physical comorbidities. All clinicians are now aware that patients with schizophrenia are at increased risk for many physical diseases, particularly prominent among them being cardiovascular diseases and diabetes mellitus, and many clinicians will at least have heard of one of the sets of guidelines produced by various organizations and associations during the past ten to fifteen years concerning the examinations to be done at baseline and then at different points of time during the follow-up of patients with schizophrenia [73–80]. However, the fact is that, unfortunately, in ordinary clinical practice, these guidelines are not frequently implemented.

Furthermore, while most clinicians will acknowledge that second-generation antipsychotics are not at all interchangeable with each other concerning their impact on physical health [27,81,82], it is not common in ordinary clinical practice for the choice of antipsychotic to be made on the basis of these considerations. The antipsychotic is often chosen solely on the basis of the doctor's preference at that particular point in time. Equally, the individual lifestyle counselling and psychoeducation interventions which should ideally be considered in all patients with schizophrenia in order to promote a healthier lifestyle, and which should certainly be considered if risk factors or actual manifestations of physical diseases emerge from the clinical characterization, are not commonly available and used in ordinary clinical practice. We argue that they should be available and used in all mental health services [83,84].

I will now consider briefly a domain very rarely considered in the clinical characterization of patients with schizophrenia which is aimed at the formulation of a personalized management plan. This is the domain of early environmental exposures.

Probably not many clinicians are aware that one of the three or four strongest non-genetic risk factors for primary psychosis is a history of childhood maltreatment and that this history is a powerful predictor of a poor response to treatment, so that it may represent an undetected source of what is called treatment resistance [85–88].

We have a very simple instrument available, the Childhood Trauma Questionnaire (CTQ) [89], whose administration takes just 10–15 min, and which can be used in ordinary clinical practice in order to assess reliably and reasonably this patient aspect. In fact, if a history of childhood trauma is prominent in the case of a particular patient, then our management will have to be particularly intensive and careful because there will be a higher risk of non-adherence and consequently non-response to both pharmacological and non-pharmacological interventions. In some of these patients, one of the validated trauma-focused CBT-based psychological interventions may be indicated [90].

I will now finally consider a domain that is acknowledged by all clinicians but which is very rarely considered in the context of the clinical characterization of the individual patient with schizophrenia aimed at the personalization of the management plan. This is the domain of internalized stigma.

It is well known that patients with schizophrenia tend to internalize social stigma and discrimination. Probably less known is that this internalized stigma may have a powerful negative impact on help-seeking and on adherence and consequently response to pharmacological and non-pharmacological interventions [91–94].

Today this aspect can be assessed reliably and reasonably in ordinary clinical practice using a validated instrument called the Internalized Stigma of Mental Illness Scale [95,96]. If this aspect emerges prominently, we could consider one of the validated group interventions, mostly with a psychoeducational component, targeting this aspect. Moreover, we will have to consider and possibly adjust the family environment and, in some cases, also the therapeutic environment, because internalized stigma may be in part iatrogenic, so that some aspects of the therapeutic relationships in that particular service may need to be reconsidered [97].

In conclusion, the management of patients with primary psychosis is today in several contexts remarkably stereotyped. What is usually done is to make a diagnosis of psychosis or schizophrenia and just on that basis to indiscriminately prescribe a second-generation antipsychotic, sometimes accompanied by a psychosocial intervention which is often non-systematic, non-personalized, and non-evidence based. This practice should be overhauled. The management of schizophrenia should become less stereotyped and more personalized. Diagnosis should always be complemented by a more detailed clinical characterization of the individual patient, covering at least the domains that I have briefly considered here.

Funding: This research received no external funding.

Conflicts of Interest: Prof. Tortorella served as speaker/consultant for Angelini and Lunbeck and received grants from Lundbeck.

References

1. American Psychiatric Association. *Diagnostic and Statistical Manual of Mental Disorders*, 5th ed.; American Psychiatric Association: Arlington, MA, USA, 2013.
2. Reed, G.M.; First, M.B.; Kogan, C.S.; Hyman, S.E.; Gureje, O.; Gaebel, W.; Maj, M.; Stein, D.J.; Maercker, A.; Tyrer, P.; et al. Innovations and changes in the ICD-11 classification of mental, behavioural and neurodevelopmental disorders. *World Psychiatry* **2019**, *18*, 3–19. [CrossRef]
3. Verdoux, H.; Tournier, M.; Bégaud, B. Antipsychotic prescribing trends: A review of pharmaco-epidemiological studies. *Acta Psychiatr. Scand.* **2010**, *121*, 4–10. [CrossRef]
4. Leamy, M.; Bird, V.; Le Boutillier, C.; Williams, J.; Slade, M. Conceptual framework for personal recovery in mental health: Systematic review and narrative synthesis. *Br. J. Psychiatry* **2011**, *199*, 445–452. [CrossRef]

5. Palmier-Claus, J.; Griffiths, R.; Murphy, E.; Parker, S.; Longden, E.; Bowe, S.; Steele, A.; French, P.; Morrison, A.; Tai, S. Cognitive behavioural therapy for thought disorder in psychosis. *Psychosis* **2017**, *9*, 347–357. [CrossRef]
6. Trower, P.; Birchwood, M.; Meaden, A.; Byrne, S.; Nelson, A.; Ross, K. Cognitive therapy for command hallucinations: Randomised controlled trial. *Br. J. Psychiatry* **2004**, *184*, 312–320. [CrossRef]
7. McKenna, P.; Leucht, S.; Jauhar, S.; Laws, K.; Bighelli, I. The controversy about cognitive behavioural therapy for schizophrenia. *World Psychiatry* **2019**, *18*, 235–236. [CrossRef]
8. Secher, R.G.; Hjorthøj, C.R.; Austin, S.F.; Thorup, A.; Jeppesen, P.; Mors, O.; Nordentoft, M. Ten-year follow-up of the OPUS specialized early intervention trial for patients with a first episode of psychosis. *Schizophr. Bull.* **2015**, *41*, 617–626. [CrossRef]
9. Sartorius, N.; Chiu, H.; Heok, K.E.; Lee, M.S.; Ouyang, W.C.; Sato, M.; Yang, Y.K.; Yu, X. Name change for schizophrenia. *Schizophr. Bull.* **2014**, *40*, 255–258. [CrossRef]
10. Maj, M. Beyond diagnosis in psychiatric practice. *Ann. Gen. Psychiatry* **2020**, *19*, 27. [CrossRef]
11. Maj, M.; van Os, J.; De Hert, M.; Gaebel, W.; Galderisi, S.; Green, M.F.; Guloksuz, S.; Harvey, P.D.; Jones, P.B.; Malaspina, D.; et al. The clinical characterization of the patient with primary psychosis aimed at personalization of management. *World Psychiatry* **2021**, *20*, 4–33. [CrossRef]
12. Kotov, R.; Jonas, K.G.; Carpenter, W.T.; Dretsch, M.N.; Eaton, N.R.; Forbes, M.K.; Forbush, K.T.; Hobbs, K.; Reininghaus, U.; Slade, T.; et al. Validity and utility of Hierarchical Taxonomy of Psychopathology (HiTOP): I. Psychosis superspectrum. *World Psychiatry* **2020**, *19*, 151–172. [CrossRef]
13. Reininghaus, U.; Böhnke, J.R.; Chavez-Baldini, U.; Gibbons, R.; Ivleva, E.; Clementz, B.A.; Pearlson, G.D.; Keshavan, M.S.; Sweeney, J.A.; Tamminga, C.A. Transdiagnostic dimensions of psychosis in the Bipolar-Schizophrenia Network on Intermediate Phenotypes (B-SNIP). *World Psychiatry* **2019**, *18*, 67–76. [CrossRef]
14. Gaebel, W.; Falkai, P.; Hasan, A. The revised German evidence- and consensus-based schizophrenia guideline. *World Psychiatry* **2020**, *19*, 117–119. [CrossRef]
15. Galderisi, S.; Rucci, P.; Mucci, A.; Rossi, A.; Rocca, P.; Bertolino, A.; Aguglia, E.; Amore, M.; Bellomo, A.; Bozzatello, P.; et al. The interplay among psychopathology, personal resources, context-related factors and real-life functioning in schizophrenia: Stability in relationships after 4 years and differences in network structure between recovered and non-recovered patients. *World Psychiatry* **2020**, *19*, 81–91. [CrossRef]
16. Kirkpatrick, B.; Fenton, W.S.; Carpenter, W.T., Jr.; Marder, S.R. The NIMH-MATRICS consensus statement on negative symptoms. *Schizophr. Bull.* **2006**, *32*, 214–219. [CrossRef]
17. Strauss, G.P.; Esfahlani, F.Z.; Galderisi, S.; Mucci, A.; Rossi, A.; Bucci, P.; Rocca, P.; Maj, M.; Kirkpatrick, B.; Ruiz, I.; et al. Network analysis reveals the latent structure of negative symptoms in schizophrenia. *Schizophr. Bull.* **2019**, *45*, 1033–1041. [CrossRef]
18. Marder, S.R.; Galderisi, S. The current conceptualization of negative symptoms in schizophrenia. *World Psychiatry* **2017**, *16*, 14–24. [CrossRef]
19. Mucci, A.; Merlotti, E.; Üçok, A.; Aleman, A.; Galderisi, S. Primary and persistent negative symptoms: Concepts, assessments and neurobiological bases. *Schizophr. Res.* **2017**, *186*, 19–28. [CrossRef]
20. Cohen, A.S.; Schwartz, E.; Le, T.P.; Fedechko, T.; Kirkpatrick, B.; Strauss, G.P. Using biobehavioral technologies to effectively advance research on negative symptoms. *World Psychiatry* **2019**, *18*, 103–104. [CrossRef]
21. Kirkpatrick, B.; Strauss, G.P.; Nguyen, L.; Fischer, B.A.; Daniel, D.G.; Cienfuegos, A.; Marder, S.R. The Brief Negative Symptom Scale: Psychometric properties. *Schizophr. Bull.* **2011**, *37*, 300–305. [CrossRef]
22. Lutgens, D.; Gariepy, G.; Malla, A. Psychological and psychosocial interventions for negative symptoms in psychosis: Systematic review and meta-analysis. *Br. J. Psychiatry* **2017**, *210*, 324–332. [CrossRef]
23. Turner, D.T.; McGlanaghy, E.; Cuijpers, P.; van der Gaag, M.; Karyotaki, E.; MacBeth, A. A meta-analysis of social skills training and related interventions for psychosis. *Schizophr. Bull.* **2018**, *44*, 475–491. [CrossRef]
24. Velthorst, E.; Koeter, M.; van der Gaag, M.; Nieman, D.H.; Fett, A.K.; Smit, F.; Staring, A.B.; Meijer, C.; de Haan, L. Adapted cognitive-behavioural therapy required for targeting negative symptoms in schizophrenia: Meta-analysis and meta-regression. *Psychol. Med.* **2015**, *45*, 453–465. [CrossRef]
25. Cella, M.; Preti, A.; Edwards, C.; Dow, T.; Wykes, T. Cognitive remediation for negative symptoms of schizophrenia: A network meta-analysis. *Clin. Psychol. Rev.* **2017**, *52*, 43–51. [CrossRef]
26. Krause, M.; Zhu, Y.; Huhn, M.; Schneider-Thoma, J.; Bighelli, I.; Nikolakopoulou, A.; Leucht, S. Antipsychotic drugs for patients with schizophrenia and predominant or prominent negative symptoms: A systematic review and meta-analysis. *Eur. Arch. Psychiatry Clin. Neurosci.* **2018**, *268*, 625–639. [CrossRef]
27. Huhn, M.; Nikolakopoulou, A.; Schneider-Thoma, J.; Krause, M.; Samara, M.; Peter, N.; Arndt, T.; Bäckers, L.; Rothe, P.; Cipriani, A.; et al. Comparative efficacy and tolerability of 32 oral antipsychotics for the acute treatment of adults with multi-episode schizophrenia: A systematic review and network meta-analysis. *Lancet* **2019**, *394*, 939–951. [CrossRef]
28. Kishimoto, T.; Hagi, K.; Nitta, M.; Kane, J.M.; Correll, C.U. Long-term effectiveness of oral second-generation antipsychotics in patients with schizophrenia and related disorders: A systematic review and meta-analysis of direct head-to-head comparisons. *World Psychiatry* **2019**, *18*, 208–224. [CrossRef]
29. Green, M.F.; Horan, W.P.; Lee, J. Nonsocial and social cognition in schizophrenia: Current evidence and future directions. *World Psychiatry* **2019**, *18*, 146–161. [CrossRef]

30. Barch, D.M. Nonsocial and social cognitive function in psychosis: Interrelationships, specificity and innovative approaches. *World Psychiatry* **2019**, *18*, 117–118. [CrossRef]
31. Davidson, M. Cognitive impairment as a diagnostic criterion and treatment target in schizophrenia. *World Psychiatry* **2019**, *18*, 171–172. [CrossRef]
32. Reichenberg, A.; Velthorst, E.; Davidson, M. Cognitive impairment and psychosis in schizophrenia: Independent or linked conditions? *World Psychiatry* **2019**, *18*, 162–163. [CrossRef]
33. Melle, I. Cognition in schizophrenia: A marker of underlying neurodevelopmental problems? *World Psychiatry* **2019**, *18*, 164–165. [CrossRef]
34. Mucci, A.; Galderisi, S.; Gibertoni, D.; Rossi, A.; Rocca, P.; Bertolino, A.; Aguglia, E.; Amore, M.; Bellomo, A.; Biondi, M.; et al. Factors associated with real-life functioning in persons with schizophrenia in a 4-year follow-up study of the Italian Network for Research on Psychoses. *JAMA Psychiatry* **2021**, *78*, 550–559. [CrossRef]
35. Sahakian, B.J.; Savulich, G. Innovative methods for improving cognition, motivation and wellbeing in schizophrenia. *World Psychiatry* **2019**, *18*, 168–170. [CrossRef]
36. Falkai, P.; Schmitt, A. The need to develop personalized interventions to improve cognition in schizophrenia. *World Psychiatry* **2019**, *18*, 170. [CrossRef]
37. Keefe, R.S.E. Why are there no approved treatments for cognitive impairment in schizophrenia? *World Psychiatry* **2019**, *18*, 167–168. [CrossRef]
38. Menon, V. Brain networks and cognitive impairment in psychiatric disorders. *World Psychiatry* **2020**, *19*, 309–310. [CrossRef]
39. Marder, S.R.; Fenton, W. Measurement and Treatment Research to Improve Cognition in Schizophrenia: NIMH MATRICS initiative to support the development of agents for improving cognition in schizophrenia. *Schizophr. Res.* **2004**, *72*, 5–9. [CrossRef]
40. Nuechterlein, K.H.; Barch, D.M.; Gold, J.M.; Goldberg, T.E.; Green, M.F.; Heaton, R.K. Identification of separable cognitive factors in schizophrenia. *Schizophr. Res.* **2004**, *72*, 29–39. [CrossRef]
41. Heinrichs, R.W.; Zakzanis, K.K. Neurocognitive deficit in schizophrenia: A quantitative review of the evidence. *Neuropsychology* **1998**, *12*, 426–445. [CrossRef]
42. Kern, R.S.; Gold, J.M.; Dickinson, D.; Green, M.F.; Nuechterlein, K.H.; Baade, L.E.; Keefe, R.S.; Mesholam-Gately, R.I.; Seidman, L.J.; Lee, C.; et al. The MCCB impairment profile for schizophrenia outpatients: Results from the MATRICS psychometric and standardization study. *Schizophr. Res.* **2011**, *126*, 124–131. [CrossRef]
43. Green, M.F.; Kern, R.S.; Braff, D.L.; Mintz, J. Neurocognitive deficits and functional outcome in schizophrenia: Are we measuring the "right stuff"? *Schizophr. Bull.* **2000**, *26*, 119–136. [CrossRef] [PubMed]
44. Grant, P.M.; Best, M.W.; Beck, A.T. The meaning of group differences in cognitive test performance. *World Psychiatry* **2019**, *18*, 163–164. [CrossRef] [PubMed]
45. Moritz, S.; Silverstein, S.M.; Dietrichkeit, M.; Gallinat, J. Neurocognitive deficits in schizophrenia are likely to be less severe and less related to the disorder than previously thought. *World Psychiatry* **2020**, *19*, 254–255. [CrossRef]
46. Hurford, I.M.; Ventura, J.; Marder, S.R.; Reise, S.P.; Bilder, R.M. A 10-minute measure of global cognition: Validation of the Brief Cognitive Assessment Tool for Schizophrenia (B-CATS). *Schizophr. Res.* **2018**, *195*, 327–333. [CrossRef] [PubMed]
47. Ventura, J.; Reise, S.P.; Keefe, R.S.; Hurford, I.M.; Wood, R.C.; Bilder, R.M. The Cognitive Assessment Interview (CAI): Reliability and validity of a brief interview-based measure of cognition. *Schizophr. Bull.* **2013**, *39*, 583–591. [CrossRef]
48. Keefe, R.S.; Poe, M.; Walker, T.M.; Kang, J.W.; Harvey, P.D. The Schizophrenia Cognition Rating Scale: An interview-based assessment and its relationship to cognition, real-world functioning, and functional capacity. *Am. J. Psychiatry* **2006**, *163*, 426–432. [CrossRef] [PubMed]
49. Bowie, C.R. Cognitive remediation for severe mental illness: State of the field and future directions. *World Psychiatry* **2019**, *18*, 274–275. [CrossRef]
50. Wykes, T.; Huddy, V.; Cellard, C.; McGurk, S.R.; Czobor, P. A meta-analysis of cognitive remediation for schizophrenia: Methodology and effect sizes. *Am. J. Psychiatry* **2011**, *168*, 472–485. [CrossRef]
51. Firth, J.; Stubbs, B.; Rosenbaum, S.; Vancampfort, D.; Malchow, B.; Schuch, F.; Elliott, R.; Nuechterlein, K.H.; Yung, A.R. Aerobic exercise improves cognitive functioning in people with schizophrenia: A systematic review and meta-analysis. *Schizophr. Bull.* **2017**, *43*, 546–556. [CrossRef]
52. Nuechterlein, K.H.; Ventura, J.; McEwen, S.C.; Gretchen-Doorly, D.; Vinogradov, S.; Subotnik, K.L. Enhancing cognitive training through aerobic exercise after a first schizophrenia episode: Theoretical conception and pilot study. *Schizophr. Bull.* **2016**, *42* (Suppl. S1), S44–S52. [CrossRef]
53. Nahum, M.; Fisher, M.; Loewy, R.; Poelke, G.; Ventura, J.; Nuechterlein, K.H.; Hooker, C.I.; Green, M.F.; Merzenich, M.; Vinogradov, S. A novel, online social cognitive training program for young adults with schizophrenia: A pilot study. *Schizophr. Res. Cogn.* **2014**, *1*, e11–e19. [CrossRef] [PubMed]
54. Kurtz, M.M.; Gagen, E.; Rocha, N.B.F.; Machado, S.; Penn, D.L. Comprehensive treatments for social cognitive deficits in schizophrenia: A critical review and effect-size analysis of controlled studies. *Clin. Psychol. Rev.* **2016**, *43*, 80–89. [CrossRef]
55. Glenthøj, L.B.; Mariegaard, L.S.; Fagerlund, B.; Jepsen, J.R.M.; Kristensen, T.D.; Wenneberg, C.; Krakauer, K.; Medalia, A.; Roberts, D.L.; Hjorthøj, C.; et al. Effectiveness of cognitive remediation in the ultra-high risk state for psychosis. *World Psychiatry* **2020**, *19*, 401–402. [CrossRef]

56. Green, M.F.; Lee, J.; Wynn, J.K. Experimental approaches to social disconnection in the general community: Can we learn from schizophrenia research? *World Psychiatry* **2020**, *19*, 177–178. [CrossRef]
57. Harvey, P.D.; Strassnig, M.T. Cognition and disability in schizophrenia: Cognition-related skills deficits and decision-making challenges add to morbidity. *World Psychiatry* **2019**, *18*, 165–167. [CrossRef]
58. Koutsouleris, N.; Kahn, R.S.; Chekroud, A.M.; Leucht, S.; Falkai, P.; Wobrock, T.; Derks, E.M.; Fleischhacker, W.W.; Hasan, A. Multisite prediction of 4-week and 52-week treatment outcomes in patients with first-episode psychosis: A machine learning approach. *Lancet Psychiatry* **2016**, *3*, 935–946. [CrossRef]
59. Mucci, A.; Rucci, P.; Rocca, P.; Bucci, P.; Gibertoni, D.; Merlotti, E.; Galderisi, S.; Maj, M. Italian Network for Research on Psychoses. The Specific Level of Functioning Scale: Construct validity, internal consistency and factor structure in a large Italian sample of people with schizophrenia living in the community. *Schizophr. Res.* **2014**, *159*, 144–150. [CrossRef] [PubMed]
60. Horan, W.P.; Dolinsky, M.; Lee, J.; Kern, R.S.; Hellemann, G.; Sugar, C.A.; Glynn, S.M.; Green, M.F. Social cognitive skills training for psychosis with community-based training exercises: A randomized controlled trial. *Schizophr. Bull.* **2018**, *44*, 1254–1266. [CrossRef]
61. Llerena, K.; Park, S.G.; McCarthy, J.M.; Couture, S.M.; Bennett, M.E.; Blanchard, J.J. The Motivation and Pleasure Scale-Self-Report (MAP-SR): Reliability and validity of a self-report measure of negative symptoms. *Compr. Psychiatry* **2013**, *54*, 568–574. [CrossRef]
62. Schlosser, D.A.; Campellone, T.R.; Truong, B.; Etter, K.; Vergani, S.; Komaiko, K.; Vinogradov, S. Efficacy of PRIME, a mobile app intervention designed to improve motivation in young people with schizophrenia. *Schizophr. Bull.* **2018**, *44*, 1010–1020. [CrossRef]
63. Drukker, M.; van Os, J.; Dietvorst, M.; Sytema, S.; Driessen, G.; Delespaul, P. Does monitoring need for care in patients diagnosed with severe mental illness impact on psychiatric service use? Comparison of monitored patients with matched controls. *BMC Psychiatry* **2011**, *11*, 45. [CrossRef]
64. Drukker, M.; van Os, J.; Bak, M.; Sytema, S.; Driessen, G.; Delespaul, P. Systematic monitoring of needs for care and global outcomes in patients with severe mental illness. *BMC Psychiatry* **2010**, *10*, 36. [CrossRef]
65. Stuart, S.R.; Tansey, L.; Quayle, E. What we talk about when we talk about recovery: A systematic review and best-fit framework synthesis of qualitative literature. *J. Ment. Health* **2017**, *26*, 291–304. [CrossRef]
66. Drukker, M.; van Dillen, K.; Bak, M.; Mengelers, R.; van Os, J.; Delespaul, P. The use of the Camberwell Assessment of Need in treatment: What unmet needs can be met? *Soc. Psychiatry Psychiatr. Epidemiol.* **2008**, *43*, 410–417. [CrossRef] [PubMed]
67. Slade, M.; Phelan, M.; Thornicroft, G.; Parkman, S. The Camberwell Assessment of Need (CAN): Comparison of assessments by staff and patients of the needs of the severely mentally ill. *Soc. Psychiatry Psychiatr. Epidemiol.* **1996**, *31*, 109–113. [CrossRef] [PubMed]
68. Phelan, M.; Slade, M.; Thornicroft, G.; Dunn, G.; Holloway, F.; Wykes, T.; Strathdee, G.; Loftus, L.; McCrone, P.; Hayward, P. The Camberwell Assessment of Need: The validity and reliability of an instrument to assess the needs of people with severe mental illness. *Br. J. Psychiatry* **1995**, *167*, 589–595. [CrossRef] [PubMed]
69. Corrigan, P.W.; Salzer, M.; Ralph, R.O.; Sangster, Y.; Keck, L. Examining the factor structure of the recovery assessment scale. *Schizophr. Bull.* **2004**, *30*, 1035–1041. [CrossRef] [PubMed]
70. Bond, G.R.; Drake, R.E.; Becker, D.R. An update on Individual Placement and Support. *World Psychiatry* **2020**, *19*, 390–391. [CrossRef]
71. Bond, G.R.; Becker, D.R.; Drake, R.E.; Rapp, C.A.; Meisler, N.; Lehman, A.F.; Bell, M.D.; Blyler, C.R. Implementing supported employment as an evidence-based practice. *Psychiatr. Serv.* **2001**, *52*, 313–322. [CrossRef]
72. Killackey, E.; Allott, K.; Jackson, H.J.; Scutella, R.; Tseng, Y.P.; Borland, J.; Proffitt, T.M.; Hunt, S.; Kay-Lambkin, F.; Chinnery, G. Individual placement and support for vocational recovery in first-episode psychosis: Randomised controlled trial. *Br. J. Psychiatry* **2019**, *214*, 76–82. [CrossRef]
73. De Hert, M.; Correll, C.U.; Bobes, J.; Cetkovich-Bakmas, M.; Cohen, D.; Asai, I.; Detraux, J.; Gautam, S.; Möller, H.J.; Ndetei, D.M.; et al. Physical illness in patients with severe mental disorders. I. Prevalence, impact of medications and disparities in health care. *World Psychiatry* **2011**, *10*, 52–77. [CrossRef]
74. Correll, C.U.; Detraux, J.; De Lepeleire, J.; De Hert, M. Effects of antipsychotics, antidepressants and mood stabilizers on risk for physical diseases in people with schizophrenia, depression and bipolar disorder. *World Psychiatry* **2015**, *14*, 119–136. [CrossRef]
75. Cimo, A.; Stergiopoulos, E.; Cheng, C.; Bonato, S.; Dewa, C.S. Effective lifestyle interventions to improve type II diabetes self-management for those with schizophrenia or schizoaffective disorder: A systematic review. *BMC Psychiatry* **2012**, *12*, 24. [CrossRef]
76. Vancampfort, D.; Stubbs, B.; Mitchell, A.J.; De Hert, M.; Wampers, M.; Ward, P.B.; Rosenbaum, S.; Correll, C.U. Risk of metabolic syndrome and its components in people with schizophrenia and related psychotic disorders, bipolar disorder and major depressive disorder: A systematic review and meta-analysis. *World Psychiatry* **2015**, *14*, 339–347. [CrossRef] [PubMed]
77. De Hert, M.; Detraux, J.; Vancampfort, D. The intriguing relationship between coronary heart disease and mental disorders. *Dialogues Clin. Neurosci.* **2018**, *20*, 31–40.
78. Vancampfort, D.; Correll, C.U.; Galling, B.; Probst, M.; De Hert, M.; Ward, P.B.; Rosenbaum, S.; Gaughran, F.; Lally, J.; Stubbs, B. Diabetes mellitus in people with schizophrenia, bipolar disorder and major depressive disorder: A systematic review and large scale meta-analysis. *World Psychiatry* **2016**, *15*, 166–174. [CrossRef]
79. Whelton, P.K.; Carey, R.M.; Aronow, W.S.; Casey, D.E., Jr.; Collins, K.J.; Dennison Himmelfarb, C.; DePalma, S.M.; Gidding, S.; Jamerson, K.A.; Jones, D.W.; et al. 2017 ACC/AHA/AAPA/ABC/ACPM/AGS/APhA/ASH/ASPC/NMA/PCNA guideline for

the prevention, detection, evaluation, and management of high blood pressure in adults: Executive summary: A report of the American College of Cardiology/American Heart Association Task Force on Clinical Practice Guidelines. *Circulation* **2018**, *138*, e426–e483.
80. Annamalai, A.; Tek, C. An overview of diabetes management in schizophrenia patients: Office based strategies for primary care practitioners and endocrinologists. *Int. J. Endocrinol.* **2015**, *2015*, 969182. [CrossRef]
81. Taipale, H.; Tanskanen, A.; Mehtala, J.; Vattulainen, P.; Correll, C.U.; Tiihonen, J. 20-year follow-up study of physical morbidity and mortality in relationship to antipsychotic treatment in a nationwide cohort of 62,250 patients with schizophrenia (FIN20). *World Psychiatry* **2020**, *19*, 61–68. [CrossRef]
82. Vancampfort, D.; Firth, J.; Correll, C.U.; Solmi, M.; Siskind, D.; De Hert, M.; Solmi, M.; Siskind, D.; De Hert, M.; Carney, R.; et al. The impact of pharmacological and non-pharmacological interventions to improve physical health outcomes in people with schizophrenia: A meta-review of meta-analyses of randomized controlled trials. *World Psychiatry* **2019**, *18*, 53–66. [CrossRef]
83. Tumiel, E.; Wichniak, A.; Jarema, M.; Lew-Starowicz, M. Nonpharmacological interventions for the treatment of cardiometabolic risk factors in people with schizophrenia—a systematic review. *Front. Psychiatry* **2019**, *10*, 566. [CrossRef]
84. Singh, S.P.; Javed, A. and WPA Expert International Advisory Panel for Early Intervention in Psychosis. Early intervention in psychosis in low- and middle-income countries: A WPA initiative. *World Psychiatry* **2020**, *19*, 122. [CrossRef]
85. Thomas, S.; Höfler, M.; Schäfer, I.; Lew-Starowicz, M. Childhood maltreatment and treatment outcome in psychotic disorders: A systematic review and meta-analysis. *Acta Psychiatr. Scand.* **2019**, *140*, 295–312. [CrossRef]
86. Bendall, S.; Alvarez-Jimenez, M.; Francey, S.M.; McGorry, P.D.; Killackey, E.; Jackson, H.; McNeil, C. TRIPP: TRauma-Informed Psychotherapy for Psychosis. *Early Interv. Psychiatry* **2014**, *8*, 18.
87. Bernstein, D.P.; Fink, L.; Handelsman, L.; Foote, J.; Lovejoy, M.; Wenzel, K.; Sapareto, E.; Ruggiero, J. Initial reliability and validity of a new retrospective measure of child abuse and neglect. *Am. J. Psychiatry* **1994**, *151*, 1132–1136. [PubMed]
88. Guloksuz, S.; Pries, L.K.; Delespaul, P.; Kenis, G.; Luykx, J.J.; Lin, B.D.; Richards, A.L.; Akdede, B.; Binbay, T.; Altınyazar, V.; et al. Examining the independent and joint effects of molecular genetic liability and environmental exposures in schizophrenia: Results from the EUGEI study. *World Psychiatry* **2019**, *18*, 173–182. [CrossRef] [PubMed]
89. Bernstein, D.P.; Fink, L.; Handelsman, L.; Foote, J. *Childhood Trauma Questionnaire (CTQ)*; American Psychiatric Association: Washington, DC, USA, 1994.
90. Brand, R.M.; McEnery, C.; Rossell, S.; Bendall, S.; Thomas, N. Do trauma-focussed psychological interventions have an effect on psychotic symptoms? A systematic review and meta-analysis. *Schizophr. Res.* **2018**, *195*, 13–22. [CrossRef] [PubMed]
91. Slade, M.; Blackie, L.; Longden, E. Personal growth in psychosis. *World Psychiatry* **2019**, *18*, 29–30. [CrossRef]
92. Ran, M.S.; Zhang, T.M.; Wong, I.Y.; Yang, X.; Liu, C.C.; Liu, B.; Luo, W.; Kuang, W.H.; Thornicroft, G.; Chan, C.L.; et al. Internalized stigma in people with severe mental illness in rural China. *Int. J. Soc. Psychiatry* **2018**, *64*, 9–16. [CrossRef]
93. Zhang, T.M.; Wong, I.Y.; Yu, Y.H.; Ni, S.G.; He, X.S.; Bacon-Shone, J.; Gong, K.; Huang, C.H.; Hu, Y.; Tang, M.M. An integrative model of internalized stigma and recovery-related outcomes among people diagnosed with schizophrenia in rural China. *Soc. Psychiatry Psychiatr. Epidemiol.* **2019**, *54*, 911–918. [CrossRef]
94. Clement, S.; Schauman, O.M.; Graham, T.; Maggioni, F.; Evans-Lacko, S.; Bezborodovs, N.; Morgan, C.; Rüsch, N.; Brown, J.S.; Thornicroft, G. What is the impact of mental health-related stigma on help-seeking? A systematic review of quantitative and qualitative studies. *Psychol. Med.* **2015**, *45*, 11–27. [CrossRef]
95. Ritsher, J.B.; Otilingam, P.G.; Grajales, M. Internalized stigma of mental illness: Psychometric properties of a new measure. *Psychiatry Res.* **2003**, *121*, 31–49. [CrossRef] [PubMed]
96. Boyd, J.E.; Adler, E.P.; Otilingam, P.G.; Peters, T. Internalized Stigma of Mental Illness (ISMI) scale: A multinational review. *Compr. Psychiatry* **2014**, *55*, 221–231. [CrossRef] [PubMed]
97. Thornicroft, G.; Mehta, N.; Clement, S.; Evans-Lacko, S.; Doherty, M.; Rose, D.; Koschorke, M.; Shidhaye, R.; O'Reilly, C.; Henderson, C. Evidence for effective interventions to reduce mental-health-related stigma and discrimination. *Lancet* **2016**, *387*, 1123–1132. [CrossRef]

Journal of
Clinical Medicine

MDPI

Review

Do Sex/Gender and Menopause Influence the Psychopathology and Comorbidity Observed in Delusional Disorders?

Alexandre González-Rodríguez [1,*], Mary V. Seeman [2], Alexandre Díaz-Pons [3,4], Rosa Ayesa-Arriola [3,4], Mentxu Natividad [1], Eva Calvo [1] and José A. Monreal [1,5]

1 Department of Mental Health, Mutua Terrassa University Hospital, Fundació Docència i Recerca Mutua Terrassa, University of Barcelona (UB), Centro de Investigación Biomédica en Red de Salud Mental (CIBERSAM), 08221 Terrassa, Spain
2 Department of Psychiatry, University of Toronto, Toronto, ON M5P 3L6, Canada
3 Department of Psychiatry, Marqués de Valdecilla University Hospital, IDIVAL, School of Medicine, University of Cantabria, 39008 Santander, Spain
4 Faculty of Psychology, National University of Distance Education (UNED), Centro de Investigación Biomédica en Red de Salud Mental (CIBERSAM), 28029 Madrid, Spain
5 Institut de Neurociències, Universitat Autònoma de Barcelona, 08221 Terrassa, Spain
* Correspondence: alexandregonzalez@mutuaterrassa.cat

Abstract: *Background*: While sex differences and gonadal hormone levels are taken seriously in the understanding and treatment of schizophrenia, their influence in the psychopathology of delusional disorders (DD) remains unknown. *Methods*: Our strategy was to conduct a narrative review of the effects of (a) sex/gender difference and (b) menopause on delusional content, affective and anxiety-related comorbidity, substance use disorders, cognition, aggressivity, and suicide risk in DD. *Results*: Because the literature is scarce, our results are tentative. We found that erotomania was more prevalent in women than in men, and especially in women with premenopausal onset. In contrast, jealous and somatic delusions were more commonly seen in DD women with postmenopausal onset. With respect to depressive comorbidity, women with premenopausal onset appear more vulnerable to depression than those with later onset. Age at menopause is reported to correlate positively with intensity of suicidal ideation. Anxiety symptoms may be related to estrogen levels. Men present with higher rates of substance use disorders, particularly alcohol use. *Conclusions*: Many male/female differences in DD may be attributable to sociocultural factors but menopause, and, therefore, levels of female hormones, influence symptom expression in women and mediate the expression of psychiatric comorbidities. Further research in this area promises to lead to improved individualized treatment.

Keywords: delusional disorders; psychosis; sex; women; psychopathology

Citation: González-Rodríguez, A.; Seeman, M.V.; Díaz-Pons, A.; Ayesa-Arriola, R.; Natividad, M.; Calvo, E.; Monreal, J.A. Do Sex/Gender and Menopause Influence the Psychopathology and Comorbidity Observed in Delusional Disorders? *J. Clin. Med.* **2022**, *11*, 4550. https://doi.org/10.3390/jcm11154550

Academic Editors: Armida Mucci and Nuri B. Farber

Received: 22 June 2022
Accepted: 2 August 2022
Published: 4 August 2022

1. Introduction

In schizophrenia studies, gender differences in the epidemiology, age of onset, psychopathology, and clinical course have been extensively reported [1]. In fact, one of the most stable findings in psychiatry research is that women with schizophrenia show a later age of onset than men, and that, while the peak of incidence in both sexes occurs in late adolescence and young adulthood, women experience a second peak at the end of their reproductive life [2]. In addition, epidemiological studies indicate that the incidence of schizophrenia is higher in men than in women [2], and that this demographic difference diminishes when age and menopausal status are controlled [3].

With respect to clinical symptoms in schizophrenia, sex/gender differences are more controversial [2,4]. Many results indicate that men suffer more 'negative' symptoms (apathy, avolition, anhedonia, and social withdrawal) while women suffer more affective symptoms (depression and mood swings) [2], but recent studies have pointed to the confounding effects on symptoms of several associated factors. A study carried out by Riecher-Rössler and colleagues [5] assessed psychopathological symptoms in 117 individuals diagnosed with an at-risk mental state (ARMS) for psychosis and 87 first-episode of psychosis (FEP) patients. No sex/gender differences in psychopathology, as measured by self-report or observer rated scales, were found. These findings are in agreement with more recent results [4] comparing psychosis patients with healthy controls.

The same is true for research that points to sex/gender differences in antipsychotic response and clinical outcomes in schizophrenia [6]. The findings are that women, in general, show a stronger response to antipsychotic medications than men during the reproductive years, but that this is no longer the case after menopause [7–9]. Response appears to worsen in women with time after menopause, suggesting that the further decline of estrogen at adrenopause contributes to the loss of effective antipsychotic response [10].

The relevance of a hormonal effect is reinforced by the success of raloxifene, a selective estrogen receptor modulator, in reducing the severity of psychotic symptoms when it is used as an adjunct to antipsychotics [11]. Using pooled data from two previous clinical trials, the Kulkarni group found that 120 mg/day of adjunctive raloxifene over a 12-week period significantly improved cognitive performance over that of placebo. After stratifying for menopausal status and adjusting for endogenous hormone levels (estrogen, progesterone, follicle stimulating hormone, and luteinizing hormone), semantic fluency, picture naming, and word list recognition were all improved by the addition of raloxifene. Aside from showing the effectiveness of hormonal treatment, this study also highlights the importance of considering menopause status when interpreting treatment effects [12].

The effect of male hormones in schizophrenia has been less often considered. A study of 120 male schizophrenia patients found that, in non-aggressive patients, lower levels of testosterone were associated with greater severity of negative symptoms [13], but association in aggressive patients remains unclear [14].

Despite accumulating evidence supporting sex differences attributable to gonadal hormones in schizophrenia, analogous differences in delusional disorders (DD) have been rarely investigated although these disorders have been known and written about since the time of Kraepelin [15] and Bleuler [16].

Several classic syndromes have been associated with DD, such as Othello syndrome [17], delusional jealousy often associated with alcohol and dementing illness and male sex. There is also de Clérambault syndrome [18] an erotomania syndrome associated with young women, and Ekbom syndrome (delusional parasitosis) [19] typically seen in middle aged women.

Because DD and schizophrenia, though related, are distinct disorders that differ in epidemiology, symptoms, and management [20,21], the investigation of DD differences between men and women is indicated. There is, for instance, significantly more functional deterioration in schizophrenia than in DD and this has been attributed to lesser neuropsychological impairment in DD [22]. More recent work, however, reports similar cognitive profiles in the two conditions [23]. While both schizophrenia and DD are characterized by the presence of delusions, in DD they generally less bizarre. DD has been classified in the Diagnostic and Statistical Manual for Mental Disorders, Fifth Edition (DSM-5), into seven subtypes according to the predominant delusional theme: persecutory, erotomanic, jealous, grandiose, somatic, mixed, and unspecified [24]. Most studies report that DD is more frequent (1.2:1–1.6:1) in women than in men; however, some have not been able to replicate these findings [24]. DSM-5 reports no major sex/gender differences in the prevalence of DD [25]. The International Statistical Classification of Diseases and Related Health Problems, 11th Edition (ICD-11) does not address sex/gender demographics but lists persistence as a characteristic of DD and unaffected affect, speech, and behavior as a requirement for diagnosis [26].

For many decades, clinical evidence has suggested that gonadal hormones may be partially responsible for the sex differences that have been found in schizophrenia [27,28]. This is because physiological estrogen fluctuations in women have been observed to affect symptom levels. Estrogens serve many neuroprotective functions, and the observations are that psychotic symptoms in women with schizophrenia wane when estrogen levels are high and rise when they are low [29].

The goal of this review is to explore the literature on the effects of sex/gender on the psychopathology of DD. Specifically, we address the following questions: (1) Are there male/female differences in delusional content in DD? What is the effect of menopause on the sex distribution of delusional themes? (2) Are there gender differences in depressive comorbidity and prevalence of anxiety disorders in patients with DD? What is the effect of menopause on the occurrence and expression of affective and/or anxiety symptoms? (3) Are there gender differences in substance use disorders in DD? What is the effect of menopause on substance use comorbidity? (4) Is suicide and aggressivity risk in DD gender-dependent? What is the effect of menopause on suicidality and aggressivity? (5) Are there gender differences in cognitive symptoms in DD? What is the effect of menopause on cognition?

We use the word 'sex' when referring to strictly biological causation of male/female difference and the word 'gender' when the differences have sociocultural roots although, in practice, the origin of difference is both biological and sociocultural.

2. Methods

A narrative review was conducted based on electronic searches through the PubMed database for English, Spanish, German, or French papers that referred in their titles or abstracts to sex/gender difference, hormones, menopause, or psychopathology in patients with DD. Additionally, we searched for further papers through the Clinicaltrials.gov database. We included papers if they addressed potential hormonal effects as explanations for male/female differences in psychopathological symptoms, psychiatric comorbidity, or suicide risk in patients with DD.

The following keywords were used: (sex OR gender OR hormones OR menopause OR women OR female) AND ("delusional disorder"). The screening and selection process was undertaken by A.G.R. and M.V.S. A total of 489 titles and abstracts were scanned. Most were excluded as they did not address the questions in which we were interested. The inclusion criteria were as follows: (1) randomized controlled trials, or (2) observational and prospective cohort studies, or (3) retrospective studies, as long as (4) they reported potential associations between sex hormones and psychopathological symptoms (including cognition) or psychiatric comorbidity or suicide risk in DD patients. Case reports were excluded.

Figure 1 shows the methodological procedure and results of the screening and selection process. After screening all accessible full-text papers, a total of 15 records were identified as relevant to our questions.

The Scale for the Assessment of Narrative Review Articles (SANRA) was used to evaluate the quality of our narrative review [30]. The scale consists of six items rated from zero (low standard) to two (high standard). Item 1 refers to the justification of the article's importance for the readership. Item 2: Presence of a statement of concrete aims or formulation of questions. Item 3: Description of the literature search. Item 4: Inclusion of references. Item 5: Demonstration of scientific reasoning. Item 6: Appropriate presentation of data. All six items were checked, and the checklist for this review is shown as Table 1.

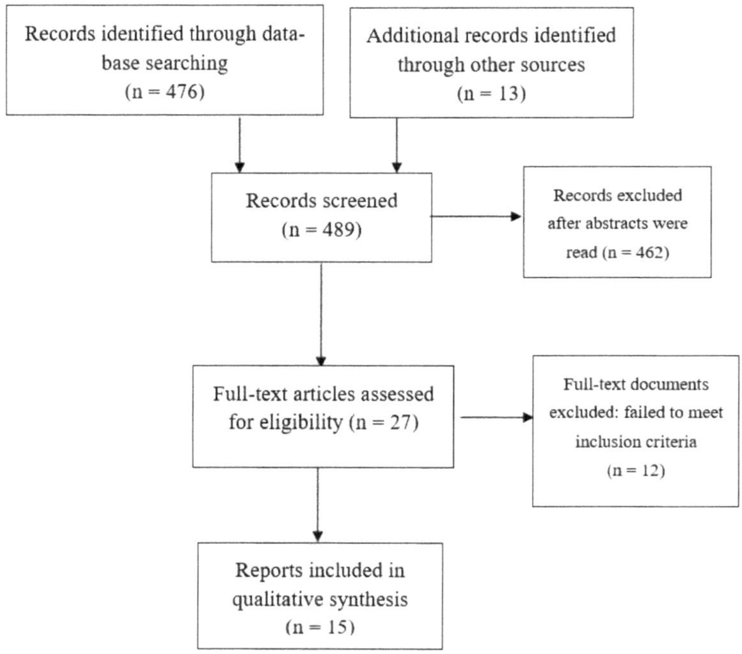

Figure 1. Flow diagram of included studies.

Table 1. Scores of the Scale for the Assessment of Narrative Review (SANRA).

Item 1	Item 2	Item 3	Item 4	Item 5	Item 6	Total Score
Justification of the article's importance	Aims and formulation of questions	Description of literature search	Referencing	Scientific reasoning	Presentation of data	Sum of scores
The importance is explicitly justified (2)	One or more concrete aims or questions are formulated (2)	The literature search is described briefly (1)	Key statements are supported by references (2)	Appropriate evidence is present (adequately described) (2)	Relevant outcome data are generally presented appropriately (2)	11

3. Results

3.1. The Effects of Sex/Gender on Delusional Themes in Delusional Disorders

Table 2 summarizes findings on the investigation of the correlation between gender and delusional content in DD.

Wustmann and collaborators carried out a gender analysis in a cohort of patients with DD as part of the Halle Delusional Syndrome Study (HADES-Study) [31]. In the first part of this study, 43 consecutive inpatients (22 m; 21 f) who fulfilled either the Diagnostic and Statistical Manual for Mental Disorders, Fourth Edition (DSM-IV) or the International Classification of Diseases 10th Edition (ICD-10) criteria for DD were followed for a minimum of three years and a maximum of 24 years. The men had more history of perinatal disturbances, lower social support and were more frequently single than women. Age at first symptom of DD and age at first hospital admission were higher in women than men, potentially due to the neuroprotective effects of estrogens. No statistically significant differences were found in the thematic content of delusions (i.e., persecutory, somatic, jealous, grandiose, and erotomanic delusions) did not differ in prevalence between men and women. Diagnostic conversion to other psychiatric conditions during the follow-up period was more frequent in men than in women. Women received psychopharmacological treatment more frequently than men. This could mean they were seen as more severely ill or, conversely, more willing to comply with medical directives and more adherent to their medication regimen.

In a similar study, Román-Avezuela and colleagues explored gender differences in a sample of 50 inpatients with DD [32]. Patients (22 m and 28 f) who fulfilled Diagnostic and Statistical Manual for Mental Disorders, 3rd Edition Revised (DSM-III-R), DSM-IV or ICD-10 criteria were consecutively recruited. Women's hospitalizations occurred at older ages than men's and women were more likely to suffer from depressive symptoms. Men presented with more persecutory, grandiose, and jealous delusions than women. Erotomania, on the other hand, was more commonly seen in women.

More recently, Kulkarni et al. [33] compared medical records of 455 patients diagnosed with DD (236 m; 219 f) with respect to age, sociodemographics, age at onset and duration of symptoms, family history, clinical and treatment details, and hospitalizations. No gender differences were found regarding age of onset or phenomenology of delusions. However, men were more likely than women to present with delusions of dysmorphophobia. In the overall sample, delusions of jealousy were the most common, followed by persecutory delusions and erotomania. Along the same lines, de Portugal and collaborators explored gender differences in DD in a cross-sectional study of 86 outpatients without finding significant differences regarding delusional content [34]. All participants were screened with the Structured Clinical Interview for the major DSM-IV Axis I diagnoses (SCID-I). Persecution was the most common delusional theme, followed by jealousy and erotomania. Men scored higher than women on symptom severity due to more frequent general and negative symptoms.

An Australian descriptive study investigated antipsychotic use, treatment outcomes, and clinical features in 55 individuals with DD aged 65 and older [35]. The patients were attending a psychiatry service, and the vast majority were postmenopausal women. The mean age at service presentation was 74.5 years, and the average age at onset was 67.5 years. The vast majority presented with persecutory delusions, six with delusional jealousy and one with delusional parasitosis. No gender difference was found with regard to delusional subtype. In another study of a psychogeriatric population, Leinonen and collaborators followed a cohort of 24 patients with major depressive disorders and 18 patients diagnosed with DD [36]. The mean age of the DD group was 75.8 and 89% were women. Five patients developed dementia. The postmenopausal women showed cognitive decline. Consistent with these findings were the results of a case register study of patients aged 60 or older [37] from a catchment area of the southern district of Amsterdam. The one-year prevalence of DD was estimated at 0.03%, and, in women, was found only in those aged 70 years and older.

A prospective study of 43 women with schizophrenia and related disorders (which includes DD) investigated the association between menstrual cycle and hospital admission. The comparison group was 14 women with other psychiatric diagnoses (affective disorder, anxiety, neurotic disorder, or personality disorder) and also non-clinical women [38]. Only 32 women with psychosis were included in the analysis because 11 (two of whom have DD) were excluded for being peri or postmenopausal. Findings were that 56% of the included patients were admitted to hospital during the low follicular phase of the menstrual cycle, which suggests that low estradiol levels were associated with an exacerbation of psychotic symptoms.

Focusing on the influence of reproductive variables on the clinical course of DD, González-Rodríguez and collaborators explored psychopathological symptoms in a cohort of 80 women with DD diagnosed using the Diagnostic and Statistical Manual for Mental Disorders, Fourth Edition, Text Revision (DSM-IV-TR) criteria [39]. Psychopathological symptoms were assessed by the Positive and Negative Syndrome Scale (PANSS) for psychotic symptoms, depressive symptoms were assessed by the 17-item Hamilton Rating Depression Scale (17-HRDS), and suicidality by the Columbia–Suicide Severity Rating Scale (C–SSRS). Fifty-seven women completed the trial. They were divided into two groups according to premenopausal and postmenopausal onset of symptoms. The women in the premenopausal onset group showed more erotomanic delusions and delusions with sexual content than those with postmenopausal onset. On the other hand, postmenopausal onset women more frequently presented with jealousy and somatic delusions.

The same research team investigated reproductive variables and use of gynecological services in a group of 25 female outpatients with DD [40]. Sociodemographic and clinical variables were recorded, as well as the following reproductive variables: age at menarche, age at menopause, use of contraceptives, menstrual patterns, gynecological disorders, and number of previous pregnancies and abortions. Utilization rates of gynecological services were also recorded. Mean age at onset was 48 years, mean age at menarche was 12.8 years, and mean age at menopause was 48.7. Persecutory delusions were most common in this sample, followed by erotomanic delusions. Age at onset of the disorder was not used as a variable.

Table 2. Putative association of sex/gender with delusional content in DD.

Potential Association	Main Findings	Reference
Negative	No differences in somatic, jealous and erotomanic delusions between men and women	Wustmann et al., 2011 [31] Kulkarni et al., 2017 [33] De Portugal et al., 2010 [34]
Positive	Erotomania more common in women than men	Román-Avezuela et al., 2015 [32]
Positive	Erotomania more likely in premenopausal than postmenopausal women	González-Rodríguez et al., 2015a [39]
Positive	Jealous and somatic delusions common in women with postmenopausal onset	González-Rodríguez et al., 2015a [39]

3.2. Potential Effects of Sex/Gender on Affective Comorbidity and Anxiety Disorders in DD

Psychiatric comorbid disorders (e.g., affective and anxiety disorders) are not rare in the context of DD. In general, affective symptoms are more frequent in women than in men. In DD, the prevalence of depressive disorders has been estimated at 21–55% [41].

Table 3 presents results of the association between sex/gender and affective comorbidity in DD.

De Portugal and collaborators carried out a cross-sectional study that included 86 outpatients with DD [34]. Sixty-two per cent of the sample were women and the mean age of the women was 55.1 (e.g., largely postmenopausal). The mean age of the men was 52.2. No statistically significant differences were found between women and men in the presence of depression, nor the severity of depressive symptoms as measured by the Montgomery–Asberg Depression Rating Scale (MADRS). The PANSS General Psychopathologic subscale was higher in men than in women. In other words, the men, though younger as a group, were more severely ill and their level of depression was equal to that of the largely postmenopausal women.

A similar study by González-Rodríguez and collaborators [39] investigated depressive symptoms in a cohort of postmenopausal women followed prospectively for 24 months and longer. The sample was divided into DD women with premenopausal and postmenopausal onset. After controlling for duration of untreated psychosis (DUP), antipsychotic dosage in chlorpromazine equivalent doses (CPZE), educational levels, and psychopathological baseline scores, women with onset in premenopause showed more depressive symptoms than those with postmenopausal onset. DD women in the perimenopausal period were not included. The same research team investigated the correlation between age at menarche, age at menopause, and psychopathology in a group of 25 female outpatients with DD [40]. Age at menopause was 48.7 years and age at menarche was 12.8 years. Neither variable was associated with psychotic or depressive symptoms.

In a tertiary care center in India, Kulkarni et al. [33] carried out a case register study by reviewing medical records of 455 patients with DD (48.1% women). Men and women were comparable in age. There were no gender differences in depressive symptoms. Leinonen and collaborators [36] followed patients with major depressive disorders and DD over 10 years and observed that psychogeriatric patients admitted to hospital for severe mental illness presented a high risk of organic dementia. In the subgroup of 18 patients with DD, the vast majority of whom were women, there was no specific mention of depressive symptoms.

Román-Avezuela and collaborators [32] retrospectively investigated cases of 50 inpatients with DSM-IV DD during their first psychiatric admission. The age of first admission was higher in women than in men (52.07 vs. 45). Women suffered more frequently from insomnia than men; however, no statistically significant differences in rates of depression were found between women and men.

Table 3. Putative sex/gender difference and affective comorbidity in DD.

Potential Association	Main Results	Reference
Negative	No difference in the presence or severity of depression between men and women with DD	Román-Avezuela et al., 2015 [32] Kulkarni et al., 2017 [33] De Portugal et al., 2010 [34]
Positive	More depression in women with premenopausal DD onset than with postmenopausal onset	González-Rodríguez et al., 2015 [39]
Negative	Ages at menarche and menopause were not associated with depressive symptoms in women with DD	González-Rodríguez et al., 2015b [40]

Abbreviations: DD, Delusional Disorder.

During the reproductive years, women experience not only depression but also anxiety symptoms at times of hormonal change (premenstrually, postpartum, perimenopause); at menopause, both anxiety and mood symptoms become more severe and occur more frequently than before [42,43].

De Portugal and collaborators evaluated 86 outpatients (33 m; 53 f) with DD who, using the Mini International Neuropsychiatry Interview (MINI), fulfilled DSM-IV criteria [44]. Almost half (46%) suffered from at least one additional psychiatric comorbidity. Anxiety disorders were diagnosed in eight patients (14%), most being women. The proportion of postmenopausal women was not reported. No differences were found between men and women in terms of functioning.

3.3. *The Effects of Sex/Gender on Substance Use Disorders in Delusional Disorder*

Many studies have reported that the rate of substance use disorder in the general population is higher in men than in women, but whether consequences distinguish men and women remains controversial [45,46].

In the context of DD, De Portugal and collaborators carried out a cross-sectional study investigating clinical features in 86 outpatients with this diagnosis [34]. A systematic inventory was used to register sociodemographic variables as well as clinical features. Premorbid substance use defined by DSM-IV criteria was also recorded. Men showed a significantly higher frequency of premorbid substance abuse than women (30.3% vs. 11.3%). No specific mention was made of the reproductive status in women participants. The higher frequency in men is in agreement with the findings of Román-Avezuela and collaborators who investigated clinical features in a sample of DD inpatients [32]. Men had more substance use disorders than women (40.9% vs. 3.6%). Cannabis abuse and dependence was more frequent (22.7% vs. 0%) in men, as was alcohol use disorder (22.7% vs. 3.6%) When analyzing substance use disorders by their onset prior or post DD, men were more likely to be diagnosed with substance use disorders at least one month before the DD diagnosis than were women (40.9% vs. 3.6%).

Along the same lines, Kulkarni et al. investigated sociodemographic and clinical characteristics in a sample of patients with DD from India [33]. The frequency of comorbid substance use disorders was significantly higher in men than in women (24.1% vs. 1.8%), which could explain the substantial occupational dysfunction found in men.

Delusional jealousy is frequently associated with neurological and psychiatric disorders [47], and alcohol use disorders. Kulkarni and collaborators [33] found that the false belief of partner's infidelity was the most common delusion, particularly in men. The high frequency of substance use disorders in men may help to explain this finding, which is consistent with the results from a cross-sectional study in first-episode treatment-naïve psychosis patients recruited in a tertiary care center in northern India [48]. The sample included 13 delusional disorder participants. A modified semi-structured interview was used to record sociodemographic and clinical characteristics, including information with regard to the use of substances: starting age, type of substance, last intake of substance, duration of substance use, and pattern of use. Tetrahydrocannabinol urine concentrations were obtained by immune assay. The Alcohol Use Disorder Identification Test (AUDIT) was used to detect alcohol use. Once again, men in the total sample were more frequently diagnosed with alcohol use disorders than were women.

3.4. The Effect of Sex/Gender on Suicide Risk and Aggressivity in Delusional Disorder

In the general population, it is well known that women make more suicide attempts than men, but men's attempts are much more often successful [49,50]. Men use more lethal means, but lethality is more common in men than women independently of the method used.

In the context of DD, González-Rodríguez and collaborators carried out a prospective observational study with a 24-month follow-up on consecutive cases of DD women attending an outpatient service [39]. Lifetime and follow-up suicidal ideation and suicidal behavior were assessed using the Columbia–Suicide Severity Rating Scale (C–SSRS). The sample was divided into two groups according to the reproductive status of the women at the time of DD onset, premenopause and postmenopause. There were no statistically significant group differences in terms of functioning, intensity of suicidal intention, or suicidal behavior. The timing of DD onset did not affect suicidality measures. The same research group carried out a case register study of 25 women with DD and found a positive correlation between age at menopause and the intensity of suicidal ideation: the older the age at menopause, the stronger the suicidal urges [40]. In an inpatient sample of 50 patients with DD, Román-Avezuela and collaborators [32] found no statistically significant differences in suicidal ideation between men and women (13.6% vs. 10.7%) [32].

De Portugal and collaborators investigated risk of aggressivity in a sample of 86 inpatients with DD [34]. No statistical gender differences were reported; however, men were more likely than women to present with an acute onset. In fact, very few studies have explored the risk of aggressivity in the DD population. Herbel and Stelmach [51] studied characteristics and behaviors of 22 DD prisoners but could not make gender comparisons because all 22 were men.

3.5. The Effect of Sex/Gender on Cognition in Delusional Disorder

Cognitive performance is considered to differ between men and women in the general population. In a study investigating cognitive functions in 21 male and 21 female students aged 19–37 years old, cognitive assessment was undertaken once in men and, in women, once during a preovulatory menstrual period and once in a postovulatory period [52]. A variety of cognitive functions were tested, and all results proved similar between men and women in their preovulatory cycle phase. During the postovulatory (high estrogen phase of the cycle), women showed advantages in the executive task (Stroop test) and disadvantages in voice response time, an attentional task. Few studies have specifically assessed neurocognitive performance in DD.

Grover and collaborators compared attention, concentration, executive functions, and memory in 20 patients with DD, as well as 20 patients with schizophrenia and 20 healthy controls [23]. Results were adjusted by taking sex, age, and level of education into account. Clinical stability of at least three months, defined by the absence of symptom exacerbation as reported by patients, relatives, or medical records review was required for participation. Dose of antipsychotic medications could not have been increased by more than 50% during those three months. The results showed that patients with DD had significantly more impairment of attention, visual learning and visual memory, verbal working memory, and executive functions, than patients with schizophrenia. No gender differences were reported.

De Portugal and colleagues found no statistically significant differences in cognitive measures between men and women with DD as measured by the Mini Mental State Examination [34].

4. Discussion

The aim of this review was to investigate the potential effects of sex/gender on the psychopathology (delusional themes, depressive and anxiety comorbidity, substance use disorders, risk of suicide and aggression, and cognition) of DD. In schizophrenia sex hormones are able to be studied directly in animal models, however this was not possible here because there are no animal models of delusional disorders and no human studies in which sex hormone levels have been assessed.

Several studies have reported that women with DD show an older age at onset of symptoms as well as age at first hospital admission than men, and their DD diagnosis is more stable, less inclined to change over time [31]. Specific delusional themes (e.g., erotomania and delusional parasitosis) have been anecdotally associated with women, but Wustmann et al. [31] found no gender differences in delusional themes, while Román-Avezuela et al. [32] reported more persecutory delusions in men and confirmed the higher rate of erotomania in women. Differences in delusional content between men and women, if they are confirmed to exist, would suggest a gender e.g., sociocultural effect rather than a biological sex effect. Kulkarni et al. [33] in a study from India, show how culture and tradition can affect delusional themes. Patient age, a biological effect, may also affect the content of delusional themes. Korner et al. [53] report that, in geriatric populations, the themes most frequently found center around persecution. This may be partially explained by the presence of incipient dementia since dementing disorders are closely associated with persecutory delusions [54].

The interest in male/female differences in depression and anxiety comorbidity in DD stems from the well-known fact that internalizing disorders (problems attributed to the self) are significantly more prevalent in women than in men [55–57]. These differences probably originate both from sex (an inherently more reactive stress reactivity in women) and from gender (socialization differences and trauma exposure differences between males and females found in many parts of the world). In most DD studies we reviewed, no sex/gender differences were found in the presence or severity of comorbid depression [32]. The lack of sex differences was consistent in samples of inpatients [32], outpatients, [34] and in mixed samples [33]. The conclusion could be that depression is such an integral part of DD that potential sex differences are obliterated or that the generally late mid-life onset of DD effaces the biological effects of sex hormone differences that are putatively responsible for depression. The latter explanation is consistent with the fact that women with premenopausal onset of DD do show more depressive symptoms than those with postmenopausal onset [39]. Another possibility is that common menopausal transition symptoms (insomnia, irritability, mood swings, and cognitive symptoms) [49] may overlap with depressive symptoms in premenopausal onset women. Age at menarche and age at menopause (indices of cumulative estrogen levels) did not correlate with the presence of depressive symptoms [40]. Rocca and collaborators [58] found long-term risk of depression and anxiety in women after bilateral oophorectomy. Thus, psychopathological effects of the loss of estrogens may differ according to the type of menopause: natural vs. surgical.

The vast majority of studies have reported a higher prevalence of substance use disorders in men suffering from DD compared to women [32,34]. Particularly, alcohol use disorders and the development of jealous delusions have been frequently found to be associated with men [38]. A higher frequency of substance use disorders prior to the onset of DD has been described in men with DD compared to women. This is probably a reflection of the relatively high substance use of men in the general population.

Suicide risk is tied to depression, but the male/female difference is probably more associated with gender than with sex. Women have more access to prescription medications than men and men have more access to guns, which means that suicidal men use more lethal means—women may thus attempt suicide more often, but men more often complete suicide [59]. Furthermore, women are more likely than men to report suicidal ideation and to, thus, receive protective social support [60,61]. However, age at menopause was positively associated with the intensity of suicidal ideation in sample of 25 women with DD [40], which suggests that neuroprotection conferred by estrogens may play a role. The onset of DD (premenopausal or postmenopausal) did not have an impact on suicidality in women with DD [39]. A recent review revealed that both individual and community level factors affect suicidal ideation in postmenopausal women [53]. In the particular context of DD, psychosocial risk factors have also been found to be associated with higher rates of DD in middle- and working-class neighborhoods than elsewhere [62].

Few studies have investigated gender differences in the risk of aggressivity in patients with DD, but men more often than women present for care in an acute state [34] and may, thus, be perceived to be more aggressive.

The pattern of cognitive function in patients with DD remains unclear. Some authors have tried to investigate cognitive performance in people with DD and compare them with those found in schizophrenia populations [63]. A recent study on the topic revealed that verbal memory and other cognitive symptoms were impaired in DD, and these were related to poor functionality.

The studies we cite considered the potential effects of depression or anxiety comorbidity as well as substance abuse and, most importantly, the menopausal state, on sex/gender difference. What they did not consider were individual genetic differences and group genetic differences between men and women. There may exist DD-associated genes that are sex-biased and that account for a substantial portion of male/female difference. This has, thus far, not been studied.

This review is limited by the paucity of relevant studies. To date, research in DD has mainly been based on observational studies, case series, and case reports. The reported findings are, therefore, tentative. A further limitation is that, though most studies report excluding organic psychoses during recruitment, they do not report what assessment tools they used to make these exclusions. As to the representativeness of our literature search, we realize that all the papers we cite were written in English although we scanned for three other languages known to the authors. Ideally, we would have wanted to review literature from around the world because it is important to know whether male/female are products of biology or of gender, or both [64].

To the best of our knowledge, however, this is the first review investigating the potential association of sex/gender and, by implication, sex hormones with clinical features of DD. It is hoped that future studies will recruit large samples and be able to directly measure levels of gonadal hormones because this could lead to improvements in treatment.

5. Conclusions

Sex and gender difference in the epidemiology, clinical expression, treatment, and outcome of psychiatric disorders is a topic of great interest and controversy. The controversy often centers around the impact of biological versus sociocultural explanations for difference, but very little of this work has been done in the field of delusional disorders. We have reviewed the sparse literature that exists and conclude that differences between men and women are relatively few, but that some differences point to the influence of menopause in symptomatic expression and comorbidity. As this field of research expands, it may lead to more individualized and, thus, more effective treatments.

Author Contributions: A.G.-R. wrote the first draft of the manuscript; M.V.S. collaborated with A.G.-R. on subsequent versions and revised the paper; A.D.-P., R.A.-A., M.N. and E.C. collaborated in writing the paper and building tables; and J.A.M. supervised and critically reviewed the content. All authors have read and agreed to the published version of the manuscript.

Funding: This research did not receive any specific grant from funding agencies in the public, commercial, or not-for-profit sectors.

Institutional Review Board Statement: Not applicable.

Informed Consent Statement: Not applicable.

Data Availability Statement: The data presented in this review are available upon request from the corresponding author.

Conflicts of Interest: A.G.-R. has received free registration or travel funds for congresses from Janssen, Lundbeck-Otsuka, and Angelini. J.A.-M. has received consultancy and/or lecture honoraria from Sanofi, Pfizer, Servier, Janssen, and Lundbeck-Otsuka.

References

1. Seeman, M.V. Sex differences in schizophrenia relevant to clinical care. *Expert. Rev. Neurother.* **2021**, *21*, 443–453. [CrossRef] [PubMed]
2. Ochoa, S.; Usall, J.; Cobo, J.; Labad, X.; Kulkarni, J. Gender differences in schizophrenia and first-episode psychosis: A comprehensive literature review. *Schizophr. Res. Treat.* **2012**, *2012*, 916198. [CrossRef] [PubMed]
3. Riecher-Rössler, A.; Butler, S.; Kulkarni, J. Sex and gender differences in schizophrenic psychoses-a critical review. *Arch. Women's Ment. Health* **2018**, *21*, 627–648. [CrossRef]
4. Menghini-Müller, S.; Studerus, E.; Ittig, S.; Heitz, U.; Egloff, L.; Andreou, C.; Valmaggia, L.R.; Kempton, M.J.; van der Gaag, M.; de Haan, L.; et al. Gender differences of patients at-risk for psychosis regarding symptomatology, drug use, comorbidity and functioning-Results from the EU-GEI study. *Eur. Psychiatry* **2019**, *59*, 52–59. [CrossRef] [PubMed]
5. González-Rodríguez, A.; Studerus, E.; Spitz, A.; Bugra, H.; Aston, J.; Borgwardt, S.; Rapp, C.; Riecher-Rossler, A. Gender differences in the psychopathology of emerging psychosis. *Isr. J. Psychiatry Relat. Sci.* **2014**, *51*, 85–92.
6. Seeman, M.V. Men and women respond differently to antipsychotic drugs. *Neuropharmacology* **2020**, *163*, 107631. [CrossRef]
7. Brzezinski, A.; Brzezinski-Sinai, N.A.; Seeman, M.V. Treating schizophrenia during menopause. *Menopause* **2017**, *24*, 582–588. [CrossRef] [PubMed]
8. Gupta, R.; Assalman, I.; Bottlender, R. Menopause and schizophrenia. *Post Menopause Int.* **2012**, *18*, 10–14. [CrossRef]
9. Seeman, M.V. Treating schizophrenia at the time of menopause. *Maturitas* **2012**, *72*, 117–120. [CrossRef]
10. González-Rodríguez, A.; Catalán, R.; Penadés, R.; Ruiz Cortés, V.; Torra, M.; Seeman, M.V.; Bernardo, M. Antipsychotic Response Worsens with Postmenopausal Duration in Women with Schizophrenia. *J. Clin. Psychopharmacol.* **2016**, *36*, 580–587. [CrossRef]
11. Kulkarni, J.; Gavrilidis, E.; Gwini, S.M.; Worsley, R.; Grigg, J.; Warren, A.; Gurvich, C.; Gilbert, H.; Berk, M.; Davis, S.R. Effect of Adjunctive Raloxifene Therapy on Severity of Refractory Schizophrenia in Women: A Randomized Clinical Trial. *JAMA Psychiatry* **2016**, *73*, 947–954. [CrossRef] [PubMed]
12. Gurvich, C.; Hudaib, A.; Gavrilidis, E.; Worsley, R.; Thomas, N.; Kulkarni, J. Raloxifene as a treatment for cognition in women with schizophrenia: The influence of menopause status. *Psychoneuroendocrinology* **2019**, *100*, 113–119. [CrossRef] [PubMed]
13. Sisek-Šprem, M.; Križaj, A.; Jukić, V.; Milošević, M.; Petrović, Z.; Herceg, M. Testosterone levels and clinical features of schizophrenia with emphasis on negative symptoms and aggression. *Nord. J. Psychiatry* **2015**, *69*, 102–109. [CrossRef] [PubMed]
14. Sisek-Šprem, M.; Gradiški, I.P.; Žaja, N.; Herceg, M. The longitudinal course of schizophrenia: Testosterone and progression of the negative symptoms. *Nord. J. Psychiatry* **2020**, *74*, 147–154. [CrossRef] [PubMed]
15. Kendler, K.S. The clinical features of paranoia in the 20th century and their representation in diagnostic criteria from DSM-III through DSM-5. *Schizophr. Bull.* **2017**, *43*, 332–343. [CrossRef] [PubMed]
16. Fried, E.I.; Koenders, M.A.; Blom, J.D. Bleuler revisited: On persecutory delusions and their resistance to therapy. *Lancet Psychiatry* **2021**, *8*, 644–646. [CrossRef]
17. Ahn, E.S. Othello syndrome: Delusional disorder–jealous type ≠ violence. *CNS Spectr.* **2021**, *26*, 160–161. [CrossRef]
18. Sampogna, G.; Zinno, F.; Giallonardo, V.; Luciano, M.; Del Vecchio, V.; Fiorillo, A. The de Clérambault syndrome: More than just a delusional disorder? *Int. Rev. Psychiatry* **2020**, *32*, 385–390. [CrossRef]
19. Orsolini, L.; Gentilotti, A.; Giordani, M.; Volpe, U. Historical and clinical considerations on Ekbom's syndrome. *Int. Rev. Psychiatry* **2020**, *32*, 424–436. [CrossRef]
20. Marneros, A.; Pillmann, F.; Wustmann, T. Delusional disorders–are they simply paranoid schizophrenia? *Schizophr. Bull.* **2012**, *38*, 561–568. [CrossRef]
21. Peralta, V.; Cuesta, M.J. Characteristics and clinical correlates of dimensions of delusional experience in schizophrenia and delusional disorder. *Schizophr. Res.* **2016**, *176*, 404–410. [CrossRef]
22. Evans, J.D.; Paulsen, J.S.; Harris, M.J.; Heaton, R.K.; Jeste, D.V. A clinical and neuropsychological comparison of delusional disorder and schizophrenia. *J. NeuroPsychiatry Clin. Neurosci.* **1996**, *8*, 281–286. [PubMed]
23. Grover, S.; Nehra, R.; Bhateja, G.; Kulhara, P.; Kumar, S. A comparative study of cognitive deficits in patients with delusional disorder and paranoid schizophrenia. *Ind. Psychiatry J.* **2011**, *20*, 107–114. [CrossRef] [PubMed]
24. American Psychiatric Association. *DSM-5 Task Force*, 5th ed.; American Psychiatric Publishing, Inc.: Washington, DC, USA, 2013.

25. González-Rodriguez, A.; Esteve, M.; Álvarez, A.; Guàrdia, A.; Monreal, J.A.; Palao, D.; Labad, J. What We Know and Still Need to Know about Gender Aspects of Delusional Disorder: A Narrative Review of Recent Work. *J. Psychiatry Brain Sci.* **2019**, *4*, e190009.
26. World Health Organization. *International Statistical Classification of Diseases and Related Health Problems*, 11th ed.; World Health Organization: Geneva, Switzerland, 2019.
27. Seeman, M.V. Gender differences in schizophrenia. *Can. J. Psychiatry* **1982**, *27*, 107–112. [CrossRef]
28. Gogos, A.; Ney, L.J.; Seymour, N.; Van Rheenen, T.E.; Felmingham, K.L. Sex differences in schizophrenia, bipolar disorder, and post-traumatic stress disorder: Are gonadal hormones the link? *Br. J. Pharmacol.* **2019**, *176*, 4119–4135. [CrossRef] [PubMed]
29. Seeman, M.V. Psychopathology in women and men: Focus on female hormones. *Am. J. Psychiatry* **1997**, *154*, 1641–1647. [CrossRef] [PubMed]
30. Baethge, C.; Goldbeck-Wood, S.; Mertens, S. SANRA—A scale for the quality assessment of narrative review articles. *Res. Integr. Peer. Rev.* **2019**, *4*, 5. [CrossRef]
31. Wustmann, T.; Pillmann, F.; Marneros, A. Gender-related features of persistent delusional disorders. *Eur. Arch. Psychiatry Clin. Neurosci.* **2011**, *261*, 29–36. [CrossRef]
32. Román Avezuela, N.; Esteve Díaz, N.; Domarco Manrique, L.; Domínguez Longás, A.; Miguélez Fernández, C.; de Portugal, E. Gender differences in delusional disorder. *Rev. Asoc. Esp. Neuropsiq.* **2015**, *35*, 37–51. [CrossRef]
33. Kulkarni, K.R.; Arasappa, R.; Prasad, M.K.; Zutshi, A.; Chand, P.K.; Murthy, P.; Muralidharan, K. Gender differences in persistent delusional disorder. *Indian J. Psychol. Med.* **2017**, *39*, 216–217. [CrossRef] [PubMed]
34. de Portugal, E.; González, N.; Miriam, V.; Haro, J.M.; Usall, J.; Cervilla, J.A. Gender differences in delusional disorder: Evidence from an outpatient sample. *Psychiatry Res.* **2010**, *177*, 235–239. [CrossRef] [PubMed]
35. Nagendra, J.; Snowdon, J. An Australian study of delusional disorder in late life. *Int. Psychogeriatr.* **2020**, *32*, 453–462. [CrossRef]
36. Leinonen, E.; Santala, M.; Hyötylä, T.; Santala, H.; Eskola, N.; Salokangas, R.K. Elderly patients with major depressive disorder and delusional disorder are at increased risk of subsequent dementia. *Nord. J. Psychiatry* **2004**, *58*, 161–164. [CrossRef] [PubMed]
37. Meesters, P.D.; de Haan, L.; Comijs, H.C.; Stek, M.L.; Smeets-Janssen, M.M.; Weeda, M.R.; Eikelenboom, P.; Smit, J.H.; Beekman, A.T. Schizophrenia spectrum disorders in later life: Prevalence and distribution of age at onset and sex in a dutch catchment area. *Am. J. Geriatr. Psychiatry* **2012**, *20*, 18–28. [CrossRef]
38. Huber, T.J.; Rollnik, J.; Wilhelms, J.; von zur Mühlen, A.; Emrich, H.M.; Schneider, U. Estradiol levels in psychotic disorders. *Psychoneuroendocrinology* **2001**, *26*, 27–35. [CrossRef]
39. González-Rodríguez, A.; Molina-Andreu, O.; Penadés, R.; Garriga, M.; Pons, A.; Catalán, R.; Bernardo, M. Delusional disorder over the reproductive life span: The potential influence of menopause on the clinical course. *Schizophr. Res. Treat.* **2015**, *2015*, 979605. [CrossRef]
40. González-Rodríguez, A.; Molina-Andreu, O.; Penadés Rubio, R.; Catalán Campos, R.; Bernardo Arroyo, M. Reproductive variables and gynaecological service use in delusional disorder outpatients. *Rev. Psiquiatr. Salud. Ment.* **2015**, *8*, 92–96. [CrossRef]
41. González-Rodríguez, A.; Molina-Andreu, O.; Navarro Odriozola, V.; Gastó Ferrer, C.; Penadés, R.; Catalán, R. Delusional disorder: An overview of affective symptoms and antidepressant use. *Eur. J. Psychiat.* **2013**, *27*, 265–276. [CrossRef]
42. Prairie, B.A.; Wisniewski, S.R.; Luther, J.; Hess, R.; Thurston, R.C.; Wisner, K.L.; Bromberger, J.T. Symptoms of depressed mood, disturbed sleep, and sexual problems in midlife women: Cross-sectional data from the Study of Women's Health Across the Nation. *J. Women's Health* **2015**, *24*, 119–126. [CrossRef]
43. Gracia, C.R.; Freeman, E.W. Onset of the Menopause Transition: The Earliest Signs and Symptoms. *Obstet. Gynecol. Clin. N. Am.* **2018**, *45*, 585–597. [CrossRef] [PubMed]
44. de Portugal, E.; Martínez, C.; González, N.; del Amo, V.; Haro, J.M.; Cervilla, J.A. Clinical and cognitive correlates of psychiatric comorbidity in delusional disorder outpatients. *Aust. N. Z. J. Psychiatry* **2011**, *45*, 416–425. [CrossRef] [PubMed]
45. Brady, K.T.; Randall, C.L. Gender differences in substance use disorders. *Psychiatr. Clin. N. Am.* **1999**, *22*, 241–252. [CrossRef]
46. Zilberman, M.; Tavares, H.; el-Guebaly, N. Gender similarities and differences: The prevalence and course of alcohol- and other substance-related disorders. *J. Addict. Dis.* **2003**, *22*, 61–74. [CrossRef] [PubMed]
47. Graff-Radford, J.; Whitwell, J.L.; Geda, Y.E.; Josephs, K.A. Clinical and imaging features of Othello's syndrome. *Eur. J. Neurol.* **2012**, *19*, 38–46. [CrossRef]
48. Banyal, N.; Bhattacharyya, D.; Yadav, P. Study to determine the prevalance of substance use and factors associated with it, in first-episode of psychosis. *Ind. Psychiatry J.* **2018**, *27*, 264–270.
49. Mergl, R.; Koburger, N.; Heinrichs, K.; Székely, A.; Tóth, M.D.; Coyne, J.; Quintão, S.; Arensman, E.; Coffey, C.; Maxwell, M.; et al. What Are Reasons for the Large Gender Differences in the Lethality of Suicidal Acts? An Epidemiological Analysis in Four European Countries. *PLoS ONE* **2015**, *10*, e0129062. [CrossRef] [PubMed]
50. Freeman, A.; Mergl, R.; Kohls, E.; Székely, A.; Gusmao, R.; Arensman, E.; Koburger, N.; Hegerl, U.; Rummel-Kluge, C. A cross-national study on gender differences in suicide intent. *BMC Psychiatry* **2017**, *17*, 234. [CrossRef]
51. Herbel, B.L.; Stelmach, H. Involuntary medication treatment for competency restoration of 22 defendants with delusional disorder. *J. Am. Acad. Psychiatry Law* **2007**, *35*, 47–59.
52. Upadhayay, N.; Guragain, S. Comparison of cognitive function between male and female medical students: A pilot study. *JCDR* **2014**, *8*, BC12–BC15. [CrossRef]
53. Kørner, A.; Lopez, A.G.; Lauritzen, L.; Andersen, P.K.; Kessing, L.V. Delusional disorder in old age and the risk of developing dementia: A nationwide register-based study. *Aging Ment. Health* **2008**, *12*, 625–629. [CrossRef] [PubMed]

54. Holt, A.E.; Albert, M.L. Cognitive neuroscience of delusions in aging. *Neuropsychiatr. Dis. Treat.* **2006**, *2*, 181–189. [CrossRef] [PubMed]
55. Kessler, R.C.; McGonagle, K.A.; Zhao, S.; Nelson, C.B.; Hughes, M.; Eshleman, S.; Wittchen, H.U.; Kendler, K.S. Lifetime and 12-month prevalence of DSM-III-R psychiatric disorders in the United States. Results from the National Comorbidity Survey. *Arch. Gen. Psychiatry* **1994**, *51*, 8–19. [CrossRef]
56. Maki, P.M.; Kornstein, S.G.; Joffe, H.; Bromberger, J.T.; Freeman, E.W.; Athappilly, G.; Bobo, W.V.; Rubin, L.H.; Koleva, H.K.; Cohen, L.S.; et al. Guidelines for the evaluation and treatment of perimenopausal depression: Summary and recommendations. *J. Women's Health* **2019**, *28*, 117–134. [CrossRef] [PubMed]
57. Allshouse, A.A.; Semple, A.L.; Santoro, N.F. Evidence for prolonged and unique amenorrhea-related symptoms in women with premature ovarian failure/primary ovarian insufficiency. *Menopause* **2015**, *22*, 166–174. [CrossRef] [PubMed]
58. Rocca, W.A.; Grossardt, B.R.; Geda, Y.E.; Gostout, B.S.; Bower, J.H.; Maraganore, D.M.; de Andrade, M.; Melton, L.J., 3rd. Long-term risk of depressive and anxiety symptoms after early bilateral oophorectomy. *Menopause* **2008**, *15*, 1050–1059. [CrossRef]
59. Callanan, V.J.; Davis, M.S. Gender differences in suicide methods. *Soc. Psychiatry Psychiatr. Epidemiol.* **2012**, *47*, 857–869. [CrossRef] [PubMed]
60. Otten, D.; Ernst, M.; Tibubos, A.N.; Brähler, E.; Fleisher, T.; Schomerus, G.; Wild, P.S.; Zöller, D.; Binder, H.; Kruse, J.; et al. Does social support prevent suicidal ideation in women and men? Gender-sensitive analyses of an important protective factor within prospective community cohorts. *J. Affect. Dis.* **2022**, *306*, 157–166. [CrossRef]
61. Kim, G.U.; Son, H.K.; Kim, M.Y. Factors affecting suicidal ideation among premenopausal and postmenopausal women. *J. Psychiatr. Ment. Health Nurs.* **2021**, *28*, 356–369. [CrossRef]
62. Tizón, J.L.; Morales, N.; Artigue, J.; Quijada, Y.; Pérez, C.; Pareja, F.; Salamero, M. Delusional disorders: Prevalence in two socially differentiated neighborhoods of Barcelona. *Psychosis* **2014**, *6*, 107–116. [CrossRef]
63. Díaz-Caneja, C.M.; Cervilla, J.A.; Haro, J.M.; Arango, C.; de Portugal, E. Cognition and functionality in delusional disorder. *Eur. Psychiatry* **2019**, *55*, 52–60. [CrossRef] [PubMed]
64. Christiansen, D.M.; McCarthy, M.M.; Seeman, M.V. Where sex meets gender: How sex and gender come together to result in sex differences in mental illness. *Front. Psychiatry* **2022**, *13*, 856436. [CrossRef] [PubMed]

Journal of
Clinical Medicine

MDPI

Article

Impact of Negative Symptoms on Functioning and Quality of Life in First Psychotic Episodes of Schizophrenia

Lorena García-Fernández [1,2,3], Verónica Romero-Ferreiro [3,4,5], Luis Sánchez-Pastor [5], Mónica Dompablo [3,5,6], Isabel Martínez-Gras [5,7], Juan Manuel Espejo-Saavedra [5,8], David Rentero [3,5], Ana Isabel Aparicio [3,9,10], Miguel Angel Alvarez-Mon [11,12], Guillermo Lahera [3,11], Jimmy Lee [13,14,15], Jose Luis Santos [3,9,10] and Roberto Rodriguez-Jimenez [3,5,8,*]

1 Clinical Medicine Department, Universidad Miguel Hernández, 03550 Alicante, Spain; lorena.garciaf@umh.es
2 Psychiatry Department, Hospital Universitario de San Juan, 03550 Alicante, Spain
3 Biomedical Research Networking Centre in Mental Health (CIBERSAM), 28029 Madrid, Spain; mvromero@ucm.es (V.R.-F.); monicadompablo@gmail.com (M.D.); davidrente7@hotmail.com (D.R.); aiaparicio@sescam.jccm.es (A.I.A.); guillermo.lahera@gmail.com (G.L.); joseluis.santosg@gmail.com (J.L.S.)
4 Quality and Academic Compliance Unit, Universidad Europea de Madrid, 28670 Madrid, Spain
5 Instituto de Investigación Sanitaria Hospital 12 de Octubre (Imas 12), 28041 Madrid, Spain; lspastor@salud.madrid.org (L.S.-P.); isabelmgras@gmail.com (I.M.-G.); juanmaespejosaavedra@gmail.com (J.M.E.-S.)
6 Cardenal Cisneros, Centro de Enseñanza Superior Adscrito a la Universidad Complutense de Madrid, 28040 Madrid, Spain
7 RETIC (Network of Addictive Conditions), Institute of Health Carlos III, 28029 Madrid, Spain
8 Legal Medicine, Psychiatry and Pathology Department, Universidad Complutense de Madrid, 28040 Madrid, Spain
9 Psychiatry Department, Hospital Virgen de la Luz, 16002 Cuenca, Spain
10 Neurobiological Research Group, Institute of Technology, Universidad de Castilla-La Mancha, 16071 Cuenca, Spain
11 Department of Medicine and Medical Specialities, Faculty of Medicine and Health Sciences, University of Alcalá, 28801 Alcalá de Henares, Spain; maalvarezdemon@icloud.com
12 Department of Psychiatry and Mental Health, Hospital Universitario Infanta Leonor, 28031 Madrid, Spain
13 Research Division, Institute of Mental Health, Singapore 539747, Singapore; jimmy_lee@imh.com.sg
14 North Region & Department of Psychosis, Institute of Mental Health, Singapore 539747, Singapore
15 Lee Kong Chian School of Medicine, Nanyang Technological University, Singapore 639798, Singapore
* Correspondence: roberto.rodriguez.jimenez@gmail.com; Tel.: +34-91-390-85-36

Citation: García-Fernández, L.; Romero-Ferreiro, V.; Sánchez-Pastor, L.; Dompablo, M.; Martínez-Gras, I.; Espejo-Saavedra, J.M.; Rentero, D.; Aparicio, A.I.; Alvarez-Mon, M.A.; Lahera, G.; et al. Impact of Negative Symptoms on Functioning and Quality of Life in First Psychotic Episodes of Schizophrenia. *J. Clin. Med.* **2022**, *11*, 983. https://doi.org/10.3390/jcm11040983

Academic Editor: Armida Mucci

Received: 5 January 2022
Accepted: 11 February 2022
Published: 14 February 2022

Abstract: Negative symptoms are not considered a unitary construct encompassing two different domains, diminished expression, and avolition-apathy. The aim of this study was to explore the relationships between each domain and psychosocial functioning and quality of life in people with a first psychotic episode of schizophrenia. In total, 61 outpatients were assessed with the Clinical Assessment Interview for Negative Symptoms (CAINS), The Functioning Assesment Short Test (FAST) and The Quality of Life Scale (QLS). The mean global score for CAINS was 21.5 (SD: 15.6), with a CAINS Avolition-Apathy (MAP) score of 17.0 (SD: 11.8), and CAINS Diminished Expression (EXP) score of 4.5 (SD: 5.0). The mean FAST score was 31.9 (SD: 18.9), and 41.1 (SD: 17.9) for QLS. Linear regression analysis revealed a significant ($F(4,53) = 15.65$, $p < 0.001$) relationship between MAP and EXP CAINS' score and FAST score. CAINS-MAP was more predictive of FAST scores ($\beta = 0.44$, $p = 0.001$) than CAINS-EXP ($\beta = 0.37$, $p = 0.007$). Linear regression analysis for QLS revealed a significant model ($F(4,56) = 29.29$, $p < 0.001$). The standardized regression weight for the CAINS-MAP was around three times greater ($\beta = -0.63$, $p < 0.001$) than for CAINS-EXP ($\beta = -0.24$, $p = 0.024$). The two different domains are associated differently with functionality and quality of life.

Keywords: negative symptoms; expressive deficits; experiential deficits; functioning; quality of life; first psychotic episode

1. Introduction

Negative symptoms of schizophrenia constitute a therapeutic challenge, as well as one of the main areas to consider in order to improve functioning (proper behaviors in real-world social situations) [1] and quality of life (the individual's perception of their position in life in the context of the culture and value systems) [2] in people with their first psychotic episodes of schizophrenia [3]. Despite the improvements achieved in the care of people with schizophrenia, up to one-third of patients might have idiopathic and stable negative symptoms [4]. From the first description of the disorder recorded by Morel in 1852 [5], negative symptoms have long been recognized as a core and clinically meaningful feature of schizophrenia. Deficit symptoms were first proposed by Kraepelin and Bleuler, referring to basic symptoms of affective blunting and weakening of emotional activities [6,7]. The subsequent identification, under a dichotomous perspective of negative symptoms as opposed to the positive ones, was defined by Crow in the 1980s including blunted affect and poverty of speech, and later revised by Andreasen with the incorporation of avolition, anhedonia, asociability and attentional deficit, suggesting the existence of a different clinical phenotype and pathophysiological substrate when negative symptoms were predominant [8,9]. Shortly after, Carpenter advanced the concept of deficit schizophrenia and, differentiated between primary and secondary negative symptoms depending on whether they were inherent to the disease or the result of additional factors such as emotional reactions, mood disorders, pharmacological treatment or the response to environmental events. The presence of at least two of the following was further suggested: restricted affect, diminished emotional range, poverty of speech, curbing of interest, diminished sense of purpose and diminished social drive, as part of the diagnostic criteria for the deficit syndrome [10,11].

With this perspective in mind, the National Institute of Mental Health (NIMH) organized in 2005, the Consensus Development Conference on Negative Symptoms with the aim of favoring the development of evidence-based measures and treatments for negative symptoms [12]. Results from the international discussion identified affective flattening, alogia, asociality, avolition and anhedonia as domains of negative symptoms and achieved a clearer definition of a hierarchical 5-factor model consistent with the NIMH-MATRICS domains with expressive and experiential domains, as second-order factors [13]. In addition, they fostered the development of new assessment instruments to address the limitations of the existing tools and encouraged the development of different therapeutic targets. As a consequence, two next-generation negative symptom scales that include an adequate sampling of expressive and experiential deficits domains were developed: The Brief Negative Symptom Scale (BNSS) [14,15] and the Clinical Assessment Interview for Negative Symptoms (CAINS) [16,17].

Negative symptoms represent a loss of normal brain functioning and have long been recognized as the most devasting among all clinical features in schizophrenia [18]. However, they are not considered a unitary construct encompassing two different domains, diminished expression including alogia and blunted affect, and avolition-apathy referring to experiential deficits, including asociality, avolition and anhedonia [19–21], that have been consistently replicated regardless of the measurement instrument used [22–24]. Negative symptoms are present in the prodromal and initial stages of the disease, are persistent, worsen with age [9], behave independently of cognition or affectivity [25], present a lack of response to pharmacological treatment [26], and importantly, are the most distressing for the family and the main determinants of impairment in functioning and quality of life, which have now become the main therapeutic targets in people with schizophrenia [27–29] both in early and chronic stages [8,27,29–32].

We hypothesize that the strength of the association between the two different domains of negative symptoms and both functionality and quality of life might be different. Unfortunately, there is a paucity of studies exploring the relationship that the expressive and experimental domains of negative symptoms exert on psychosocial functioning and quality of life in people with a first psychotic episode of schizophrenia using the Clinical

Assessment Interview for Negative Symptoms (CAINS). Given this interest, the aim of the present study was to explore the strength of the relationships between each domain of negative symptoms as separate constructs and psychosocial functioning and quality of life in people with a first psychotic episode of schizophrenia.

2. Materials and Methods

2.1. Sample

The present cross-sectional study was carried out with the participation of 61 Caucasian outpatients with a first psychotic episode of schizophrenia, who were consecutively included in the First Episode Programs of the Universitary "12 de Octubre" Hospital (Madrid, Spain) and "Virgen de la Luz" Hospital (Cuenca, Spain). The inclusion criteria included: (1) diagnosis of schizophrenia or schizophreniform disorder according to DSM-5 criteria [33], using the Structured Clinical Interview for DSM-5 (SCID-5) [34], (2) a minimum of eight consecutive weeks of stabilization on their antipsychotic medication after discharge from the hospitalization unit, (3) aged from 18 to 55 years and (4) fluent Spanish speaking that enables the protocol to be completed. Exclusion criteria were: (1) substance use disorder diagnosed in the past eight weeks (excluding nicotine and caffeine), and (2) traumatic head injury. All participants were clinically assessed by psychiatrists with more than 5 years of experience in the use of the scales. The study was approved by the Clinical Research Ethics Committee and all participants signed the informed consent. Demographic and clinical characteristics of participants are described in Table 1.

Table 1. Demographic and clinical characteristics of participants with a first psychotic episode of schizophrenia.

	Patients (*n* = 61)
Age years mean (SD)	26.5 (8.2)
Gender *n* (% men)	44 (72.1)
Education years mean (SD)	12.3 (3.0)
Second Generation Antipsychotics *n* (%)	59 (96.7%)
Clorpromazine equivalents-mg mean (SD)	413.2 (238.0)
PANSS	
Positive mean (SD)	11.2 (4.8)
Negative mean (SD)	16.8 (7.3)
General Psychopathology mean (SD)	28.0 (8.5)
Total mean (SD)	56.0 (17.2)
CAINS	
Avolition-apathy mean (SD)	17.0 (11.8)
Diminish expression mean (SD)	4.5 (5.0)
Total mean (SD)	21.5 (15.6)
FAST mean (SD)	31.9 (18.9)
QLS mean (SD)	41.1 (17.9)

PANSS: The Positive and Negative Syndrome Scale. CAINS: The Clinical Assessment Interview for Negative Symptoms. FAST: The Functioning Assessment Short Test. QLS: The Quality of Life Scale.

2.2. Assessment Instruments

2.2.1. Symptoms Were Assessed Using the Positive and Negative Syndrome Scale (PANSS) [35] applied only for descriptive purposes.

2.2.2. The Clinical Assessment Interview for Negative Symptoms (CAINS)

The Clinical Assessment Interview for Negative Symptoms (CAINS) is a 13-item tool designed to address the limitations inherent to previous assessment instruments used to evaluate negative symptoms [36,37]. The scale provides both a single summary score, and two scores for the two negative symptom domains [17] reporting the emotional experience (motivation and pleasure) and emotional expression subscales separately. The first nine items, the motivation and pleasure (MAP) subscale, relate to experiential deficits, assessing the motivation, anticipation and experience of pleasure in occupational and recreational activities, and social contacts with partners, friends and family. The last four items, the expression (EXP) subscale, relate to expressive deficits, assessing both vocal and gestural features. All items are rated on a scale of 0–4, with higher scores reflecting greater impairment.

2.2.3. The Functioning Assessment Short Test (FAST)

The Functioning Assessment Short Test (FAST) is a 24-item instrument divided into 6 specific areas of operation (autonomy, occupational functioning, cognitive functioning, financial aspects, relationships and free time) designed to address functioning in patients with mental disorders [38–40]. All items are rated on a scale of 0–3, with higher scores reflecting greater operating difficulties.

2.2.4. The Quality of Life Scale (QLS)

The Quality of Life Scale (QLS) is a 21-item semi-structured interview designed to measure quality of life specifically in patients with schizophrenia [41–43]. The scale obtains information about symptoms and functioning in relation to four areas: interpersonal relationships, instrumental role, intrapsychic functions, and use of common objects and daily activities. It provides an overall score as well as single scores on each of the 4 factors. Each item is scored from 0 (greater degree of dysfunction) to 6 (normality). The higher the score, the better the patient's functioning in that category.

2.3. Statistical Analysis

Data were managed and analyzed with SPSS v.24. Mean and SD were used for continuous variables and percentages for categorical variables. Multiple regression analysis (ENTER method) was employed to develop a predictive model of FAST total scores for the MAP and EXP subscales of the CAINS, included as predictor variables. Second, another regression model was performed, this time considering QLS scores as the response variable. Age and gender (0 = female, 1 = male) were included as covariates in the regression models. Collinearity diagnostics were based on the variance inflation factor (VIF). The absence of collinearity was considered when VIF values were lower than 4 [44].

3. Results

3.1. Relationship between Negative Symptoms and Functioning

Linear regression analysis revealed a statistically significant ($F(4,53) = 15.65$, $p < 0.001$) relationship between CAINS' MAP and EXP subscales and FAST scores. The proportion of variance in FAST scores explained by the model was substantial (adjusted $r^2 = 0.507$). None of the two independent variables were correlated, as the variance inflation factor is closer to 1 (VIF = 1.84 and 1.99, respectively). Based on the results of the above model, the formula to calculate the predicted FAST score is: Predicted FAST = [34.15 + 0.72 CAINS-MAP + 1.40 CAINS-EXP − 6.14 Gender − 0.62 Age].

From the standardized regression weights (β) in the model, the CAINS-MAP had a slightly greater effect on FAST scores ($\beta = 0.44$, $p = 0.001$) than the CAINS-EXP ($\beta = 0.37$, $p = 0.007$).

3.2. Relationship between Negative Symptoms and Quality of Life

A linear regression analysis using the QLS overall score was performed. Results revealed a statistically significant model ($F(4,56) = 29.29$, $p < 0.001$) between the CAINS' MAP and EXP subscales and QLS scores. The proportion of variance explained by the model was large (adjusted $r^2 = 0.654$). Regarding collinearity diagnostic, none of the two independent variables proved to be correlated, as the variance inflation factor is, again, closer to 1 (VIF = 1.82 and 1.89, respectively). Based on the results of the above model, the formula to calculate the predicted QLS score is: Predicted QLS = [80.65 − 1.36 CAINS-MAP − 1.21 CAINS-EXP − 3.13 Gender − 0.56 Age].

Negative weights indicate that higher scores on quality of life are associated with lower CAINS scores. From the standardized regression weights, CAINS-MAP had a larger effect on QLS ($\beta = -0.63$, $p < 0.001$) than CAINS-EXP ($\beta = -0.24$, $p = 0.024$).

Table 2 shows the relationship between negative symptoms and functioning and quality of life.

Table 2. Negative symptoms as predictive variables for functioning and quality of life.

Response Variable	Parameter	Unstandardized Coefficient (Std. Error)	Beta (Standardized)	*p*-Value
FAST $r^2 = 0.507$	Intercept	34.15 (7.23)		<0.001
	CAINS-MAP	0.72 (0.20)	0.443	0.001
	CAINS-EXP	1.40 (0.50)	0.37	0.007
	Sex	−6.14 (4.29)	−0.143	0.159
	Age (years)	−0.62 (0.22)	−0.274	0.006
QLS $r^2 = 0.654$	Intercept	80.65 (7.54)		<0.001
	CAINS-MAP	−1.36 (0.22)	−0.634	<0.001
	CAINS-EXP	−1.21 (0.52)	−0.242	0.024
	Sex	−3.13 (4.43)	−0.056	0.484
	Age (years)	0.56 (0.24)	0.181	0.023

CAINS-MAP: Avolition-apathy domain. CAINS-EXP: Diminish expression domain. FAST: The Functioning Assessment Short Test. QLS: The Quality of Life Scale.

4. Discussion

This study highlights the need to put higher emphasis on understanding the structure of negative symptoms and its influence on the psychosocial functioning and quality of life of people with a first psychotic episode of schizophrenia, which is essential to improve their future.

The aim of the present study was to explore the strength of the relationship between each domain of negative symptoms as separate constructs and psychosocial functioning and quality of life in people with a first psychotic episode of schizophrenia. Our results have shown that both MAP and EXP subscales, explored through the CAINS, are associated with functioning and quality of life.

Regarding psychosocial functioning, both domains of negative symptoms are independently related to functional performance with a slightly greater predictive weight for the MAP subscale, suggesting that it may represent a more severe aspect of psychopathology. In line with this, findings from chronic schizophrenia, first episode psychosis and clinical high risk for psychosis have also found experiential deficits to be linked to various aspects of functioning, both cross-sectionally [3,45–49] and longitudinally [50–54].

Similar to functioning, our study has evaluated the different negative symptoms' domains, both expressive and experimental, and correlated them with quality of life. We found that both the MAP and EXP subscales were independently associated with quality of life. Moreover, the impact of MAP's score on QLS compared with the EXP score was almost triple in people with a first psychotic episode, which makes this domain of negative symptoms a priority intervention target to improve quality of life in early stages and also in chronic schizophrenia [55].

In line with the obtained results, it could be proposed that the two symptomatic domains of negative symptoms explore different psychopathological areas. On the one hand, the EXP subscale is related to the observation of emotional expression, whereas the MAP subscale is related to more internal aspects of the emotional experience such as lack of will, lack of pleasure and absence of motivational goals that will further limit successful interaction between people with a first psychotic episode and society.

Globally, the pattern of findings across relationships between negative symptoms' domains and both functioning and quality of life represents a distinct and greater predictive power for the MAP subscale compared with the EXP subscale, which gives the experential deficits domain higher impact on severity and greater weight in outcome, enriching previous research showing that those patients with a predominant MAP subscale score had, in addition, significantly more severe conceptual disorganization, greater social cognition impairment, higher rates of hospitalization and poorer social functioning [56]. These data bring consistency to previous findings [57–60] and provide the novelty of showing a different link for each domain within the construct of negative symptoms with both functional outcomes and quality of life in people with a first psychotic episode of schizophrenia. However, the specific weight of each domain, a novelty provided by the study presented, has not been evaluated separately.

Moreover, our results give support to DSM 5 [33,61] positioning diminished expression and avolition, anhedonia and asociality as the two prominent domains of negative symptoms [21], given their importance in the prodromal and residual phases and the huge burden they impose on functioning and quality of life across the life course of people with schizophrenia.

The main strengths of the present study are: first, the use of a rigorous negative symptom assessment instrument that systematically measures experiential and expressive symptoms following DSM 5's 2 factors model; second, the evaluation of people in early stages of psychosis avoiding bias due to chronicity; and finally, the use of two main clinically variables, functioning and quality of life, as outcome. Despite the above, some limitations should be mentioned: first, the cross-sectional design preclude determination of direct causal relationships; second, a larger sample of participants could have provided more robust conclusions; and finally, participants' cognitive performance might have been impacting on the functioning and quality of life.

Advances in the understanding of negative symptoms have led to the identification of two interrelated yet separable domains, diminished expression and experiential deficits, both in patients' first psychotic episodes [58] and chronic schizophrenia [19,59] that might necessitate different therapeutic approaches [19,20,62,63] emphasizing the benefit of measuring them separately [16]. We believe that more emphasis should be placed on rigorously assessing negative symptoms and the development of specific treatments for each domain as part of the clinical protocols for patients with a first psychotic episode in order to improve their functioning and quality of life.

Author Contributions: Conceptualization, R.R.-J., L.G.-F. and J.L.S.; methodology, R.R.-J. and J.L.S.; formal analysis, V.R.-F.; investigation, M.D., A.I.A., J.M.E.-S., D.R., I.M.-G., M.A.A.-M. and L.S.-P.; resources, V.R.-F., J.L. and G.L.; data curation, V.R.-F.; writing—original draft preparation, R.R.-J., L.G.-F., J.L.S., V.R.-F., M.A.A.-M., G.L. and J.L.; writing—review and editing, R.R.-J. and L.G.-F. All authors have read and agreed to the published version of the manuscript.

Funding: This research was supported in part by the by the Instituto de Salud Carlos III (grants PI16/00359, PI19/00766; Fondo de Investigaciones Sanitarias/FEDER), by the European Development Regional Fund "A way to achieve Europe" (ERDF), by Madrid Regional Government (R&D activities in Biomedicine S2017/BMD-3740 (AGES cm 2-CM)) and Structural Funds of the European Union. JL was supported by the Singapore Ministry of Health National Medical Research Council Clinician Scientist Award (MOH-000013).

Institutional Review Board Statement: The study was conducted in accordance with the Declaration of Helsinki, and approved by the Comité de Ética e Investigación Clínica del Hospital Universitario 12 de Octubre (protocol code 16/329 and date of approval 25 February 2020).

Informed Consent Statement: Informed consent was obtained from all subjects involved in the study.

Data Availability Statement: The data from this study will be made publicly available following the completion of all publications and following the removal of all identifiers by request.

Acknowledgments: Authors would like to thank all the participants for their time and dedication.

Conflicts of Interest: R. Rodriguez-Jimenez has been a consultant for, spoken in activities of, or received grants from: Instituto de Salud Carlos III, Fondo de Investigación Sanitaria (FIS), Centro de Investigación Biomédica en Red de Salud Mental (CIBERSAM), Madrid Regional Government (S2010/BMD-2422 AGES; S2017/BMD-3740), JanssenCilag, Lundbeck, Otsuka, Pfizer, Ferrer, Juste, Takeda, Exeltis, Casen-Recordati, Angelini. J Lee has received honoraria from JanssenCilag and Otsuka. G. Lahera has been a consultant to or has received honoraria or grants from Janssen-Cilag, Otsuka-Lundbeck, Lilly, Astra-Zeneca, CIBERSAM and Instituto de Salud Carlos III. All other authors declare that they have no conflict of interest.

References

1. Abel, D.B.; Minor, K.S. Social functioning in schizophrenia: Comparing laboratory-based assessment with real-world measures. *J. Psychiatr. Res.* **2021**, *138*, 500–506. [CrossRef]
2. World Health Organization. *WHOQOL: Measuring Quality of Life*; World Health Organization: Geneva, Switzerland, 2020; Retrieved 22 May 2020.
3. Foussias, G.; Agid, O.; Fervaha, G.; Remington, G. Negative symptoms of schizophrenia: Clinical features, relevance to real world functioning and specificity versus other CNS disorders. *Eur. Neuropsychopharmacol.* **2014**, *24*, 693–709. [CrossRef]
4. López-Díaz, Á.; Lara, I.; Lahera, G. Is the Prevalence of the Deficit Syndrome in Schizophrenia Higher than Estimated? Results of a Meta-Analysis. *Psychiatry Investig.* **2018**, *15*, 94–98. [CrossRef]
5. Morel, M. *Traité Théorique et Pratique des Maladies Mentales Considérées dans Leur Nature, Leur Traitement, et dans Leur Rapport avec la Médecine Légale des Aliénés*; Grimblot et Veuve Raybois: Nancy, France, 1852.
6. Bleuler, E. *Dementia Praecox Oder Gruppe der Schizophrenien*; Deiticke: Leipzig, Germany, 1911.
7. Kraepelin, E. *Psychiatrie: Ein Lehrbuch Fur Studirende Und Aerzte*, 4th ed.; Barth: Leipzig, Germany, 1893.
8. Andreasen, N.C.; Olsen, S. Negative v Positive Schizophrenia: Definition and Validation. *Arch. Gen. Psychiatry* **1982**, *39*, 789–794. [CrossRef]
9. Crow, T.J. Molecular pathology of schizophrenia: More than one disease process? *Br. Med. J.* **1980**, *280*, 66–68. [CrossRef]
10. Carpenter, W.T.; Heinrichs, D.W.; Wagman, A.M.I. Deficit and nondeficit forms of schizophrenia: The concept. *Am. J. Psychiatry* **1988**, *145*, 578–583. [CrossRef]
11. Kirkpatrick, B.; Galderisi, S. Deficit schizophrenia: An update. *World Psychiatry* **2008**, *7*, 143–147. [CrossRef]
12. Kirkpatrick, B.; Fenton, W.S.; Carpenter, W.T., Jr.; Marder, S.R. The NIMH-MATRICS consensus statement on negative symptoms. *Schizophr. Bull.* **2006**, *32*, 214–219. [CrossRef]
13. Ahmed, A.O.; Kirkpatrick, B.; Galderisi, S.; Mucci, A.; Rossi, A.; Bertolino, A.; Rocca, P.; Maj, M.; Kaiser, S.; Bischof, M.; et al. Cross-cultural Validation of the 5-Factor Structure of Negative Symptoms in Schizophrenia. *Schizophr. Bull.* **2019**, *45*, 305–314. [CrossRef]
14. Kirkpatrick, B.; Strauss, G.P.; Nguyen, L.; Fischer, B.A.; Daniel, D.G.; Cienfuegos, A.; Marder, S.R. The brief negative symptom scale: Psychometric properties. *Schizophr. Bull.* **2011**, *37*, 300–305. [CrossRef]
15. Strauss, G.P.; Keller, W.R.; Buchanan, R.W.; Gold, J.M.; Fischer, B.A.; McMahon, R.P.; Catalano, L.T.; Culbreth, A.J.; Carpenter, W.T.; Kirkpatrick, B. Next-generation negative symptom assessment for clinical trials: Validation of the Brief Negative Symptom Scale. *Schizophr. Res.* **2012**, *142*, 88–92. [CrossRef]
16. Horan, W.P.; Kring, A.M.; Gur, R.E.; Reise, S.P.; Blanchard, J.J. Development and psychometric validation of the Clinical Assessment Interview for Negative Symptoms (CAINS). *Schizophr. Res.* **2011**, *132*, 140–145. [CrossRef]
17. Kring, A.M.; Gur, R.E.; Blanchard, J.J.; Horan, W.P.; Reise, S.P. The Clinical Assessment Interview for Negative Symptoms (CAINS): Final development and validation. *Am. J. Psychiatry* **2013**, *170*, 165–172. [CrossRef] [PubMed]
18. Azorin, J.M.; Belzeaux, R.; Adida, M. Negative symptoms in schizophrenia: Where we have been and where we are heading. *CNS Neurosci. Ther.* **2014**, *20*, 801–808. [CrossRef]
19. Blanchard, J.J.; Cohen, A.S. The structure of negative symptoms within schizophrenia: Implications for assessment. *Schizophr. Bull.* **2006**, *32*, 238–245. [CrossRef]
20. Kirkpatrick, B.; Mucci, A.; Galderisi, S. Primary, Enduring Negative Symptoms: An Update on Research. *Schizophr. Bull.* **2017**, *43*, 730–736. [CrossRef]
21. Strauss, G.P.; Nuñez, A.; Ahmed, A.O.; Barchard, K.A.; Granholm, E.; Kirkpatrick, B.; Gold, J.M.; Allen, D.N. The Latent Structure of Negative Symptoms in Schizophrenia. *JAMA Psychiatry* **2018**, *75*, 1303. [CrossRef]
22. Kelley, M.E.; van Kammen, D.P.; Allen, D.N. Empirical validation of primary negative symptoms: Independence from effects of medication and psychosis. *Am. J. Psychiatry* **1999**, *156*, 406–411. [CrossRef]
23. Liemburg, E.; Castelein, S.; Stewart, R.; van der Gaag, M.; Aleman, A.; Knegtering, H. Genetic Risk and Outcome of Psychosis (GROUP) Investigators. Two subdomains of negative symptoms in psychotic disorders: Established and confirmed in two large cohorts. *J. Psychiatr. Res.* **2013**, *47*, 718–725. [CrossRef]
24. Richter, J.; Hesse, K.; Schreiber, L.; Burmeister, C.P.; Eberle, M.C.; Eckstein, K.N.; Zimmermann, L.; Wildgruber, D.; Klingberg, S. Evidence for two distinct domains of negative symptoms: Confirming the factorial structure of the CAINS. *Psychiatry Res.* **2019**, *271*, 693–701. [CrossRef]

25. Stouten, L.H.; Veling, W.; Laan, W.; van der Helm, M.; van der Gaag, M. Psychotic symptoms, cognition and affect as predictors of psychosocial problems and functional change in first-episode psychosis. *Schizophr. Res.* **2014**, *158*, 113–119. [CrossRef] [PubMed]
26. Stahl, S.M.; Buckley, P.F. Negative symptoms of schizophrenia: A problem that will not go away. *Acta Psychiatr. Scand.* **2007**. [CrossRef] [PubMed]
27. Watson, P.; Zhang, J.P.; Rizvi, A.; Tamaiev, J.; Birnbaum, M.L.; Kane, J. A meta-analysis of factors associated with quality of life in first episode psychosis. *Schizophr. Res.* **2018**, *202*, 26–36. [CrossRef] [PubMed]
28. Wójciak, P.; Rybakowski, J. Clinical picture, pathogenesis and psychometric assessment of negative symptoms of schizophrenia. *Psychiatr. Pol.* **2018**, *52*, 185–197. [CrossRef]
29. Woolverton, C.B.; Bell, E.K.; Moe, A.M.; Harrison-Monroe, P.; Breitborde, N.J.K. Social cognition and the course of social functioning in first-episode psychosis. *Early Interv. Psychiatry* **2018**, *12*, 1151–1156. [CrossRef]
30. Hunter, R.; Barry, S. Negative symptoms and psychosocial functioning in schizophrenia: Neglected but important targets for treatment. *Eur. Psychiatry* **2012**, *27*, 432–436. [CrossRef]
31. Perlick, D.A.; Rosenheck, R.A.; Kaczynski, R.; Bingham, S.; Collins, J. Association of symptomatology and cognitive deficits to functional capacity in schizophrenia. *Schizophr. Res.* **2008**, *99*, 192–199. [CrossRef]
32. Savill, M.; Orfanos, S.; Reininghaus, U.; Wykes, T.; Bentall, R.; Priebe, S. The relationship between experiential deficits of negative symptoms and subjective quality of life in schizophrenia. *Schizophr. Res.* **2016**, *176*, 387–391. [CrossRef]
33. American Psychiatric Association. *Diagnostic and Statistical Manual of Mental Disorders (DSM-5®)*; American Psychiatric Publising: Arlington, VA, USA, 2013.
34. First, M.; Williams, J.M.G.; Karg, R.; Spitzer, R. *Structured Clinical Interview for DSM-5 Disorders–Research Version (SCID-5-RV)*; American Psychiatric Association: Arlington, VA, USA, 2015.
35. Kay, S.R.; Fiszbein, A.; Opfer, L.A. The positive and negative syndrome scale (PANSS) for schizophrenia. *Schizophr. Bull.* **1987**, *13*, 261–276. [CrossRef]
36. Blanchard, J.J.; Kring, A.M.; Horan, W.P.; Gur, R. Toward the next generation of negative symptom assessments: The collaboration to advance negative symptom assessment in schizophrenia. *Schizophr. Bull.* **2011**, *37*, 291–299. [CrossRef]
37. Valiente-Gómez, A.; Mezquida, G.; Romaguera, A.; Vilardebò, I.; Andrés, H.; Granados, B.; Larrubia, J.; Pomarol-Clotet, E.; McKenna, P.J.; Sarró, S.; et al. Validation of the Spanish version of the Clinical Assessment for Negative Symptoms (CAINS). *Schizophr. Res.* **2015**, *166*, 104–109. [CrossRef] [PubMed]
38. Amoretti, S.; Mezquida, G.; Rosa, A.R.; Bioque, M.; Cuesta, M.J.; Pina-Camacho, L.; Garcia-Rizo, C.; Barcones, F.; González-Pinto, A.; Merchán-Naranjo, J.; et al. The functioning assessment short test (FAST) applied to first-episode psychosis: Psychometric properties and severity thresholds. *Eur. Neuropsychopharmacol.* **2021**. [CrossRef] [PubMed]
39. González-Ortega, I.; Rosa, A.; Alberich, S.; Barbeito, S.; Vega, P.; Echeburúa, E.; Vieta, E.; González-Pinto, A. Validation and use of the functioning assessment short test in first psychotic episodes. *J. Nerv. Ment. Dis.* **2010**, *198*, 836–840. [CrossRef] [PubMed]
40. Rosa, A.R.; Sánchez-Moreno, J.; Martínez-Aran, A.; Salamero, M.; Torrent, C.; Reinares, M.; Comes, M.; Colom, F.; Van Riel, W.; Ayuso-Mateos, J.; et al. Validity and reliability of the Functioning Assessment Short Test (FAST) in bipolar disorder. *Clin. Pract. Epidemiol. Ment. Health* **2007**, *3*, 5. [CrossRef] [PubMed]
41. Heinrichs, D.W.; Hanlon, T.E.; Carpenter, W.T. The Quality of Life Scale: An Instrument for Rating the Schizophrenic Deficit Syndrome. *Schizophr. Bull.* **1984**, *10*, 388–398. [CrossRef] [PubMed]
42. Karow, A.; Wittmann, L.; Schöttle, D.; Schäfer, I.; Lambert, M. The assessment of quality of life in clinical practice in patients with schizophrenia. *Dialogues Clin. Neurosci.* **2014**, *16*, 185–195. [CrossRef]
43. Rodríguez, A.; Soler, R.; Rodríguez, M.A.; Jarne Esparcia, A.; Miarons, R. Estudio factorial y adaptación de la Escala de Calidad de Vida en la Esquizofrenia (QLS). *Rev. Psicol. Gen. Apl. Rev. Fed. Española Asoc. Psicol.* **1995**, *48*, 353–364.
44. Hair, J.F., Jr.; Black, W.C.; Babin, B.J.; Anderson, R.E. *Multivariate Data Analysis. A Global Perspective*, 7th ed.; Pearson Education: Upper Saddle River, NJ, USA, 2010.
45. Kiang, M.; Christensen, B.K.; Remington, G.; Kapur, S. Apathy in schizophrenia: Clinical correlates and association with functional outcome. *Schizophr. Res.* **2003**, *63*, 79–88. [CrossRef]
46. Faerden, A.; Friis, S.; Agartz, I.; Barrett, E.A.; Nesvåg, R.; Finset, A.; Melle, I. Apathy and functioning in first-episode psychosis. *Psychiatr. Serv.* **2009**, *60*, 1495–1503. [CrossRef]
47. Konstantakopoulos, G.; Ploumpidis, D.; Oulis, P.; Patrikelis, P.; Soumani, A.; Papadimitriou, G.N.; Politis, A.M. Apathy, cognitive deficits and functional impairment in schizophrenia. *Schizophr. Res.* **2011**, *133*, 193–198. [CrossRef]
48. Ang, M.S.; Rekhi, G.; Lee, J. Validation of the Brief Negative Symptom Scale and its association with functioning. *Schizophr. Res.* **2019**, *208*, 97–104. [CrossRef] [PubMed]
49. Yang, Z.; Lee, S.H.; Abdul Rashid, N.A.; See, Y.M.; Dauwels, J.; Tan, B.L.; Lee, J. Predicting Real-World Functioning in Schizophrenia: The Relative Contributions of Neurocognition, Functional Capacity, and Negative Symptoms. *Front. Psychiatry* **2021**, *12*, 639536. [CrossRef] [PubMed]
50. Foussias, G.; Remington, G. Negative symptoms in schizophrenia: Avolition and occam's razor. *Schizophr. Bull.* **2010**, *36*, 359–369. [CrossRef] [PubMed]
51. Faerden, A.; Finset, A.; Friis, S.; Agartz, I.; Barrett, E.A.; Nesvåg, R.; Andreassen, O.A.; Marder, S.R.; Melle, I. Apathy in first episode psychosis patients: One year follow up. *Schizophr. Res.* **2010**, *116*, 20–26. [CrossRef]

52. Evensen, J.; Røssberg, J.I.; Barder, H.; Haahr, U.; Ten Velden Hegelstad, W.; Joa, I.; Johannessen, J.O.; Larsen, T.K.; Melle, I.; Opjordsmoen, S.; et al. Apathy in first episode psychosis patients: A ten year longitudinal follow-up study. *Schizophr. Res.* **2012**, *136*, 19–24. [CrossRef]
53. Fervaha, G.; Foussias, G.; Agid, O.; Remington, G. Impact of primary negative symptoms on functional outcomes in schizophrenia. *Eur. Psychiatry* **2014**, *29*, 449–455. [CrossRef]
54. Lam, M.; Abdul Rashid, N.A.; Lee, S.A.; Lim, J.; Foussias, G.; Fervaha, G.; Ruhrman, S.; Remington, G.; Lee, J. Baseline social amotivation predicts 1-year functioning in UHR subjects: A validation and prospective investigation. *Eur. Neuropsychopharmacol.* **2015**, *25*, 2187–2196. [CrossRef]
55. Rocca, P.; Montemagni, C.; Zappia, S.; Piterà, R.; Sigaudo, M.; Bogetto, F. Negative symptoms and everyday functioning in schizophrenia: A cross-sectional study in a real world-setting. *Psychiatry Res.* **2014**, *218*, 284–289. [CrossRef]
56. Green, M.F.; Hellemann, G.; Horan, W.P.; Lee, J.; Wynn, J.K. From perception to functional outcome in schizophrenia: Modeling the role of ability and motivation. *Arch. Gen. Psychiatry* **2012**, *69*, 1216–1224. [CrossRef]
57. Gard, D.E.; Kring, A.M.; Gard, M.G.; Horan, W.P.; Green, M.F. Anhedonia in schizophrenia: Distinctions between anticipatory and consummatory pleasure. *Schizophr. Res.* **2007**, *93*, 253–260. [CrossRef]
58. Hovington, C.L.; Bodnar, M.; Joober, R.; Malla, A.K.; Lepage, M. Identifying persistent negative symptoms in first episode psychosis. *BMC Psychiatry* **2012**, *12*, 224. [CrossRef] [PubMed]
59. Okada, H.; Hirano, D.; Taniguchi, T. Impact of Negative Symptom Domains and Other Clinical Characteristics on Functional Outcomes in Patients with Schizophrenia. *Schizophr. Res. Treat.* **2021**, *2021*, 8864352. [CrossRef] [PubMed]
60. Strauss, G.P.; Harrow, M.; Grossman, L.S.; Rosen, C. Periods of recovery in deficit syndrome schizophrenia: A 20-year multi-follow-up longitudinal study. *Schizophr. Bull.* **2010**, *36*, 788–799. [CrossRef] [PubMed]
61. Messinger, J.W.; Trémeau, F.; Antonius, D.; Mendelsohn, E.; Prudent, V.; Stanford, A.D.; Malaspina, D. Avolition and expressive deficits capture negative symptom phenomenology: Implications for DSM-5 and schizophrenia research. *Clin. Psychol. Rev.* **2011**, *31*, 161–168. [CrossRef] [PubMed]
62. Malla, A.K.; Takhar, J.J.; Norman, R.M.G.; Manchanda, R.; Cortese, L.; Haricharan, R.; Verdi, M.; Ahmed, R. Negative symptoms in first episode non-affective psychosis. *Acta Psychiatr. Scand.* **2002**, *105*, 431–439. [CrossRef] [PubMed]
63. Strauss, G.P.; Horan, W.P.; Kirkpatrick, B.; Fischer, B.A.; Keller, W.R.; Miski, P.; Buchanan, R.W.; Green, M.F.; Carpenter, W.T. Deconstructing negative symptoms of schizophrenia: Avolition-apathy and diminished expression clusters predict clinical presentation and functional outcome. *J. Psychiatr. Res.* **2013**, *47*, 783–790. [CrossRef]

Journal of
Clinical Medicine

MDPI

Article

Correlation of Health-Related Quality of Life with Negative Symptoms Assessed with the Self-Evaluation of Negative Symptoms Scale (SNS) and Cognitive Deficits in Schizophrenia: A Cross-Sectional Study in Routine Psychiatric Care

Jonas Montvidas [1,*], Virginija Adomaitienė [1], Darius Leskauskas [1] and Sonia Dollfus [2]

[1] Psychiatry Department, Lithuanian University of Health Sciences, LT-50162 Kaunas, Lithuania
[2] Psychiatry Department, University of Caen Normandy, 14000 Caen, France
* Correspondence: jonas.montvidas@lsmu.lt

Abstract: (1) Background: Schizophrenia is a severe mental disorder characterized by various symptom groups that tremendously affect health-related quality of life (HRQoL). We aimed to specify whether negative symptoms and cognitive deficits of schizophrenia correlate and can predict HRQoL. (2) Methods: Patients diagnosed with paranoid schizophrenia were invited to participate in the study. Participants were evaluated using the Montreal Cognitive Assessment (MoCA) and the Brief Psychiatric Rating Scale (BPRS) and were asked to fill out the Self-evaluation of Negative Symptoms scale (SNS) and the Medical Outcomes Short Form Survey (SF-36). Pearson's and Spearman's correlations were used to calculate the correlations between cognitive deficits and negative symptoms. We performed the receiver operating characteristic (ROC) analysis for the variables correlated with SF-36 scores. (3) Results: HRQoL correlated significantly with the negative symptoms; however, it did not correlate with cognitive deficits. ROC analysis showed that the abulia subscore of the SNS showed the most significant predictive potential of HRQoL. (4) Conclusions: Negative symptoms correlate more significantly with the HRQoL than cognitive symptoms. The SNS offers the possibility of predicting the HRQoL of patients with schizophrenia and is useful as a screening tool in clinical practice.

Keywords: schizophrenia; negative symptoms; cognitive deficits; self-evaluation of negative symptoms; health-related quality of life

Citation: Montvidas, J.; Adomaitienė, V.; Leskauskas, D.; Dollfus, S. Correlation of Health-Related Quality of Life with Negative Symptoms Assessed with the Self-Evaluation of Negative Symptoms Scale (SNS) and Cognitive Deficits in Schizophrenia: A Cross-Sectional Study in Routine Psychiatric Care. *J. Clin. Med.* **2023**, *12*, 901. https://doi.org/10.3390/jcm12030901

Academic Editor: Jerzy Samochowiec

Received: 15 December 2022
Revised: 15 January 2023
Accepted: 16 January 2023
Published: 23 January 2023

1. Introduction

Schizophrenia is a debilitating mental disorder characterized by an insidious course with relapsing-remitting positive symptoms (hallucinations, delusions, disorganized thought process), chronically present negative symptoms (blunted affect, anhedonia, alogia, avolition, social withdrawal), and cognitive deficits (attention, speed of processing, memory, working memory, reasoning, and problem-solving, as well as social cognition domains, such as emotion processing and theory of mind) [1]. According to data published by the World Health Organization, schizophrenia affects approximately one person out of every 300 and mostly starts at a young age [2].

Around 90 percent of patients diagnosed with schizophrenia have cognitive deficits, and approximately 50 to 60 percent have negative symptoms [3,4]. Both cognitive deficits and negative symptoms have predictive value for the onset of psychosis and the severity and the outcomes of the disease [5–7]. Moreover, negative symptoms are present in 50–70% of first-episode psychosis patients later diagnosed with schizophrenia, and around 10 to 30% of them develop at least one persistent negative symptom [8,9]. Cognitive deficits and negative symptoms remain chronically present during the illness [10]. Neither cognitive deficits nor negative symptoms significantly correlate with the severity of positive symptoms or the duration of untreated psychosis [11,12].

Schizophrenia significantly impacts the objective social, occupational, and everyday functioning and the subjective Health-Related Quality of Life (HRQoL) of schizophrenia patients and their caretakers [13]. Objective everyday functioning refers to how well a person performs various tasks. Subjective HRQoL refers to how health influences the perceived well-being in 3 domains of life: physical, mental, and social [14,15]. HRQoL has been found to be an independent predictor of relapse in schizophrenia [16]. A phenomenon called the "insight paradox" was described that greater insight in schizophrenia was negatively correlated with the subjective HRQoL [17]. Among the 3 domains of HRQoL, the social domain was reported to have the lowest score [18]. Therefore, assessing HRQoL in schizophrenia is necessary to understand how this disorder impacts the life of the patients and to set the main treatment targets to minimize the impact of this mental disorder [18].

Most studies that evaluated negative symptoms of schizophrenia used extensive and challenging to use questionnaires. The most widely used instruments for negative symptoms assessment were the Positive and Negative Symptoms Scale (PANSS) for the Assessment of Negative Symptoms (SANS) [19]. These scales take at least 45 min to complete, and PANSS needs special training to be administered and scored correctly, which significantly impedes its use in daily bedside practice [20–23]. Moreover, PANSS and SANS have proven content validity problems [24]. The European Psychiatrists Association (EPA) Guidance on assessing negative symptoms advocates the so-called 'second generation' scales. It encourages using self-assessment tools such as the Self-assessment scale of Negative Symptoms (SNS) [19].

Most research articles about the relationship between cognitive deficits and functioning or HRQoL employed expensive, corporation-owned, complicated questionnaires that took a long time to complete. The most often used tools were Cambridge Neuropsychological Test Automated Battery (CANTAB), CogState, and Repeatable Battery for the Assessment of Neuropsychological Status (BRANS) [25]. The NIMH-Measurement and Treatment Research to Improve Cognition in Schizophrenia (MATRICS) Consensus Cognitive Battery (MCCB) is a diagnostic tool that is recommended by the EPA to be used for cognitive function assessment for patients with schizophrenia [26]. However, MCCB takes at least 60–90 min to complete, making it difficult to use in a bedside practice [27,28]. Moreover, none of the tools recommended for cognitive symptoms assessment by the EPA are available in Lithuanian.

Recognizing the need for further research on the relationship between HRQoL and negative symptoms and cognitive deficits of schizophrenia conducted using tools applicable in daily practice, we aimed to evaluate negative symptoms and cognitive deficits of schizophrenia with easily administered scales and to assess the correlations between negative symptoms, cognitive deficits, and subjective health-related quality of life.

2. Materials and Methods

2.1. Participants

Patients of the Lithuanian University of Health Sciences Hospital Kaunas Clinics Psychiatry department diagnosed with paranoid schizophrenia (according to the ICD-10 AM diagnostic criteria, diagnostic code F20.0) were invited to participate in the study during routine clinical care. The period of data collection was between the beginning of March 2019 and January 2020. The authors of this study worked as psychiatrists in the inpatient and outpatient psychiatric wards of the study center. The authors of this study asked other psychiatrists to inform them about patients with schizophrenia without active psychotic symptoms. Patients on the last day of their hospitalization and without active psychotic symptoms were informed about our study and invited to join. Outpatients that visited their psychiatrists for a routine visit and were evaluated by the treating psychiatrist as presenting no active psychotic symptoms were informed about the study and were asked to join. One of the researchers screened participants who were asked to join our study for inclusion and exclusion criteria. Inclusion criteria were diagnosis of schizophrenia with no acute psychotic symptoms present during the evaluation and aged 18–65. Exclusion criteria were intellectual disability, addiction to psychoactive substances, and acute psychotic symptoms during the primary assessment. We screened the patients for active psychotic symptoms with the Lithuanian version of the Mini International Neuropsychiatric Interview (MINI) module L, "Psychotic disorders." We wanted to test the relationship between negative symptoms, cognitive deficits and the subjective HRQoL; therefore, we controlled for psychosis and did not include patients with active, positive symptoms that can induce secondary negative symptoms. Depression was evaluated using the Brief Psychiatric Rating scale-18 item 9 "Depression". We did not control for the number of medications, the dosage, and the duration of treatment. Participants deemed appropriate to be included in the study were asked to sign an informed consent form. Around 150 patients with schizophrenia were treated in the study center during the period of data collection; out of them, around 100 were recommended to our team and were screened, and 67 met the inclusion criteria and signed the informed consent form to participate in the study. We did not collect the data of screened patients.

2.2. Bioethics

Bioethics approval No. BE-2-22 was received from the Kaunas Regional Biomedical Research Ethics Committee on 1 March 2019.

2.3. Procedure and Measures

After the participants signed the informed consent form, they were included in the study. Participants were screened during routine clinical care; therefore, short and quick evaluation tools were selected—the Montreal Cognitive Assessment (MoCA) and the Brief Psychiatric Rating Scale (BPRS). After screening, they were asked to complete the Medical Outcomes Short Form Survey (SF-36) and the Self-evaluation of Negative Symptoms Scale (SNS). Sociodemographic data regarding the sex, age, and years of education of participants were collected. Patients were also asked to rate their general well-being from 1 (feeling horrible) to 10 (feeling wonderful).

The MoCA is a screening tool developed to detect mild cognitive impairments. It evaluates short-term memory, visuospatial abilities, executive functions, attention, language, and orientation. It has a highest score of 30 points and takes 10–15 min to complete. The MoCA evaluates visuospatial/executive (MoCA-VE), naming (MoCA-N), attention (MoCA-A), language (MoCA-L), abstraction (MoCA-AB), delayed recall (MoCA-DR), and orientation (MoCA-O) subscores and the total score (MoCA-TS) [29]. The MoCA is considered sensitive to detect mild and severe cognitive impairment in patients with schizophrenia, therefore validating it as an appropriate cognitive deficit screening tool for patients with schizophrenia. It has been validated in a schizophrenia patient sample that scoring below 26 points indicates a mild cognitive impairment, and scoring below 23 points indicates severe cognitive impairment [30–32]. Even though the MoCA is not a tool that is widely accepted to use for the assessment of cognitive symptoms, it is the only alternative to the Mini-Mental Examination Scale (MMSE) available in Lithuania.

The BPRS is one of the most widely used psychiatric rating scales. We used a version of the BPRS consisting of 18 items evaluating symptoms of depression, anxiety, agitation, and psychosis, as well as negative symptoms. Every item is scored from 1 (not present) to 7 (extremely severe) [33]. The scoring is based on the clinical interview and the patient's behavior. Depressive symptoms are evaluated with the ninth item, "Depressive mood" (BPRS-D) [34,35]. Most researchers employed the negative symptoms of schizophrenia subscores (BPRS-N) consisting of a sum of the scores of items 3, "Emotional withdrawal," 13, "Motor retardation," and 16, "Blunted affect" [36].

The SNS is a 'second generation' subjective negative symptoms evaluation tool that evaluates all five domains of negative symptoms of schizophrenia [37]. It is recommended in the current EPA Guidance paper on negative symptom assessment [19]. A patient is asked to read the 20 statements listed in the SNS and then mark whether they agree (2 points), mildly agree (1 point), or disagree (0 points) with each of the statements. The maximum score is 40 points, with each subdomain of negative symptoms having a top score of 8 points. Questions 1 to 4 evaluate social withdrawal (SNS-SW), 5 to 8 evaluate reduced emotional range (SNS-RER), 9 to 12 evaluate alogia (SNS-A), 13 to 16 evaluate avolition (SNS-AV), and questions 17 to 20 assess anhedonia (SNS-AN). We can add the five subscores to obtain a total score (SNS-TS) [37]. It only takes around 5 min to complete and score the SNS. The Lithuanian version of SNS has been validated and shown good psychometric properties [38].

The SF-36 is one of the most widely used HRQoL evaluation tools. It is free and easy to self-administer and takes about 7–10 min [39]. The SF-36 measures eight HRQoL aspects: physical functioning (SF-36-PF), physical role-functioning (SF-36-RP), bodily pain (SF-36-BP), general health (SF-36-GH), vitality (SF-36-VT), social functioning (SF-36-SF), role emotional (SF-36-RE), and mental health (SF-36-MH). Component analyses showed that there are two distinct concepts measured by the SF-36: a physical dimension, represented by the Physical Component Summary (PCS), and a mental dimension, represented by the Mental Component Summary (MCS) [40]. Every HRQoL aspect is assessed by a score varying from 0 to 100, with a higher score meaning better HRQoL. These subscales are not disease or treatment specific. The SF-36 subscales were found suitable to administer, and the scores were reliable for patients with schizophrenia [41].

2.4. Statistical Analysis

We used the Chi-square test to see if there were statistically significant differences in sample distribution according to different variables. Internal consistency was calculated for the BPRS-N, MoCA-TS, and SNS-TS. The means of BPRS-D and BPRS-N scores, five SNS subscores and the SNS-TS, MoCA subscores, and MoCA-TS and SF-36 scores were calculated. We grouped the sample into groups according to the SNS total score ($\leq$20 or >20), MoCA total score ($\geq$26 or <26), and SF-36 scores (<50 or $\geq$50) in order to evaluate for demographic differences between different patient groups. We chose the middle of the score range for SNS and SF-36 because we did not find data regarding cut-off scores between severe and mild negative symptoms and good and bad HRQoL. All scores and subscores were tested for normality of distribution using the Shapiro–Wilk test. Student t-test was used for normally distributed and parametric variables, and the Mann–Whitney test was used for the not normally distributed and nonparametric variables. Our main null hypothesis was that the subjective HRQoL did not correlate with negative symptoms and/or cognitive deficits of schizophrenia. Pearson's correlation was used to calculate the correlations between normally distributed variables, and Spearman's correlation was used for variables that were not distributed normally. We performed the receiver operating characteristic (ROC) analysis for the variables correlated with SF-36 scores. We set SF-36 <50 as an expected outcome. An area under the curve (AUC) of 0.5 would tell us that our test was not able to distinguish the true positives (where the SF-36 score is actually <50) and false positives (where SF-36 is >50 even though we expected it to be $\geq$50). An AUC of 1 would tell us that all of the positives are true positives. An excellent test would be an AUC of 0.9 or more, a good one would be an AUC of 0.8 or more, and a fair one would be an AUC of 0.7 or more.

The level of significance was kept at 95% ($p < 0.05$). A total of 56 correlation analyses were performed; therefore, the Bonferroni correction for *p*-values was 0.018. We used the Statistical Package for the Social Sciences version 27 for the statistical analysis.

3. Results

3.1. Demographic Data

The sample consisted of 67 respondents. It included significantly ($p = 0.02$) more females ($n = 43$, 64.2%) than males ($n = 24$, 35.8%). The mean age was 41.51 (SD 13.76, CI 95% 38.15–44.86). Age was not normally distributed ($p = 0.005$). There were no age differences between the sexes ($z = -1.564$, $p = 0.118$). The mean of years of education was 14.9 (SD 3.34, CD95% 14.08–15.71). Years of education were not normally distributed

(p = 0.024) and did not differ between sexes (z = −0.251, p = 0.802). The mean score of general well-being was 6.27 (SD 1.871, CD95% 5.81–6.73) and was not normally distributed (p = 0.005). The general well-being score did not differ between the sexes (z = −0.967, p = 0.334).

There were no significant differences in the number of participants between SNS-TS ≤20 or >20 groups (p = 0.282). There was a significant difference between respondent count in MoCA-TS ≥26 (n = 20; 29.9%) and <26 (n = 47; 70.1%) groups (p < 0.001). There were statistically significant differences in SF-36 <50 and ≥50 groups in SF-36-PF (12 vs. 55, p <0.001), SF-36-RP (20 vs. 47, p <0.001), and SF-36-BP (54 vs. 13, p < 0.001).

3.2. Internal Consistency, Mean Scores and Mean Ranks

Cronbach's alpha of the BPRS-N (α = 0.857), SNS-TS (α = 0.82), and the five subscores (α = 0.76), MoCA-TS (α = 0.769) and the SF-36 (α = 0.858) showed good internal consistency.

The mean scores of the BPRS-D, BPRS-N, SNS subscores, SNS-TS, MoCA subscores, and MoCA-TS and SF-36 scores are given in Table 1. None of the scores differed significantly between the sexes.

Table 1. Mean scores of SNS, BPRS, MoCA, and SF-36.

Scale	Mean Score	CI 95 Proc.
SNS-SW	4.33 (2.642)	3.68–4.97
SNS-RER	3.49 (1.691)	3.08–3.91
SNS-A	4.03 (2.933)	3.33–4.75
SNS-AV	4.03 (2.202)	3.49–4.57
SNS-AN	3.27 (2.1)	2.76–3.78
SNS-TS	18.61 (8.792)	16.47–20.76
BPRS-D	2.39 (1.255)	2.08–2.69
BPRS-N	10.42 (3.947)	9.46–11.38
MoCA-VE	3.18 (1.476)	2.82–3.54
MoCA-N	2.84 (0.51)	2.71–2.96
MoCA-A	4.36 (1.544)	3.98–4.73
MoCA-L	1.58 (0.781)	1.39–1.77
MoCA-AB	1.31 (0.763)	1.13–1.5
MoCA-DR	2.93 (1.418)	2.58–3.27
MoCA-O	5.81 (0.557)	5.67–5.91
MoCA-TS	22.82 (4.376)	21.75–23.89
SF-36-PF	75.75 (24.313	69.82–81.68
SF-36-RP	52.24 (20.749)	47.18–57.30
SF-36-BP	26.63 (26.863)	20.07–33.18
SF-36-GH	43.28 (20.954)	38.17–48.39
SF-36-VT	41.79 (21.047)	26.66–46.92
SF-36-SF	45.36 (24.742)	39.32–51.93
SF-36-RE	37.76 (37.159)	28.7–46.83
SF-36-MH	52.54 (18.94)	47.92–57.16

3.3. Correlations

None of the scores correlated with age, except for MoCA-N (rho = −0.364, p = 0.002) and MoCA-TS (rho = −0.345, p = 0.004). None of the scores correlated with years of education. None of the MoCA or BRPS-D scores correlated with the general well-being score. However, all five SNS subscores, SNS-TS and BPRS-N, correlated significantly with the general well-being score. Most of the SF-36 scores correlated significantly with the general well-being score. Correlations with the general well-being score are provided in Table 2.

Table 2. Correlation of SNS-TS and subscores, BPRS-N and SF-36 subscores with the general well-being score.

Scale	Pearson r/Spearman Rho	p
SNS-SW	−0.459	<0.001
SNS-RER	−0.428	<0.001
SNS-A	−0.414	<0.001
SNS-AV	−0.592	<0.001
SNS-AN	−0.395	<0.001
SNS-TS	−0.593	<0.001
BPRS-N	−0.443	<0.001
SF-36-PF	0.497	<0.001
SF-36-RP	0.253	0.039
SF-36-BP	−0.159	0.2
SF-36-GH	0.585	<0.001
SF-36-VT	0.619	<0.001
SF-36-SF	0.407	<0.001
SF-36-RE	0.451	<0.001
SF-36-MH	0.478	<0.001

The MoCA did not correlate with BPRS-N, BPRS-D, and SNS scores, except for MoCA-L with BPRS-N (rho = −0.3, p = 0.014), MoCA-AB with BPRS-N (rho = −0.349, p = 0.004), MoCA-TS with SNS-A (rho = −0.243, p = 0.048), MoCA-VE with SNS-AN (rho = −0.408, $p < 0.001$) and MoCA-TS with SNS-AN (rho = −0.319, p = 0.008). The MoCA did not correlate with SF-36 scores. The BPRS-D had only one statistically significant correlation with SF-36-PF (rho = −0.324, p = 0.008).

We found that SF-36-PF correlated with BPRS-N, SNS-TS, and every SNS subscore except for SNS-BA. SF-36-RP did not correlate with any of the SNS scores or BPRS-N. SF-36-BP correlated with SNS-AV and SNS-AN. SF-36-RE correlated with SNS-AV. SF-36-GH, SF-36-VT, SF-36-SF, and SF-36-MH correlated with every SNS score and BPRS-N. SNS, BPRS, and SF-36 correlations are provided in Table 3.

Table 3. SF-36, SNS, and BPRS-N correlations.

SF-36 Score	SNS/BPRS Score	Pearson r/Spearman Rho	p
SF-36-PF	SNS-TS	−0.531	<0.001
SF-36-RP	SNS-TS	−0.129	0.263
SF-36-BP	SNS-TS	0.288	0.018
SF-36-GH	SNS-TS	−0.589	<0.001
SF-36-VT	SNS-TS	−0.627	<0.001
SF-36-SF	SNS-TS	−0.496	<0.001
SF-36-RE	SNS-TS	−0.229	0.062
SF-36-MH	SNS-TS	−0.59	<0.001
SF-36-PF	SNS-SW	−0.427	<0.001
SF-36-RP	SNS-SW	−0.121	0.329
SF-36-BP	SNS-SW	0.172	0.164
SF-36-GH	SNS-SW	−0.38	0.002
SF-36-VT	SNS-SW	−0.49	<0.001
SF-36-SF	SNS-SW	−0.482	<0.001
SF-36-RE	SNS-SW	−0.198	0.109
SF-36-MH	SNS-SW	−0.51	<0.001
SF-36-PF	SNS-RER	−0.188	0.129
SF-36-RP	SNS-RER	0.053	0.667
SF-36-BP	SNS-RER	0.086	0.491
SF-36-GH	SNS-RER	−0.342	0.005
SF-36-VT	SNS-RER	−0.44	<0.001
SF-36-SF	SNS-RER	−0.394	<0.001
SF-36-RE	SNS-RER	−0.245	0.046
SF-36-MH	SNS-RER	−0.509	<0.001

Table 3. *Cont.*

SF-36 Score	SNS/BPRS Score	Pearson r/Spearman Rho	*p*
SF-36-PF	SNS-A	−0.373	0.002
SF-36-RP	SNS-A	−0.085	0.492
SF-36-BP	SNS-A	0.218	0.077
SF-36-GH	SNS-A	−0.448	<0.001
SF-36-VT	SNS-A	−0.375	0.002
SF-36-SF	SNS-A	−0.413	<0.001
SF-36-RE	SNS-A	−0.177	0.153
SF-36-MH	SNS-A	−0.427	<0.001
SF-36-PF	SNS-AV	−0.518	<0.001
SF-36-RP	SNS-AV	−0.238	0.053
SF-36-BP	SNS-AV	0.323	0.008
SF-36-GH	SNS-AV	−0.568	<0.001
SF-36-VT	SNS-AV	−0.629	<0.001
SF-36-SF	SNS-AV	−0.329	0.007
SF-36-RE	SNS-AV	−0.368	0.002
SF-36-MH	SNS-AV	−0.458	<0.001
SF-36-PF	SNS-AN	−0.469	<0.001
SF-36-RP	SNS-AN	−0.146	0.238
SF-36-BP	SNS-AN	0.284	0.02
SF-36-GH	SNS-AN	−0.442	<0.001
SF-36-VT	SNS-AN	−0.388	0.001
SF-36-SF	SNS-AN	−0.374	0.002
SF-36-RE	SNS-AN	−0.163	0.188
SF-36-MH	SNS-AN	−0.467	<0.001
SF-36-PF	BPRS-N	−0.375	0.002
SF-36-RP	BPRS-N	−0.007	0.955
SF-36-BP	BPRS-N	0.175	0.157
SF-36-GH	BPRS-N	−0.415	<0.001
SF-36-VT	BPRS-N	−0.417	<0.001
SF-36-SF	BPRS-N	−0.354	0.003
SF-36-RE	BPRS-N	−0.155	0.209
SF-36-MH	BPRS-N	−0.486	<0.001

3.4. Receiver Operating Characteristic (ROC) Analysis

Because MoCA scores did not correlate with SF-36 scores, we did not perform a ROC analysis for the MoCA. The ROC analysis for BPRS-D, BPRS-N, and SNS scores had mixed results. The ROC analysis with a statistically significant AUC ≥ 0.7 is given in Table 4.

Table 4. The area under the curve (AUC) ≥ 0.7.

SF-36 Score	SNS/BPRS Score	AUC	*p*
SF-36-PF	SNS-AV	0.711	0.023
	BPRS-D	0.719	0.018
SF-36-RP	SNS-AV	0.709	0.007
SF-36-GH	SNS-A	0.729	0.001
	SNS-AV	0.823	<0.001
	SNS-TS	0.776	<0.001
SF-36-VT	SNS-AV	0.762	<0.001
	SNS-TS	0.749	0.001
SF-36-SF	SNS-A	0.728	0.002
SF-36-MH	BPRS-N	0.737	0.001
	SNS-SW	0.786	<0.001
	SNS-RER	0.759	<0.001
	SNS-A	0.706	0.004
	SNS-AV	0.743	0.001
	SNS-AN	0.745	0.001
	SNS-TS	0.809	<0.001

No AUC $\geq$ 0.9 was found. Only SNS-AV with SF-36-GH (AUC = 0.823) and SNS-TS with SF-36-MH (AUC = 0.809) had AUC $\geq$ 0.8. We found that the SNS-AV score of 3.5 predicted that SF-36-GH would be less than 50, with a sensitivity of 79.5% and specificity of 75%. SNS-TS score of 20.5 predicted that SF-36-MH would be less than 50 with a sensitivity of 70% and specificity of 73%.

4. Discussion

We found that negative symptoms of schizophrenia had a stronger correlation with HRQoL than cognitive deficits when evaluated with quick bedside tools SNS, BPRS and MoCA. The correlation between cognitive deficits of schizophrenia and the HRQoL was insignificant. We also found that negative symptoms of schizophrenia, assessed with a short self-evaluation scale, were predictive of the HRQoL in schizophrenia.

The unique finding of our study is that the avolition subdomain of negative symptoms was the most predictive of reduced HRQoL. To our knowledge, this is the first study where ROC analysis was performed for HRQoL prediction using a scale for negative symptom assessment. Dollfus et al. performed a ROC analysis in a study with SNS and found that scoring 7 points or more on the SNS separated healthy controls and patients with schizophrenia with a sensitivity of 92.7% and specificity of 85.9% [42]. We believe that the findings of our ROC analysis of the SNS results complement the results of Dollfus et al. and further prove the validity of SNS as a screening tool regarding the prediction of poor life quality for patients with schizophrenia.

Our results of an insignificant correlation between the subjective HRQoL and cognitive deficits in schizophrenia are similar to the results of other authors, who found that cognitive deficits were closely linked to poorer everyday functioning but not subjective HRQoL. A relationship between cognitive functioning and real-life functioning has been found in a 5-year large-scale longitudinal study by Mucci et al. [43]. The EPA Guidance paper on the evaluation of cognitive deficits of schizophrenia described that cognitive deficits of schizophrenia are closely linked to everyday functioning but not to the subjective HRQoL [26]. A meta-analysis by Arielle et al. showed that cognitive deficits had a non-statistically significant relationship with self-reported HRQoL [44]. Various other authors also conclude that schizophrenia is characterized by deficits in various cognitive domains that have a more significant effect on objective functioning compared to negative or positive symptoms but have less influence on the subjective HRQoL [26,45,46]. Moreover, Domenech et al. found that patients with more significant cognitive deficits reported higher HRQoL on the SF-36 scale [47].

On the other hand, some authors find different results. For example, Apteinin et al. found that executive functions and working memory deficits were associated with lower self-reported quality of life [48]. Kurtz et al. found similar results in a 5-year follow-up study; however, they found that negative and positive symptoms but not cognitive deficits were independent predictors of objective psychosocial status. However, they managed to find a link between cognitive deficits and "life satisfaction" [49]. This could be explained by much greater sample sizes and different methodologies and warrants further research.

We found that negative symptoms correlated strongly and significantly with the HRQoL. Many other authors have reported similar findings. Greater PANSS negative symptoms scores were associated with worse SF-36 physical and mental scores [47,50]. Pukrop et al. found that the reduction of negative symptoms severity significantly improved SF-36 scores [41]. Rabinowitz et al. found that negative symptoms were more correlated to the reduction of QoL. However, a combination of prominent negative and prominent positive symptoms had the greatest correlation with reduced QoL [6].

On the other hand, Chou et al. found that psychosocial factors had the most significant effect on the HRQoL, and depressive symptoms had the most significant effect out of the psychopathological factors [46]. This might be explained by different assessment tools used to assess depressive and negative symptoms of schizophrenia. Chou et al. used PANSS, a hetero-assessment tool, to evaluate negative symptoms and a self-assessment scale (Beck

Depression Inventory-II, BDI-II) to assess depressive symptoms, while we did the opposite and used hetero-assessment of depressive symptoms with the BPRS and used self-rating for negative symptoms with SNS. Chemerinski et al. found that using only specific few items within BDI-II and not the entire BDI-II provides a more clinically accurate assessment of depression in schizophrenia [51]. Additionally, other authors found that depressive and negative symptoms often overlap, and depressive symptoms often constitute secondary negative symptoms [52]. Even though Dollfus et al. found that SNS is an appropriate tool to screen negative symptoms regardless of the severity of depressive symptoms, we believe that further investigation into the ability of self-assessment tools to distinguish between secondary negative symptoms caused by depression and primary negative symptoms is required [42].

There is an ongoing discussion about what type of HRQoL measures are applicable for patients with schizophrenia. HRQoL measures can be divided into two groups: specific disease-targeted measures and generic measures. The disease-targeted measures are created to evaluate a particular disorder, whereas generic measures can be applied to any disorder. Generic measures can be further specified as profile-based (evaluating multiple aspects) or preference-based (producing a single score). We used the SF-36, which is a generic profile measure [14]. The SF-36 was proven applicable in schizophrenia research by some researchers [7,47]. However, other researchers found unclear results about the applicability of generic HRQoL measures for patients with schizophrenia [53,54]. Therefore, we recognize that using a generic HRQoL measure can be considered one of the limitations of our study.

Another limitation of our study is the use of the MoCA for the evaluation of cognitive deficits of schizophrenia because this scale is not among the tools that are recommended for the assessment of cognitive deficits [26]. However, we had to comply with the fact that only the MoCA and MMSE are currently available in Lithuania. The MoCA is more effective than the MMSE when evaluating cognitive deficits in a sample of patients with schizophrenia [55–57]. Moreover, Belvederi et al. have compared the MoCA to the Screen for Cognitive Impairment in Psychiatry (SCIP), which is recognized and recommended for the evaluation of cognitive deficits by the EPA. The MoCA showed similar, albeit worse, results compared to the SCIP [58]. Our research team is currently in the process of validating the Lithuanian version of the SCIP.

Other limitations are a relatively small sample size, broad inclusion criteria, not using a 'second-generation' rater-based assessment tools for negative symptom assessment, and using a short-form evaluation of depressive symptoms. A bigger sample size might have improved the normality of the distribution of the variables and increased the significance of some correlations between HRQoL and cognitive deficits. Making the inclusion criteria narrower and controlling for medications used, years of disease, and other criteria might have helped make our results more reliable. Using a 'second-generation' hetero-assessment tool for evaluating negative symptoms might have helped to increase the validity of our negative symptom assessment. However, the ability of patients with schizophrenia to self-evaluate was proven extensively [59–61]. Direct comparison of precision for prediction of the HRQoL of such tools as the Brief Negative Symptoms Scale and SNS would be recommended. Moreover, using a more detailed evaluation of depressive symptoms could have yielded a more pronounced correlation of depression symptoms with other symptom groups.

5. Conclusions

We may conclude that HRQoL correlated significantly with negative symptoms but did not correlate with cognitive deficits of patients diagnosed with schizophrenia. Negative symptoms evaluated with both 'first generation' observer-rated and 'second generation' self-assessment tools correlated significantly with HRQoL. A reduction of HRQoL can be predicted with SNS, especially the avolition subscore of SNS, which warrants further investigation of SNS as a screening tool for the quality of life of patients with schizophrenia.

Author Contributions: S.D., V.A., D.L. and J.M. contributed to the conception and design of the study. J.M. organized the database. J.M. performed the statistical analysis. J.M. wrote the first draft of the manuscript. V.A. and D.L. performed manuscript revisions. All authors have read and agreed to the published version of the manuscript.

Funding: Publication of this article was funded by the Lithuanian university of Health Sciences.

Institutional Review Board Statement: Bioethics approval No. BE-2-22 was received from the Kaunas Regional Biomedical Research Ethics Committee on 1 March 2019.

Informed Consent Statement: Informed consent was obtained from all subjects involved in the study.

Data Availability Statement: Data are stored in the personal storage of the corresponding author and is not available online.

Conflicts of Interest: The authors declare no conflict of interest.

References

1. Owen, M.J.; Sawa, A.; Mortensen, P.B. Schizophrenia. *Lancet* **2016**, *388*, 86–97. [CrossRef]
2. The World Health Organization. Schizophrenia. Available online: https://www.who.int/news-room/fact-sheets/detail/schizophrenia (accessed on 6 March 2019).
3. Bobes, J.; Arango, C.; Garcia-Garcia, M.; Rejas, J. Prevalence of negative symptoms in outpatients with schizophrenia spectrum disorders treated with antipsychotics in routine clinical practice: Findings from the CLAMORS study. *J. Clin. Psychiatry* **2010**, *71*, 280–286. Available online: https://pubmed-ncbi-nlm-nih-gov.ezproxy.dbazes.lsmuni.lt/19895779/ (accessed on 26 November 2022). [CrossRef]
4. Zhang, H.; Wang, Y.; Hu, Y.; Zhu, Y.; Zhang, T.; Wang, J.; Ma, K.; Shi, C.; Yu, X.; Li, C. Meta-analysis of cognitive function in Chinese first-episode schizophrenia: MATRICS Consensus Cognitive Battery (MCCB) profile of impairment. *Gen. Psychiatry* **2019**, *32*, e100043. [CrossRef]
5. Addington, J.; Heinssen, R. Prediction and Prevention of Psychosis in Youth at Clinical High Risk. *Annu. Rev. Clin. Psychol.* **2012**, *8*, 269–289. [CrossRef]
6. Rabinowitz, J.; Berardo, C.G.; Bugarski-Kirola, D.; Marder, S. Association of prominent positive and prominent negative symptoms and functional health, well-being, healthcare-related quality of life and family burden: A CATIE analysis. *Schizophr. Res.* **2013**, *150*, 339–342. [CrossRef]
7. Azaiez, C.; Millier, A.; Lançon, C.; Clay, E.; Auquier, P.; Llorca, P.-M.; Toumi, M. Health related quality of life in patients having schizophrenia negative symptoms—A systematic review. *J. Mark. Access Health Policy* **2018**, *6*, 1517573. [CrossRef]
8. Lyne, J.; O'Donoghue, B.; Owens, E.; Renwick, L.; Madigan, K.; Kinsella, A.; Clarke, M.; Turner, N.; O'Callaghan, E. Prevalence of item level negative symptoms in first episode psychosis diagnoses. *Schizophr. Res.* **2012**, *135*, 128–133. [CrossRef]
9. Galderisi, S.; Mucci, A.; Buchanan, R.W.; Arango, C. Negative symptoms of schizophrenia: New developments and unanswered research questions. *Lancet Psychiatry* **2018**, *5*, 664–677. [CrossRef]
10. Tripathi, A.; Kar, S.K.; Shukla, R. Cognitive Deficits in Schizophrenia: Understanding the Biological Correlates and Remediation Strategies. *Clin. Psychopharmacol. Neurosci.* **2018**, *16*, 7–17. [CrossRef]
11. Lewandowski, K.E.; Cohen, B.M.; Öngur, D. Evolution of neuropsychological dysfunction during the course of schizophrenia and bipolar disorder. *Psychol. Med.* **2010**, *41*, 225–241. [CrossRef]
12. Davidson, M.; Harvey, P.D.; Powchik, P.; Parrella, M.; White, L.; Knobler, H.Y.; Losonczy, M.F.; Keefe, R.S.; Katz, S.; Frecska, E. Severity of symptoms in chronically institutionalized geriatric schizophrenic patients. *Am. J. Psychiatry* **1995**, *152*, 197–207. [CrossRef]
13. Caqueo-Urízar, A.; Gutiérrez-Maldonado, J.; Miranda-Castillo, C. Quality of life in caregivers of patients with schizophrenia: A literature review. *Health Qual. Life Outcomes* **2009**, *7*, 84. [CrossRef]
14. Hays, R.D.; Morales, L.S. The RAND-36 measure of health-related quality of life. *Ann. Med.* **2001**, *33*, 350–357. [CrossRef]
15. Narvaez, J.M.; Twamley, E.W.; McKibbin, C.L.; Heaton, R.K.; Patterson, T.L. Subjective and objective quality of life in schizophrenia. *Schizophr. Res.* **2008**, *98*, 201–208. [CrossRef]
16. Boyer, L.; Millier, A.; Perthame, E.; Aballea, S.; Auquier, P.; Toumi, M. Quality of life is predictive of relapse in schizophrenia. *BMC Psychiatry* **2013**, *13*, 15. [CrossRef]
17. Margariti, M.; Ploumpidis, D.; Economou, M.; Christodoulou, G.N.; Papadimitriou, G.N. Quality of life in schizophrenia spectrum disorders: Associations with insight and psychopathology. *Psychiatry Res.* **2015**, *225*, 695–701. [CrossRef]
18. Desalegn, D.; Girma, S.; Abdeta, T. Quality of life and its association with psychiatric symptoms and socio-demographic characteristics among people with schizophrenia: A hospital-based cross-sectional study. *PLoS ONE* **2020**, *15*, e0229514. [CrossRef]
19. Galderisi, S.; Mucci, A.; Dollfus, S.; Nordentoft, M.; Falkai, P.; Kaiser, S.; Giordano, G.M.; Vandevelde, A.; Nielsen, M.; Glenthøj, L.B.; et al. EPA guidance on assessment of negative symptoms in schizophrenia. *Eur. Psychiatry* **2021**, *64*, e23. [CrossRef]
20. Kay, S.R.; Flszbeln, A.; Qpjer, L.A. The Positive and Negative Syndrome Scale (PANSS) for Schizophrenia. Volume 13. 1967. Available online: https://academic.oup.com/schizophreniabulletin/article/13/2/261/1919795 (accessed on 1 January 2023).
21. Opler, M.; Yavorsky, C.; Daniel, D.G. Positive and Negative Syndrome Scale (PANSS) Training Challenges, Solutions, and Future Directions copy. *Innov. Clin. Neurosci.* **2017**, *14*, 77–81.

22. Kumari, S.; Malik, M.; Florival, M.C.; Manalai, M.P.; Sonje, S. An Assessment of Five (PANSS, SAPS, SANS, NSA-16, CGI-SCH) commonly used Symptoms Rating Scales in Schizophrenia and Comparison to Newer Scales (CAINS, BNSS). *J. Addict. Res. Ther.* **2017**, *8*, 324. [CrossRef]
23. Rabany, L.; Weiser, M.; Werbeloff, N.; Levkovitz, Y. Assessment of negative symptoms and depression in schizophrenia: Revision of the SANS and how it relates to the PANSS and CDSS. *Schizophr. Res.* **2011**, *126*, 226–230. [CrossRef] [PubMed]
24. Garcia-Portilla, M.P.; Garcia-Alvarez, L.; Saiz, P.A.; Al-Halabí, S.; Bascaran, M.-T.; Muñiz, J.; Bobes, J. Psychometric evaluation of the negative syndrome of schizophrenia. *Eur. Arch. Psychiatry Clin. Neurosci.* **2015**, *265*, 559–566. [CrossRef] [PubMed]
25. Bakkour, N.; Samp, J.; Akhras, K.; El Hammi, E.; Soussi, I.; Zahra, F.; Duru, G.; Kooli, A.; Toumi, M. Systematic review of appropriate cognitive assessment instruments used in clinical trials of schizophrenia, major depressive disorder and bipolar disorder. *Psychiatry Res.* **2014**, *216*, 291–302. [CrossRef]
26. Vita, A.; Gaebel, W.; Mucci, A.; Sachs, G.; Erfurth, A.; Barlati, S.; Zanca, F.; Giordano, G.M.; Glenthøj, L.B.; Nordentoft, M.; et al. European Psychiatric Association guidance on assessment of cognitive impairment in schizophrenia. *Eur. Psychiatry* **2022**, *65*, e58. [CrossRef] [PubMed]
27. Jędrasik-Styła, M.; Ciołkiewicz, A.; Styła, R.; Linke, M.; Parnowska, D.; Gruszka, A.; Denisiuk, M.; Jarema, M.; Green, M.F.; Wichniak, A. The Polish Academic Version of the MATRICS Consensus Cognitive Battery (MCCB): Evaluation of Psychometric Properties. *Psychiatr. Q.* **2015**, *86*, 435–447. [CrossRef]
28. August, S.M.; Kiwanuka, J.N.; McMahon, R.P.; Gold, J.M. The MATRICS Consensus Cognitive Battery (MCCB): Clinical and cognitive correlates. *Schizophr. Res.* **2012**, *134*, 76–82. [CrossRef] [PubMed]
29. Nasreddine, Z.S.; Phillips, N.A.; Bédirian, V.; Charbonneau, S.; Whitehead, V.; Collin, I.; Cummings, J.L.; Chertkow, H. The Montreal Cognitive Assessment, MoCA: A Brief Screening Tool for Mild Cognitive Impairment. 2005. Available online: www.mocatest (accessed on 20 November 2022).
30. Rosca, E.C.; Cornea, A.; Simu, M. Montreal Cognitive Assessment for evaluating the cognitive impairment in patients with schizophrenia: A systematic review. *Gen. Hosp. Psychiatry* **2020**, *65*, 64–73. [CrossRef]
31. Wu, C.; Dagg, P.; Molgat, C. A pilot study to measure cognitive impairment in patients with severe schizophrenia with the Montreal Cognitive Assessment (MoCA). *Schizophr. Res.* **2014**, *158*, 151–155. [CrossRef]
32. Yang, Z.; Rashid, N.A.A.; Quek, Y.F.; Lam, M.; See, Y.M.; Maniam, Y.; Dauwels, J.; Tan, B.L.; Lee, J. Montreal Cognitive Assessment as a screening instrument for cognitive impairments in schizophrenia. *Schizophr. Res.* **2018**, *199*, 58–63. [CrossRef]
33. Overall, J.E.; Gorham, D.R. *The Brief Psychiatric Rating Scale*; Psychological Reports; Southern Universiites Press: Carbondale, IL, USA, 1962; Volume 10.
34. Shafer, A. Meta-analysis of the Brief Psychiatric Rating Scale factor structure. *Psychol. Assess.* **2005**, *17*, 324–335. [CrossRef]
35. Overall, J.E. The Brief Psychiatric Rating Scale in Psychopharmacology Research. *Psychol. Meas. Psychopharmacol.* **2015**, *7*, 67–78. [CrossRef]
36. Papers, R.; Nicholson, I.R.; Chapman, J.E.; Neufeld, R.W.J. Variability in BPRS definitions of positive and negative symptoms. *Schizophr. Res.* **1995**, *17*, 177–185.
37. Dollfus, S.; Mach, C.; Morello, R. Self-Evaluation of Negative Symptoms. *Schizophr. Bull.* **2016**, *42*, 571–578. [CrossRef] [PubMed]
38. Montvidas, J.; Adomaitienė, V.; Leskauskas, D.; Dollfus, S. Validation of the lithuanian version of the self-evaluation of negative symptoms scale (SNS). *Nord. J. Psychiatry* **2020**, *75*, 351–355. [CrossRef] [PubMed]
39. Newnham, E.A.; Harwood, K.E.; Page, A.C. Evaluating the clinical significance of responses by psychiatric inpatients to the mental health subscales of the SF-36. *J. Affect. Disord.* **2007**, *98*, 91–97. [CrossRef] [PubMed]
40. Pukrop, R.; Schlaak, V.; Möller-Leimkühler, A.M.; Albus, M.; Czernik, A.; Klosterkötter, J.; Möller, H.-J. Reliability and validity of Quality of Life assessed by the Short-Form 36 and the Modular System for Quality of Life in patients with schizophrenia and patients with depression. *Psychiatry Res.* **2003**, *119*, 63–79. [CrossRef]
41. Leese, M.; Schene, A.; Koeter, M.; Meijer, K.; Bindman, J.; Mazzi, M.A.; Puschner, B.; Burti, L.; Becker, T.; Moreno, M.; et al. SF-36 scales, and simple sums of scales, were reliable quality-of-life summaries for patients with schizophrenia. *J. Clin. Epidemiol.* **2008**, *61*, 588–596. [CrossRef]
42. Dollfus, S.; Delouche, C.; Hervochon, C.; Mach, C.; Bourgeois, V.; Rotharmel, M.; Tréhout, M.; Vandevelde, A.; Guillin, O.; Morello, R. Specificity and sensitivity of the Self-assessment of Negative Symptoms (SNS) in patients with schizophrenia. *Schizophr. Res.* **2019**, *211*, 51–55. [CrossRef]
43. Mucci, A.; Galderisi, S.; Gibertoni, D.; Rossi, A.; Rocca, P.; Bertolino, A.; Aguglia, E.; Amore, M.; Bellomo, A.; Biondi, M.; et al. Factors Associated With Real-Life Functioning in Persons with Schizophrenia in a 4-Year Follow-up Study of the Italian Network for Research on Psychoses Supplemental content. *JAMA Psychiatry* **2021**, *78*, 550–559. Available online: https://jamanetwork.com/ (accessed on 1 January 2023). [CrossRef]
44. Tolman, A.W.; Kurtz, M.M. Neurocognitive Predictors of Objective and Subjective Quality of Life in Individuals With Schizophrenia: A Meta-Analytic Investigation. *Schizophr. Bull.* **2010**, *38*, 304–315. [CrossRef]
45. Green, M.F.; Horan, W.P.; Lee, J. Nonsocial and social cognition in schizophrenia: Current evidence and future directions. *World Psychiatry* **2019**, *18*, 146–161. [CrossRef]
46. Chou, C.-Y.; Ma, M.-C.; Yang, T.-T. Determinants of subjective health-related quality of life (HRQoL) for patients with schizophrenia. *Schizophr. Res.* **2014**, *154*, 83–88. [CrossRef]

47. Domenech, C.; Pastore, A.; Altamura, A.C.; Bernasconi, C.; Corral, R.; Elkis, H.; Evans, J.; Malla, A.; Margari, F.; Krebs, M.-O.; et al. Correlation of Health-Related Quality of Life in Clinically Stable Outpatients with Schizophrenia. *Neuropsychiatr. Dis. Treat.* **2019**, *15*, 3475–3486. [CrossRef]
48. Alptekin, K.; Akvardar, Y.; Akdede, B.B.K.; Dumlu, K.; Işik, D.; Pirinçci, F.; Yahssin, S.; Kitiş, A. Is quality of life associated with cognitive impairment in schizophrenia? *Prog. Neuropsychopharmacol. Biol. Psychiatry* **2005**, *29*, 239–244. [CrossRef]
49. Kurtz, M.M.; Gopal, S.; John, S.; Thara, R. Objective psychosocial function vs. subjective quality-of-life in schizophrenia within 5-years after diagnosis: A study from southern India. *Psychiatry Res.* **2018**, *272*, 419–424. [CrossRef]
50. Gaur, V.; Jagawat, T.; Gupta, S.; Ahmad Khan, P.; Souza, M.D.; Sharan, A. Quality of life in outpatient Schizophrenics: Correlation with illness severity and psychopathology. *Delhi Psychiatry J.* **2015**, *18*, e0229514.
51. Chemerinski, E.; Bowie, C.; Anderson, H.; Harvey, P.D. Depression in Schizophrenia: Methodological Artifact or Distinct Feature of the Illness? *J. Neuropsychiatr.* **2008**, *20*, 431–440. [CrossRef]
52. Gupta, T.; Strauss, G.P.; Cowan, H.R.; Pelletier-Baldelli, A.; Ellman, L.M.; Schiffman, J.; Mittal, V.A. Secondary Sources of Negative Symptoms in Those Meeting Criteria for a Clinical High-Risk Syndrome. *Biol. Psychiatry Glob. Open Sci.* **2021**, *1*, 210–218. [CrossRef] [PubMed]
53. Mulhern, B.; Mukuria, C.; Barkham, M.; Knapp, M.; Byford, S.; Soeteman, D.; Brazier, J. Using generic preference-based measures in mental health: Psychometric validity of the EQ-5D and SF-6D. *Br. J. Psychiatry* **2014**, *205*, 236–243. [CrossRef]
54. Boyer, L.; Baumstarck, K.; Boucekine, M.; Blanc, J.; Lançon, C.; Auquier, P. Measuring quality of life in patients with schizophrenia:an overview. *Expert Rev. Pharm. Outcomes Res.* **2013**, *13*, 343–349. [CrossRef]
55. Fisekovic, S.; Memic, A.; Pasalic, A. Correlation Between MoCA and MMSE For the Assessment of Cognition in Schizophrenia. *Acta Inform. Med.* **2012**, *20*, 186–189. [CrossRef] [PubMed]
56. Rossetti, H.C.; Lacritz, L.H.; Cullum, C.M.; Weiner, M.F. Normative Data for the Montreal Cognitive Assessment (MoCA) in a Population-Based Sample. 2011. Available online: www.mocatest.org (accessed on 20 November 2022).
57. Damian, A.M.; Jacobson, S.A.; Hentz, J.G.; Belden, C.M.; Shill, H.A.; Sabbagh, M.N.; Caviness, J.N.; Adler, C.H. The Montreal Cognitive Assessment and the Mini-Mental State Examination as Screening Instruments for Cognitive Impairment: Item Analyses and Threshold Scores. *Dement. Geriatr. Cogn. Disord.* **2011**, *31*, 126–131. [CrossRef]
58. Murri, M.B.; Folesani, F.; Costa, S.; Biancosino, B.; Colla, C.; Zerbinati, L.; Caruso, R.; Nanni, M.G.; Purdon, M.E.; Grassi, L. Screening for cognitive impairment in non-affective psychoses: A comparison between the SCIP and the MoCA. *Schizophr. Res.* **2020**, *218*, 188–194. [CrossRef] [PubMed]
59. Bell, M.; Fiszdon, J.; Richardson, R.; Lysaker, P.; Bryson, G. Are self-reports valid for schizophrenia patients with poor insight? Relationship of unawareness of illness to psychological self-report instruments. *Psychiatry Res.* **2007**, *151*, 37–46. [CrossRef] [PubMed]
60. Hamera, E.K.; Schneider, J.K.; Potocky, M.; Casebeer, M.A. Validity of self-administered symptom scales in clients with schizophrenia and schizoaffective disorders. *Schizophr. Res.* **1996**, *19*, 213–219. [CrossRef]
61. Dollfus, S.; Mucci, A.; Giordano, G.M.; Bitter, I.; Austin, S.F.; Delouche, C.; Erfurth, A.; Fleischhacker, W.W.; Movina, L.; Glenthøj, B.; et al. European Validation of the Self-Evaluation of Negative Symptoms (SNS): A Large Multinational and Multicenter Study. *Front. Psychiatry* **2022**, *13*, 826465. [CrossRef]

Journal of
Clinical Medicine

MDPI

Article

Switching Antipsychotic Medications in People with Schizophrenia: A 4-Year Naturalistic Study

Giammarco Cascino [1], Rossella Ceres [1], Alessio Maria Monteleone [2], Paola Bucci [2], Giulia Maria Giordano [2], Silvana Galderisi [2] and Palmiero Monteleone [1,*]

1 Department of Medicine, Surgery and Dentistry, 'Scuola Medica Salernitana', University of Salerno, 84131 Salerno, Italy
2 Department of Psychiatry, University of Campania 'L. Vanvitelli', 80138 Naples, Italy
* Correspondence: pmonteleone@unisa.it

Abstract: Although generally effective in ameliorating the core manifestations of schizophrenia, antipsychotics (APs) may lead to only suboptimal responses or may be associated with a variety of treatment-related adverse events which require additional treatment strategies. Under such clinical circumstances, switching APs represents a rational treatment option. The present study aimed to identify the variables that predict AP switch and to quantify the frequency of this phenomenon in people with schizophrenia in real-life. A secondary analysis was conducted on the data collected at baseline and at a 4-year follow-up from a large sample of community-dwelling Italian people with schizophrenia. Demographic and clinical variables as well as information about AP treatment were recorded at two time points. Over the 4-year period, 34.9% of the 571 participants switched the AP; in particular, 8.4% of participants switched from first-generation APs (FGAs) to second-generation APs or vice versa, while 8.2% of them switched to clozapine. Logistic regression models showed that combination of APs at baseline was negatively associated with AP switch, while treatment with FGAs and the presence of extrapyramidal symptoms at baseline were associated with AP class switch. Although the aim of the present study was not to assess predictors of clinical relapse in people with schizophrenia, we might speculate that switching APs represents a surrogate indicator of treatment failure in some patients and could lead into relapse, which is a costly aspect of schizophrenia management in both economic and human terms. The sooner such a negative outcome can be predicted and managed, the sooner the treatment can be optimized to avoid it.

Keywords: schizophrenia; antipsychotics; switch; extrapyramidal symptoms; treatment

Citation: Cascino, G.; Ceres, R.; Monteleone, A.M.; Bucci, P.; Giordano, G.M.; Galderisi, S.; Monteleone, P. Switching Antipsychotic Medications in People with Schizophrenia: A 4-Year Naturalistic Study. *J. Clin. Med.* **2022**, *11*, 5965. https://doi.org/10.3390/jcm11195965

Academic Editor: Armida Mucci

Received: 7 September 2022
Accepted: 8 October 2022
Published: 10 October 2022

1. Introduction

Since 1952, with the development of chlorpromazine, antipsychotic (AP) medications have been mainstays in the treatment of schizophrenia to both manage its acute symptoms and prevent its relapse. Until clozapine was approved by the US Food and Drug Administration for treatment-resistant schizophrenia and second-generation APs (SGAs) were developed, first-generation antipsychotics (FGAs) were widely used as first choice treatment for schizophrenia. Unfortunately, the use of FGAs is associated with side effects, especially extrapyramidal symptoms (EPS) that may increase disease-induced disability and stigma and may require additional treatments [1].

The introduction of clozapine and other SGAs broadened treatment options for patients with schizophrenia since these medications have been shown to be as effective as FGAs in relieving the positive symptoms of schizophrenia [2]. Moreover, compared to FGAs, SGAs are associated with a different side effect profile, characterized by weight gain and disturbances in glucose and lipid metabolism [3–6] as well as other emerging effects (e.g., [7]) but with a less frequent occurrence of EPS [8].

Although generally effective in ameliorating the core manifestations of the disease, both FGAs and SGAs could lead to only suboptimal responses or may be associated with a variety of treatment-related adverse events which require additional treatment strategies. Partial response with persistent positive and negative symptoms and/or the presence of residual symptoms is common even in first-episode patients [9], and relapses frequently occur [10]. Under such clinical circumstances, a switch of APs represents a rational treatment option, in the hope that it results in better treatment outcomes, even if a recent meta-analysis showed that continuing AP treatment at standard doses or switching to a different AP are similarly effective strategies to prevent relapses [11]. Similarly, both life-threatening and other non-dangerous adverse effects, which could shorten the patient's life expectancy [12] or may impair the patient's adherence to treatment, could be a reason for changing APs after a benefit/tolerability profile with the patient has been established [13].

Few studies have investigated so far the frequency of AP switching and the predictors of APs changes in naturalistic clinical settings. Weinmann et al. [14] evaluated switching from FGAs to SGAs among inpatients with schizophrenia, which is not representative of patients treated in usual outpatient care settings. They found that patients who switched from FGAs to SGAs had fewer previous psychiatric admissions, a shorter illness duration, and fewer comorbid substance disorders. Sernyak et al. [15] used the Veterans Affairs national administrative data to identify predictors of medication switching among patients with schizophrenia. After controlling for independent sociodemographic, diagnostic, and functional variables, the frequency of clinical contact was the most robust predictor of AP switch. Finally, Nyhuis et al. [16] conducted a post hoc analysis of data from a one-year randomized, open-label, multisite study of APs in the treatment of schizophrenia. They found that about one-third of patients switched APs before the end of the study, and that lack of antipsychotic use in the prior year, pre-existing depression, female gender, worsening of AP-induced akathisia, and worsening of symptoms of depression/anxiety during the first 2 weeks of AP therapy were the best predictors of AP switch.

These results cannot be considered conclusive since those studies have several methodological limitations, such as the relatively low number of investigated variables, the poor representativeness of study populations and of outpatient clinical practice settings, and the relatively short follow-up period. Since the identification of treatment switching predictors can help the clinician to tailor effective treatment regimens to patients and optimize early treatment responses, further studies aiming to identify the variables that predict AP switch and the frequency of this phenomenon in people with schizophrenia in the real-life are warranted. To accomplish these aims, a secondary analysis was conducted on the data collected from a large and well-characterized sample of community-dwelling Italian people with schizophrenia, recruited in the context of a multicenter study of the Italian Network for Research on Psychoses (NIRP) [17,18]. In that study sociodemographic and illness-related variables, personal resources and context-related factors that could affect the functional outcome of people with schizophrenia in real-life were recorded. Based on the above literature studies focusing on the possible role of clinical factors in predicting AP switch, we included in the present analysis only the available sociodemographic and illness-related variables.

2. Materials and Methods

2.1. Participants

The NIRP conducted a large multicenter study (baseline study) involving 921 community-dwelling, clinically stable patients with schizophrenia, aiming to investigate illness-related variables, personal resources, and context-related factors that could affect the social functioning of people with schizophrenia in the real-life [17]. After 4 years from the baseline study, all the 921 patients were asked to participate in a follow-up study aiming to investigate the natural evolutions of the patterns of relationships among illness-related variables, personal resources, context-related factors and real-life functioning [18]. The inclusion criterion was a diagnosis of schizophrenia according to DSM-IV, confirmed by the Structured Clinical Interview for DSM-IV-Patient version (SCID-I-P). Exclusion criteria were: (1) a history of head trauma with loss of consciousness in the 4-year interval between baseline and follow-up; (2) progressive cognitive deterioration possibly due to dementia or other neurological illness diagnosed in the last 4 years; (3) alcohol and/ or substance abuse in the last 6 months according to the SCID-I-P; (4) current pregnancy or lactation; (5) inability to provide an informed consent; (6) treatment modifications and/or hospitalization due to symptom exacerbation in the last 3 months in order to assess patients who were in a stable state of the disorder.

After receiving a comprehensive explanation of the study procedures and goals, all the subjects signed a written informed consent to participate. All the study procedures complied with the ethical standards of the relevant national and institutional committees on human experimentation and with the Helsinki Declaration of 1975, as revised in 2008. The study was approved by the Ethics Committees of participating centers. Recruitment took place from March 2016 to December 2017.

2.2. Clinical Assessment

Positive and disorganization symptoms were assessed by the Positive and Negative Syndrome Scale (PANSS) [19]. Scores for "positive symptoms" were calculated based on the 7 consensus, 5-factor solution proposed by Wallwork et al. [20]. "Disorganization" was the PANSS item P2, to avoid overlap with cognitive impairment. Since the PANSS is not considered an adequate instrument for the assessment of avolition, does not assess anhedonia, and the evaluation of asociality overlaps with measures of functioning [21–25], negative symptoms were measured by means of the Brief Negative Symptom Scale (BNSS) [26] that allows the identification of two separate factors: (a) avolition, consisting of anhedonia, asociality, and avolition and (b) expressive deficit, including blunted affect and alogia. The Italian version of the BNSS was validated as part of the Italian Network project [27]. Depressive symptoms were evaluated using the Calgary Depression Scale for Schizophrenia (CDSS) [28]. EPS were assessed by the St. Hans Rating Scale (SHRS), which allowed us to assess dyskinesia, parkinsonism, dystonia, and akathisia [29].

All included subjects had a stable drug treatment dose and were on the same AP drug/s within the 3 months before both the baseline and the follow-up assessment.

Patients were treated with different FGAs and/or SGAs according to judgment of the referring clinicians. For each patient, APs taken at baseline and at follow-up were recorded. Patients who took at follow-up an AP different from that taken at baseline were considered switchers. This categorization was carried out first for any change in APs, then for a switch from FGAs to SGAs or vice versa and finally for a switch to clozapine. Daily chlorpromazine equivalent doses (CED) of APs were calculated as suggested by Gardner et al. [30].

2.3. Statistical Analysis

All statistical analyses were performed through R, Version 4.2 (R core Team, Vienna, Austria).

Multivariate analyses of variance (MANOVAs) were run to investigate differences in demographic and clinical variables between participants who switched APs and those who did not according to the above categorization. Group differences in categorical variables were investigated by the Pearson's chi square test.

Different logistic regression models were performed to identify factors associated with AP switch: dependent variable was the first switch for any APs, then a switch between APs generation, and last a switch to clozapine, while patient age, gender, duration of illness, psychopathology severity, presence of any EPS, class and combination of APs taken at baseline, long-acting AP formulation, and the CED of AP taken at follow-up were included as independent variables. Class of AP taken at baseline was categorized as FGA or SGA, in case of a combination of an FGA with an SGA, FGA was assigned; combination of AP was a dummy variable in which any combination of AP, of both same and different class, was indicated with '1'; the long-acting AP formulation was also a dummy variable.

Finally, to obtain the magnitude of the variation on the probability scale, marginal effects at the mean, in which the covariates are kept at their mean values, were used.

3. Results

Of the 921 subjects recruited at baseline, 618 joined the follow-up study. No significant differences in baseline variables emerged between participants joining the follow-up study and those who did not (n = 303) [18]. Complete assessments were available for 571 participants who were included in this analysis. They were 391 men (mean age ± SD: 44.6 ± 10.1) and 180 women (mean age ± SD: 46.1 ± 11.1). At baseline, 406 patients were treated with SGAs (339 with single SGA, 67 with two or more different SGAs), 85 were treated with FGAs (66 with single FGA, 89 with two or more FGAs), and 80 with a combination of FGAs and SGAs. At the follow-up assessment, 413 participants were treated with SGAs (341 with single SGA, 72 with two or more different SGAs), 77 with FGAs (71 with single FGA, 6 with two or more FGAs), and 81 with a combination of FGAs and SGAs, respectively. At baseline, 85 patients were treated with long-acting AP, while at follow-up, the number treated with long-acting AP was 135. At baseline, the mean (±SD) daily CED of APs was 516.45 ± 347.01 mg, while at follow-up it was 353.13 ± 273.28 mg.

Over the 4-year period, 199 (34.9%) participants switched AP; 105 (18.4%) participants switched the class of AP. In particular, 49 (8.6%) participants switched from FGAs to SGAs, while 56 (9.8%) patients had the opposite switch; finally, 47 (8.2%) patients switched to clozapine.

Demographic and clinical characteristics of participants at baseline according to the AP switch are reported in Table 1. Number and percentages of patients who switched the baseline AP at the study end point according to the medication at baseline are reported in Supplementary Table S1.

Table 1. Demographic and clinical characteristics of study participants at baseline according to the occurrence of antipsychotic switch. AP, antipsychotics; CDSS, Calgary Depression Scale for Schizophrenia; CED, chlorpromazine equivalent doses; EPS, extrapyramidal symptoms; FGA, first-generation antipsychotics; SGA, second-generation antipsychotics.

	No AP Switch (n = 372)	**AP Switch**		
		Total Group (n = 199)	**AP Class Switch (n = 105)**	**Clozapine Switch (n = 47)**
Age, years	40.6 ± 10.1	40.1 ± 11.1	42.8 ± 9.5	35.8 ± 10.6 *
Gender, m (%)	248 (66.7)	143 (71.8)	77 (73.3)	33 (70.2)
Illness duration, yrs	16.4 ± 10.1	16.6 ± 10.7	19.4 ± 10.4	13.8 ± 9.5
AP generation, FGA (%)	110 (29.6)	55 (27.6)	56 (53.3)	14 (29.8)
SGA (%)	262 (70.4)	144 (72.4)	49 (46.7)	33 (70.2)
AP combination, n (%)	118 (31.7)	48 (24.1)	45 (42.8)	12 (25.5)
AP long-acting, n (%)	50 (13.4)	35 (17.6)	15 (14.3)	7 (14.9)
Daily CED	516.6 ± 350.1	361.2 ± 302.1	424.5 ± 309.8	549.5 ± 388.7
Positive symptoms	9.7 ± 4.9	9.8 ± 4.4	10.7 ± 5.0	11.1 ± 5.2
Disorganization	2.6 ± 1.5	2.6 ± 1.4	2.9 ± 1.5	2.7 ± 1.5
Expression deficits	12.7 ± 8.3	12.9 ± 7.3	13.7 ± 8.0	13.8 ± 7.4
Avolition	20.7 ± 9.9	21.1 ± 8.9	21.2 ± 8.7	21.3 ± 8.7
CDSS	3.8 ± 3.9	4.1 ± 4.0	4.2 ± 3.8	4.4 ± 4.4
Any EPS, n (%)	145 (39)	86 (43.2)	59 (56.2)	19 (40.4)

* p = 0.001 vs. no AP switch.

At baseline assessment, the MANOVA on demographic and clinical measures comparing the group who switched the AP with the group who did not switch did not show a significant overall group effect (Pillai trace = 0.01, $F_{8, 406} = 0.48$, $p = 0.87$). The MANOVA comparing the group who switched from FGA to SGA or vice versa and the group who did not switch AP class did not show a significant group effect (Pillai trace = 0.01, $F_{8, 406} = 0.57$, $p = 0.8$). Finally, the MANOVA comparing the group who switched to clozapine with the group who did not switch to clozapine showed a significant overall group effect (Pillai trace = 0.04, $F_{8, 406} = 2.09$, $p = 0.03$). Indeed, a significant difference emerged between the two groups in age ($F_{1, 413} = 10.2$, $p = 0.001$), since the group who switched to clozapine over the 4-year period was younger (35.81 ± 10.68 years) than the group who did not switch (40.85 ± 10.35 years).

The Pearson's chi square test showed a significant association between the switch of AP class and the AP class taken at baseline ($\chi^2 = 37.4$, $p = 9.7 \times 10^{-10}$) and the presence of any EPS at baseline ($\chi^2 = 13.2$, $p = 2.7 \times 10^{-4}$), while no significant association emerged between the switch of AP class and gender as well as between the switch to any AP or to clozapine and all the categorical variables.

The first logistic regression model with any AP switch as dependent variable showed that any AP switch was negatively associated with the combination of APs at baseline ($b = -0.44$, $p = 0.04$), indicating that participants taking more than one AP at baseline were less likely to switch APs over the follow-up period (Figure 1). The logistic regression model with AP class switch as dependent variable showed that treatment with FGAs ($b = 1.09$, $p = 3.75 \times 10^{-5}$) and the presence of any EPS ($b = 0.52$, $p = 0.02$) at baseline were significantly associated to AP class switch, indicating that participants taking FGA and showing EPS at baseline were more likely to switch AP class over the follow-up period (Figure 2). Finally, the logistic regression model with switch to clozapine as dependent variable showed that age was negatively associated to clozapine switch ($b = -0.08$, $p = 0.01$), while the severity of positive symptoms was positively associated to clozapine switch ($b = 0.1$, $p = 0.04$), indicating that younger participants with more severe positive symptoms at baseline were more likely to switch to clozapine over the follow-up period.

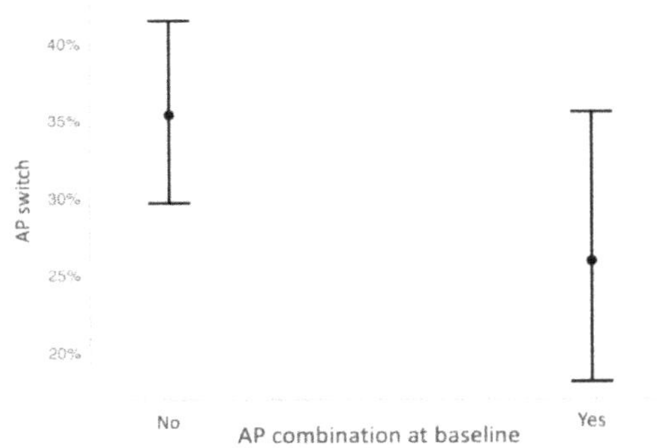

Figure 1. Predicted probabilities of antipsychotic (AP) switch associated with APs combination at baseline.

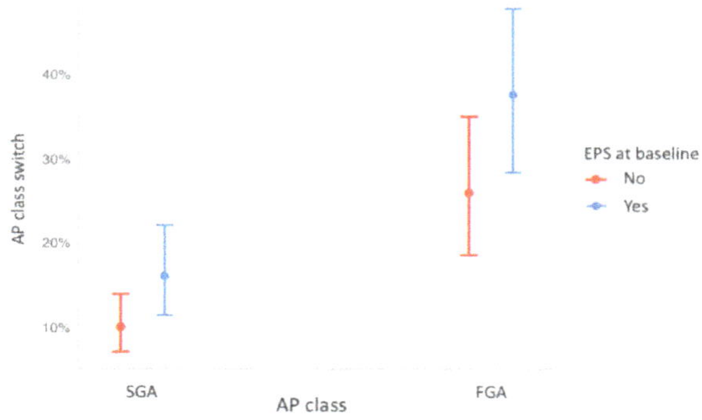

Figure 2. Predicted probabilities of switching antipsychotic (AP) class associated with AP class taken at baseline and the occurrence of extrapyramidal symptoms (EPS) at baseline. FGA = first-generation antipsychotics; SGA = second-generation antipsychotics.

4. Discussion

The first finding of the present secondary analysis of data from the naturalistic multicentre study of the NIRP was that approximately one-third (34.9%) of the participants switched AP over the 4-year follow-up period. This finding is in line with two previous studies showing that at 1-year follow-up, AP switch occurred in 26.3% and 29.5% of participants, respectively [15,16]. Different from these results, the CATIE study reported that 74% of patients discontinued AP medication within 18 months from starting treatment and switched to a different AP in phase II of the study. In addition to the clear methodological differences between the CATIE study and the present one, it has been suggested that such a high rate of switching may be due to the CATIE study protocol, which encouraged patients and clinicians to switch drugs too soon with the hope that a new drug might produce better results than that originally assigned [31], although subsequent analyses on the CATIE trial data showed that switching to a new medication yielded no advantage over staying on the previous medication [32].

We found that none of the variables assessed at baseline predicted the switch to any AP at follow-up except for the presence of multiple AP therapy. Indeed, participants who took more than one AP at baseline were less likely to switch AP medication over the 4-year naturalistic treatment. The discrepancy in our findings with those of the previous studies [15,16] may be due, at least in part, to differences in the variables entered in the regression model and/or to the longer follow-up period of our study, which could have an impact on the effect of some clinical variables. The finding of a negative association between combination of APs at baseline and AP switch over the follow-up suggests that the combination of APs is considered by clinician an alternative to AP switch in case of an unsatisfactory response despite most of the evidence and treatment guidelines recommending AP monotherapy and acknowledging the feasibility of AP combination only in specific conditions, such as for clozapine-resistant patients [33–37]. In support of this possible explanation, at baseline participants with AP polytherapy showed positive and disorganization symptoms higher than those with AP monotherapy (post hoc analysis: t = 4.4, $p < 0.001$; t = 2.85; $p = 0.005$, respectively).

Our second study finding was that 18.4% of the total sample switched AP class with 8.6% of participants switching from FGAs to SGAs and 9.8% of them having the opposite switch. Inconsistent with our data, the CUtLASS study showed that 35% of patients switched from an SGA to an FGA, while 46% had the opposite switching within 1 year from the treatment randomization [38]. Differences in the study designs and the length of the follow-up periods may be the major determinants of such a discrepancy. Moreover, we found that treatment with FGA and the presence of EPS at baseline were significantly associated to the AP class switch. The latter associations were expected since FGAs are associated with a prevalence of EPS higher than SGA and the occurrence of EPS may be considered a valid reason to switch from FGAs to SGAs since EPS increase disease-induced disability and stigma, impair the patients' adherence to treatment, and may require additional treatments, which, in turn, may impair the drug treatment tolerability [8,39]. Consistent with our findings, Nyhuis et al. [16] found that worsening of akathisia in the first 2 weeks of AP treatment predicted AP switch in a sample composed almost completely of outpatients from a randomized open-label study conducted in a naturalistic setting. On the contrary, Weinmann et al. [14] found that a short disease duration, fewer previous psychiatric hospitalizations, voluntary admission, and pronounced thought disorder were significantly associated with switching from FGAs to SGAs. This discrepancy may be due to the different clinical setting and the different follow-up duration, as Weissman et al. [14] focused on inpatients with 1-year follow-up.

Our last study finding was that 8.2% of participants switched to clozapine. Younger age and more severe positive symptoms were associated with clozapine switch. These findings are in line with clinical recommendations to offer clozapine monotherapy as soon as the criteria for treatment resistance are fulfilled [37].

Some limitations of the present study need to be acknowledged. First, detailed information about drug treatments over the 4-year follow-up is lacking, so we were not able to establish when the switch occurred over follow-up or to identify the reasons for switching or to verify whether patients underwent multiple AP switches. Second, the patients' adherence to treatment was not assessed and this may have affected the switch rate since clinicians could have switched the AP in the presence of an apparent non-clinical response to the ongoing treatment. Moreover, anamnestic information about substance abuse may be quite unreliable and nicotine abuse, which significantly affects the pharmacokinetics of clozapine [40], was not assessed. Information regarding psychopharmacological treatments other than AP, in particular antidepressants, was lacking. In order to overcome this issue, since depressive symptoms were found to be the best predictors of AP switch [16], we included CDSS, as a measure of depressive symptoms, in the analysis. Finally, side effects of AP, such as the increase in weight or diabetes, were not reported, although they may be a reason to switch AP.

The strengths of our study include its naturalistic nature, the large sample of participants who were recruited in specialist mental health services distributed throughout the whole national territory, and the long follow-up duration.

5. Conclusions

In conclusion, the present findings, showing that approximately one-third of the participants switched AP over the 4-year follow-up period and that combination of APs was negatively associated with AP switch, while treatment with an FGA and the presence of EPS at baseline were associated to the AP class switch, might help inform clinical decision-making in usual practice. The current management of patients with primary psychosis worldwide is often stereotyped, since in almost all cases an AP is prescribed, with SGA usually preferred to FGA [41–43]. Tailoring effective treatment regimens to patients and optimizing early treatment responses are pivotal challenges in psychiatry [44–47]. Although the aim of the present study was not to assess predictors of clinical relapse in people with schizophrenia living in the community, we might speculate that switching APs represents a surrogate indicator of treatment failure in some patients. As treatment failure often leads into relapse, which is one of the costliest aspects of schizophrenia management in both economic and human terms [48,49], the sooner such a negative outcome can be predicted and managed, the sooner the treatment can be optimized to avoid it.

Supplementary Materials: The following supporting information can be downloaded at: https://www.mdpi.com/article/10.3390/jcm11195965/s1. Table S1. Number and percentages of patients who switched the baseline antipsychotic (AP) at the study end point according to the medication at baseline.

Author Contributions: Conceptualization, S.G. and P.M.; methodology, G.C., R.C. and P.B.; formal analysis, G.M.G. and G.C..; investigation, R.C., A.M.M., P.B. and G.M.G.; data curation, P.B., G.M.G. and R.C.; writing—original draft preparation, G.C. and P.M.; writing—review and editing, S.G., P.B. and P.M.; supervision, S.G. and P.M. All authors have read and agreed to the published version of the manuscript.

Funding: This research received no external funding.

Institutional Review Board Statement: The study was conducted in accordance with the Declaration of Helsinki and approved by the Ethics Committee of participating centers: C.E. Seconda Università degli Studi di Napoli, Approval Code: 323, Approval Date: 2 August 2013; Ethic Committee Name: C.E. Campania Sud, Approval Code: n. 54_r.p.s.o., Approval Date: 18 September 2015.

Informed Consent Statement: Informed consent was obtained from all subjects involved in the study.

Data Availability Statement: The data presented in this study are available on request from the corresponding author.

Conflicts of Interest: The authors declare no conflict of interest. The funders had no role in the design of the study; in the collection, analyses, or interpretation of data; in the writing of the manuscript; or in the decision to publish the results.

References

1. Taipale, H.; Tanskanen, A.; Mehtälä, J.; Vattulainen, P.; Correll, C.U.; Tiihonen, J. 20-year follow-up study of physical morbidity and mortality in relationship to antipsychotic treatment in a nationwide cohort of 62,250 patients with schizophrenia (FIN20). *World Psychiatry* **2020**, *19*, 61–68. [CrossRef] [PubMed]
2. Lieberman, J.A.; Stroup, T.S.; McEvoy, J.P.; Swartz, M.S.; Rosenheck, R.A.; Perkins, D.O.; Keefe, R.S.; Davis, S.M.; Davis, C.E.; Lebowitz, B.D.; et al. Clinical Antipsychotic Trials of Intervention Effectiveness (CATIE) Investigators. Effectiveness of antipsychotic drugs in patients with chronic schizophrenia. *N. Eng. J. Med.* **2005**, *353*, 1209–1223. [CrossRef] [PubMed]
3. Ebenbichler, C.F.; Laimer, M.; Eder, U.; Mangweth, B.; Weiss, E.; Hofer, A.; Hummer, M.; Kemmler, G.; Lechleitner, M.; Patsch, J.R.; et al. Olanzapine induces insulin resistance: Results from a prospective study. *J. Clin. Psychiatry* **2003**, *64*, 1436–1439. [CrossRef] [PubMed]
4. Sernyak, M.J.; Leslie, D.L.; Alarcon, R.D.; Losonczy, M.F.; Rosenheck, R. Association of Diabetes Mellitus With Use of Atypical Neuroleptics in the Treatment of Schizophrenia. *Am. J. Psychiatry* **2002**, *159*, 561–566. [CrossRef]
5. Solmi, M.; Fornaro, M.; Ostinelli, E.G.; Zangani, C.; Croatto, G.; Monaco, F.; Krinitski, D.; Fusar-Poli, P.; Correll, C.U. Safety of 80 antidepressants, antipsychotics, anti-attention-deficit/hyperactivity medications and mood stabilizers in children and adolescents with psychiatric disorders: A large scale systematic meta-review of 78 adverse effects. *World Psychiatry* **2020**, *19*, 214–232. [CrossRef]
6. Correll, C.U.; Sikich, L.; Reeves, G.; Johnson, J.; Keeton, C.; Spanos, M.; Kapoor, S.; Russell, K.; Miller, L.; Chandrasekhar, Y.; et al. Metformin add-on vs. antipsychotic switch vs. continued antipsychotic treatment plus healthy lifestyle education in overweight or obese youth with severe mental illness: Results from the IMPACT trial. *World Psychiatry* **2020**, *19*, 69–80. [CrossRef]
7. de Leon, J.; Sanz, E.J.; Noren, N.; De las Cuevas, C. Pneumonia may be more frequent and have more fatal outcomes with clozapine than with other second-generation antipsychotics. *World Psychiatry* **2020**, *19*, 120–121. [CrossRef]
8. Monteleone, P.; Cascino, G.; Monteleone, A.M.; Rocca, P.; Rossi, A.; Bertolino, A.; Aguglia, E.; Amore, M.; Collantoni, E.; Corrivetti, G.; et al. Prevalence of antipsychotic-induced extrapyramidal symptoms and their association with neurocognition and social cognition in outpatients with schizophrenia in the "real-life". *Prog. Neuro-Psychopharmacol. Biol. Psychiatry* **2021**, *109*, 110250. [CrossRef]
9. Meltzer, H.Y.; Lee, M.; Cola, P. The Evolution of Treatment Resistance: Biologic Implications. *J. Clin. Psychopharmacol.* **1998**, *18*, 5S–11S. [CrossRef]
10. Alvarez-Jimenez, M.; Priede, A.; Hetrick, S.E.; Bendall, S.; Killackey, E.; Parker, A.G.; McGorry, P.D.; Gleeson, J.F. Risk factors for relapse following treatment for first episode psychosis: A systematic review and meta-analysis of longitudinal studies. *Schizophr. Res.* **2012**, *139*, 116–128. [CrossRef]
11. Ostuzzi, G.; Vita, G.; Bertolini, F.; Tedeschi, F.; De Luca, B.; Gastaldon, C.; Nosé, M.; Papola, D.; Purgato, M.; Del Giovane, C.; et al. Continuing, reducing, switching, or stopping antipsychotics in individuals with schizophrenia-spectrum disorders who are clinically stable: A systematic review and network meta-analysis. *Lancet Psychiatry* **2022**, *9*, 614–624. [CrossRef]
12. Correll, C.U.; Solmi, M.; Croatto, G.; Schneider, L.K.; Rohani-Montez, S.C.; Fairley, L.; Smith, N.; Bitter, I.; Gorwood, P.; Taipale, H.; et al. Mortality in people with schizophrenia: A systematic review and meta-analysis of relative risk and aggravating or attenuating factors. *World Psychiatry* **2022**, *21*, 248–271. [CrossRef] [PubMed]
13. Edlinger, M.; Baumgartner, S.; Eltanaihi-Furtmüller, N.; Hummer, M.; Fleischhacker, W.W. Switching Between Second-Generation Antipsychotics. *CNS Drugs* **2005**, *19*, 27–42. [CrossRef] [PubMed]

14. Weinmann, S.; Janssen, B.; Gaebel, W. Switching Antipsychotics in Inpatient Schizophrenia Care. *J. Clin. Psychiatry* **2004**, *65*, 1099–1105. [CrossRef]
15. Sernyak, M.J.; Leslie, D.; Rosenheck, R. Predictors of antipsychotic medication change. *J. Behav. Health Serv. Res.* **2005**, *32*, 85–94. [CrossRef] [PubMed]
16. Nyhuis, A.W.; Faries, D.E.; Ascher-Svanum, H.; Stauffer, V.L.; Kinon, B.J. Predictors of switching antipsychotic medications in the treatment of schizophrenia. *BMC Psychiatry* **2010**, *10*, 75. [CrossRef] [PubMed]
17. Galderisi, S.; Rossi, A.; Rocca, P.; Bertolino, A.; Mucci, A.; Bucci, P.; Rucci, P.; Gibertoni, D.; Aguglia, E.; Amore, M.; et al. The influence of illness-related variables, personal resources and context-related factors on real-life functioning of people with schizophrenia. *World Psychiatry* **2014**, *13*, 275–287. [CrossRef]
18. Galderisi, S.; Rucci, P.; Mucci, A.; Rossi, A.; Rocca, P.; Bertolino, A.; Aguglia, E.; Amore, M.; Bellomo, A.; Bozzatello, P.; et al. The interplay among psychopathology, personal resources, context-related factors and real-life functioning in schizophrenia: Stability in relationships after 4 years and differences in network structure between recovered and non-recovered patients. *World Psychiatry* **2020**, *19*, 81–91. [CrossRef]
19. Kay, S.R.; Fiszbein, A.; Opler, L.A. The Positive and Negative Syndrome Scale (PANSS) for Schizophrenia. *Schizophr. Bull.* **1987**, *13*, 261–276. [CrossRef]
20. Wallwork, R.S.; Fortgang, R.; Hashimoto, R.; Weinberger, D.R.; Dickinson, D. Searching for a consensus five-factor model of the Positive and Negative Syndrome Scale for schizophrenia. *Schizophr. Res.* **2012**, *137*, 246–250. [CrossRef]
21. Kirkpatrick, B.; Fenton, W.S.; Carpenter, W.T.; Marder, S.R. The NIMH-MATRICS consensus statement on negative symptoms. *Proc. Schizophr. Bull.* **2006**, *32*, 214–219. [CrossRef] [PubMed]
22. Galderisi, S.; Mucci, A.; Dollfus, S.; Nordentoft, M.; Falkai, P.; Kaiser, S.; Giordano, G.M.; Vandevelde, A.; Nielsen, M.Ø.; Glenthøj, L.B.; et al. EPA guidance on assessment of negative symptoms in schizophrenia. *Eur. Psychiatry* **2021**, *64*, e23. [CrossRef] [PubMed]
23. Kotov, R.; Jonas, K.G.; Carpenter, W.T.; Dretsch, M.N.; Eaton, N.R.; Forbes, M.K.; Forbush, K.T.; Hobbs, K.; Reininghaus, U.; Slade, T.; et al. Validity and utility of Hierarchical Taxonomy of Psychopathology (HiTOP): I. Psychosis superspectrum. *World Psychiatry* **2020**, *19*, 151–172. [CrossRef] [PubMed]
24. Peralta, V.; Gil-Berrozpe, G.J.; Sanchez-Torres, A.; Cuesta, M.J. Clinical relevance of general and specific dimensions in bifactor models of psychotic disorders. *World Psychiatry* **2021**, *20*, 306–307. [CrossRef]
25. Moritz, S.; Silverstein, S.M.; Dietrichkeit, M.; Gallinat, J. Neurocognitive deficits in schizophrenia are likely to be less severe and less related to the disorder than previously thought. *World Psychiatry* **2020**, *19*, 254–255. [CrossRef]
26. Kirkpatrick, B.; Strauss, G.P.; Nguyen, L.; Fischer, B.A.; Daniel, D.G.; Cienfuegos, A.; Marder, S.R. The Brief Negative Symptom Scale: Psychometric Properties. *Schizophr. Bull.* **2011**, *37*, 300–305. [CrossRef]
27. Mucci, A.; Galderisi, S.; Merlotti, E.; Rossi, A.; Rocca, P.; Bucci, P.; Piegari, G.; Chieffi, M.; Vignapiano, A.; Maj, M. The Brief Negative Symptom Scale (BNSS): Independent validation in a large sample of Italian patients with schizophrenia. *Eur. Psychiatry* **2015**, *30*, 641–647. [CrossRef]
28. Addington, D.; Addington, J.; Maticka-tyndale, E. Assessing Depression in Schizophrenia: The Calgary Depression Scale. *Br. J. Psychiatry* **1993**, *163*, 39–44. [CrossRef]
29. Gerlach, J.; Korsgaard, S.; Clemmesen, P.; Lauersen, A.-M.L.; Magelund, G.; Noring, U.; Povlsen, U.J.; Bech, P.; Casey, D.E. The St. Hans Rating Scale for extrapyramidal syndromes: Reliability and validity. *Acta Psychiatr. Scand.* **1993**, *87*, 244–252. [CrossRef]
30. Gardner, D.M.; Murphy, A.L.; O'Donnell, H.; Centorrino, F.; Baldessarini, R.J. International Consensus Study of Antipsychotic Dosing. *Am. J. Psychiatry* **2010**, *167*, 686–693. [CrossRef]
31. Naber, D.; Lambert, M. The CATIE and CUtLASS Studies in Schizophrenia. *CNS Drugs* **2009**, *23*, 649–659. [CrossRef] [PubMed]
32. Rosenheck, R.A.; Davis, S.; Covell, N.; Essock, S.; Swartz, M.; Stroup, S.; McEvoy, J.; Lieberman, J. Does switching to a new antipsychotic improve outcomes? Data from the CATIE Trial. *Schizophr. Res.* **2009**, *107*, 22–29. [CrossRef] [PubMed]
33. Gallego, J.A.; Nielsen, J.; De Hert, M.; Kane, J.M.; Correll, C.U. Safety and tolerability of antipsychotic polypharmacy. *Expert Opin. Drug Saf.* **2012**, *11*, 527–542. [CrossRef] [PubMed]
34. Taylor, D.M.; Smith, L.; Gee, S.H.; Nielsen, J. Augmentation of clozapine with a second antipsychotic—A meta-analysis. *Acta Psychiatr. Scand.* **2012**, *125*, 15–24. [CrossRef] [PubMed]
35. Galling, B.; Roldán, A.; Hagi, K.; Rietschel, L.; Walyzada, F.; Zheng, W.; Cao, X.-L.; Xiang, Y.-T.; Zink, M.; Kane, J.M.; et al. Antipsychotic augmentation vs. monotherapy in schizophrenia: Systematic review, meta-analysis and meta-regression analysis. *World Psychiatry* **2017**, *16*, 77–89. [CrossRef]
36. Baandrup, L. Polypharmacy in schizophrenia. *Basic Clin. Pharmacol. Toxicol.* **2020**, *126*, 183–192. [CrossRef]
37. Gaebel, W.; Falkai, P.; Hasan, A. The revised German evidence- and consensus-based schizophrenia guideline. *World Psychiatry* **2020**, *19*, 117–119. [CrossRef]
38. Jones, P.B.; Barnes, T.R.E.; Davies, L.; Dunn, G.; Lloyd, H.; Hayhurst, K.P.; Murray, R.M.; Markwick, A.; Lewis, S.W. Randomized Controlled Trial of the Effect on Quality of Life of Second- vs First-Generation Antipsychotic Drugs in Schizophrenia. *Arch. Gen. Psychiatry* **2006**, *63*, 1079–1087. [CrossRef]
39. Hugenholtz, G.W.K.; Heerdink, E.R.; Meijer, W.E.; Stolker, J.-J.; Egberts, A.C.G.; Nolen, W.A. Reasons for Switching between Antipsychotics in Daily Clinical Practice. *Pharmacopsychiatry* **2005**, *38*, 122–124. [CrossRef]

40. Qurashi, I.; Stephenson, P.; Nagaraj, C.; Chu, S.; Drake, R.; Couchman, L.; Flanagan, R. Changes in smoking status, mental state and plasma clozapine concentration: Retrospective cohort evaluation. *BJPsych. Bull.* **2019**, *43*, 271–274. [CrossRef]
41. Maj, M.; van Os, J.; De Hert, M.; Gaebel, W.; Galderisi, S.; Green, M.F.; Guloksuz, S.; Harvey, P.D.; Jones, P.B.; Malaspina, D.; et al. The clinical characterization of the patient with primary psychosis aimed at personalization of management. *World Psychiatry* **2021**, *20*, 4–33. [CrossRef] [PubMed]
42. Carpenter, W.T. Primary psychosis: More to know, much more to do. *World Psychiatry* **2021**, *20*, 1–2. [CrossRef] [PubMed]
43. Cannon, T.D. Delivering on the public health promise of the psychosis risk paradigm. *World Psychiatry* **2020**, *19*, 391–392. [CrossRef]
44. Swift, J.K.; Mullins, R.H.; Penix, E.A.; Roth, K.L.; Trusty, W.T. The importance of listening to patient preferences when making mental health decision. *World Psychiatry* **2021**, *20*, 316–319. [CrossRef]
45. Unutzer, J.; Carlo, A.D.; Collins, P.Y. Leveraging collaborative care to improve access to mental health care on a global scale. *World Psychiatry* **2020**, *19*, 36–37. [CrossRef]
46. Singh, S.P.; Javed, A.; on behalf of the WPA Expert International Advisory Panel for Early Intervention in Psychosis. Early intervention in psychosis in low- and middle-income countries: A WPA initiative. *World Psychiatry* **2020**, *19*, 122. [CrossRef] [PubMed]
47. Drake, R.E.; Xie, H.; McHugo, G.J. A 16-year follow-up of patients with serious mental illness and co-occurring substance use disorder. *World Psychiatry* **2020**, *19*, 397–398. [CrossRef]
48. Almond, S.; Knapp, M.; Francois, C.; Toumi, M.; Brugha, T. Relapse in schizophrenia: Costs, clinical outcomes and quality of life. *Br. J. Psychiatry* **2004**, *184*, 346–351. [CrossRef]
49. Knapp, M.; Wong, G. Economics and mental health: The current scenario. *World Psychiatry* **2020**, *19*, 3–14. [CrossRef]

Journal of
Clinical Medicine

MDPI

Review

Second-Generation Antipsychotics' Effectiveness and Tolerability: A Review of Real-World Studies in Patients with Schizophrenia and Related Disorders

Michele Fabrazzo *, Salvatore Cipolla, Alessio Camerlengo, Francesco Perris and Francesco Catapano

Department of Psychiatry, University of Campania "Luigi Vanvitelli", Largo Madonna Delle Grazie 1, 80138 Naples, Italy; salvatore2211@gmail.com (S.C.); alessiocamerlengo90@gmail.com (A.C.); francesco.perris@unicampania.it (F.P.); francesco.catapano@unicampania.it (F.C.)

* Correspondence: michele.fabrazzo@unicampania.it; Tel.: +39-(0)-81-566-65-29; Fax: +39-(0)-81-566-65-23

Abstract: Despite methodological limitations, real-world studies might support clinicians by broadening the knowledge of antipsychotics' (APs) effectiveness and tolerability in different clinical scenarios and complement clinical trials. We conducted an extensive literature search in the PubMed database to evaluate the effectiveness and tolerability profiles of second-generation antipsychotics (SGAs) from real-world studies to aid clinicians and researchers in selecting the proper treatment for patients with schizophrenia and related disorders. The present review evidenced that SGAs demonstrated superior effectiveness over first-generation antipsychotics (FGAs) in relapse-free survival and psychiatric hospitalization rate and for treating negative symptoms. Persistence and adherence to therapy were higher in SGAs than FGAs. Most studies concluded that switching to long-acting injectables (LAIs) was significantly associated with a lower treatment failure rate than monotherapy with oral SGAs. Considerable improvements in general functionality, subjective well-being, and total score on global satisfaction tests, besides improved personal and social performance, were reported in some studies on patients treated with LAI SGAs. Clozapine was also associated with the lowest rates of treatment failure and greater effectiveness over the other SGAs, although with more severe side effects. Effectiveness on primary negative symptoms and cognitive deficits was rarely measured in these studies. Based on the data analyzed in the present review, new treatments are needed with better tolerability and improved effectiveness for negative, affective, and cognitive symptoms.

Keywords: schizophrenia; negative symptoms; real-world studies; real-world effectiveness; tolerability; treatment adherence; second-generation antipsychotics; long-acting injectable antipsychotics

Citation: Fabrazzo, M.; Cipolla, S.; Camerlengo, A.; Perris, F.; Catapano, F. Second-Generation Antipsychotics' Effectiveness and Tolerability: A Review of Real-World Studies in Patients with Schizophrenia and Related Disorders. *J. Clin. Med.* **2022**, *11*, 4530. https://doi.org/10.3390/jcm11154530

Academic Editor: Armida Mucci

Received: 13 June 2022
Accepted: 1 August 2022
Published: 3 August 2022

1. Introduction

Schizophrenia is among the most disabling mental health conditions [1] and affects approximately 24 million people worldwide [2,3]. In addition, subjects affected by schizophrenia and related disorders have a 10–25-year reduction in life expectancy than the general population due to the increased rates of comorbid physical illnesses, smoking, and substance abuse, rates of suicide as common causes of death, and reduced health-seeking behavior [4–6].

Patients with schizophrenia and related disorders may experience positive, negative, affective, and cognitive symptoms influencing many aspects of their daily functioning [7–13].

The psychopharmacological treatment of schizophrenia and other psychotic disorders relies mainly on antipsychotics (APs), which are traditionally divided into two classes: first-generation antipsychotics (FGAs) and second-generation antipsychotics (SGAs) [14–16]. Both classes of drugs are effective in relieving the positive symptoms of schizophrenia. Instead, evidence of the efficacy on negative, affective, and cognitive symptoms is inconclusive, and these dimensions remain the unmet needs of schizophrenia treatment [17–19].

APs may also induce different side-effect profiles [20], occasionally perceived by patients as distressing and disabling [21]. In general, side effects include extrapyramidal side effects (EPS), increased prolactin plasma levels, metabolic complications such as weight gain, metabolic syndrome, hyperlipidemia, and type 2 diabetes, which may reduce life expectancy [22–24]. Specifically, FGAs might induce hyperprolactinemia and frequent adverse motor effects, such as EPS, as well as increasing disability and stigma related to the disease [24].

SGAs are associated, although not consistently [25–27], with a reduced incidence of EPS, compared to FGAs, with a few distinctions between both medications [28,29]. However, the difference between the two classes of APs is clinically relevant, as EPSs are associated with reduced treatment adherence, depression, suicide, secondary negative symptoms, worse cognitive performance, deficits in motor skills and verbal learning, attention, and working memory [30–33]. Furthermore, EPSs often require additional treatment with anticholinergic drugs, burdening patients with adverse effects such as memory impairment, delirium, and autonomic nervous system dysfunctions.

APs may prove to be ineffective for many patients [34]. In addition, a few of them experience at least one relapse over the five years after the beginning of therapy [35]. Between a quarter and a third of affected patients manifest treatment resistance, and only 17.5% might respond to clozapine [34,36]. Therefore, a key component of the long-term management of schizophrenia and related disorders is to select an appropriate antipsychotic treatment for the needs of each individual [37,38]. The efficacy and tolerability of antipsychotic treatment might profoundly affect adherence to therapy and clinical response, with the risk of relapses [39,40].

Adverse effects are also a frequent cause for discontinued treatment, besides lack of insight, disease severity, and treatment characteristics. In addition, adverse effects may impact environmental factors such as patient's erroneous belief in the effectiveness of medication, and substance abuse [39]. For this reason, there is a need for new treatments with improved tolerability and efficacy for negative, affective, and cognitive symptoms.

In the last 15 years, some studies have investigated the effectiveness of SGAs compared to FGAs for schizophrenia and related disorders, leading to reconceiving trials' design using APs, as in the US Clinical Antipsychotic Trials of Intervention Effectiveness (CATIE) [26] and the UK Cost Utility of the Latest Antipsychotic Drugs in Schizophrenia Study (CUtLASS) [17]. The two trials measured short- and mid-term outcomes, not always considering the real-world clinical practice and outcome measures besides positive symptoms (e.g., exclusion of comorbidity with substance abuse, predominance of chronic patients, and lack of quality of life/well-being measures) [40]. Furthermore, the European First Episode Schizophrenia Trial (EUFEST) compared the effectiveness of some SGAs with that of a low dose of haloperidol in first-episode schizophrenia at 1-year follow-up. SGAs were associated with a higher retention rate than haloperidol (primary outcome). However, the psychopathological scores' mean reduction did not vary [41]. A secondary analysis showed that most SGAs had higher response and remission rates than haloperidol [42]. All treatment groups were associated with worsened hypertriglyceridemia or hyperglycemia. Only ziprasidone was less associated with weight gain [43]. These results disagreed with those reported in a chart review demonstrating that SGAs in first-episode patients had a three times higher incidence of metabolic syndrome with respect to FGAs [44]. However, the study had a longer follow-up period (3 years) than the EUFEST trial. Overall, the available evidence does not coherently indicate superior effectiveness and tolerability for SGAs.

One of the most considerable challenges in treating patients with schizophrenia and related disorders is the life-long functional disability associated with negative symptoms, cognitive impairment, and increased treatment resistance after each acute episode. Consequently, the primary goal of antipsychotic treatment should be not only to achieve a partial (or optimal) remission of symptoms in the acute phase but also to improve long-term outcomes and reduce the risk of secondary negative symptoms and worsening of cognitive impairment [45,46].

Harmonizing the results of randomized clinical trials (RCTs) with those of observational studies remains a challenge for clinical medicine. Although RCTs are considered the "gold standard" for evaluating the efficacy and safety of an intervention, observational studies conducted in a real-world scenario help provide evidence of the intervention in clinical practice effectiveness. Ref. [47], indeed, reported that "real-world effectiveness" is one of the last five years' significant research trends [47].

For a clinician, assessing both efficacy and effectiveness remains a crucial factor. Indeed, observational studies are beneficial in clinical situations rarely tested in RCTs and provide reliable real-world evidence. Specifically, RCTs evaluate interventions under ideal conditions in highly selected populations, whereas observational studies examine effects in naturalistic settings. Furthermore, RCTs results might not apply to the entire population of patients due to complex clinical presentations and poor responses to standard treatments in "real-world" settings.

On the other hand, dissimilar findings may arise due to such issues as selection bias, confounding, statistical power, and differential adherence and follow-up. Furthermore, real-world studies encompass a wide range of research methods and data sources and can be broadly categorized as non-interventional studies, patient registries, claims database studies, patient surveys, and electronic health record studies. Real-world studies can also be categorized into prospective studies, which generally require primary data collection, and retrospective studies, which use secondary data gathered over a long period (i.e., data initially collected for other purposes). Nevertheless, a recent Cochrane review showed little evidence that the results of observational studies and RCTs are systematically discordant [48]. Thus, studies on clinical effectiveness and naturalistic outcomes cannot replace RCTs, which remain complementary and fundamental to gathering helpful information.

This review aims to provide an update of the primary therapeutic and side-effect profiles of SGAs, focusing on real-world studies to enable clinicians and researchers to select the most appropriate treatment for adult patients $\geq$ 18 years diagnosed with schizophrenia or related disorders.

2. Methods

We conducted an extensive literature search in the PubMed database from inception until May 2022, with English as a language filter. This review was conducted according to the Preferred Reporting Items for Systematic Review and Meta-Analysis (PRISMA) statement, as applicable [49]. The search was conducted with the following terms (MeSH headings): (("Adult"[Mesh]) AND ("Humans"[Mesh]) AND ("Real-World") AND (("Schizophrenia"[Mesh]) OR ("Schizophrenia Spectrum and Other Psychotic Disorders"[Mesh])) AND (("Antipsychotic Agents/adverse effects"[Mesh]) OR ("Antipsychotic Agents/therapeutic use"[Mesh])) NOT ("Electroconvulsive Therapy"[Mesh]) NOT ("Transcranial Magnetic Stimulation"[Mesh])). In addition, we hand-searched the reference lists of included articles of any study on our topic of interest.

We focused on real-world studies, including prevalently longitudinal comparative studies (i.e., cohort or case–control studies). We identified schizophrenia and/or schizophrenia spectrum and other psychotic disorders as the mental disorders of interest for the scoping review, including only studies on psychopathological symptoms assessment through standardized rating scales. Furthermore, we included studies on patients treated with SGAs, or co-treated with FGAs and SGAs in the oral or long-acting injectable (LAI) formulations. Specifically, we selected studies containing data on individual drugs or grouped SGAs that reported the effectiveness and tolerability outcomes for adult participants $\geq$18 years. Moreover, we included studies evaluating both effectiveness and/or tolerability in patients switching from oral SGAs or FGAs to LAI SGAs.

The primary outcomes of interest were the effectiveness of oral and/or LAI formulations of SGAs on positive, negative, affective, and cognitive symptoms and their tolerability profile. In particular, we considered of interest studies reporting one or more of the following elements: (1) ≤20% reduction on the psychopathology assessment scale (i.e., BPRS); (2) improvements in quality of life rated by specific scales (i.e., Subjective Well-Being under Neuroleptics Scale [SWN-S] and the Treatment Satisfaction Questionnaire for Medication [TSQM]); (3) magnitude of treatment effects on severity measures (i.e., the Positive and Negative Syndrome Scale [PANSS], the Brief Psychiatric Rating Scale [BPRS], the Clinical Global Impression—Severity scale [CGI-S], and Quality of Life [QoL] scores); (4) improvement in negative symptoms; (5) effects on cognitive performance (evaluated by standard neuropsychological instruments); (6) improvement in global and social functioning, self-care, and disturbing/aggressive behavior (i.e., evaluated by the Global Assessment of Functioning [GAF] or the Personal and Social Performance [PSP] scale scores or defined as an increase in at least one activity in which the patient participated, compared to the baseline activity); (7) assessment of rate and time to treatment discontinuation, defined as stopping the AP medication started in baseline conditions and/or adding a new AP; (8) persistence/compliance/adherence on medications (measured as pill counts, pharmacy records, and proportion of adherent/non-adherent patients); (9) occurrence of any mental health events (suicide, hospitalization, or emergency department visits); (10) risk of rehospitalization and treatment failure (suicide attempt, discontinuation or switch to other medications, or death).

In addition, we considered of interest studies reporting any new onset or worsening side effects, i.e., EPS, hyperprolactinemia, diabetes, ketoacidosis, hyperglycemic state, weight gain/overweight/obesity, hyperlipidemia or hypercholesterolemia, hypertriglyceridemia, hypertension, and metabolic syndrome. We considered suitable and recorded any definition of these clinical entities, including diagnoses based on any coding system (e.g., ICD-10) and exposure to specific treatments (e.g., antihypertensives).

We excluded studies on pregnant women and considered only studies containing results on at least one outcome of interest (effectiveness or tolerability, or both).

S.C. and A.C. extracted the relevant data, and synthesized them in a tabular format; F.M., F.P. and F.C. triple-checked the extracted data for accuracy; M.F., S.C. and A.C extracted the data on study characteristics (type of study, number of participants/sample size, and psychopathological diagnostic tools), outcome measures (proportion of patients with schizophrenia and related disorders, psychopathological assessment tools used to evaluate the severity of disease), and therapeutic intervention types (oral vs. LAI SGAs).

Two authors of the present review (S.C. and A.C.) independently assessed the quality and risk of bias in the non-randomized studies of interventions (NRSIs) included in the present review through the ROBINS-I tool (Risk of Bias in Non-randomized Studies of Interventions). Such a tool [50] comprises three main domains for bias evaluation: pre-intervention, during the intervention, and post-intervention. The risk of bias was judged for each domain and sub-domain and classified as low, moderate, high, or no information (Supplementary Table S1).

The two authors resolved disagreements through discussion or involving a third author (F.P.). In line with the ROBINS-I tool, the authors considered an NRSI at low risk if judged at low risk of bias for all domains; at moderate risk if judged at moderate risk for at least one domain; at high risk if judged at high risk of bias for at least one domain but not at critical risk of bias in any domain; and at critical risk if judged at critical risk in at least one domain. In addition, we indicated "no information" for an NRSI in case no clear judgment of high or critical risk of bias was possible and in case information about one or more key domains was missing.

3. Results

As shown in Supplementary Figure S1, we retrieved 188 articles and excluded 115 by initial screening of titles and abstracts as not addressing the topics of interest. We included the remaining 73 articles in the final analysis as relevant for the full-text screening. We excluded 39 of them after careful reading: 10/73 were narrative reviews or reviews that did not analyze studies on patients in real-world conditions or therapeutic and/or tolerability outcomes, 26/73 were studies including patient populations different from the target ones, and 3 were studies with only abstracts written in the English language. The remaining 34 articles were eligible to be included in our review.

We further subdivided the 34 studies according to the outcome analyzed regarding effectiveness and tolerability, which were examined based on the type of AP formulation (oral vs. LAI) used to treat enrolled patients, as reported in Supplementary Figure S1. Thus, the studies reporting the effectiveness of SGAs were sub-grouped into oral SGAs (15/34) and LAI SGAs (19/34) subgroups. Finally, only 11 studies reported data on the tolerability profile of SGAs, namely 3 studies involving oral SGAs and 8 LAI SGAs (Supplementary Figure S1).

The overall risk of bias was moderate for most non-randomized clinical studies (20/34). Instead, the risk of bias appeared low for one study, with those remaining (13/34) presenting a high risk (Supplementary Table S1).

3.1. Studies Investigating the Effectiveness of SGAs

All the 34 retrieved studies reported the effectiveness of SGAs in patients with a diagnosis of schizophrenia or related disorders. A total of 15 studies evaluated the effectiveness of SGAs in patients treated with oral formulations and the other 19 in patients treated with LAI SGAs.

SGAs included amisulpride, clozapine, olanzapine, quetiapine, risperidone, paliperidone, ziprasidone, aripiprazole, brexpiprazole, and lurasidone, as a monotherapy or in combination. All the studies emphasized that clozapine was not to be used in combination with other SGAs.

FGAs were prevalently used as an all-drug comparison group and included haloperidol, zuclopenthixol, flupentixol, and sulpiride. In some studies, FGAs were also used in combination therapy with SGAs.

3.1.1. Studies Investigating the Effectiveness of Oral SGAs Treatments

In Table 1, we summarized the results of our literature search on effectiveness outcomes. We described the effectiveness of each treatment and subdivided the 15 studies we analyzed as follows: six studies were on SGAs vs. FGAs, four on olanzapine vs. risperidone, two on ziprasidone not compared with other SGAs or FGAs, one on clozapine vs. other SGAs or FGAs, and one on lurasidone and brexpiprazole, each drug vs. other SGAs.

Table 1. Real-world population-based studies investigating the effectiveness of oral SGAs in patients with schizophrenia and related disorders.

Authors, Year of Publication, Country of Study	Type of Study	No. Included Patients, Target Population	Duration of Follow-Up	Outcome Measures of Effectiveness	Treatment Arms	Results
Taylor et al., 2005 UK [51]	Prospective comparative outcome study, no pharmaceutical industry sponsorship	373 In- and out-patients recruited in 2022	6 months	CGI, positive and negative psychotic symptoms, quality of life.	SGAs treatment groups: Ami, Clo, Ola, Que, Ris	Clinical effectiveness: all SGAs produced similar out-comes; Ola and Ris significantly reduced all ratings at 6 months vs. other SGAs.
Ritsner et al., 2007 Israel [52]	Open-label, observational study, funded by Pfizer Pharmaceuticals Israel	70 patients recruited from 2004 to 2006	1 year	Q-LES-Q, severity of symptoms, distress level	Zipra flexible dosage regimen (40–160 mg/day).	Dropout rate: 54.3% Satisfaction with general activity: increased from month 6 onwards. Severity of clinical symptoms and emotional distress: moderate improvements

Table 1. *Cont.*

Authors, Year of Publication, Country of Study	Type of Study	No. Included Patients, Target Population	Duration of Follow-Up	Outcome Measures of Effectiveness	Treatment Arms	Results
Ratner et al., 2007 Israel [53]	Open-label, observational trial, funded by Pfizer Pharmaceuticals Israel	70 patients previously treated with FGAs or other SGAs, recruited from 2004 to 2006	1 year	PANSS, CGI-S, and GAF scales; Rate and mean time of discontinuation treatment.	Zipra flexible-dose monotherapy	All PANSS factors and GAF scores: improved ($p < 0.05$). Effect sizes for changes: moderate from baseline to endpoint: PANSS negative (d = 0.58), positive and activation (for both d = 0.64), dysphoric mood (d = 0.54), autistic preoccupations (d = 55) factors, and general functioning (d = 0.78). Discontinuation treatment: 54.3%; Mean time to discontinuation: 4.4 ± 2.7 months.
Kilzieh et al., 2008 USA [54]	Retrospective study, funded by Eli Lilly	495 patients recruited from1999 to 2000	2 years	Medication discontinuation	Ola vs. Ris	Discontinuation rates: lower for Ola (70%) than Ris (76%) ($p = 0.12$). Median time to discontinuation: longer for Ola (150 days) than Ris (90 days) ($p = 0.04$). Self-discontinuation: no significant difference between Ola (50%) and Ris (46%). Switching rate: more likely to occur in Ris (30%) than Ola (20%) group.
Cortesi et al., 2013 Italy [55]	Longitudinal, retrospective/prospective multicenter cohort study (COMETA), funded by Janssen-Cilag Italy SpA	637 patients enrolled from 2006 to 2007 in 86 mental health centers	mean 14.4 (3.0–17.9) months	PANSS, CGI-S, GAF scales; Persistence, compliance, costs and HRQoL	SGAs, FGAs, and SGAs +FGAs vs. untreated patients.	Relapse rate: 17.1% of patients. Switching rate: 13.4% of SGAs treated patients switched to FGAs, combined SGAs and FGAs, or no treatment. Overall, 22.9% of the cohort switched to another class of drugs at least once, 11% at least twice, and 1.3% four or five times. Persistence on treatment: higher with SGAs than FGAs; on average, 402.8 days for SGAs, 263.0 days for FGAs. The naïve patients had an improvement higher than the non-naïve patients on HRQoL (SF-36 PCS and MCS scores).

Table 1. *Cont.*

Authors, Year of Publication, Country of Study	Type of Study	No. Included Patients, Target Population	Duration of Follow-Up	Outcome Measures of Effectiveness	Treatment Arms	Results
Novick et al., 2016 UK [56]	Prospective study (SOHO study), no pharmaceutical industry sponsorship	3712 patients from Europe, Latin America, North Africa, Middle East and East Asia, enrolled from 2000 to 2001	3 years	CGI-SCH negative and positive symptoms. Improvement in social functioning.	Oral Ola vs. other oral SGAs (Ris, Que, Ami, Clo, other SGAs) vs. FGAs.	Negative symptoms and social functioning: SGAs likely superior to FGAs; Overall, negative and depressive symptoms: Ola more effective. Rates of treatment discontinuation: at 36 months lower in Ola-treated patients (38.4%)
Vanasse et al., 2016 Canada [57]	Retrospective cohort study, no pharmaceutical industry sponsorship	18,869 patients enrolled from 1998 to 2005	2 years	Risk of AP discontinuation, switch/add-on AP treatment; combination discontinuation and switching of APs.	All FGAs as single category vs. SGAs (Ola, Ris, Que, Clo)	Risk of stopping or changing medication: lower for Clo, Que, Ola, and Ris vs. FGAs. Clo was the most effective SGA, and Que was the least.
Misawa et al., 2017 Tokyo, Japan [58]	Retrospective mirror-image study, chart review study, no pharmaceutical industry sponsorship	35 patients treated with Clo before 2015, who had taken any SGAs for at least 1 year before initiating Clo.	1 year	Hospitalization and seclusion rates.	Clo vs. other SGAs (Ola, Ris, Ari, Que, Blon, Pali, Peros, PP1M) or FGAs (oral or LAI formulation)	Length of hospitalization: Clo more effective than other SGAs (median value for SGA 110 days and 80 days for Clo; $p = 0.054$). Total days of seclusion: no days during the Clo phase ($p < 0.001$) compared to SGAs (5 days). The number of patients who were secluded at least once was significantly lower ($p = 0.005$) in the Clo phase ($n = 5$; 17.2%) than in the SGA phase ($n = 17$; 58.2%).
Tiihonen et al., 2017 Sweden [59]	Prospectively, nationwide study, funded by Janssen-Cilag	29,823 Patients diagnosed with schizophrenia from 2006 to 2013	Mean 5.7 years (median, 6.9 years).	Risk of rehospitalization; treatment failure	Oral FGAs (Flup, Halo, Perph, and Zuclo) vs. oral SGAs (Ari, Clo, and Ola).	Risk of psychiatric rehospitalization: lowest with Clo monotherapy vs. no use of APs; highest risk with oral Fluph, Que, and Perph; Clo associated with the lowest rates vs. oral Ola.
Rajagopalan et al., 2017 USA [60]	Retrospective study, funded by Sunovion Pharmaceuticals Inc.	1413 patients with a first SGAs prescription claim from 2009 to 2012	6 months	Adherence/medication possession; ratio/proportion of adherent/non-adherent patients; discontinuation rate/mean time to discontinuation	Lura vs. other oral SGAs (Ari, Ola, Que, Ris, and Zipra)	Discontinuation rate: lower for Lura vs. all other SGAs (49.3% vs. 62.3–68.3%, all $p < 0.05$), except for Ris ($p < 0.05$). Mean time to discontinuation: longer for Lura than for other SGAs. Adherence: greater for Lura vs. other SGAs.

Table 1. *Cont.*

Authors, Year of Publication, Country of Study	Type of Study	No. Included Patients, Target Population	Duration of Follow-Up	Outcome Measures of Effectiveness	Treatment Arms	Results
Zhang et al., 2019 Shanghai, China [61]	Prospective, multicenter study (SALT-C study), no pharmaceutical industry sponsorship	373 patients receiving Ola, Ris, or Ari monotherapy at least 13 weeks after the baseline visit, recruited from 2011 to 2014	Follow-up times: 13, 26, 52, 78, 104, 130, and 156 weeks after baseline	Discontinuation rate; changes in social functioning (PSP score)	Three SGAs (Ola, Ris, and Ari) as monotherapy.	All-cause discontinuation rate: higher for Ris, lower for Ola and Ari before 24 months but higher in patients taking Ari after 24 months. PSP improvement: maximum value of 80.3% at weeks 56.7 after treatment with Ola, 68.2% at weeks 29.2 with Ris, and 23.9% at weeks 36.8 with Ari.
Stam et al., 2020 The Netherlands [62]	Nationwide pharmacy drug dispensing database; prescription data from 1996 to 2017 from ~ 60 community pharmacies, no pharmaceutical industry sponsorship	321 patients previously treated with Clo for ≥90 days, then discontinued due to undefined reasons, recruited from 1996 to 2017	Analysis of database prescriptions from 60 community pharmacies	Persistence time, discontinuation rate in patients stopping Clo	SGAs (Clo, Ola, Que, Ris, and Ari) or FGAs (Halo, Zuclo, Flu, and Sulp) in monotherapy or in combination therapy. LAI therapy included only PP1M or Zuclo LAI	Persistence time: SGAs better than FGAs; restarting Clo or switching to Ris or Ola significantly better than other APs.
Yan et al., 2020 USA [63]	Retrospective cohort study, funded by Otsuka and Lundbeck	6254 patients identified as having at least one claim for either Brex or another oral SGAs, recruited from 2015 to 2016	12 months	Risk of psychiatric inpatient hospitalization rate	Brex vs. other oral SGAs (Zipra, Pali, Lura, Ari, Que, Ola, Ris)	Psychiatric hospitalizations rate/year: Pali and Que users worse than Brex users. No significant differences emerged among other SGAs users.
Barbosa et al., 2021 Brazil [64]	Open, non-concurrent, paired and nationwide cohort study, no pharmaceutical industry sponsorship	3416 patients, 1708 treated with Ola, 1708 with Ris, recruited from 2000 to 2015	15 years	Discontinuation treatment	Ola vs. Ris in monotherapy or in combination therapy with other SGAs (including Clo)	Discontinuation rate: 84.4% of total patients, 82.1% of Ola treated patients, and 86.8% for those prescribed Ris; Median time to discontinuation: overall 63 months, Ola 66 months, and Ris 59 months; Relapse-free survival and psychiatric hospitalization: Ola better than Ris (HR = 1.22; 95% CI = 0.99–1.51; $p = 0.06$).
Hatta et al., 2022 Japan [65]	Multicenter, prospective, cohort study, no pharmaceutical industry sponsorship	1011 patients acutely hospitalized from 2019 to 2021	1 year after discharge	CGI-S score, PANSS-8 derived from PANSS-30; Risk of treatment failure	SGAs (Pal, Ola, Ris, Ari, Brex, Blon, Que) or FGAs (Halo, Fluph) in monotherapy or polytherapy.	Treatment failure: 588 patients, due to rehospitalization (513 patients), discontinuation (17 patients), death (11 patients), prolonged hospitalization for one year (47 patients); lower risk with combined Ola and Pali, higher risk with combined Ari and Ola.

Table 1. *Cont.*

Authors, Year of Publication, Country of Study	Type of Study	No. Included Patients, Target Population	Duration of Follow-Up	Outcome Measures of Effectiveness	Treatment Arms	Results
						Risk of Switching to LAIs and APs polytherapy: 23.4% (237 patients) during follow-up, 74.3% (176/237) patients during hospitalization.

Q-LES-Q = Quality of Life Enjoyment and Satisfaction Questionnaire; PANSS = Positive and Negative Syndrome Scale; CGI-S = Clinical Global Impression—Severity scale; GAF = Global Assessment of Functioning Scale; AP = Antipsychotic; FGAs = First-Generation Antipsychotics; Chlorpro = Chlorpromazine; Fluph= Fluphenazine; Flup = Flupentixol; Halo = Haloperidol; Perph = Perphenazine; Peros = Perospirone; Zuclo = Zuclopenthixol; Sulp = Sulpiride; SGAs = Second-Generation Antipsychotics; Blo = Blonanserin; Zipra = Ziprasidone; Ami = Amisulpride; Clo = Clozapine; Ola = Olanzapine; Que = Quetiapine; Ris = Risperidone; Pali = Paliperidone; Ari = Aripiprazole; Brex = Brexpiprazole; Lura = Lurasidone; Zote = Zotepine; COMETA = COMpliance, costs and quality of life-clinical experience in antipsychotic therapy; HRQoL = Health-Related Quality of Life; SF-36 PCS and MCS = Physical (PCS) and Mental (MCS) Component Summary scores of SF-36; SOHO = Schizophrenia Outpatient Health Outcomes; SALT-C = Schizophrenia by Atypical Antipsychotic Treatment in China; CGI-SCH = Clinical Global Impressions Severity Scale—Schizophrenia version; PSP = Personal and Social Performance.

Most studies evaluated the effectiveness of SGAs vs. FGAs [55–57,59,62,65]. Olanzapine, in particular, emerged as an effective treatment option among the atypical agents [51].

Only a few studies directly evaluated the therapeutic effects of SGAs on positive, negative, and affective symptoms [41,42,46,55,56], and none reported antipsychotic effectiveness in disabling cognitive symptoms.

Persistence, adherence, or failure to treatment, as well as the rate of SGAs discontinuation or risk of hospitalization, were analyzed in most studies [52–55,57–62,64,65]. Overall, olanzapine demonstrated superior real-world effectiveness vs. risperidone in relapse-free survival and psychiatric hospitalization [61]. Moreover, switching to clozapine, to risperidone or to olanzapine oral monotherapy was also associated with significantly better persistence in treatment [62]. In addition, Hatta et al. (2022) [65] suggested that switching to LAIs or APs polytherapy might be more likely associated with a low treatment failure rate [65]. Clozapine, as well, was associated with the lowest rates of treatment failure and more marked effects vs. other SGAs in reducing the period of hospitalization [58].

Refs. [52,53] reported on ziprasidone effectiveness, concluding that the improvement in PANSS factors and GAF scores was significant but associated with a discontinued treatment for any cause in more than 50% of patients [52,53]. Discontinuation due to lack of clinical effectiveness was linked more to patients' perceptions (25.7%) than to physicians' conclusions (8.6%). However, both studies did not include a control group for comparison. Differently, the study by [60] reported that patients treated with lurasidone demonstrated greater adherence when compared to patients treated with other SGAs [60]. Finally, when brexpiprazole treatment was examined compared to other SGAs, it was found to be associated with fewer psychiatric hospitalizations per year than paliperidone and quetiapine. No significant differences in other efficacy measures emerged between patients treated with brexpiprazole and those with other SGAs [63].

The overall risk of bias for most non-randomized clinical studies reporting the effectiveness of oral SGAs was moderate (11/15).

3.1.2. Studies Investigating the Effectiveness of LAI SGAs Treatments

Most studies reporting on LAI APs treatments included patients that had been previously treated with oral FGAs or SGAs or switched from one LAI FGA/SGA to another LAI SGA treatment (Table 2). Some studies described patients previously treated with the corresponding oral formulation and then shifting to LAI therapy. Furthermore, most studies included patients treated with once-monthly paliperidone palmitate (PP1M) and aripiprazole LAI (Table 2). On the other hand, only a few studies compared the effectiveness of LAI SGAs vs. LAI FGAs, or oral FGAs/SGAs vs. LAI FGAs/SGAs, or oral SGAs vs. LAI SGAs [66].

Table 2. Real-world population-based studies investigating the effectiveness of SGAs LAI formulations in patients with schizophrenia and related disorders.

Authors, Year of Publication, Country of Study	Type of Study	No. Included Patients, Target Population	Duration of Follow-Up	Outcome Measures of Effectiveness	Treatment Arms	Results
Schreiner et al., 2014 21 European countries [67]	Prospective Multicenter study (from 160 sites in 21 countries); sponsored by Janssen-Cilag	593 patients switched from oral APs who received at least 1 dose of PP1M during the study, recruited from 2010 to 2013	6 months	PANSS total score, PANSS subscale scores, PANSS Marder factor scores; CGI-C scores; PSP total score; PSP domain scores; and subjective well-being (SWN-S and TSQM).	PP1M	PANSS total: decreased from 71.5 (14.6) at baseline to 59.7 (18.1) at the endpoint; 64% of patients showed a ≥20% improvement in PANSS total score. CGI-S score: increased from 31.8% of patients to 63.2% of patients rating mildly ill or less Mean personal and social performance total score: improved significantly for all patients from baseline to endpoint ($p \leq 0.0001$).
Hargarter et al., 2015 21 European countries [68]	Prospective multicenter, open-label study [PALMFlexS], sponsored by Janssen Cilag International NV	149 patients with acute symptoms, switching from oral APs due to lack of efficacy, recruited from 2010 to 2013	6 months	PANSS total score PANSS subscale and Marder factor, CGI-S score, CGI-C score, PSP total score, and four PSP domain scores (socially useful activities, personal and social relationships, self-care, and disturbing and aggressive behavior); Mini-ICF-APP; SWN-S-short form, and TSQM scale.	Patients switching from oral APs to PP1M.	CGI-C: severity significantly decreased; percentage of patients rated markedly ill or worse decreased from 75.1% at baseline to 20.5% at last observation; patients categorized as minimally (26.5%), much (41.3%), or very much (14.3%) improved. SWN-S total score, TSQM global satisfaction score, TSQM satisfaction scores related to medication effectiveness: significant improvements PSP total score: significantly increased from baseline to last observation.
Chan et al., 2015 Taiwan [69]	Retrospective cohort study, supported by grants from the E-Da Hospital	379 patients recruited from 2011 to 2012	12 months	Rehospitalization rate, length of hospital stay, emergency room visits and medical expenditures.	Oral SGAs (Que, Ola, Ami, Zipra, Pali, Clo, Zote) or FGAs (Chlorpro, Sulp, Halo, Fluph) or oral Ris vs. LAI Ris	Hospitalization rate before enrolment: all-oral APs group 32.1%, oral Ris group 35.9%, and LAI Ris group 88.4% ($p < 0.0001$). After a 1-year follow-up: all three groups showed similar rehospitalization rates (all-oral APs group 28.9%, oral Ris group 30.1%, LAI Ris group, 30.2%, $p > 0.999$);

Table 2. *Cont.*

Authors, Year of Publication, Country of Study	Type of Study	No. Included Patients, Target Population	Duration of Follow-Up	Outcome Measures of Effectiveness	Treatment Arms	Results
						Length of hospital stay, and number of emergency room visits during follow-up: LAI Ris reduced the severity of disease more significantly than oral APs and medical expenditures.
Alphs et al., 2015 USA [70]	Randomized, prospective, multicenter study (PRIDE study), funded by Janssen Scientific Affairs LLC.	444 patients recruited from 2010 to 2013	15 months	First treatment failure in patients treated with PP1M vs. daily oral APs; time to first psychiatric hospitalization or arrest/incarceration; functionality measured by PSP; severity of psychopathology by CGI-S; adherence to treatment	PP1M vs. daily oral APs (Ari, Halo, Ola, Pali, Perph, Que, Ris)	First treatment failure: PP1M significantly delay in time vs. oral APs ($p = 0.011$); observed treatment failure rates were 39.8% and 53.7%. Arrest/incarceration and psychiatric hospitalization, most common reasons for treatment failure in the PP1M and oral APs groups (21.2% vs. 29.4% and 8.0% vs. 11.9%). No significant differences in PSP and CGI-S scale scores.
Fernández-Miranda et al., 2017 Spain [71]	Prospective observational study, no pharmaceutical industry sponsorship	30 patients resistant to previous Aps treatment, recruited from 2012 to 2015	3 years	CGI-S, WHO-DAS, CAN, MARS, laboratory tests, weight measurement, treatment discontinuation	32 months with 150 mg Eq PP1M, then on average dose of PP: 228, 7 mg Eq/ 28 days; range between 175 and 400 mEq	CGI-S, WHO-DAS, CAN, and MARS: significant improvements ($p < 0.05$) from baseline to month 6. Discontinuation rate: 2/30 due to lack of effectiveness. Significant decrease in the use of other Aps and other psychiatric medications ($p < 0.05$).
Pilon et al., 2017 USA [72]	Retrospective longitudinal cohort study, funded by Janssen Scientific Affairs, LLC.	24,662 patients from Claims data for Medicaid beneficiaries recruited from 2009 to 2015	12 months	Adherence; persistence; health care resource utilization; Medicaid spending	LAI SGAs (Ari, Ola, Pali, Ris) vs. oral SGAs (Ari, Asena, Ilop, Lura, Ola, Pali, Que, Ris, Zipra)	Adherence and persistence to therapy: increased in PP-LAI patients, whereas Ari-LAI and Ris-LAI patients similar to oral SGAs patients; persistence significantly better for PP1M and Ris-LAI, whereas Ari-LAI was similar to oral SGAs. Health care resource utilization: fewer long-term care admissions, long-term care length of stay, and home care services with LAI-SGAs; mental health institute admissions and visits were significantly more frequent with oral SGAs. Medical costs: SGA-LAIs lower than oral SGAs, but higher pharmacy costs.

Table 2. *Cont.*

Authors, Year of Publication, Country of Study	Type of Study	No. Included Patients, Target Population	Duration of Follow-Up	Outcome Measures of Effectiveness	Treatment Arms	Results
Tiihonen et al., 2017 Sweden [59]	Prospective study from nationwide databases, funded by Janssen-Cilag	29,823 patients recruited from 2006 to 2013	Mean 5.7 years (median, 6.9 years).	Time receiving monotherapy; Time receiving any therapy; Risk of rehospitalization; Treatment failure (suicide attempt, discontinuation or switch to other medication, or death)	LAI FGAs (Fluph, Flupent, Halo, Perph, Zuclo) vs. LAI SGAs (Ola, Pali, Ris)	Risk of psychiatric rehospitalization: lowest during monotherapy with PP1M, LAI Zuclo, LAI Perph, and LAI Ola vs. no use of APs and vs. equivalent oral APs (20–30% lower); Relapse prevention: LAI APs highest rates; treatment failure: All LAI APs had the lowest rates vs. oral Ola.
Schöttle et al., 2018 Germany [73]	Multicenter, prospective study, sponsored by Lundbeck GmbH and Otsuka GmbH.	242 patients recruited from 2014 to 2016	6 months	BPRS, CGI-S, and CGI-I	Patients pre-treated with oral Ari vs. transition to LAI Ari 1-monthly	CGI-S score: proportion of patients with high CGI-S scores decreased and with low scores increased significantly ($p < 0.001$); decreased significantly more in patients $\leq$35 years; BPRS scores improved, especially in younger patients $\leq$35 years.
Patel et al., 2019 USA [74]	Retrospective claims-based study, funded by Janssen Scientific Affairs, LLC.	122 Veterans' Health Administration patients with Schizophrenia, initiating treatment with PP1M between 2015 and 2017	12-month pre- and post-PP3M initiation	Treatment patterns, healthcare resource use, and costs	Pre- and post-PP3M transition: patients treated with PP1M vs. patients transited to PP3M	Outpatient and pharmacy visits: reduced during transition to PP3M. Adherence to treatment: 64.8% (proportion of days covered 80%) in patients treated with PP1M and 61.5% in those treated with PP3M. Healthcare resource use: outcomes pre- and post-PP3M transition showed lower all-cause outpatient (37.5 vs. 31.1, $p \leq 0.0001$) and pharmacy visits (56.1 vs. 46.7, $p \leq 0.0001$): substantial decrease also in concomitant medication use (i.e., antidepressants) in patients during the post-PP3M transition.
Devrimci-Ozguven et al., 2019 Turkey [75]	National, multicenter, retrospective, and mirror-image study; no pharmaceutical industry sponsorship	205 patients who presented their first psychotic attack 1 year or more before the initial PP1M injection, recruitment initiated in 2016	12 months	PANSS, CGI-S, BPRS, PSP, and GAF scores	Before vs. after treatment with PP1M.	Relapse and median number of hospitalizations: reduced. Effects on functionality: positive. Rate of patients readmitted to the hospital for relapse: 79.5% vs. 28.9% ($p < 0.001$) with median number of hospitalizations (2 vs. 0, $p < 0.001$) lower during PP1M treatment vs. the period before PP1M treatment.

Table 2. *Cont.*

Authors, Year of Publication, Country of Study	Type of Study	No. Included Patients, Target Population	Duration of Follow-Up	Outcome Measures of Effectiveness	Treatment Arms	Results
						PANSS score: decreased by 20% or more during treatment in 75.7% of patients. Functionality: higher when the disease duration was 5 years or less.
Takàcs et al., 2019 Hungary [76]	Nationwide, longitudinal study, no pharmaceutical industry sponsorship	12,232 patients recruited from 2012 to 2013, followed up to 2015	2 years	All-cause treatment discontinuation	All patients with newly initiated SGAs during the inclusion period: oral SGAs (Ami, Ari, Clo, Ola, Que, Ris, Pali, Zipra) vs. LAI SGAs (Ris, Ola, PP1M).	Persistence on treatment after 1 year: oral APs varied between 17% (oral Ris) and 31% (oral Ola), LAIs between 32% (Ris LAI) and 64% (PP1M). The 2-year data were similarly in favor of LAIs. Median time to discontinuation: in the oral group, between 57 days (Clo) and 121 days (Ola); in the LAI group between 176 and 287 days.
Fagiolini et al., 2019 Italy [77]	Observational, retrospective study, no pharmaceutical industry sponsorship	261 patients who had started LAI Ari (at least one injection) at least 6 months before the inclusion visit, recruited from 2015 to 2017	6 months	CGI-S, evaluation of schizophrenia dimensions (symptoms and clusters of symptoms) assessed by the LDPS and SCI-PSY questionnaire	Patients treated with LAI Ari.	Persistence on treatment: 225 patients (86%) for at least 6 months; all patients with baseline CGI-S of 1 or 2,95% with CGI-S of 3, 86% with CGI-S of 4, 82% with CGI-S of 5, 73% with CGI of 6, and 90% with CGI of 7. LAI Ari continuation rate: higher (86.2%) in patients with: (1) baseline CGI score $\leq$ 4; (2) LDPS mania score $\leq$ 5; (3) psychotic spectrum schizoid score $\leq$ 11.
Fernández-Miranda et al., 2020 Spain [78]	Observational, mirror-image study, no pharmaceutical industry sponsorship.	150 patients resistant to previous APs treatment, recruited from 2014 to 2016	6 years	CGI-S, WHO-DAS, MARS, laboratory tests, weight measurement	60 patients treated with LAI Ris $\geq$ 75 mg; 60 treated with 75 mg/month PP1M; 30 treated with $\geq$600 mg/month LAI Ari	Clinical effectiveness: global improvement on all the scales. Hospital admissions and suicide attempts: statistically significant decrease
Magliocco et al., 2020 Italy [79]	Longitudinal prospective study, no pharmaceutical industry sponsorship	32 patients previously treated with oral SGAs, recruited from 2016 to 2018	12 months	Cognitive performance: SCWT and ROCF tests; PANSS, QOLS, PSP	PP1M vs. oral Pali LAI Ari vs. oral Ari	Neurocognitive function: improved significantly after 12 months of treatment with SGA LAI.

Table 2. *Cont.*

Authors, Year of Publication, Country of Study	Type of Study	No. Included Patients, Target Population	Duration of Follow-Up	Outcome Measures of Effectiveness	Treatment Arms	Results
						Clinical improvement: on psychotic symptoms, psychosocial functioning, and quality of life, and no differences emerged between PP1M and LAI Ari; Functional recovery, adherence to treatment, dropout rate, further social and cognitive improvements: improved in patients who had already experienced relief when on oral SGA therapy.
Iwata et al., 2020 Japan [80]	Retrospective, observational cohort study based on a claims database, supported by Otsuka Pharmaceutical Co., Ltd.	198 LAI Ari group; 1240 oral Ari group, receiving a prescription from 2015 to 2017	Between 2 and 3 years	Treatment persistence	LAI Ari vs. oral Ari group	Treatment persistence: in LAI Ari-treated patients significantly longer than those treated with oral Ari. Discontinuation treatment: LAI Ari group significantly less likely to discontinue than the oral group (adjusted HR 0.54, 95% confidence interval [CI] 0.43–0.68).
Fernández-Miranda et al., 2021 Spain [66]	Observational, longitudinal study, no pharmaceutical industry sponsorship	688 patients with severe schizophrenia in standard care treatments in mental health units (MHU) and on specific program for people with severe mental illness (SMIP), recruited from 2012 to 2014 and followed between 2015 and 2019	5 years	Treatment discontinuation, hospital admissions, and suicide attempts	LAI-FGAs/LAI-SGAs vs. oral FGAS/SGAs	Adherence to treatment: all LAI-APs achieved higher adherence ($p < 0.001$), fewer relapses ($p < 0.001$) and suicide attempts ($p < 0.01$) than oral APs in severe schizophrenia patients.
Lauriello et al., 2021 USA [81]	Retrospective observational cohort study funded by Alkermes, Inc.	485 who had used APs in the 60 days preceding the index date, recruited from 2015 to 2017	6 months	Treatment patterns, healthcare resource use, costs before and after initiating LAI Ari	Recent AP LAI group vs. recent oral AP vs. neither an LAI nor oral AP ("no recent AP").	All-cause inpatient admissions: decreased by 22.4%, along with emergency room visits. All-cause inpatient costs: decreased by an average of USD 2836 per patient ($p < 0.05$) in the 6-month follow-up; outpatient pharmacy costs: increased by US $4121 ($p < 0.05$), resulting in no significant difference in overall costs between the pre- and post-treatment periods.

Table 2. *Cont.*

Authors, Year of Publication, Country of Study	Type of Study	No. Included Patients, Target Population	Duration of Follow-Up	Outcome Measures of Effectiveness	Treatment Arms	Results
						Discontinuation rate: 29.0%, 40.0%, and 32.9% in the three study subgroups.
Mahabaleshwarkar et al. (2021) USA [82]	Retrospective mirror-image study, funded by Janssen Scientific Affairs, LLC.	210 in patients with at least one oral APs prescription during the 12-month pre-index period, recruited from 2008 to 2020	12-month pre- and post-index periods	Rate of healthcare use: inpatient, emergency room, and outpatient visits	PP1M treatment	Acute healthcare use: reduced significantly from 61.4% to 20.5%, ($p \leq 0.001$). A more substantial reduction was observed in patients with a prior relapse vs. the overall cohort.
Hatta et al., 2022 Japan [65]	Multicenter, prospective, cohort study, no pharmaceutical industry sponsorship	1011 patients with acute onset or exacerbation of schizophrenia and other psychotic disorders, recruited from 2019 to 2021 and followed up to March 2021	19 months	Risk of treatment failure	Oral SGAs (Pali, Ola, Ris, Ari, Brex, Blon, Que) or FGAs (Halo, Fluph) in monotherapy or polytherapy (excluded Clo) vs. LAI group (Pali, Ari, Halo, Ris, Fluph).	Treatment failure: low rate (588 patients, 58.2%); rehospitalization (513 patients), discontinued medication (17 patients), death (11 patients), and continued hospitalization for one year (47 patients); lower risk in about 19% of patients treated with LAIs and 17% in those with APs polytherapy, vs. patients treated with oral APs. Switching to LAIs or APs polytherapy (no Clo allowed): in early non-responders, it appeared beneficial for preventing treatment failure in acutely hospitalized patients; Ola combined with Pali was significantly associated with a lower risk of treatment failure than monotherapy.

AP = Antipsychotic; FGAs = First-Generation Antipsychotics; SGAs = Second-Generation Antipsychotics; PANSS = Positive and Negative Syndrome Scale; QOLS = Quality of Life scale; PSP = Personal and Social Performance Scale; SWN-S = Subjective Well-being under Neuroleptics Scale; TSQM = Treatment Satisfaction Questionnaire for Medication; PALMFlexS = Paliperidone Palmitate Flexible Dosing in Schizophrenia; CGI-C = Clinical Global Impression—Change; CGI-S = Clinical Global Impression Severity Scale; BPRS = Brief Psychiatric Rating Scale; GAF = Global Assessment of Function; Mini-ICF-APP = Mini-ICF (International Classification of Functionality, Disability and Health) rating for Activity and Participation Disorders in Psychological Illnesses; PP1M = once-monthly paliperidone palmitate; PRIDE = Paliperidone Palmitate Research in Demonstrating Effectiveness; PP3M = once-every-3-months paliperidone palmitate; LDPS = Lifetime Dimensions of Psychosis Scale; SCI-PSY = Structured Clinical Interview for the Psychotic Spectrum; SCWT = Stroop Color and Word Test; ROCF = Rey–Osterrieth Complex Figure Test.

Finally, only the study by [69] presented results on the effectiveness of LAI risperidone in a retrospective cohort study vs. all-oral SGAs and FGAs and vs. oral risperidone [69]. All the studies, including patients treated with PP1M, reported significant improvements in subjective well-being and global satisfaction, and improved personal and social performance [59,65,67,68,70–72,74–76,78,79,82]. Furthermore, functionality improvement was more remarkable in patients with a disease duration of 5 years or less [75]. Finally, in a longitudinal prospective study, Ref. [79] reported that PP1M and once-monthly aripiprazole

LAI improved social and cognitive functioning in patients who had already experienced relief compared with the corresponding oral formulations of SGAs [79]. In addition, a few studies reported that high doses of PP1M (175 mg equivalent/28 days) in patients with severe schizophrenia improved the drug's effectiveness [71]. Furthermore, when patients receiving doses of PP1M ≥175 mg Eq were compared to patients treated with high doses of risperidone-LAI (dose ≥ 75 mg) or aripiprazole-LAI (dose ≥ 600 mg/month), PP1M showed better clinical effectiveness, besides reducing the risk of hospital admissions and suicide attempts [78].

Additionally, patients enrolled in other studies showed a low dropout rate, reduced acute healthcare use, and significantly improved neurocognitive function after 12 months of treatment with LAI SGAs, besides better effects on positive, negative, and affective symptoms, psychosocial functioning, and quality of life [79,82]. Furthermore, the transition from PP1M to PP3M evidenced a substantial decrease in combined medications and healthcare resource use, and increased adherence [74].

Treatment with once-monthly aripiprazole LAI improved BPRS and CGI-S scores, especially in younger patients (age ≤ 35 years) [71] and was less likely to be associated with discontinuation of treatment when compared with the corresponding oral group or other SGAs [65,72,73,77,79–81]. Thus, adherence and the hospitalization rate appeared to be improved. Such a pharmacological pattern indicates the potential for greater clinical stability in patients who initiated aripiprazole LAI than that achieved with their previous treatments [60].

The risk of bias for non-randomized clinical studies reporting the effectiveness of LAI SGAs was almost equally distributed between moderate (9/19) and high (10/19) risk.

3.2. Studies Investigating Tolerability of Oral or LAI SGAs

Table 3 illustrates real-world studies investigating the tolerability of oral or LAI SGAs in patients with schizophrenia and related disorders.

Table 3. Real-world population-based studies investigating the tolerability of oral and/or LAI formulations of SGAs in patients with schizophrenia and related disorders.

Authors (Year of Publication), Country of Study	Type of Study	No. of Analyzed Patients	Duration of Follow-Up	Tolerability Results
Taylor et al. (2005) UK [51]	Prospective comparative outcome study with Ami, Clo, Ola, Que, and Ris., no pharmaceutical industry sponsorship	373 In- and out- patients recruited in 2022	6 months	Rate of side effects: 50% (Ami), 60% (Clo), 25% (Ola), 37.5% (Que), 63.3% (Ris).
Ratner et al. (2007) Israel [53]	Open-labeled, flexible-dose, large-scale, observational trial of oral ziprasidone monotherapy, funded by Pfizer Pharmaceuticals Israel	32/70 completed ziprasidone treatment, recruited from 2004 to 2006	1 year	Vital signs, ECGs, or clinical laboratory variables associated with treatment: no significant changes; ESRS, DSAS, weight, and DAI-30: no significant differences during the three follow-up visits (p values ≤ 0.05). Adverse events from baseline to endpoint: mild or moderate fatigue (22–28%), sleep disturbances (12–22%), headache (12–16%), somnolence (16–12%).

Table 3. *Cont.*

Authors (Year of Publication), Country of Study	Type of Study	No. of Analyzed Patients	Duration of Follow-Up	Tolerability Results
Iqbal et al. (2020) UK [83]	Data from de-identified EHRs of three mental health trusts in the UK no pharmaceutical industry sponsorship	2835 selected patients under clozapine treatment from 2007 to 2016	Not applicable	Highest recorded adverse effects: sedation, fatigue, agitation, dizziness, hypersalivation, weight gain, tachycardia, headache, constipation, and confusion in the three months following the treatment start; higher percentages of all adverse effects displayed in the first month of therapy; ADRs' significant association of gender and ethnicity in 7/33, smoking status in 21/33 and hospital admission in 30/33.
Schreiner et al. (2014) 21 European countries [67]	Prospective, interventional, single-arm, multicenter study, sponsored by Janssen-Cilag	593 non-acute symptomatic patients unsuccessfully treated with oral APs; all patients were treated with flexible-dose PP1M, recruited from 2010 to 2013	6 months	Follow-up side effects: 59.7% of patients experienced at least 1 treatment-related side effect; 93.1% of side effects were rated mild or moderate in intensity; 75.8% of adverse effects resulted in no dosage change. Treatment-related adverse effects occurring in ≥5% of patients: injection site pain (2.3%), insomnia (8.6%), anxiety (6 7%), psychotic disorder (6.1%), and headache (5.6%); 18 patients (3.0%) reported at least one potentially prolactin-related side effect, four (0.7%) hyperprolactinemia, and seven (1.2%) potentially prolactin-related side effects as well as hyperprolactinemia. Mean increase of 0.4 kg/m^2 (95% CI, 0.3–0.6) in BMI and mean weight change between baseline and endpoint of 1.2 kg (95% CI, 0.7–1.6) in the whole group; 81 patients (15.4%) had a ≥7% increase in weight from baseline to endpoint. No EPS were evidenced in all groups.

Table 3. *Cont.*

Authors (Year of Publication), Country of Study	Type of Study	No. of Analyzed Patients	Duration of Follow-Up	Tolerability Results
Hargarter et al. (2015) 21 European countries [68]	Prospective, multicenter, open-label study [PALMFlexS], sponsored by Janssen Cilag International NV	149 patients treated with PP1M flexible dosing, recruited from 2010 to 2013	6 months	Treatment-related side effects: 63.7% of patients experienced at least one, the majority (89.1%) of which were rated as mild or moderate in intensity and did not result in a PP1M dose change (69.7%). Treatment-related side effects reported in ≥5% of patients: injection site pain (13.7%), insomnia (10.8%), psychotic disorder (10.4%), headache, and anxiety (6.1%). Discontinuation treatment: overall, 19 patients (9.0%) reported one or more adverse effects that led to early termination of treatment; most frequent adverse effects leading to discontinuation were psychotic disorder (n = 4, 1.9%), acute episode of schizophrenia (n = 2; 0.9%) and amenorrhea (n = 2; 0.9%). In the total cohort, 12 patients (5.7%) had a potentially prolactin-related adverse effect, 2 (0.9%) hyperprolactinemia, and 1 (0.5%) both. Adverse effects reported as potentially prolactin-related: amenorrhea (2.4%), galactorrhea (0.5%), erectile dysfunction (1.4%), gynecomastia (0.5%), and sexual dysfunction (1.4%). Overall, 40 patients (22.5%) had a ≥7% increase in body weight.
Alphs et al. (2015) USA [70]	Randomized, prospective, open-label, parallel-group, multicenter study (PRIDE study), funded by Janssen Scientific Affairs LLC.	444 patients under flexible monthly maintenance doses of PP1M within a range of 78–234 mg, recruited from 2010 to 2013	15 months	The five most common treatment-related side effects were: pain in the site of injection (18.6%); insomnia (16.8%); weight increase (11.9%); akathisia (11.1%); and anxiety (10.6%). The incidence of hyperprolactinemia was 23.5%, associated with sexual dysfunctions.

Table 3. *Cont.*

Authors (Year of Publication), Country of Study	Type of Study	No. of Analyzed Patients	Duration of Follow-Up	Tolerability Results
Rosso et al. (2016) Italy [84]	Multicenter prospective observational study, no pharmaceutical industry sponsorship	60 inpatients and outpatients treated with PP1M flexible maintenance dosage within the range of 50 to 150 mg Eq, recruited from 2013 to 2014	12 months	The proportion of patients with MetS did not significantly change at 6 (39.0%) and 12 months (29.5%) of PP1M treatment vs. baseline (33%); no significant variation emerged between MetS individual components at baseline and 6 and 12 months. Among the study completers without MetS at baseline ($n = 30$), only two patients (6.6%) fulfilled MetS criteria at the end of the study period (12 months); among study completers with MetS at baseline ($n = 14$), four patients (28 5%) did not fulfill MetS criteria at the end of the study period. A significant increase in BMI (26.3 ± 6.0 vs. 27.1 ± 4.6, $p = 0.031$) and waist circumference (98.2 ± 17.9 vs. 100.3 ± 15.9, $p = 0.021$) from baseline to endpoint. Weight gain in approximately 15% of patients. Rate of ADR: At least one mild or moderate ADR in 71 3% of patients (at baseline), 88.0% (at 6 months), and 52.1% (at 12 months); at each assessment point, no significant differences were found in blood pressure, glycemia, triglycerides, total cholesterol, and HDL cholesterol mean scores. Hyperprolactinemia: in four patients (6.6%) at baseline, six patients (10.1%) at T1, and six patients (13.6%) at T2; symptomatic in two women that showed amenorrhea.

Table 3. *Cont.*

Authors (Year of Publication), Country of Study	Type of Study	No. of Analyzed Patients	Duration of Follow-Up	Tolerability Results
Fernández-Miranda et al. (2017) Spain [71]	Prospective, observational study, patients resistant to previous oral or LAI FGAs and/or SGAs, no pharmaceutical industry sponsorship	30 patients treated with 150 mg Eq PP1M, then on average dose of PP1M 228,7 mEq/ 28 days; range between 175 and 400 mEq, recruited from 2012 to 2015	3 years	ADR rate: no patients experienced serious adverse events. Discontinuation rate: only one patient due to metabolic syndrome. General tolerability: significant weight loss ($p < 0.05$), decreased glucose, total cholesterol, triglycerides, PRL levels and EPS
Schöttle et al. (2018) Germany [73]	Multicenter, prospective, non-interventional study, sponsored by Lundbeck GmbH and Otsuka GmbH.	242 patients switching from oral-Ari to Ari-LAI, recruited from 2014 to 2016	6 months	Side effects: weight gain (0.4%), experiencing EPS (2.9%), hyperprolactinemia-related side effects (0%) (such as sexual dysfunction), EPS in patients > 35 years who were diagnosed with schizophrenia more than 5 years before.
Devrimci-Ozguven et al. (2019) Turkey [75]	National, multicenter, retrospective, and mirror-image study with PP1M, no pharmaceutical industry sponsorship	205 patients who presented their first psychotic attack 1 year or more before the initial PP1M injection, recruitment initiated in 2016	12 months	Frequency of adverse events: no significant difference before and during PP1M treatment. Side effects: hyperlipidemia, EPS (Parkinsonism, acute dystonia, and akathisia), sedation, and constipation decreased post-PP1M treatment phase; prolactin elevation, amenorrhea/menstrual irregularity in female patients, and sexual dysfunction increased; body weight increased slightly in both female and male patients.
Fernández-Miranda et al. (2020) Spain [78]	Observational, mirror-image study, no pharmaceutical industry sponsorship	150 patients resistant to previous APs: 60 patients treated with LAI Ris $\geq$ 75 mg; 60 treated with 75 mg/month PP1M; 30 treated with $\geq$ 600 mg/month LAI Ari, recruited from 2014 to 2016	6 years	Tolerability profile: good for all LAIs, especially Ari-LAI; two patients discontinued treatment due to side effects (akathisia) with Ari-LAI, five with PP1M (three EPS, one hyper-PRL, and one sedation), nine with Ris-LAI (four EPS, one hyper-PRL, three sedation, and one hyperlipemia). Discontinuation rate: four with Ris-LAI, two with PP1m, and one with Ari-LAI due to a lack of effectiveness.

EPS = Extrapyramidal Symptoms; ESRS = Extrapyramidal Symptom Rating Scale; DSAS = Distress Scale for Adverse Symptoms; ADR = Adverse Drug Reaction; DAI-30= Drug Attitude Inventory; EHR = Electronic Health Records; PP1M = Paliperidone palmitate once-monthly; MetS = Metabolic Syndrome; PRIDE study = Paliperidone Palmitate Research in Demonstrating Effectiveness study.

Ref. [51] sustained that the number of patients presenting side effects when treated with SGAs (amisulpride, clozapine, olanzapine, quetiapine, and risperidone) was in the range of 25–63.3%. However, the authors did not specify the secondary or adverse effects reported by patients [51]. On the other hand, among all patients who completed treatment with oral ziprasidone monotherapy, the most common adverse events from baseline to endpoint were mild/moderate [53].

Ref. [83] reported that most frequent adverse effects in patients treated with clozapine (N = 2835) were observed in the three months following treatment start [83]. However, higher percentages of all adverse effects appeared in the first month of clozapine therapy. Furthermore, the data analysis showed a significant negative association between most adverse drug reactions and smoking status, hospital admission conditions, gender, ethnicity, and age of the included patients [83].

Among studies on the tolerability profile of LAI SGAs, six out of eight studies included patients under PP1M treatment. Most studies evidenced treatment-related adverse effects occurring in $\geq$5% of patients and mainly represented by pain in the injection site (2.3%), insomnia (8.6%), anxiety (6.7%), psychotic disorder (6.1%), headache (5.6%), weight increase (11.9%), and akathisia (11.1%) [67,68,70,71,73,75,78]. Instead, at each assessment point, no significant differences arose in blood pressure, glycemia, triglycerides, total cholesterol, and HDL cholesterol mean scores [71,84]. In the total patient population, 5.7% had a potentially prolactin-related adverse effect (prolactin elevation, amenorrhea/menstrual irregularity in female patients, galactorrhea, gynecomastia, erectile dysfunction, and decreased general sexual function in males) which greatly affected compliance to treatment [67,68,70,75,78,84]. Furthermore, when used at higher doses than standard ones ($\geq$175 mg Eq), PP1M showed a good tolerability profile [71].

The overall risk of bias for non-randomized clinical studies reporting the tolerability results of oral or LAI SGAs was moderate (6/11) and high (5/11).

4. Discussion

Overall, the real-world studies analyzed in the present review evidenced that SGAs effectiveness proved superior vs. FGAs, in terms of relapse-free survival, discontinuation rate, and psychiatric hospitalization rate. Furthermore, SGAs were likely superior to FGAs for treating negative symptoms.

On the contrary, RCT results showed that SGAs did not appear to have a better efficacy on negative symptoms than FGAs, although some other studies showed a good efficacy associated with a favorable side-effect profile [85–87]. The CATIE study evidenced that all APs had limitations. Therefore, 74% of patients discontinued their randomized treatment over 18 months due to inefficacy or intolerable side effects. Additionally, SGAs differed neither from each other nor from perphenazine (an FGA) concerning effectiveness or EPS. Several studies included in the present review compared SGAs prevalently to haloperidol, which has an increased propensity to cause drug-induced EPS. Accordingly, there was no evidence that SGAs were better for negative symptoms and cognitive deficits. Individual drugs differed in specific side effects. Olanzapine, for example, proved to be the most effective concerning discontinuation rate (64%), although causing the highest side-effect burden [26].

Furthermore, from studies examined in the present review, LAI APs appeared as the pharmacologic treatments with the highest prevention rates of relapse in patients with schizophrenia and related disorders. The risk of psychiatric rehospitalization was the lowest during monotherapy with once-monthly paliperidone LAI, zuclopenthixol, perphenazine, and olanzapine compared with no use of APs [44]. In addition, all LAI APs appeared to be associated with a lower risk of rehospitalization also when compared with the equivalent oral formulations (i.e., oral olanzapine) [44]. Switching from oral SGAs or FGAs to LAIs or APs polytherapy in early non-responders appeared beneficial for preventing treatment failure in hospitalized patients with acute schizophrenia [46,65]. Better relapse prevention and clinical stability were achieved by switching from one LAI to another when deemed necessary [65]. Finally, a more favorable tolerability profile was described in patients switching from oral aripiprazole to aripiprazole LAI [73]. Side effects, such as weight gain, EPS, those related to hyperprolactinemia, and sexual dysfunction, rarely emerged [71,78]. Overall, EPS were present only in patients > 35 years diagnosed with schizophrenia more than 5 years before.

Different long-term SGAs efficacy and tolerability patterns emerged prevalently from meta-analyses of RCTs, which indicated that: (1) regarding all-cause discontinuation, clozapine, olanzapine, and risperidone were significantly superior to several other SGAs, while quetiapine was inferior to several other SGAs [88,89]; (2) as to psychopathology, clozapine and olanzapine were superior to several other SGAs, while quetiapine and ziprasidone were inferior to several other SGAs [90,91]; (3) regarding intolerability-related discontinuation, risperidone was superior and clozapine inferior to several other SGAs [20,92,93]. Concerning weight gain, olanzapine was worse than all the other compared non-clozapine SGAs, and risperidone was significantly worse than several other SGAs. Regarding prolactin increase, risperidone and amisulpride were significantly worse than several other SGAs. Regarding parkinsonism, olanzapine was superior to risperidone, without significant differences about akathisia. Concerning sedation and somnolence, clozapine and quetiapine were significantly worse than a few other SGAs.

However, the apparent improvement in key clinical domains (e.g., negative symptoms) reported by meta-analyses may be largely attributable to improvements in a related clinical domain, such as positive symptoms or fewer AP-related side effects (e.g., EPS), a problem often referred to as pseudospecificity [94].

Our analysis evidenced that SGAs therapy persistence and adherence to treatment were higher than with FGAs. Furthermore, some studies concluded that switching to LAIs or APs polytherapy was associated with a lower treatment failure. In addition, general functionality, subjective well-being, global satisfaction, and improved personal and social performance were reported in patients treated with LAI formulations of SGAs (namely, PP1M and once-monthly aripiprazole LAI) when compared with the corresponding oral formulations.

Clozapine, as well, was associated with the lowest rates of treatment failure and greater efficacy vs. the other SGAs, despite being administered exclusively for intolerant and/or non-responder patients and presenting neurocognitive compromise (mainly reduced performance on attention and memory), plus an unfavorable metabolic and hematological adverse-event profile [83,95]. In the 99% of patients entering CATIE phase 2, clozapine also emerged as significantly more effective than the other SGAs, with a median time to discontinuation of 10 months, twice the length of the following best AP, namely olanzapine [96]. Thus, in both CATIE and CUtLASS studies, SGAs were not found to be more effective (except for olanzapine in CATIE) and did not produce measurably fewer EPS overall. Furthermore, clozapine was the most effective for treatment-resistant patients [26,27].

Among the real-world studies we analyzed, only a few reported on new SGAs, such as lurasidone and brexpiprazole. However, patients treated with lurasidone displayed greater adherence when compared to patients treated with other SGAs [60]. Furthermore, one study analyzed the efficacy of brexpiprazole, and no significant differences emerged when treated patients were compared with those treated with other SGAs [63].

No real-world studies on the effectiveness and tolerability outcomes of patients treated with cariprazine were retrieved by our literature search, although the FDA had approved the drug in 2015.

Most studies selected in this literature review present a few methodological limitations relating to the standard use of medical data from insurance companies, patient registries, administrative and healthcare claims database. Such limitations include no verification of the psychiatric diagnosis and treatments received, high polypharmacy rates, limited knowledge of earlier treatment conditions, and emerging side effects. Furthermore, these studies typically do not present measures of laboratory biological parameters, relying on surrogate markers for the presence of a disease (i.e., for diabetes, the prescription of a hypoglycemic agent, or an ICD code for diabetes). Furthermore, the heterogeneity of the studies conducted in different populations over several decades will likely introduce relevant biases. One of the significant limitations of some studies was the limited or absent control over the data collection quality, which reduced the internal validity of the results. Other potential biases may result from unmeasured confounders and insufficient statistical adjustment of confounders. In this respect, retrospective study data do not meet the criteria of reliability and accuracy required by the methodological rigor of RCTs.

5. Conclusions

The present review evidenced that SGAs demonstrated superior effectiveness over FGAs in relapse-free survival and psychiatric hospitalization rate and for treating negative symptoms, while no clear evidence emerged regarding the effectiveness on cognitive deficits. In addition, persistence and adherence to therapy were higher with SGAs than FGAs. Most studies concluded that switching to LAIs was significantly associated with a low treatment failure rate than monotherapy with oral SGAs. Significant improvements in general functionality, subjective well-being, and global satisfaction, besides improved personal and social performance, were reported in some studies on patients treated with LAI SGAs. Furthermore, considering safety and tolerability, our literature review suggests that in adult patients with schizophrenia and related disorders, there may be a lower association of weight gain and adverse metabolic effects with ziprasidone, aripiprazole, and some FGAs compared with olanzapine, clozapine, quetiapine, and risperidone.

Finally, it is crucial for the clinicians to be familiar with the various therapeutic options, not neglecting the old medications, which are still in use with acceptable effectiveness.

Supplementary Materials: The following supporting information can be downloaded at: https://www.mdpi.com/article/10.3390/jcm11154530/s1, Table S1: Risk of bias assessments in non-randomized clinical studies. Figure S1: Flow diagram showing study selection process of included articles.

Author Contributions: Conceptualization, M.F. and F.C.; methodology, M.F., S.C., A.C. and F.P.; software, S.C. and A.C.; validation, S.C. and A.C.; formal analysis, S.C.; investigation, M.F. and F.C.; resources, M.F., F.C. and F.P.; data curation, M.F., F.C. and F.P.; writing—original draft preparation, M.F.; writing—review and editing, M.F. and F.C.; visualization, A.C. and S.C.; supervision, F.C.; project administration, M.F.; funding acquisition, M.F. and F.C. All authors have read and agreed to the published version of the manuscript.

Funding: This research received no external funding.

Institutional Review Board Statement: Not applicable.

Informed Consent Statement: Not applicable.

Data Availability Statement: All data relevant to this paper are included in the article.

Acknowledgments: We would like to thank Marinella Simioli for her professional language and editing assistance.

Conflicts of Interest: The authors declare no conflict of interest.

References

1. Thornicroft, G.; Tansella, M.; Becker, T.; Knapp, M.; Leese, M.; Schene, A.; Vazquez-Barquero, J.L.; EPSILON Study Group. The personal impact of schizophrenia in Europe. *Schizophr. Res.* **2004**, *69*, 125–132. [CrossRef]
2. Abi-Dargham, A. Schizophrenia: Overview and dopamine dysfunction. *J. Clin. Psychiatry* **2014**, *75*, e31. [CrossRef] [PubMed]
3. Singh, S.P.; Javed, A.; on behalf of the WPA Expert International Advisory Panel for Early Intervention in Psychosis. Early intervention in psychosis in low- and middle-income countries: A WPA initiative. *World Psychiatry* **2020**, *19*, 122. [CrossRef]
4. Drake, R.E.; Xie, H.; McHugo, G.J. A 16-year follow-up of patients with serious mental illness and co-occurring substance use disorder. *World Psychiatry* **2020**, *19*, 397–398. [CrossRef] [PubMed]
5. Plana-Ripoll, O.; Musliner, K.L.; Dalsgaard, S.; Momen, N.C.; Weye, N.; Christensen, M.K.; Agerbo, E.; Iburg, K.M.; Laursen, T.M.; Mortensen, P.B.; et al. Nature and prevalence of combinations of mental disorders and their association with excess mortality in a population-based cohort study. *World Psychiatry* **2020**, *19*, 339–349. [CrossRef]

6. Green, M.F.; Lee, J.; Wynn, J.K. Experimental approaches to social disconnection in the general community: Can we learn from schizophrenia research? *World Psychiatry* **2020**, *19*, 177–178. [CrossRef]
7. Galderisi, S.; Rucci, P.; Mucci, A.; Rossi, A.; Rocca, P.; Bertolino, A.; Aguglia, E.; Amore, M.; Bellomo, A.; Bozzatello, P.; et al. The interplay among psychopathology, personal resources, context-related factors and real-life functioning in schizophrenia: Stability in relationships after 4 years and differences in network structure between recovered and non-recovered patients. *World Psychiatry* **2020**, *19*, 81–91. [CrossRef]
8. Kotov, R.; Jonas, K.G.; Carpenter, W.T.; Dretsch, M.N.; Eaton, N.R.; Forbes, M.K.; Forbush, K.T.; Hobbs, K.; Reininghaus, U.; Slade, T.; et al. HiTOP Utility Workgroup. Validity and utility of Hierarchical Taxonomy of Psychopathology (HiTOP): I. Psychosis superspectrum. *World Psychiatry* **2020**, *19*, 151–172. [CrossRef] [PubMed]
9. Menon, V. Brain networks and cognitive impairment in psychiatric disorders. *World Psychiatry* **2020**, *19*, 309–310. [CrossRef]
10. Moritz, S.; Silverstein, S.M.; Dietrichkeit, M.; Gallinat, J. Neurocognitive deficits in schizophrenia are likely to be less severe and less related to the disorder than previously thought. *World Psychiatry* **2020**, *19*, 254–255. [CrossRef] [PubMed]
11. Lysaker, P.H.; Hasson-Ohayon, I. Metacognition in psychosis: A renewed path to understanding of core disturbances and recovery-oriented treatment. *World Psychiatry* **2021**, *20*, 359–361. [CrossRef] [PubMed]
12. Lahey, B.B.; Moore, T.M.; Kaczkurkin, A.N.; Zald, D.H. Hierarchical models of psychopathology: Empirical support, implications, and remaining issues. *World Psychiatry* **2021**, *20*, 57–63. [CrossRef] [PubMed]
13. Jones, I. Postpartum psychosis: An important clue to the etiology of mental illness. *World Psychiatry* **2020**, *19*, 334–336. [CrossRef]
14. Maj, M.; van Os, J.; De Hert, M.; Gaebel, W.; Galderisi, S.; Green, M.F.; Guloksuz, S.; Harvey, P.D.; Jones, P.B.; Malaspina, D.; et al. The clinical characterization of the patient with primary psychosis aimed at personalization of management. *World Psychiatry* **2021**, *20*, 4–33. [CrossRef]
15. Gaebel, W.; Falkai, P.; Hasan, A. The revised German evidence- and consensus-based schizophrenia guideline. *World Psychiatry* **2020**, *19*, 117–119. [CrossRef]
16. McCutcheon, R.A.; Krystal, J.H.; Howes, O.D. Dopamine and glutamate in schizophrenia: Biology, symptoms and treatment. *World Psychiatry* **2020**, *19*, 15–33. [CrossRef]
17. Lasalvia, A.; Tansella, M. Young people at high risk for psychosis: Conceptual framework, research evidence and treatment opportunities. *Epidemiol. Psychiatr. Sci.* **2012**, *21*, 317–322. [CrossRef] [PubMed]
18. Patel, K.R.; Cherian, J.; Gohil, K.; Atkinson, D. Schizophrenia: Overview and treatment options. *Pharm. Ther.* **2014**, *39*, 638–645.
19. Egerton, A.; Grace, A.A.; Stone, J.; Bossong, M.G.; Sand, M.; McGuire, P. Glutamate in schizophrenia: Neu-rodevelopmental perspectives and drug development. *Schizophr. Res.* **2020**, *223*, 59–70. [CrossRef] [PubMed]
20. Leucht, S.; Cipriani, A.; Spineli, L.; Mavridis, D.; Orey, D.; Richter, F.; Samara, M.; Barbui, C.; Engel, R.R.; Geddes, J.R.; et al. Comparative efficacy and tolerability of 15 antipsychotic drugs in schizophrenia: A multiple-treatments meta-analysis. *Lancet* **2013**, *382*, 951–962. [CrossRef]
21. Kaar, S.J.; Natesan, S.; McCutcheon, R.; Howes, O.D. Antipsychotics: Mechanisms underlying clinical response and side-effects and novel treatment approaches based on pathophysiology. *Neuropharmacology* **2020**, *172*, 107704. [CrossRef] [PubMed]
22. Peluso, M.J.; Lewis, S.W.; Barnes, T.R.; Jones, P.B. Extrapyramidal motor side-effects of first- and second-generation antipsychotic drugs. *Br. J. Psychiatry* **2012**, *200*, 387–392. [CrossRef] [PubMed]
23. Üçok, A.; Gaebel, W. Side effects of atypical antipsychotics: A brief overview. *World Psychiatry* **2008**, *7*, 58–62. [CrossRef] [PubMed]
24. Taipale, H.; Tanskanen, A.; Mehtala, J.; Vattulainen, P.; Correll, C.U.; Tiihonen, J. 20-year follow-up study of physical morbidity and mortality in relationship to antipsychotic treatment in a nationwide cohort of 62,250 patients with schizophrenia (FIN20). *World Psychiatry* **2020**, *19*, 61–68. [CrossRef] [PubMed]
25. Fabrazzo, M.; Monteleone, P.; Prisco, V.; Perris, F.; Catapano, F.; Tortorella, A.; Monteleone, A.M.; Steardo, L.; Maj, M. Olanzapine is faster than haloperidol in inducing metabolic abnormalities in schizophrenic and bipolar patients. *Neuropsychobiology* **2015**, *72*, 29–36. [CrossRef] [PubMed]
26. Lieberman, J.A.; Stroup, T.S.; McEvoy, J.P.; Swartz, M.S.; Rosenheck, R.A.; Perkins, D.O.; Keefe, R.S.; Davis, S.M.; Davis, C.E.; Lebowitz, B.D.; et al. Clinical Antipsychotic Trials of Intervention Effectiveness (CATIE) Investigators. Effectiveness of antipsychotic drugs in patients with chronic schizophrenia. *N. Engl. J. Med.* **2005**, *353*, 1209–1223. [CrossRef] [PubMed]
27. Jones, P.B.; Barnes, T.R.; Davies, L.; Dunn, G.; Lloyd, H.; Hayhurst, K.P.; Murray, R.M.; Markwick, A.; Lewis, S.W. Randomized controlled trial of the effect on Quality of Life of second- vs. first-generation antipsychotic drugs in schizophrenia: Cost Utility of the Latest Antipsychotic Drugs in Schizophrenia Study (CUtLASS 1). *Arch. Gen. Psychiatry* **2006**, *63*, 1079–1087. [CrossRef] [PubMed]
28. Rybakowski, J.K.; Vansteelandt, K.; Remlinger-Molenda, A.; Fleischhacker, W.W.; Kahn, R.S.; Peuskens, J.; EUFEST Study Group. Extrapyramidal symptoms during treatment of first schizophrenia episode: Results from EUFEST. *Eur. Neuropsychopharmacol.* **2014**, *24*, 1500–1505. [CrossRef] [PubMed]
29. Kapur, S.; Remington, G. Atypical antipsychotics: Patients value the lower incidence of extrapyramidal side effects. *BMJ* **2001**, *321*, 1360–1361. [CrossRef] [PubMed]
30. Geddes, J.; Freemantle, N.; Harrison, P.; Bebbington, P.; for the National Schizophrenia Guideline Development Group. Atypical antipsychotics in the treatment of schizophrenia: Systematic overview and meta-regression analysis. *BMJ* **2001**, *321*, 1371–1376. [CrossRef] [PubMed]

31. Cuesta, M.J.; Sánchez-Torres, A.M.; de Jalón, E.G.; Campos, M.S.; Ibáñez, B.; Moreno-Izco, L.; Peralta, V. Spontaneous parkinsonism is associated with cognitive impairment in antipsychotic-naive patients with first-episode psychosis: A 6-month follow-up study. *Schizophr. Bull.* **2014**, *40*, 1164–1173. [CrossRef] [PubMed]
32. Fervaha, G.; Agid, O.; Takeuchi, H.; Lee, J.; Foussias, G.; Zakzanis, K.K.; Graff-Guerrero, A.; Remington, G. Extrapyramidal symptoms and cognitive test performance in patients with schizophrenia. *Schizophr. Res.* **2015**, *161*, 351–356. [CrossRef]
33. Demjaha, A.; Lappin, J.M.; Stahl, D.; Patel, M.X.; MacCabe, J.H.; Howes, O.D.; Heslin, M.; Reininghaus, U.A.; Donoghue, K.; Lomas, B.; et al. Antipsychotic treatment resistance in first-episode psychosis: Prevalence, subtypes and predictors. *Psychol. Med.* **2017**, *47*, 1981–1989. [CrossRef]
34. Emsley, R.; Chiliza, B.; Asmal, L.; Harvey, B.H. The nature of relapse in schizophrenia. *BMC Psychiatry* **2013**, *13*, 50. [CrossRef]
35. Lally, J.; Gaughran, F.; Timms, P.; Curran, S.R. Treatment-resistant schizophrenia: Current insights on the pharmacogenomics of antipsychotics. *Pharmgenomics Pers. Med.* **2016**, *9*, 117–129. [CrossRef] [PubMed]
36. Chekroud, A.M.; Bondar, J.; Delgadillo, J.; Doherty, G.; Wasil, A.; Fokkema, M.; Cohen, Z.; Belgrave, D.; DeRubeis, R.; Iniesta, R.; et al. The promise of machine learning in predicting treatment outcomes in psychiatry. *World Psychiatry* **2021**, *20*, 154–170. [CrossRef] [PubMed]
37. Carpenter, W.T. Primary psychosis: More to know, much more to do. *World Psychiatry* **2021**, *20*, 1–2. [CrossRef] [PubMed]
38. Higashi, K.; Medic, G.; Littlewood, K.J.; Diez, T.; Granström, O.; De Hert, M. Medication adherence in schizophrenia: Factors influencing adherence and consequences of nonadherence, a systematic literature review. *Ther. Adv. Psychopharmacol.* **2013**, *3*, 200–218. [CrossRef] [PubMed]
39. Crawford, M.J.; Thana, L.; Evans, R.; Carne, A.; O'Connell, L.; Claringbold, A.; Saravanamuthu, A.; Case, R.; Munjiza, J.; Jayacodi, S.; et al. Switching antipsychotic medication to reduce sexual dysfunction in people with psychosis: The REMEDY RCT. *Health Technol. Assess.* **2020**, *24*, 1–54. [CrossRef]
40. Lewis, S.; Lieberman, J. CATIE and CUtLASS: Can we handle the truth? *Br. J. Psychiatry* **2008**, *192*, 161–163. [CrossRef] [PubMed]
41. Kahn, R.S.; Fleischhacker, W.W.; Boter, H.; Davidson, M.; Vergouwe, Y.; Keet, I.P.; Gheorghe, M.D.; Rybakowski, J.K.; Galderisi, S.; Libiger, J.; et al. Effectiveness of antipsychotic drugs in first-episode schizophrenia and schizophreniform disorder: An open randomised clinical trial. *Lancet* **2008**, *371*, 1085–1097.
42. Boter, H.; Peuskens, J.; Libiger, J.; Fleischhacker, W.W.; Davidson, M.; Galderisi, S.; Kahn, R.S.; EUFEST study group. Effectiveness of antipsychotics in first-episode schizophrenia and schizophreniform disorder on response and remission: An open randomized clinical trial (EUFEST). *Schizophr. Res.* **2009**, *115*, 97–103. [CrossRef] [PubMed]
43. Fleischhacker, W.W.; Siu, C.O.; Bodén, R.; Pappadopulos, E.; Karayal, O.N.; Kahn, R.S.; EUFEST study group. Metabolic risk factors in first-episode schizophrenia: Baseline prevalence and course analysed from the European First-Episode Schizophrenia Trial. *Int. J. Neuropsychopharmacol.* **2013**, *16*, 987–995. [CrossRef] [PubMed]
44. De Hert, M.; Schreurs, V.; Sweers, K.; Van Eyck, D.; Hanssens, L.; Sinko, S.; Wampers, M.; Scheen, A.; Peuskens, J.; van Winkel, R. Typical and atypical antipsychotics differentially affect long-term incidence rates of the metabolic syndrome in first-episode patients with schizophrenia: A retrospective chart review. *Schizophr. Res.* **2008**, *101*, 295–303. [CrossRef] [PubMed]
45. Altamura, A.C.; Glick, I.D. Designing outcome studies to determine efficacy and safety of antipsychotics for 'real world' treatment of schizophrenia. *Int. J. Neuropsychopharmacol.* **2010**, *13*, 971–973. [CrossRef] [PubMed]
46. Palumbo, D.; Caporusso, E.; Piegari, G.; Mencacci, C.; Torriero, S.; Giuliani, L.; Fabrazzo, M.; Pinto, D.; Galderisi, S. Social Cognition Individualized Activities Lab for Social Cognition Training and Narrative Enhancement in Patients With Schizophrenia: A Randomized Controlled Study to Assess Efficacy and Generalization to Real-Life Functioning (Prot. n°: NCT05130853). *Front. Psychiatry* **2022**, *13*, 833550. [CrossRef] [PubMed]
47. Sabe, M.; Pillinger, T.; Kaiser, S.; Chen, C.; Taipale, H.; Tanskanen, A.; Tiihonen, J.; Leucht, S.; Correll, C.U.; Solmi, M. Half a century of research on antipsychotics and schizophrenia: A scientometric study of hotspots, nodes, bursts, and trends. *Neurosci. Biobehav. Rev.* **2022**, *36*, 104608. [CrossRef] [PubMed]
48. Anglemyer, A.; Horvath, H.T.; Bero, L. Healthcare outcomes assessed with observational study designs compared with those assessed in randomized trials. *Cochrane Database Syst. Rev.* **2014**, *2014*, MR000034. [CrossRef] [PubMed]
49. Liberati, A.; Altman, D.G.; Tetzlaff, J.; Mulrow, C.; Gøtzsche, P.C.; Ioannidis, J.P.; Clarke, M.; Devereaux, P.J.; Kleijnen, J.; Moher, D.L. The PRISMA statement for reporting systematic reviews and meta-analyses of studies that evaluate healthcare interventions: Explanation and elaboration. *BMJ* **2009**, *339*, b2700. [CrossRef] [PubMed]
50. Sterne, J.A.C.; Hernán, M.A.; McAleenan, A.; Reeves, B.C.; Higgins, J.P.T. Chapter 25: Assessing risk of bias in a non-randomized study. In *Cochrane Handbook for Systematic Reviews of Interventions Version 6.1*; Higgins, J.P.T., Thomas, J., Chandler, J., Cumpston, M., Li, T., Page, M.J., Welch, V.A., Eds.; John Wiley & Sons: New York, NY, USA, 2020; Available online: www.training.cochrane.org/handbook (accessed on 1 June 2022).
51. Taylor, M.; Turner, M.; Watt, L.; Brown, D.; Martin, M.; Fraser, K. Atypical anti-psychotics in the real world—A naturalistic comparative outcome study. *Scott. Med. J.* **2005**, *50*, 102–106. [CrossRef]
52. Ritsner, M.S.; Yorkov, V.; Ratner, Y.; Soifer, P.; Gibel, A. The effectiveness of ziprasidone in treating impaired quality of life in schizophrenia: A 12-month, open-label, flexible-dose, naturalistic observational study of patients undergoing usual care. *Prog. Neuropsychopharmacol. Biol. Psychiatry* **2007**, *31*, 1470–1477. [CrossRef] [PubMed]

53. Ratner, Y.; Gibel, A.; Yorkov, V.; Ritsner, M.S. Effectiveness, safety, and tolerability of ziprasidone for treating schizophrenia patients undergoing usual care: A 12-month, open-label, flexible-dose, naturalistic observational trial. *Prog. Neuropsychopharmacol. Biol. Psychiatry* **2007**, *31*, 1401–1409. [CrossRef] [PubMed]
54. Kilzieh, N.; Todd-Stenberg, J.A.; Kennedy, A.; Wood, A.E.; Tapp, A.M. Time to discontinuation and self-discontinuation of olanzapine and risperidone in patients with schizophrenia in a naturalistic outpatient setting. *J. Clin. Psychopharmacol.* **2008**, *28*, 74–77. [CrossRef] [PubMed]
55. Cortesi, P.A.; Mencacci, C.; Luigi, F.; Pirfo, E.; Berto, P.; Sturkenboom, M.C.; Lopes, F.L.; Giustra, M.G.; Mantovani, L.G.; Scalone, L. Compliance, persistence, costs and quality of life in young patients treated with antipsychotic drugs: Results from the COMETA study. *BMC Psychiatry* **2013**, *13*, 98. [CrossRef]
56. Novick, D.; Montgomery, W.; Treuer, T.; Moneta, M.V.; Haro, J.M. Real-world Effectiveness of Antipsychotics for the Treatment of Negative Symptoms in Patients with Schizophrenia with Predominantly Negative Symptoms. *Pharmacopsychiatry* **2017**, *50*, 56–63. [CrossRef] [PubMed]
57. Vanasse, A.; Blais, L.; Courteau, J.; Cohen, A.A.; Roberge, P.; Larouche, A.; Grignon, S.; Fleury, M.J.; Lesage, A.; Demers, M.F.; et al. Comparative effectiveness and safety of antipsychotic drugs in schizophrenia treatment: A real-world observational study. *Acta Psychiatr.Scand.* **2016**, *134*, 374–384. [CrossRef]
58. Misawa, F.; Suzuki, T.; Fujii, Y. Effect of Clozapine vs. Other Second-Generation Antipsychotics on Hospitalization and Seclusion: A Retrospective Mirror-Image Study in a Japanese Public Psychiatric Hospital. *J. Clin. Psychopharmacol.* **2017**, *37*, 664–668. [CrossRef] [PubMed]
59. Tiihonen, J.; Mittendorfer-Rutz, E.; Majak, M.; Mehtälä, J.; Hoti, F.; Jedenius, E.; Enkusson, D.; Leval, A.; Sermon, J.; Tanskanen, A.; et al. Real-World Effectiveness of Antipsychotic Treatments in a Nationwide Cohort of 29 823 Patients With Schizophrenia. *JAMA Psychiatry* **2017**, *74*, 686–693. [CrossRef]
60. Rajagopalan, K.; Wade, S.; Meyer, N.; Loebel, A. Real-world adherence assessment of lurasidone and other oral atypical antipsychotics among patients with schizophrenia: An administrative claims analysis. *Curr. Med. Res. Opin.* **2017**, *33*, 813–820. [CrossRef] [PubMed]
61. Zhang, L.; Li, Y.G.; He, S.; Zhang, Y.; Yu, Y.M.; Li, Y.; Wen, H.; Qiao, Y.; Shen, Y.F.; Li, H.F. Quantitative efficacy of three antipsychotic drugs for schizophrenia based on a real-world study in China. *Acta Pharmacol. Sin.* **2019**, *40*, 1611–1620. [CrossRef] [PubMed]
62. Stam, N.; Taipale, H.; Tanskanen, A.; Isphording, L.; Okhuijsen-Pfeifer, C.; Schuiling-Veninga, C.C.M.; Bos, J.H.J.; Bijker, B.J.; Tiihonen, J.; Luykx, J.J. Persistence of Antipsychotic Use After Clozapine Discontinuation: A Real-World Study Across Antipsychotics. *Clin. Transl. Sci.* **2020**, *13*, 1170–1177. [CrossRef]
63. Yan, T.; Greene, M.; Chang, E.; Houle, C.R.; Waters, H.C.; Tarbox, M.H.; Broder, M.S. Health Care Cost in Patients With Schizophrenia Treated With Brexpiprazole Versus Other Oral Atypical Antipsychotic Therapy. *Clin. Ther.* **2020**, *42*, 77–93. [CrossRef] [PubMed]
64. Barbosa, W.B.; Gomes, R.M.; Godman, B.; Acurcio, F.A.; Guerra Júnior, A.A. Real-world effectiveness of olanzapine and risperidone in the treatment of schizophrenia in Brazil over a 16-year follow-up period; findings and implications. *Expert. Rev. Clin. Pharmacol.* **2021**, *14*, 269–279. [CrossRef]
65. Hatta, K.; Katayama, S.; Ishizuka, T.; Sudo, Y.; Nakamura, M.; Hasegawa, H.; Imai, A.; Morikawa, F.; Shimada, T.; Misawa, F.; et al. Real-world effectiveness of antipsychotic treatments in 1011 acutely hospitalized patients with schizophrenia: A one-year follow-up study. *Asian J. Psychiatr.* **2022**, *67*, 102917. [CrossRef] [PubMed]
66. Fernández-Miranda, J.J.; Díaz-Fernández, S.; López-Muñoz, F. Oral Versus Long-Acting Injectable Antipsychotic Treatment for People With Severe Schizophrenia: A 5-Year Follow-up of Effectiveness. *J. Nerv. Ment. Dis.* **2021**, *209*, 330–335. [CrossRef] [PubMed]
67. Schreiner, A.; Bergmans, P.; Cherubin, P.; Keim, S.; Rancans, E.; Bez, Y.; Parellada, E.; Carpiniello, B.; Vidailhet, P.; Hargarter, L. A prospective flexible-dose study of paliperidone palmitate in nonacute but symptomatic patients with schizophrenia previously unsuccessfully treated with oral antipsychotic agents. *Clin. Ther.* **2014**, *36*, 1372–1388. [CrossRef] [PubMed]
68. Hargarter, L.; Cherubin, P.; Bergmans, P.; Keim, S.; Rancans, E.; Bez, Y.; Parellada, E.; Carpiniello, B.; Vidailhet, P.; Schreiner, A. Intramuscular long-acting paliperidone palmitate in acute patients with schizophrenia unsuccessfully treated with oral antipsychotics. *Prog. Neuropsychopharmacol. Biol. Psychiatry* **2015**, *58*, 1–7. [CrossRef]
69. Chan, H.W.; Huang, C.Y.; Feng, W.J.; Yen, Y.C. Risperidone long-acting injection and 1-year rehospitalization rate of schizophrenia patients: A retrospective cohort study. *Psychiatry Clin. Neurosci.* **2015**, *69*, 497–503. [CrossRef] [PubMed]
70. Alphs, L.; Benson, C.; Cheshire-Kinney, K.; Lindenmayer, J.P.; Mao, L.; Rodriguez, S.C.; Starr, H.L. Real-world outcomes of paliperidone palmitate compared to daily oral antipsychotic therapy in schizophrenia: A randomized, open-label, review board-blinded 15-month study. *J. Clin. Psychiatry* **2015**, *76*, 554–561. [CrossRef] [PubMed]
71. Fernández-Miranda, J.J.; Díaz-Fernández, S. Tolerability of effective high doses of paliperidone palmitate in patients with severe resistant schizophrenia. *Int. Clin. Psychopharmacol.* **2017**, *32*, 6–12. [CrossRef] [PubMed]
72. Pilon, D.; Tandon, N.; Lafeuille, M.H.; Kamstra, R.; Emond, B.; Lefebvre, P.; Joshi, K. Treatment Patterns, Health Care Resource Utilization, and Spending in Medicaid Beneficiaries Initiating Second-generation Long-acting Injectable Agents Versus Oral Atypical Antipsychotics. *Clin. Ther.* **2017**, *39*, 1972–1985. [CrossRef]

73. Schöttle, D.; Janetzky, W.; Luedecke, D.; Beck, E.; Correll, C.U.; Wiedemann, K. Effectiveness of aripiprazole once-monthly in schizophrenia patients pretreated with oral aripiprazole: A 6-month, real-life non-interventional study. *BMC Psychiatry* **2018**, *18*, 365.
74. Patel, C.; El Khoury, A.; Huang, A.; Wang, L.; Baser, O.; Joshi, K. Health Outcomes Among Patients Diagnosed with Schizophrenia in the US Veterans Health Administration Population Who Transitioned from Once-Monthly to Once-Every-3-Month Paliperidone Palmitate: An Observational Retrospective Analysis. *Adv. Ther.* **2019**, *36*, 2941–2953. [CrossRef] [PubMed]
75. Devrimci-Ozguven, H.; Atmaca, M.; Baran, Z.; Cengisiz, C.; Çinar, C.; Erol, A.; Genç, Y.; Karadağ, H.; Karakülah, K.; Karasu, U.; et al. Efficacy and Safety of Paliperidone Palmitate Treatment in Patients With Schizophrenia: A Real-World Multicenter, Retrospective, Mirror-Image Study. *J. Clin. Psychopharmacol.* **2019**, *39*, 604–610. [CrossRef] [PubMed]
76. Takács, P.; Czobor, P.; Fehér, L.; Gimesi-Országh, J.; Fadgyas-Freyler, P.; Bacskai, M.; Rakonczai, P.; Borsi, A.; Hegyi, R.; Németh, T.; et al. Comparative effectiveness of second generation long-acting injectable antipsychotics based on nationwide database research in Hungary. *PLoS ONE* **2019**, *14*, e0218071. [CrossRef]
77. Fagiolini, A.; Aguglia, E.; Ballerini, A.; Callista, G.; Carpiniello, B.; Clerici, M.; Corrivetti, G.; De Fazio, P.; De Filippis, S.; De Giorgi, S.; et al. Real-world effectiveness of long acting aripiprazole: Treatment persistence and its correlates in the Italian clinical practice. *Psychiatry Res.* **2019**, *272*, 698–706. [CrossRef]
78. Fernández-Miranda, J.J.; Díaz-Fernández, S.; López-Muñoz, F. High Doses of Second-Generation Long-Acting Antipsychotics in the Treatment of Patients with Severe Resistant Schizophrenia: A Six-Year Mirror-Image Study. *Psychiatr. Clin. Psychopharmacol.* **2020**, *30*, 335–345.
79. Magliocco, F.; de Filippis, R.; Aloi, M.; Staltari, F.A.; Gaetano, R.; Segura-Garcia, C.; De Fazio, P. Second-generation long-acting injections anti-psychotics improve executive functions in patients with schizophrenia: A 12-month real-world study. *Int. J. Psychiatry Clin. Pract.* **2020**, *24*, 201–207. [CrossRef]
80. Iwata, N.; Inagaki, A.; Sano, H.; Niidome, K.; Kojima, Y.; Yamada, S. Treatment Persistence Between Long-Acting Injectable Versus Orally Administered Aripiprazole Among Patients with Schizophrenia in a Real-World Clinical Setting in Japan. *Adv. Ther.* **2020**, *37*, 3324–3336. [CrossRef] [PubMed]
81. Lauriello, J.; Weiden, P.J.; Gleeson, C.D.; Shah, A.; Boulanger, L.; Jariwala-Parikh, K.; Hedgeman, E.; O'Sullivan, A.K. Real-World Outcomes and Costs Following 6 Months of Treatment with the Long-Acting Injectable (LAI) Aripiprazole Lauroxil for the Treatment of Schizophrenia. *CNS Drugs* **2021**, *35*, 1123–1135. [CrossRef]
82. Mahabaleshwarkar, R.; Lin, D.; Fishman, J.; Blair, T.; Hetherington, T.; Palmer, P.; Patel, C.; Benson, C.; Joshi, K.; Krull, C.; et al. The Impact of Once-Monthly Paliperidone Palmitate on Healthcare Utilization Among Patients With Schizophrenia Treated in an Integrated Healthcare System: A Retrospective Mirror-Image Study. *Adv. Ther.* **2021**, *38*, 1958–1974. [CrossRef] [PubMed]
83. Iqbal, E.; Govind, R.; Romero, A.; Dzahini, O.; Broadbent, M.; Stewart, R.; Smith, T.; Kim, C.H.; Werbeloff, N.; MacCabe, J.H.; et al. The side effect profile of Clozapine in real world data of three large mental health hospitals. *PLoS ONE* **2020**, *15*, e0243437. [CrossRef] [PubMed]
84. Rosso, G.; Pessina, E.; Martini, A.; Di Salvo, G.; Maina, G. Paliperidone Palmitate and Metabolic Syndrome in Patients With Schizophrenia: A 12-Month Observational Prospective Cohort Study. *J. Clin. Psychopharmacol.* **2016**, *36*, 206–212. [CrossRef] [PubMed]
85. Möller, H.J.; Czobor, P. Pharmacological treatment of negative symptoms in schizophrenia. *Eur. Arch. Psychiatry Clin. Neurosci.* **2015**, *265*, 567–578. [CrossRef]
86. Prisco, V.; Iannaccone, T.; Tusciano, A.; Boccardi, M.; Perris, F.; Capuano, A.; Catapano, F.; Fabrazzo, M. Safety warning dei farmaci in psichiatria: Segnalazioni di reazioni avverse ai farmaci dal 2002 al 2014 [Drug safety warnings in psychiatry: Adverse drug reactions' signaling from 2002 to 2014]. *Riv. Psichiatr.* **2016**, *51*, 96–103.
87. Fabrazzo, M.; Fuschillo, A.; Perris, F.; Catapano, F. The unmasking of hidden severe hyponatremia after long-term combination therapy in exacerbated bipolar patients: A case series. *Int. Clin. Psychopharmacol.* **2019**, *34*, 206–210. [CrossRef] [PubMed]
88. Leucht, S.; Tardy, M.; Komossa, K.; Heres, S.; Kissling, W.; Salanti, G.; Davis, J.M. Antipsychotic drugs versus placebo for relapse prevention in schizophrenia: A systematic review and meta-analysis. *Lancet* **2012**, *379*, 2063–2071. [CrossRef]
89. Kishimoto, T.; Agarwal, V.; Kishi, T.; Leucht, S.; Kane, J.M.; Correll, C.U. Relapse prevention in schizophrenia: A systematic review and meta-analysis of second-generation antipsychotics versus first-generation antipsychotics. *Mol. Psychiatry* **2013**, *18*, 53–66. [CrossRef]
90. Leucht, S.; Arbter, D.; Engel, R.R.; Kissling, W.; Davis, J.M. How effective are second-generation antipsychotic drugs? A meta-analysis of placebo-controlled trials. *Mol. Psychiatry* **2009**, *14*, 429–447. [CrossRef]
91. Kishimoto, T.; Hagi, K.; Nitta, M.; Leucht, S.; Olfson, M.; Kane, J.M.; Correll, C.U. Effectiveness of Long-Acting Injectable vs Oral Antipsychotics in Patients With Schizophrenia: A Meta-analysis of Prospective and Retrospective Cohort Studies. *Schizophr. Bull.* **2018**, *44*, 603–619. [CrossRef] [PubMed]
92. Kishimoto, T.; Hagi, K.; Nitta, M.; Kane, J.M.; Correll, C.U. Long-term effectiveness of oral second-generation antipsychotics in patients with schizophrenia and related disorders: A systematic review and meta-analysis of direct head-to-head comparisons. *World Psychiatry* **2019**, *18*, 208–224. [CrossRef]
93. Wagner, E.; Siafis, S.; Fernando, P.; Falkai, P.; Honer, W.G.; Röh, A.; Siskind, D.; Leucht, S.; Hasan, A. Efficacy and safety of clozapine in psychotic disorders-a systematic quantitative meta-review. *Transl. Psychiatry* **2021**, *11*, 487. [CrossRef]

94. Hopkins, S.C.; Ogirala, A.; Loebel, A.; Koblan, K.S. Understanding Antipsychotic Drug Treatment Effects: A Novel Method to Reduce Pseudospecificity of the Positive and Negative Syndrome Scale (PANSS) Factors. *Innov. Clin. Neurosci.* **2017**, *14*, 54–58.
95. Fabrazzo, M.; Prisco, V.; Sampogna, G.; Perris, F.; Catapano, F.; Monteleone, A.M.; Maj, M. Clozapine versus other antipsychotics during the first 18 weeks of treatment: A retrospective study on risk factor increase of blood dyscrasias. *Psychiatry Res.* **2017**, *256*, 275–282. [CrossRef] [PubMed]
96. Swartz, M.S.; Stroup, T.S.; McEvoy, J.P.; Davis, S.M.; Rosenheck, R.A.; Keefe, R.S.; Hsiao, J.K.; Lieberman, J.A. What CATIE found: Results from the schizophrenia trial. *Psychiatr. Serv.* **2008**, *59*, 500–506. [CrossRef]

Journal of
Clinical Medicine

MDPI

Article

Impaired Effort Allocation in Patients with Recent-Onset Schizophrenia and Its Relevance to Negative Symptoms Assessments and Persistent Negative Symptoms

Ezgi Ince Guliyev [1,*], Sinan Guloksuz [2,3] and Alp Ucok [4]

1 Department of Psychiatry, Erenkoy Training and Research Hospital for Mental and Neurological Diseases, University of Health Sciences, Istanbul 34736, Turkey
2 Department of Psychiatry and Neuropsychology, Maastricht University Medical Centre, 6202 Maastricht, The Netherlands
3 Department of Psychiatry, Yale School of Medicine, New Haven, CT 06510, USA
4 Department of Psychiatry, Faculty of Medicine, Istanbul University, Istanbul 34093, Turkey
* Correspondence: ezgi.ince@yahoo.com

Abstract: (1) Background: Our aims in this study were (i) to compare effort allocation capacity measured between patients with recent-onset schizophrenia (SCZ) and healthy controls (HCs), (ii) within the SCZ, to investigate the association of effort allocation capacity with negative symptoms (NS), and (iii) to compare this association with the type of NS scale used. (2) Methods: Thirty-one patients with SCZ and 30 HCs participated in the study. The NS was examined using an older-generation (Scale for the Assessment of Negative Symptoms, SANS), a newer-generation (Brief Negative Symptoms Scale, BNSS), and a self-rated (Self-evaluation of Negative Symptoms Scale, SNS) negative symptom scale, as well as longitudinally by using persistent NS (PNS) distinction. (3) Results: The SCZ group was less willing to expend effort in high/moderate-probability and -magnitude conditions but more in low-probability and -magnitude conditions. A general reduction in effort allocation capacity was also present. Patients with PNS were less likely to choose hard tasks than non-PNS patients. Clinician-rated scales correlated with 50% probability and moderate-reward-magnitude conditions. Correlations with the SNS were minimal. (4) Conclusions: Our findings suggest that patients with SCZ may show a general reduction in effort allocation capacity and make inefficient choices, although they are not totally reward-insensitive. The effects of NS on effort expenditure can be more pronounced when the rewarding stimulus is vague.

Keywords: effort expenditure; negative symptoms; recent-onset schizophrenia; persistent negative symptoms; motivation

Citation: Ince Guliyev, E.; Guloksuz, S.; Ucok, A. Impaired Effort Allocation in Patients with Recent-Onset Schizophrenia and Its Relevance to Negative Symptoms Assessments and Persistent Negative Symptoms. *J. Clin. Med.* **2022**, *11*, 5060. https://doi.org/10.3390/jcm11175060

Academic Editor: Nuri B. Farber

Received: 3 August 2022
Accepted: 27 August 2022
Published: 28 August 2022

1. Background

Negative symptoms (NS) are core features of schizophrenia (SCZ), which appear in the early stages and may persist significantly throughout the disease process [1]. They are linked to poor functional and treatment outcomes [2] and represent an unmet therapeutic need [3]. Studies showed that more than half of the individuals with SCZ have at least one NS [4,5]. Among them, motivational deficits have been consistently associated with functional or vocational impairments [6–9]. Despite their frequency and the burden they impose on patients' lives, there are still challenges in identifying and conceptualizing motivation deficits [10,11].

Several behavioral paradigms based on reward processing mechanisms have been proposed to identify and conceptualize motivation deficits in patients with SCZ [12–14]. Among these, the paradigms related to effort–cost computation [15], which measure how much physical effort an individual is willing to exert to obtain varying magnitudes of reward, stand out with a more solid translational neuroscientific background [16]. Current evidence suggests that individuals with SCZ show impairments in effort allocation for rewards compared to healthy controls (HC), which means they are failing to maximize their reward by not choosing the high-effort options when the reward magnitude or probability of getting the reward is higher [17–24]. Only a few studies reported otherwise [25].

Studies examining the relationship between inefficient effort allocation and NS produced inconsistent findings. For example, there are studies reporting a negative correlation between NS measured by clinical scales and effort-based decision making paradigm performances [21,23,26–28], supporting the hypothesis that patients with more NS exert less effort to obtain a reward. However, some studies found only a negative trend-level correlation [19], a positive correlation [20], or no correlation [18,22,24,25,29–31] between NS and effort allocation capacity. NS was also investigated categorically in studies that found differences in effort expenditure performances across high- and low-NS groups [24,28,31]. Only one study considered the endurance of NS, and they found a group difference in the effort allocation between the deficit syndrome and non-deficit syndrome [29]. To our knowledge, no study has investigated effort-based decision-making differences in SCZ patients employing the proposed persistent negative symptoms (PNS) criteria [32].

A closer examination of mixed results reveals methodological differences between these studies. For example, task performances were sometimes correlated with NS total score [19,30], but sometimes with amotivation score [20,27]. Moreover, some studies used an older-generation scale [19,21,24,30], while others used a newer-generation scale such as the Clinical Assessment Interview for Negative Symptoms (CAINS) or the Brief Negative Symptoms Scale (BNSS) [20,22,31] or a scale specific to apathy or anhedonia [21,23,24,30]. Very few studies evaluated self-report NS [22,29]. Selection of the NS scale is particularly important as the conceptualization of NS has evolved since the development of earlier scales, and different scales might reflect/cover different aspects of the NS construct, although correlated in validation studies [1,33]. In fact, a recently published European Psychiatric Association (EPA) guidance on the assessment of NS recommended against the use of older-generation scales alone and supported the inclusion of newer-generation and self-report scales to better evaluate the experiential domains [33]. There is also no consensus on the measures of the task performance. The most consistently used ones were the rate of hard task choice in the high-reward-magnitude or high-probability trials, but other parameters were also present. The majority of the studies were conducted with chronic SCZ, which increases the likelihood of confounding factors. In fact, only one study included subjects with first-episode psychosis [24].

As it is hypothetically expected that effort motivation has a strong relationship with NS, assessments of NS and choice of the parameter that represents the effort task may have a role in these conflicting results. Therefore, in this study, we aimed to investigate effort-based decision-making in patients with recent-onset SCZ compared to HC using the Effort Expenditure for Reward Task (EEfRT) [15]. We also examined the association of NS with effort allocation capacity using an older-generation (Scale for the Assessment of Negative Symptoms, SANS), a newer-generation (BNSS), and a self-rated (Self-Evaluation of Negative Symptoms Scale, SNS) NS scale, as well as longitudinally by using PNS distinction. Lastly, we aimed to compare this association with the type of NS scale used.

2. Materials and Methods

2.1. Participants

Participants of the study were 31 patients with recent-onset SCZ recruited from Istanbul University Faculty of Medicine, Department of Psychiatry, and 30 healthy volunteers matched in terms of age, gender, and education year recruited through advertisements in the local communities. Inclusion criteria for the SCZ group were a diagnosis of SCZ according to DSM-5, clinical stabilization with antipsychotics for at least 3 months, illness duration of fewer than 5 years, age > 18, and consent to participate. Participants with a history of substance abuse in the past year, intellectual disability, a neurological disorder, or a health condition that might compromise the evaluation process or course of disease were excluded. For the HC group, in addition to the above exclusion criteria, current psychiatric diagnosis, lifelong diagnosis of psychotic disorder, and family history of psychotic disorders were also sought. Patients were also excluded if they were stabilized with a first-generation antipsychotic to minimize extrapyramidal or secondary symptoms. All patients were using second-generation antipsychotics in both interviews. Olanzapine equivalent doses were calculated according to Leucht et al. [34].

The authors assert that all procedures contributing to this work comply with the ethical standards of the relevant national and institutional committees on human experimentation and with the Helsinki Declaration of 1975, as revised in 2008. All procedures involving human subjects were approved by the Clinical Research Ethics Committee of Istanbul University Faculty of Medicine (approval number 1032). All adult participants provided written informed consent to participate in this study.

2.2. Clinical and Cognitive Measures

NS patients were evaluated with the BNSS [35,36], SANS [37,38], and SNS [39,40]. A categorical approach for assessing NS was also considered using the criteria proposed by Buchanan for the Persistent Negative Symptoms (PNS) [32]. Accordingly, patients with at least moderate levels of NS persisting for at least 6 months with no or mild levels of positive, depressive, and extrapyramidal symptoms were categorized into the PNS group. In this study, the persistence of NS was assessed with BNSS. To measure other symptom domains, we used the Scale for the Assessment of Positive Symptoms (SAPS) [41,42], Calgary Depression Scale for Schizophrenia (CDSS) [43,44], and Extrapyramidal Symptoms Rating Scale (ESRS) [45]. The level of psychosocial functioning was evaluated with the Personal and Social Performance Scale (PSP) [46,47]. The Brief Cognitive Assessment Tool for Schizophrenia (B-CATS) comprising Trail Making Test-B [48], Category Fluency [49], and Digit Symbol Substitution [50] tests was administered to both groups to determine their cognitive functions [51]. All clinical and cognitive assessment tools have been translated into and validated for Turkish, except for ESRS. All clinical assessments, except for the cognitive battery and the Effort Expenditure for the Rewards Task (EEfRT), were performed at two timepoints at least 6 months apart. The mean interval between the two interviews was 10.32 (2.56) months.

2.3. Effort Expenditure for the Rewards Task (EEfRT)

EEfRT is a computer-based behavioral paradigm developed by Treadway et al. that assesses effort-based decision making by measuring how much physical effort individuals exert to obtain varying amounts of monetary rewards [15]. EEfRT was programmed in the Inquisit Millisecond software package 5 (https://www.millisecond.com/download/, accessed on 2 June 2019) and administered using Inquisit Player. In order to be consistent with the previous literature, we did not make any changes to the task. The original task consists of consecutive trials that require participants to choose between two difficulty levels ("hard task" and "easy task"). In each trial, participants are given the option to choose between easy and hard tasks. To complete the easy task, the participant had to press the specified key of the computer 30 times in succession with the index finger of the active hand within 7 s. A fixed 1 TRY was offered for each easy task. To complete the difficult task, the participant had to press the specified key of the computer 100 times in a row with the pinky finger of his passive hand within 21 s. Reward amounts ranging from 1.24 TRY to 4.30 TRY were offered for each difficult task. The amount of reward offered for the hard task differed in each trial, and, at the start of the trial, the participant was shown how much reward was provided for the hard task in that trial. There were three different probability levels for receiving the reward after successful completion of each trial: 88%, 50%, and 12%. These probability levels varied from trial to trial, and the level applicable to that trial applied to hard and easy tasks. There were equal proportions of tasks from all probability levels throughout the experiment. Probability levels were evenly distributed over the rewards for difficult tasks. All participants were offered the same randomized order of challenge reward amount. All trials began with a 5 s selection period, during which participants were shown the amount of reward they could earn for easy and difficult tasks, and the probability of winning the reward for that trial was shown. After the task was completed, a feedback screen appeared for 2 s, reporting whether the participant had completed the task or not. Then, if the participant had successfully completed the task, a second 2 s feedback screen appeared, stating whether the person was given the reward in that trial and, if so, how much reward money was given. At the beginning of the task, all participants were given instructions on how to play the task, and four test trials were completed. They were offered a fixed payment for their participation, plus additional payment depending on their performance on the task. Participants had 20 min to complete the entire task.

2.4. Statistical Analysis

The EEfRT was evaluated considering the percentage of total hard task selection across different probability (88%, 50%, and 12%) and reward magnitude levels (low, medium, and high). The reward magnitude was divided into three categories: low reward 1.24–2 TL, medium reward 2.01–3 TL, and high reward 3.01–4.12 TL. A 2 (group: SCZ and HC or PNS vs. non-PNS) × 3 (reward probability: 88%, 50%, and 12%) × 3 (reward magnitude: high, medium, and low reward) repeated-measures analysis of variance (ANOVA) test was used to investigate the main effects and interactions of probability level, reward magnitude, and diagnostic group on participants' hard task choices. In the repeated-measures ANOVA test, the percentage of choosing the difficult task was the independent variable. Probability and reward levels, the dependent variables, were assigned as within-subject factors; and the diagnosis group was assigned as a between-subject factor. In cases where sphericity could not be achieved in factors with three levels, the Greenhouse–Geisser correction was applied.

Pearson or Spearman correlation tests were used to analyze the association of clinical measurements with EEfRT performance, depending on the normality of the distribution as assessed by the Shapiro–Wilk test. The composite cognitive scores were calculated by averaging *z*-scores of individual cognitive tests. Then, *z*-scores were standardized on the basis of the cognitive scores of HC. Although the mean hard task selection rate in 88% probability trials, the mean hard task selection rate in high reward trials, the difference in hard task selection rate between 88% and 12% trials, and the difference in hard task selection rates of high and low reward trials were frequently used in the literature [15,19–21,23,24,29,52], due to the exploratory nature of this study, we used the mean hard task selection rate in all conditions including all levels of reward probability and reward magnitude. The statistical significance level was set at $p < 0.05$. Statistical analyses were performed using the IBM SPSS (Statistical Package for Social Sciences) program version 21.0 (IBM, Armonk, NY, USA).

A priori power analyses were conducted using G*Power Software version 3.1.9.6. (University of Kiel, Kiel, Germany) to determine the minimum sample size [53]. A total of forty participants were required for repeated-measures ANOVA with two groups and nine (3 × 3) measurements to achieve 80% power for detecting an effect size of 0.15 at 0.05 significance. As for correlations, 67 participants were required to achieve 80% power for detecting an effect size of 0.3 at 0.05 significance.

3. Results

3.1. Sociodemographic Variables

The groups did not differ in age, gender, or marital status, but there was a significant difference in education ($t = 2.269$; $p = 0.027$). The pairwise comparisons of sociodemographic and clinical variables between the study groups are presented in Table 1.

Table 1. Sociodemographic, cognitive, and clinical characteristics.

	SCZ (n = 31)	HC (n = 30)	Test Statistics (t, χ^2)	p-Value	PNS (+) (n = 13)	PNS (−) (n = 18)	Test Statistics (t, χ^2)	p-Value
Sociodemographic characteristics								
Age, years	25.45 (5.46)	26.00 (2.44)	0.503	0.614	23.30 (4.8)	26.63 (5.55)	1.746	0.091
Gender, % female	8 (25.8)	8 (26.7)	0.006	0.939	2 (15.4)	6 (33.3)	0.412	0.242
Education, years	12.32 (3.00)	13.83 (2.10)	2.269	0.027 *	11.00 (2.70)	13.21 (2.83)	2.203	0.035 *
Cognitive assessment								
TMT-B	119.21 (63.96)	60.25 (21.24)	4.061	<0.001 *	153.45 (72.73)	97.66 (46.28)	2.278	0.038 *
CFT	15.60 (3.17)	22.48 (3.87)	7.275	<0.001 *	14.09 (6.94)	16.57 (3.22)	2.223	0.035 *
DSST	55.85 (19.61)	87.50 (14.09)	6.933	<0.001 *	47.72 (61.50)	19.10 (18.12)	1.946	0.062
Clinical characteristics								
Age at onset, years	22.71 (5.5)	-	-	-	20.46 (4.33)	23.94 (5.87)	1.824	0.078
Duration of illness, years	2.93 (1.19)	-	-	-	3.07 (1.32)	2.78 (1.08)	0.674	0.505
OLZ equivalent doses, mg	17.07 (7.88)	-	-	-	21.86 (7.32)	13.9 (6.55)	3.150	0.004 *

* $p < 0.05$. CFT, Category Fluency Test; DSST, Digit Symbol Substitution Test; HC, healthy controls; OLZ, olanzapine; PNS, persistent negative symptoms; SCZ, schizophrenia; TMT-B, Trail Making Test-B.

3.2. Results of SCZ vs. HC Comparison

In the EEfRT, the SCZ group chose the hard task in 31.13% of all trials (SD = 10.98), whereas HCs chose the hard task in 38.37% of all trials (SD = 10.34). None of the participants had a percentage of choosing the total difficult task above 90% or below 10%. No significant difference was observed in total trials attempted (SCZ: mean = 71.93, SD = 10.36; HC: mean = 75.53, SD = 7.80; t = 1.503; p = 0.134), but patients with SCZ completed significantly fewer trials compared to HCs (SCZ: mean = 63.93, SD = 9.49; HC: mean = 74.80, SD = 8.01; t = 3.593; p = 0.001). There was no significant difference in mean reaction time between the two groups (SCZ: mean = 2271.37, SD = 547.76; HC: mean = 2074.60, SD = 360.59; t = 1.635; p = 0.111).

3.2.1. Main Effects

The repeated-measures ANOVA test indicated a statistically significant main effect of the group (F(1;50) = 10.801; p = 0.002; $p\eta^2$ = 0.076), with SCZ engaged in overall less effortful choices compared to HC. Furthermore, the main effects of the reward probability (F(1.6;98) = 99.451; p = 0.0005; $p\eta^2$ = 0.628) and the reward magnitude (F(1.4;86.2) = 166.47; p = 0.0005; $p\eta^2$ = 0.738) were significant, which means that, overall, participants' likelihood of choosing the hard task increased as the level of reward probability and reward magnitude increased.

3.2.2. Group Effects and Interactions

The group × reward probability interaction was statistically significant (F(1.66;98) = 16.192; p = 0.0001; $p\eta^2$ = 0.215). Post hoc comparisons revealed that the SCZ group chose the hard task more in the 12% probability level compared to HC (F(1;59) = 9.337; p = 0.003; $p\eta^2$ = 0.137), whereas HCs made more hard task choices compared to SCZ in the 88% and 50% probability levels (F(1;59) = 18.922; p = 0.0001; $p\eta^2$ = 0.243 and F(1;59) = 5.388; p = 0.024; $p\eta^2$ = 0.084, respectively). In both groups, the percentage of choosing the hard task increased as the reward probability increased (Figure 1). That is, the percentage of choosing the hard task was significantly different in the 12% to 50% (p = 0.002 in SCZ; p = 0.0005 in HC) and 50% to 88% comparisons (p = 0.0005 in SCZ; p = 0.0005 in HC) in both groups.

The group × reward magnitude interaction was also significant (F(1.46;86.21) = 19.861; p = 0.0005; $p\eta^2$ = 0.252). Post hoc comparisons revealed that SCZ group made significantly more hard task choices in the low-reward-magnitude trials compared to HCs (F(1;59) = 5.715; p = 0.02; $p\eta^2$ = 0.088), whereas HCs made more effortful choices in the medium- and high-reward-magnitude trials compared to the SCZ group (F(1;59) = 4.937;

$p = 0.03$; $p\eta^2 = 0.077$ and F(1;59) = 24.336; $p = 0.0005$; $p\eta^2 = 0.292$, respectively). In both groups, the percentage of choosing the hard task increased as the reward magnitude increased. That is, the percentage of choosing the hard task was significantly different in comparisons of low to medium reward magnitude ($p = 0.0001$ in SCZ; $p = 0.0001$ in HC) and medium to high magnitude ($p = 0.0001$ in SCZ; $p = 0.0001$ in HC) in both groups. The group × reward probability × reward magnitude interaction was also statistically significant (F(2;100) = 1.693; $p = 0.189$; $p\eta^2 = 0.109$).

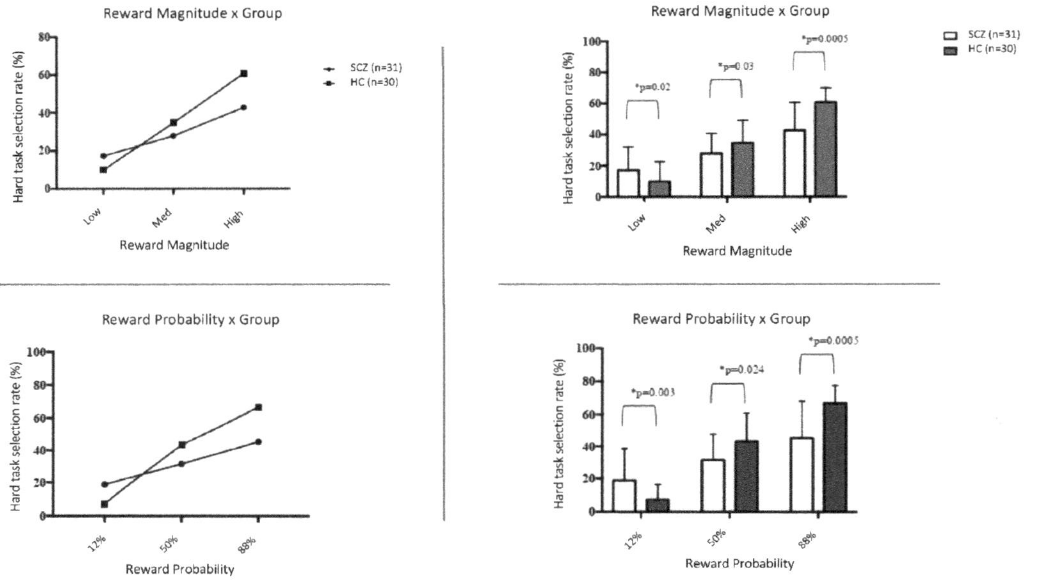

Figure 1. The proportions of hard task selection across patient groups in different reward probability and reward magnitude conditions. * Significance level at $p < 0.05$.

3.3. *The Association of Effort Allocation Capacity with NS*

3.3.1. Results of PNS vs. Non-PNS Comparison

Comparisons of the sociodemographic and clinical features of the patient groups can be found in Table 2. Patients with PNS attempted slightly more trials compared to patients without PNS ($t = 2.389$, $p = 0.024$). Nevertheless, there was no difference between the patient groups in the total number of trials completed ($t = 1.547$, $p = 0.133$). Overall, the patients with PNS chose the hard task in 25.06% (SD = 10.76) of the trials, whereas HCs chose the hard task in 35.52% (SD = 9.08) of the trials. The mean reaction time did not differ between the patient groups (PNS: mean = 2163.47 SD = 514.76; non-PNS: mean = 2347.53, SD = 572.72; $t = 0.888$; $p = 0.374$).

There were significant main effects of the group (F(1;25) = 11.108; $p = 0.002$; $p\eta^2 = 0.277$), reward probability F(1.43;41.71) = 11.817; $p = 0.0001$; $p\eta^2 = 0.290$), and reward magnitude (F(1.29;37.42) = 26.454; $p = 0.0001$; $p\eta^2 = 0.477$) in the repeated-measures ANOVA analysis. However, there were no significant group × reward probability, group × reward magnitude, or three-way interactions.

3.3.2. Correlations of EEfRT Performances with NS

Correlations with the NS total scores and motivation and pleasure (MAP) subdomain scores are presented in Table 3. The BNSS total score was significantly negatively correlated with the total rate of hard task selection, hard task selection rate at 50% reward probability, and hard task selection rate at medium reward magnitude. The SANS total score and the

SNS total score were significantly correlated with the hard task selection rate at 50% reward probability, with the direction of correlation being negative and positive, respectively.

Table 2. Mean clinical scale scores and their comparisons between patients with and without PNS.

	SCZ ($n = 31$)	PNS(+) ($n = 13$)	PNS(−) ($n = 18$)	Test Statistics (t)	p-Value
BNSS					
BNSS Total	38.82 (15.90)	44.53 (8.21)	29.00 (11.91)	4.298	<0.0001 *
BNSS MAP	28.04 (10.10)	29.38 (5.14)	19.11 (8.35)	4.145	<0.0001 *
BNSS ED	10.82 (7.52)	12.00 (5.35)	8.11 (4.59)	2.091	0.047
SANS					
SANS Total	47.81 (18.93)	52.41 (12.10)	38.50 (14.43)	2.752	0.010 *
SANS MAP	27.32 (8.76)	33.00 (4.61)	23.22 (8.82)	4.001	<0.0001 *
SANS ED	16.77 (8.74)	19.75 (9.19)	14.77 (8.07)	1.563	0.129
SNS					
SNS Total	24.78 (8.26)	17.84 (6.68)	27.68 (7.35)	3.853	0.001 *
SNS MAP	14.84 (5.29)	11.61 (4.25)	17.05 (4.84)	3.271	0.003 *
SNS ED	9.88 (3.27)	8.75 (3.46)	10.9 (2.81)	1.727	0.098
SAPS	12.0	12.0 (12.44)	9.16 (8.06)	0.719	0.481
CDSS	1.33 (1.09)	2.53 (3.01)	1.72 (1.56)	0.983	0.334
ESRS	6.33 (4.67)	7.38 (3.30)	5.77 (3.07)	1.391	0.175
PSP	46.25 (16.03)	40.76 (15.52)	51.38 (14.83)	1.929	0.064

* $p < 0.05$. BNSS, Brief Negative Symptoms Scale; CDSS, Calgary Depression Scale for Schizophrenia; ED, expressive deficits; EEfRT, Effort Expenditure for the Rewards Task; ESRS; Extrapyramidal Symptoms Rating Scale; MAP, motivation and pleasure deficits; NS, negative symptoms; PNS, persistent negative symptoms; PSP, Personal and Social Performance Scale; SANS, Scale for the Assessment of Negative Symptoms; SAPS, Scale for the Assessment of Positive Symptoms; SCZ, schizophrenia; SNS, Self-Evaluation of Negative Symptoms Scale.

Table 3. Correlations of EEfRT performance measures with different negative symptoms scale scores.

Variables	88%	50%	12%	High Reward	Mid Reward	Low Reward
NS Total Scores						
BNSS	−0.313	−0.497 **	−0.191	−0.309	−0.528 **	−0.184
SANS	−0.325	−0.368 *	−0.032	−0.253	−0.352	−0.055
SNS	0.051	0.360 *	0.132	0.102	0.284	0.086
MAP Subdomain						
BNSS	−0.434 *	−0.477 **	−0.152	−0.250	−0.462 *	−0.163
SANS	−0.258	−0.496 **	−0.030	−0.357	−0.453 *	−0.068
SNS	−0.102	0.245	0.138	0.007	0.093	−0.032

* $p < 0.05$, ** $p < 0.01$. BNSS, Brief Negative Symptoms Scale; EEfRT, Effort Expenditure for the Rewards Task; MAP, motivation and pleasure deficits; NS, negative symptoms; SANS, Scale for the Assessment of Negative Symptoms; SNS, Self-Evaluation of Negative Symptoms Scale.

As for the correlations with the MAP subdomains, MAP subdomains of BNSS and SANS were significantly negatively correlated with the total rate of hard task selection and hard task selection rate at 50% reward probability. Additionally, the BNSS MAP subdomain was negatively correlated with the hard task selection rate at 88% and hard task selection rate in medium-reward conditions, whereas SANS MAP was negatively correlated with the hard task selection rate in the medium-reward condition. The MAP subdomain of SNS did not correlate with any EEfRT performance measures. No correlations were observed with the difference-score analyses (Supplementary Table S1).

3.4. Correlations with Other Clinical Parameters

No significant correlations were observed between any EEfRT measures and SAPS, CDSS, ESRS, and mean antipsychotic doses (Supplementary Table S2). Significant positive correlations were found between the composite cognition score and the total rate of hard task selection ($r = 0.406$, $p = 0.032$) and hard task selection rate at medium-reward levels ($r = 0.382$, $p = 0.045$). The PSP score was also positively correlated with the hard task selection rate at 50% ($r = 0.394$; $p = 0.031$).

4. Discussion

4.1. Main Findings

This study investigated effort-based decision-making differences between patients with recent-onset SCZ and HC. Furthermore, we examined the relationship between the effort allocation capacity and NS both continuously by using different NS scales and categorically by using the PNS distinction. Our findings suggested that patients with SCZ showed a general reduction in effort allocation for monetary rewards compared to HC, which was more pronounced in high- and moderate-probability and -magnitude trials. Secondly, we found that the NS, particularly amotivation, negatively correlated with effort expenditure when the magnitude of the reward and the possibility of getting the reward were moderate. Thirdly, patients with PNS showed a more significant reduction in effort allocation compared to patients without PNS.

4.2. SCZ vs. HC Comparison

When the participants' choices under different conditions were examined in detail, we found that, while the reward magnitude and probability levels were medium and high, patients with SCZ chose the difficult task at a lower rate than HC. This difference between the two groups was especially evident when the reward magnitude and probability levels were highest. Unlike studies revealing reduced effort allocation only when the reward magnitude and probability were higher [23,24,31], we also observed a general reduction in the proportion of high-effort trials in patients with recent-onset SCZ compared to HC. Examples of such a group difference also exist in the literature [20,30]. In addition, we observed that patients with SCZ chose the hard task more often than HC in the low-probability and -magnitude trials, as also found in some previous studies. [19–21,24]. In other words, patients with SCZ preferred the easy task with low reward more in trials where it would be advantageous to exert more effort, but the hard task in trials where effort was expected to be strategically minimized. Overall, adding to the evidence in the literature, these findings suggest that patients with SCZ both have a general reduction in effort capacity and make inefficient choices in terms of effort allocation. It is important to note that, in our study, the percentage of choosing the hard task increased significantly with the increasing amount of reward and the probability of winning a reward in both groups. There are studies in the literature that found this trend only in HC [20]. However, the fact that the increase in the tendency to choose the hard task with the increase in the magnitude of rewards that can be won and the probability of winning the reward has also been observed in SCZ may indicate two possibilities. The first one is that the patients did not make arbitrary choices and were able to understand and apply the rules of the EEfRT task. The second one is that the reward valuation may at least partially be spared in SCZ as the patients were responsive to increasing levels of reward yet still were willing to exert less effort than HC. In line with this, a relatively preserved value-guided decision-making was found in previous studies [54].

4.3. Association of Effort Allocation Capacity with NS

One of the main aims of the present study was to investigate the relationship between effort allocation and NS using different types of NS assessments (old- vs. new-generation scales; clinician vs. self-report; cross-sectional vs. longitudinal assessment) and different EEfRT performances. Interestingly, apart from SNS-MAP, all scales and MAP subscales were correlated with hard task selection rate in medium-reward-magnitude and/or medium-reward-probability conditions. Only the MAP domain of BNSS was associated with the high-probability condition, whereas none of the NS scales or subscales correlated with the high-reward-magnitude, low-reward-magnitude, or low-reward-probability conditions.

These findings may indicate that patients exhibit effort-related attitudes independent of NS in situations where it is more certain whether a reward will be obtained or not. Similarly, a rewarding stimulus of very high or very low potency may reduce the impact of NS on effort-based decision making. However, the more moderate precision and potency of the stimulus may cause people with NS to perform differently than those without NS. In the literature, very few studies considered moderate-level trials as a performance parameter [21,22]. Fervaha et al. (2013) found that apathy was significantly correlated to hard task selection rate in high-reward (50%) trials [21]. Additionally, similar to NS, there was a positive correlation between functioning and effort expenditure only in the 50% probability condition, which is in line with previous research that found an association between functioning and various EEfRT parameters [23,24,26]. It is known that NS, especially motivation/pleasure deficits, are closely related to functioning [6,7]. Overall, our results may indicate that, despite NS, sufficiently high-potency stimuli may trigger reward responses in people with schizophrenia. However, further studies investigating the effort-based attitudes in response to vague rewarding stimuli in patients with NS and functioning are needed.

As far as we know, this is the first study to evaluate effort-based decision making in the context of a longitudinal evaluation of NS in SCZ. Our results suggested that patients with PNS were less willing to exert effort than patients without PNS. Fervaha et al. (2015) also found a group-level difference in EEfRT performance between patients with and without deficit syndrome [29]. A critical difference was that the evaluation of persistence was cross-sectional and retrospective in the DS assessment, whereas it was prospective in the PNS assessment [55].

4.4. Comparisons of Different NS Measurements

In the comparison of NS scales, there was a clear difference between the scores of self-report and clinician-rated scales, as correlations between self-report scales and EEfRT parameters were very limited. This also supports a recent meta-analysis comparing self-reported, clinician-rated, and performance-based motivation measures in SCZ, although only two studies were included in the self-report vs. performance-based measure comparison [56]. On the other hand, in our study, none of the clinician-rated scales vastly outperformed the other. Overall, the correlations between the clinician-rated scale scores and EEfRT performance measures were low to medium. However, BNSS demonstrated a slightly more consistent association with effort allocation capacity, with more correlations (including one with high probability conditions) and more robust correlation coefficients for total scores compared to SANS. This difference was less pronounced in the correlations conducted with MAP subdomains. Conceptually, new-generation scales, which were developed after the NIMH-MATRICS Consensus Statement, provide a more detailed assessment of amotivation by separating internal experience from behavior and including aspects such as anticipatory and consummatory pleasure. In the literature, no correlation was found between SANS and EEfRT task measures [21,23,24], except for a trend-level association when covarying for medication dose [19]. Plus, there is an equal number of studies that did [27,28] and did not [25,57] find correlations with SANS in cognitive or physical effort exertion tasks other than EEfRT. We observed correlations between SANS and EEfRT scores only when the rewarding stimuli were vague. This may be due to the fact that other studies generally did not include correlations with medium-level conditions. The EEfRT studies that used BNSS were relatively few. In one study, BNSS and SANS were merged to obtain composite scores of avolition and anhedonia correlated with reward magnitude and probability differences [23]. Strauss et al. (2021) found a correlation between BNSS total and MAP subdomain scores and effort expenditure in the very-high-reward-magnitude condition in individuals at clinical high risk for psychosis [52]. In studies conducted with other cognitive or physical effort tasks and using BNSS, NS patients were found to be significantly associated with effort performance when considered continuous or categorical variables [27,31,58,59]. There was also a cognitive effort study in which no correlation was found when BNSS was used [57]. Another new-generation scale, CAINS, was also used in effort-based decision-making paradigms and resulted in significant correlations with task performances [20,26,60], although one study reported otherwise [22]. Putting all these together, the use of new-generation scales may enable a more accurate evaluation of NS in relation to effort-based decision making.

4.5. Strengths, Limitations, and Future Recommendations

The present study had some strengths. First, we recruited patients with recent-onset SCZ to reduce the confounding effects of the chronicity of the disease and prolonged medication exposure, which may have affected the effort allocation process. Secondly, we extensively investigated NS including different types of scales and a temporal approach by considering PNS. Furthermore, to minimize the secondary negative symptoms, we only included patients using second-generation antipsychotic medications. There were several limitations of the study that should be considered. Firstly, the sample size was small, especially after dividing the group with respect to their PNS statuses. Increasing the sample size would have increased the statistical power. Plus, we did not apply a correction for multiple comparisons because it was too restrictive considering the sample size. Future studies with more samples could use such corrections. Secondly, our participants were not medication-free. Although we only included patients on second-generation antipsychotics and did not find an association with medication dose, a possible contribution of antipsychotic medication cannot be excluded. Thirdly, the patient group was slightly less educated than HC, which is an expected phenomenon considering the diagnosis could impair the education process. Furthermore, in line with the original study, we did not individually calibrate the number of button presses during the EEfRT task. This might have led to lower task completion rates in individuals with motor impairments. However, Barch et al. (2014) demonstrated that the easy or hard task selection process was independent of finger tapping speed [23]. Regarding measurement tools, ESRS has not yet been validated in the Turkish language. Additionally, future studies could implement more direct measurement methods such as ecological momentary assessments (EMAs). Although the small number of existing studies regarding EEfRT and EMA gave contradictory findings [22,61], novel digital phenotyping methods can be promising in terms of effort expenditure research in patients with SCZ [62].

5. Conclusions

Our findings contribute to the existing literature suggesting that patients with SCZ may show a general reduction in effort allocation capacity and make inefficient choices in terms of effort allocation, although they are not totally reward-insensitive. The effects of NS on effort expenditure can be more pronounced in situations where the probability or the magnitude of the effort is moderate. Future studies are needed to evaluate the relationship among the real-life correspondences of NS, effort expenditure for the rewards, and reward valuation.

Supplementary Materials: The following supporting information can be downloaded at: https://www.mdpi.com/article/10.3390/jcm11175060/s1, Table S1. Correlations of EEfRT difference measures with different negative symptoms scale scores. Table S2. Correlations of EEfRT performance measures with other clinical measures.

Author Contributions: E.I.G., S.G. and A.U. conceptualized the study and contributed to its design. E.I.G. and A.U. were included in the data collection process. E.I.G. conducted the literature review, managed the data, performed the statistical analysis, and drafted the manuscript. A.U. and S.G. contributed to the interpretation of the data. All authors have read and agreed to the published version of the manuscript.

Funding: This research received no external funding.

Institutional Review Board Statement: The study was conducted in accordance with the Declaration of Helsinki, and approved by the Clinical Research Ethics Committee of Istanbul University Faculty of Medicine (date: August 2019; number 1032).

Informed Consent Statement: Informed consent was obtained from all subjects involved in the study.

Data Availability Statement: The data that support the findings of this study are available from the corresponding author (E.I.G.) upon reasonable request.

Acknowledgments: We would like to thank all participants who volunteered in the study.

Conflicts of Interest: The authors declare no conflict of interest.

References

1. Galderisi, S.; Mucci, A.; Buchanan, R.W.; Arango, C. Negative Symptoms of Schizophrenia: New Developments and Unanswered Research Questions. *Lancet Psychiatry* **2018**, *5*, 664–677.
2. Milev, P.; Ho, B.C.; Arndt, S.; Andreasen, N.C. Predictive Values of Neurocognition and Negative Symptoms on Functional Outcome in Schizophrenia: A Longitudinal First-Episode Study with 7-Year Follow-Up. *Am. J. Psychiatry* **2005**, *162*, 495–506. [CrossRef]
3. Correll, C.U.; Schooler, N.R. Negative Symptoms in Schizophrenia: A Review and Clinical Guide for Recognition, Assessment, and Treatment. *Neuropsychiatr. Dis. Treat.* **2020**, *16*, 519–534.
4. Bobes, J.; Arango, C.; Garcia-Garcia, M.; Rejas, J. Prevalence of Negative Symptoms in Outpatients with Schizophrenia Spectrum Disorders Treated with Antipsychotics in Routine Clinical Practice: Findings from the CLAMORS Study. *J. Clin. Psychiatry* **2009**, *70*, 15446. [CrossRef]
5. Lyne, J.; O'Donoghue, B.; Owens, E.; Renwick, L.; Madigan, K.; Kinsella, A.; Clarke, M.; Turner, N.; O'Callaghan, E. Prevalence of Item Level Negative Symptoms in First Episode Psychosis Diagnoses. *Schizophr. Res.* **2012**, *135*, 128–133. [CrossRef]
6. Foussias, G.; Remington, G. Negative Symptoms in Schizophrenia: Avolition and Occam's Razor. *Schizophr. Bull.* **2010**, *36*, 359–369. [CrossRef]
7. Fervaha, G.; Foussias, G.; Agid, O.; Remington, G. Amotivation and Functional Outcomes in Early Schizophrenia. *Psychiatry Res.* **2013**, *210*, 665–668. [CrossRef]
8. Strauss, G.P.; Horan, W.P.; Kirkpatrick, B.; Fischer, B.A.; Keller, W.R.; Miski, P.; Buchanan, R.W.; Green, M.F.; Carpenter, W.T. Deconstructing Negative Symptoms of Schizophrenia: Avolition-Apathy and Diminished Expression Clusters Predict Clinical Presentation and Functional Outcome. *J. Psychiatr. Res.* **2013**, *47*, 783–790. [CrossRef]
9. Galderisi, S.; Rossi, A.; Rocca, P.; Bertolino, A.; Mucci, A.; Bucci, P.; Rucci, P.; Gibertoni, D.; Aguglia, E.; Amore, M.; et al. The Influence of Illness-Related Variables, Personal Resources and Context-Related Factors on Real-Life Functioning of People with Schizophrenia. *World Psychiatry* **2014**, *13*, 275–287. [CrossRef]
10. Sicras-Mainar, A.; Maurino, J.; Ruiz-Beato, E.; Navarro-Artieda, R. Impact of Negative Symptoms on Healthcare Resource Utilization and Associated Costs in Adult Outpatients with Schizophrenia: A Population-Based Study. *BMC Psychiatry* **2014**, *14*, 225. [CrossRef]
11. Marder, S.R.; Galderisi, S. The Current Conceptualization of Negative Symptoms in Schizophrenia. *World Psychiatry* **2017**, *16*, 14–24. [CrossRef]
12. Barch, D.M.; Dowd, E.C. Goal Representations and Motivational Drive in Schizophrenia: The Role of Prefrontal-Striatal Interactions. *Schizophr. Bull.* **2010**, *36*, 919–934. [CrossRef]
13. Kring, A.M.; Elis, O. Emotion Deficits in People with Schizophrenia. *Annu. Rev. Clin. Psychol.* **2013**, *9*, 409–433. [CrossRef]
14. Kring, A.M.; Barch, D.M. The Motivation and Pleasure Dimension of Negative Symptoms: Neural Substrates and Behavioral Outputs. *Eur. Neuropsychopharmacol.* **2014**, *24*, 725–736. [CrossRef]
15. Treadway, M.T.; Buckholtz, J.W.; Schwartzman, A.N.; Lambert, W.E.; Zald, D.H. Worth the "EEfRT"? The Effort Expenditure for Rewards Task as an Objective Measure of Motivation and Anhedonia. *PLoS ONE* **2009**, *4*, e6598. [CrossRef]
16. Markou, A.; Salamone, J.D.; Bussey, T.J.; Mar, A.C.; Brunner, D.; Gilmour, G.; Balsam, P. Measuring Reinforcement Learning and Motivation Constructs in Experimental Animals: Relevance to the Negative Symptoms of Schizophrenia. *Neurosci. Biobehav. Rev.* **2013**, *37*, 2149–2165.
17. Green, M.F.; Horan, W.P.; Barch, D.M.; Gold, J.M. Effort-Based Decision Making: A Novel Approach for Assessing Motivation in Schizophrenia. *Schizophr. Bull.* **2015**, *41*, 1035–1044. [CrossRef]
18. Reddy, L.F.; Horan, W.P.; Barch, D.M.; Buchanan, R.W.; Dunayevich, E.; Gold, J.M.; Lyons, N.; Marder, S.R.; Treadway, M.T.; Wynn, J.K.; et al. Effort-Based Decision-Making Paradigms for Clinical Trials in Schizophrenia: Part 1-Psychometric Characteristics of 5 Paradigms. *Schizophr. Bull.* **2015**, *41*, 1045–1054. [CrossRef]
19. Treadway, M.T.; Peterman, J.S.; Zald, D.H.; Park, S. Impaired Effort Allocation in Patients with Schizophrenia. *Schizophr. Res.* **2015**, *161*, 382–385. [CrossRef]
20. McCarthy, J.M.; Treadway, M.T.; Bennett, M.E.; Blanchard, J.J. Inefficient Effort Allocation and Negative Symptoms in Individuals with Schizophrenia. *Schizophr. Res.* **2016**, *170*, 278–284. [CrossRef]
21. Fervaha, G.; Graff-Guerrero, A.; Zakzanis, K.K.; Foussias, G.; Agid, O.; Remington, G. Incentive Motivation Deficits in Schizophrenia Reflect Effort Computation Impairments during Cost-Benefit Decision-Making. *J. Psychiatr. Res.* **2013**, *47*, 1590–1596. [CrossRef]

22. Moran, E.K.; Culbreth, A.J.; Barch, D.M. Ecological Momentary Assessment of Negative Symptoms in Schizophrenia: Relationships to Effort-Based Decision Making and Reinforcement Learning. *J. Abnorm. Psychol.* **2017**, *126*, 96–105. [CrossRef]
23. Barch, D.M.; Treadway, M.T.; Schoen, N. Effort, Anhedonia, and Function in Schizophrenia: Reduced Effort Allocation Predicts Amotivation and Functional Impairment. *J. Abnorm. Psychol.* **2014**, *123*, 387–397. [CrossRef]
24. Chang, W.C.; Chu, A.O.K.; Treadway, M.T.; Strauss, G.P.; Chan, S.K.W.; Lee, E.H.M.; Hui, C.L.M.; Suen, Y.N.; Chen, E.Y.H. Effort-Based Decision-Making Impairment in Patients with Clinically-Stabilized First-Episode Psychosis and Its Relationship with Amotivation and Psychosocial Functioning. *Eur. Neuropsychopharmacol.* **2019**, *29*, 629–642. [CrossRef]
25. Docx, L.; De La Asuncion, J.; Sabbe, B.; Hoste, L.; Baeten, R.; Warnaerts, N.; Morrens, M. Effort Discounting and Its Association with Negative Symptoms in Schizophrenia. *Cogn. Neuropsychiatry* **2015**, *20*, 172–185. [CrossRef]
26. Horan, W.P.; Felice Reddy, L.; Barch, D.M.; Buchanan, R.W.; Dunayevich, E.; Gold, J.M.; Marder, S.R.; Wynn, J.K.; Young, J.W.; Green, M.F. Effort-Based Decision-Making Paradigms for Clinical Trials in Schizophrenia: Part 2-External Validity and Correlates. *Schizophr. Bull.* **2015**, *41*, 1055–1065. [CrossRef]
27. Hartmann, M.N.; Hager, O.M.; Reimann, A.V.; Chumbley, J.R.; Kirschner, M.; Seifritz, E.; Tobler, P.N.; Kaiser, S. Apathy but Not Diminished Expression in Schizophrenia Is Associated with Discounting of Monetary Rewards by Physical Effort. *Schizophr. Bull.* **2015**, *41*, 503–512. [CrossRef]
28. Serper, M.; Payne, E.; Dill, C.; Portillo, C.; Taliercio, J. Allocating Effort and Anticipating Pleasure in Schizophrenia: Relationship with Real World Functioning. *Eur. Psychiatry* **2017**, *46*, 57–64. [CrossRef]
29. Fervaha, G.; Duncan, M.; Foussias, G.; Agid, O.; Faulkner, G.E.; Remington, G. Effort-Based Decision Making as an Objective Paradigm for the Assessment of Motivational Deficits in Schizophrenia. *Schizophr. Res.* **2015**, *168*, 483–490. [CrossRef]
30. Huang, J.; Yang, X.H.; Lan, Y.; Zhu, C.Y.; Liu, X.Q.; Wang, Y.F.; Cheung, E.F.C.; Xie, G.R.; Chan, R.C.K. Neural Substrates of the Impaired Effort Expenditure Decision Making in Schizophrenia. *Neuropsychology* **2016**, *30*, 685–696. [CrossRef]
31. Gold, J.M.; Strauss, G.P.; Waltz, J.A.; Robinson, B.M.; Brown, J.K.; Frank, M.J. Negative Symptoms of Schizophrenia Are Associated with Abnormal Effort-Cost Computations. *Biol. Psychiatry* **2013**, *74*, 130–136. [CrossRef]
32. Buchanan, R.W. Persistent Negative Symptoms in Schizophrenia: An Overview. *Schizophr. Bull.* **2007**, *33*, 1013–1022. [CrossRef]
33. Galderisi, S.; Mucci, A.; Dollfus, S.; Nordentoft, M.; Falkai, P.; Kaiser, S.; Giordano, G.M.; Vandevelde, A.; Nielsen, M.Ø.; Glenthøj, L.B.; et al. EPA Guidance on Assessment of Negative Symptoms in Schizophrenia. *Eur. Psychiatry* **2021**, *64*, 1–91. [CrossRef]
34. Leucht, S.; Samara, M.; Heres, S.; Davis, J.M. Dose Equivalents for Antipsychotic Drugs: The DDD Method. *Schizophr. Bull.* **2016**, *42*, S90–S94. [CrossRef]
35. Kirkpatrick, B.; Strauss, G.P.; Nguyen, L.; Fischer, B.A.; Daniel, D.G.; Cienfuegos, A.; Marder, S.R. The Brief Negative Symptom Scale: Psychometric Properties. *Schizophr. Bull.* **2011**, *37*, 300–305. [CrossRef]
36. Polat Nazlı, I.; Ergül, C.; Aydemir, Ö.; Chandhoke, S.; Üçok, A.; Gönül, A.S. Validation of Turkish Version of Brief Negative Symptom Scale. *Int. J. Psychiatry Clin. Pract.* **2016**, *20*, 265–271. [CrossRef]
37. Andreasen, N.C. The Scale for the Assessment of Negative Symptoms (SANS): Conceptual and Theoretical Foundations. *Br. J. Psychiatry* **1989**, *155*, 49–52. [CrossRef]
38. Erkoç, Ş.; Arkonac, O.; Atakli, C.; Ozmen, E. Negatif Semptomları Değerlendirme Ölçeğinin Güvenilirliği ve Geçerliliği. *Düsünen Adam* **1991**, *4*, 14–15.
39. Dollfus, S.; Mach, C.; Morello, R. Self-Evaluation of Negative Symptoms: A Novel Tool to Assess Negative Symptoms. *Schizophr. Bull.* **2016**, *42*, 571–578. [CrossRef]
40. Polat, I.; Ince Guliyev, E.; Elmas, S.; Karakaş, S.; Aydemir, Ö.; Üçok, A. Validation of the Turkish Version of the Self-Evaluation of Negative Symptoms Scale (SNS). *Int. J. Psychiatry Clin. Pract.* **2022**. [CrossRef]
41. Andreasen, N.C. *Scale for the Assessment of Positive Symptoms (SAPS)*; University of Iowa: Iowa City, IA, USA, 1984.
42. Erkoç, Ş.; Arkonac, O.; Atakli, C.; Ozmen, E. Pozitif Semptomları Değerlendirme Ölçeğinin Güvenilirliği ve Geçerliliği. *Dusunen Adam* **1991**, *4*, 20–24.
43. Addington, D.; Addington, J.; Maticka-Tyndale, E. Assessing Depression in Schizophrenia: The Calgary Depression Scale. *Br. J. Psychiatry* **1993**, *163*, 39–44.
44. Aydemir, O.; Danacı, A.E.; Deveci, A.; Icelli, I. Calgary Şizofrenide Depresyon Ölçeği'nin Türkçe Versiyonunun Güvenilirliği ve Geçerliliği. *Nöropsikiyatri Arşivi* **2000**, *37*, 82–86.
45. Chouinard, G.; Margolese, H.C. Manual for the Extrapyramidal Symptom Rating Scale (ESRS). *Schizophr. Res.* **2005**, *76*, 247–265. [CrossRef]
46. Morosini, P.L.; Magliano, L.; Brambilla, L.; Ugolini, S.; Pioli, R. Development, Reliability and Acceptability of a New Version of the DSM-IV Social and Occupational Functioning Assessment Scale (SOFAS) to Assess Routine Social Funtioning. *Acta Psychiatr. Scand.* **2000**, *101*, 323–329. [CrossRef]
47. Aydemir, O.; Ucok, A.; Esen-Danacı, A.; Canpolat, T.; Karadayi, G.; Emiroglu, B.; Sarioz, F. Bireysel ve Sosyal Performans Ölçeği'nin Türkçe Sürümünün Geçerlilik ve Güvenilirlik Çalışması. *Klin. Psikofarmakol. Bul.* **2009**, *19*, 93–100.
48. Türkeş, N.; Can, H.; Kurt, M.; Elmastaş Dikeç, B. İz Sürme Testi'nin 20-49 Yaş Aralığında Türkiye İçin Norm Belirleme Çalışması. *Turk Psikiyatr. Derg.* **2015**, *26*, 189–196.
49. Akİ, Ö.E.; Alkan, B.; Demİrsöz, T.; Velİbaşoğlu, B.; Taşdemİr, T.; Erbaş, S.P.; Selvİ, K.; Ergenç, İ.; Barişkin, E.; Özdemİr, P.; et al. Effects of Age, Gender and Education on Phonemic and Semantic Verbal Fluency. *Turk Psikiyatr. Derg.* **2022**, *33*, 53. [CrossRef]

50. Sezgin, N.; Baştuğ, G.; Karaağaç, S.Y.; Yilmaz, B. Wechsler Yetişkinler Için Zekâ Ölçeği Gözden Geçirilmiş Formu (WAIS-R) Türkiye Standardizasyonu: Ön Çalışma. *Ank. Üniversitesi Üniversitesi Dil Tar.-Coğrafya Fakültesi Derg.* **2014**, *54*, 451–480. [CrossRef]
51. Hurford, I.M.; Ventura, J.; Marder, S.R.; Reise, S.P.; Bilder, R.M. A 10-Minute Measure of Global Cognition: Validation of the Brief Cognitive Assessment Tool for Schizophrenia (B-CATS). *Schizophr. Res.* **2018**, *195*, 327–333. [CrossRef]
52. Strauss, G.P.; Bartolomeo, L.A.; Luther, L. Reduced Willingness to Expend Effort for Rewards Is Associated with Risk for Conversion and Negative Symptom Severity in Youth at Clinical High-Risk for Psychosis. *Psychol. Med.* **2021**. [CrossRef]
53. Faul, F.; Erdfelder, E.; Lang, A.-G.; Buchner, A. G*Power 3: A flexible statistical power analysis program for the social, behavioral, and biomedical sciences. *Behav. Res. Methods* **2007**, *39*, 175–191.
54. Chang, W.C.; Waltz, J.A.; Gold, J.M.; Chan, T.C.W.; Chen, E.Y.H. Mild Reinforcement Learning Deficits in Patients with First-Episode Psychosis. *Schizophr. Bull.* **2016**, *42*, 1476–1485. [CrossRef]
55. Mucci, A.; Merlotti, E.; Üçok, A.; Aleman, A.; Galderisi, S. Primary and Persistent Negative Symptoms: Concepts, Assessments and Neurobiological Bases. *Schizophr. Res.* **2017**, *186*, 19–28.
56. Luther, L.; Firmin, R.L.; Lysaker, P.H.; Minor, K.S.; Salyers, M.P. A Meta-Analytic Review of Self-Reported, Clinician-Rated, and Performance-Based Motivation Measures in Schizophrenia: Are We Measuring the Same "Stuff"? *Clin. Psychol. Rev.* **2018**, *61*, 24–37.
57. Gold, J.M.; Kool, W.; Botvinick, M.M.; Hubzin, L.; August, S.; Waltz, J.A. Cognitive Effort Avoidance and Detection in People with Schizophrenia. *Cogn. Affect Behav. Neurosci.* **2014**, *15*, 145–154. [CrossRef]
58. Strauss, G.P.; Whearty, K.M.; Morra, L.F.; Sullivan, S.K.; Ossenfort, K.L.; Frost, K.H. Avolition in Schizophrenia Is Associated with Reduced Willingness to Expend Effort for Reward on a Progressive Ratio Task. *Schizophr. Res.* **2016**, *170*, 198–204. [CrossRef]
59. Culbreth, A.; Westbrook, A.; Barch, D. Negative Symptoms Are Associated with an Increased Subjective Cost of Cognitive Effort. *J. Abnorm. Psychol.* **2016**, *125*, 528–536. [CrossRef]
60. Wolf, D.H.; Satterthwaite, T.D.; Kantrowitz, J.J.; Katchmar, N.; Vandekar, L.; Elliott, M.A.; Ruparel, K. Amotivation in Schizophrenia: Integrated Assessment with Behavioral, Clinical, and Imaging Measures. *Schizophr. Bull.* **2014**, *40*, 1328–1337. [CrossRef]
61. Culbreth, A.J.; Westbrook, A.; Braver, T.S.; Barch, D.M. Effort in Daily Life: Relationships between Experimental Tasks and Daily Experience. *Motiv. Sci.* **2020**, *6*, 303–308. [CrossRef]
62. Strauss, G.P.; Raugh, I.M.; Zhang, L.; Luther, L.; Chapman, H.C.; Allen, D.N.; Kirkpatrick, B.; Cohen, A.S. Validation of Accelerometry as a Digital Phenotyping Measure of Negative Symptoms in Schizophrenia. *Schizophrenia* **2022**, *8*, 37. [CrossRef]

Journal of
Clinical Medicine

MDPI

Article

Relationship of Neuropeptide S (NPS) with Neurocognitive, Clinical, and Electrophysiological Parameters of Patients during Structured Rehabilitation Therapy for Schizophrenia

Agnieszka Markiewicz-Gospodarek [1,*], Renata Markiewicz [2], Beata Dobrowolska [3], Mansur Rahnama [4] and Bartosz Łoza [5]

1 Department of Human Anatomy, Medical University of Lublin, 20-090 Lublin, Poland
2 Department of Neurology, Neurological and Psychiatric Nursing, Medical University of Lublin, 20-093 Lublin, Poland
3 Department of Holistic Care and Management in Nursing, Medical University of Lublin, 20-081 Lublin, Poland
4 Department of Oral Surgery, Medical University of Lublin, 20-093 Lublin, Poland
5 Department of Psychiatry, Medical University of Warsaw, 02-091 Warsaw, Poland
* Correspondence: agnieszkamarkiewiczgospodarek@umlub.pl

Abstract: Introduction: Neuropeptide S is a biomarker related to various neuropsychiatric and neurocognitive functions. Since the need to improve cognitive functions in schizophrenia is unquestionable, it was valuable to investigate the possible relationships of plasma levels of NPS with neurocognitive, psychopathological and EEG parameters in patients with schizophrenia. Aim: Relationships between the serum NPS level and neurocognitive, clinical, and electrophysiological parameters were investigated in patients diagnosed with schizophrenia who underwent structured rehabilitation therapy. Methods: Thirty-three men diagnosed with schizophrenia were randomized into two groups. The REH group (N16) consisted of patients who underwent structured rehabilitation therapy, the CON group (N17) continued its previous treatment. Additionally, the reference NPS serum results were checked in a group of healthy people (N15). In the study several tests assessing various neurocognitive functions were used: d2 Sustained-Attention Test (d2), Color Trails Test (CTT), Beck Cognitive Insight Scale (BCIS), Acceptance of Illness Scale (AIS), and General Self-Efficacy Scale (GSES). The clinical parameters were measured with Positive and Negative Syndrome Scale (PANSS) and electrophysiological parameters were analyzed with auditory evoked potentials (AEPs) and quantitative electroencephalography (QEEG). The NPS, neurocognitive, clinical, and electrophysiological results of REH and CON groups were recorded at the beginning (T1) and after a period of 3 months (T2). Results: A decreased level of NPS was associated with the improvement in specific complex indices of d2 and BCIS neurocognitive tests, as well as the improvement in the clinical state (PANSS). No correlation was observed between the level of NPS and the results of AEPs and QEEG measurements. Conclusions: A decreased level of NPS is possibly related to the improvement in metacognition and social cognition domains, as well as to clinical improvement during the rehabilitation therapy of patients with schizophrenia.

Keywords: neuropeptide S; schizophrenia; cognitive functioning; rehabilitation; AEP; QEEG

Citation: Markiewicz-Gospodarek, A.; Markiewicz, R.; Dobrowolska, B.; Rahnama, M.; Łoza, B. Relationship of Neuropeptide S (NPS) with Neurocognitive, Clinical, and Electrophysiological Parameters of Patients during Structured Rehabilitation Therapy for Schizophrenia. *J. Clin. Med.* **2022**, *11*, 5266. https://doi.org/10.3390/jcm11185266

Academic Editor: Armida Mucci

Received: 15 July 2022
Accepted: 3 September 2022
Published: 6 September 2022

1. Introduction

While Bleuler assumed from the very beginning that schizophrenia has a multilayered and especially neurocognitive origin, his idea was updated at the end of 20th century by Andreasen et al., in the neo-Bleulerian cognitive dysmetria model and served as an umbrella concept for the dozens of more specific cognitive hypotheses for the origins of schizophrenia, such as neurodevelopmental theory, frontal dysconnectivity, dorsolateral hypo-frontality, sensory gating deficits, and other domain-specific models [1–3]. All such "misconnection" theories identify the disturbances in basic cognitive and behavioral domains (e.g., speed of processing, attention, working memory, learning, and problem solving), but at the same time their biological substrates remain at best in the realm of well-formulated but isolated observations [4]. As a result, there are currently no neurocognitive methods enabling individual and specific schizophrenia diagnosis, and no approved pro-cognitive drugs or therapies exist [5].

Various abnormalities of the neuropeptide system have been demonstrated in schizophrenic patients [6]. However, there is no evidence of a true primary or secondary relationship between neuropeptides and schizophrenia that contributes directly to its etiopathogenesis. On the other hand, the need to improve cognitive functions in schizophrenia is fundamental and unquestionable and there are studies showing the beneficial effect of neuropeptides on cognitive functioning. Neuropeptides and typical neurotransmitters are usually co-released; however, the neuropeptides require high-frequency burst firing, which enables both the coordinated and independent neurotransmitter activity [6]. Neuropeptides act through metabotropic G-protein-coupled receptors (GPCRs), changing cell excitability, signaling, and gene expression.

Neuropeptide S (NPS) has multiple neuropsychiatric functions [7], and it has been postulated that it may play an important role in regulating cognitive functioning [8]. The problem is that so far, the studies have been conducted almost exclusively on animals [9]. Neuropeptide S (NPS) is a 20-amino-acid ligand, which name originates from its N-terminal serine residue. It is found in human beings and nearly all tetrapods [10,11]. The precursor mRNA of NPS is found in only a limited number of regions of the brain (trigeminal nucleus, lateral parabrachial nucleus, locus coeruleus, and amygdala), and in contrast, NPSR1 mRNA is widely expressed in the entire central nervous system (CNS) [11,12]. NPS fibers project to limbic and thalamic areas such as the amygdala, hypothalamus, and paraventricular thalamic nucleus [13]. In humans, the neurons expressing NPS and NPSR1 mRNA were mainly found in the regions important for integration of autonomous information and emotional behavior like the parabrachial area [14].

Preclinical and clinical studies of the NPS/NPSR1 system have remained separated thus far, and there is no comprehensive description of the role of this system neither in humans nor in rodents [11]. The NPS/NPSR1 system seems to play a significant role in stress responsiveness and the activation of the hypothalamic–pituitary–adrenal axis in rodents [11,15]. NPS activity is associated with inhibitors of neurons which gate the amygdala output [16]. The NPS/NPSR1 system also participates in regulating the wakefulness–sleep cycle [17]. It is, therefore, assumed that since the NPS metabolism is highly conservative across different species, research on animals may be accurately extrapolated to humans [16]. While such assumptions can be true in the case of the behavioral regulation of anxiety [10], arousal [10], or pain [16,18], it is difficult to simply extrapolate this way with the assumed role of NPS/NPSR1 in drug addiction [19,20], memory consolidation, conceptual generalization [19], or especially personality formation [20].

The therapeutic use of the NPS/NPSR1 system in humans has been suggested since the discovery of NPS [10]. NPS/NPSR1 activity could potentially be useful in the treatment of various anxiety disorders [21]. The authors of animal studies predicted that the NPS/NPSR1 system would facilitate the extinction of conditioned fear [11,22]. Specifically, the anxiolytic effect is not related to excessive sedation, but rather to an increase in activity ("novel activating anxiolytic"), which is a pharmacologically unique feature [21]. The median plasma NPS level was found to be significantly higher in generalized anxiety disorder (GAD) patients [23]. While NPS may have a beneficial effect on anxiety, no direct effect on depression has been demonstrated thus far in animal models [24]. The NPS/NPSR1 system could be the target for the development of drugs for wakefulness–sleep disorders [16], to alleviate motor and non-motor dysfunctions of Parkinson's diseases [12], to improve learning and memory, e.g., in Alzheimer's disease [9], and to treat substance abuse disorders [25,26].

There are only preliminary data on the relationship between the NPS/NPSR1 system and the course of schizophrenia [7]. A case–control comparison revealed that the low functioning NPSR1 Asn107 variant was significantly associated with schizophrenia [27]. However, another study revealed no genetic association of NPSR1 alleles with schizophrenia (and ADHD), suggesting a rather specific relationship of NPSR1 with anxiety disorders [28]. There are various separate animal patterns for specific dysfunctions that could support the diagnostic and/or therapeutic potential of the NPS/NPSR1 system in schizophrenia research, for example, the acoustic startle response [27], but there is no comprehensive animal model to directly transfer these data to human pre-clinical or clinical models. The mechanism of the psychopharmacological effect of NPS on schizophrenia psychopathology may result from blocking the NMDA antagonist-induced deficits in prepulse inhibition [27–29]. NPS blocks MK-810 NMDA antagonism, suggesting a potential antipsychotic effect of NPS, such as MK-801, which blocks NMDA transmission and serves as a pharmacological model of schizophrenia [28,29]. Nevertheless, the similarity of NPS to anti-psychotics is not complete as haloperidol and sulpiride, both being dopamine D2 receptor antagonists, inhibit NPS-induced anti-nociceptive activity [17]. Long-term olanzapine administration led to the upregulation of NPS and downregulation of the NPSR expression in the rat hypothalamus [30]. Chronic haloperidol administration led to the upregulation of NPS and NPSR in the rat brainstem [31]. These animal results suggest that anti-psychotics may work by affecting peptidergic signaling. However, they do not provide answers about the real impact of the NPS/NPSR1 system on schizophrenia.

The impact of intensive rehabilitation, especially with the use of the neurofeedback (NF) technique, on the level of peptide factors such as BDNF, as well as on the clinical state, has already been shown in human studies [32,33]. However, no studies on the relationship between plasma NPS in patients with schizophrenia and any type of treatment have been published so far. Although investigations of NPS's permeability from the blood–brain barrier have not been conducted on human subjects, the rationality of measuring plasma NPS level in patients with mental disorders has been demonstrated [23].

The purpose of the study was to examine the relationship between NPS serum level cognitive parameters during the structured rehabilitation therapy of patients with schizophrenia. In addition, this evaluation was performed in relation to the clinical condition and results of electrophysiological tests.

2. Materials and Methods

2.1. Study Design

This study was a randomized, controlled 3-month trial reported with the use of CONsolidated Standards of Reporting Trials (CONSORT) guidelines [34]. The trial is registered in the ISRCTN registry (Trial ID: ISRCTN78612833) where the full protocol can be found. Thirty-three male patients with paranoid schizophrenia (according to ICD-10-DCR [ICD]) were divided into two groups: a group in an intensive rehabilitation programme (REH, N16), and a control group with standard social support (CON, N17). In the study, the sample size (N) was calculated for the test power of the NPS level in the range of not less than 0.8, which criterion is considered strong and adequate in behavioral sciences [35].

The N for 0.8 test power was set to 15 and respectively: 16 for 0.83 and 17 for 0.85. Members of both REH and CON groups were recruited from participants of a city day-care center programme. They continued their antipsychotic treatment and usual clinical management. Additionally, a group of healthy (H), non-clinical males (N15) with comparable characteristics was considered to check NPS reference results.

2.2. Participants

The inclusion criteria (CON and REH groups) were patients' consent, male gender, clinical diagnosis of paranoid schizophrenia [ICD], age 18–50, right-handedness (writing), no current neurological diseases, mental disability, or alcohol and/or psychoactive substance addiction. The inclusion criteria in the non-clinical group (H) were the same as above, but all the participants were mentally healthy. The study was limited only to male participants to reduce the risk of potential gender differences in NPS levels which could not be corrected reliably between relatively small groups. Previous NPS studies with a limited number of participants clearly indicated difficulties in interpreting the results in relation to gender [23,24,28]. Moreover, PANSS results can also be influenced by gender differences [36].

Subjects, after meeting the inclusion criteria, were randomly assigned to two groups (REH, CON), without the researchers participating in the drawing process.

All recruited patients had remained relatively stable, i.e., without active psychotic episodes for not less than 18 months. The patients cannot be treated as clinically "residual" according to ICD-10-DCR, as they were quite young, active, and multi-episodic, so they fit the pattern of episodic schizophrenia with stable or progressive development of negative symptoms in the intervals between psychotic episodes (ICD-10-DCR: F20.01/F20.02) [8]. No current suicidal risk was diagnosed.

As can be seen from Table 1A, all the significant study parameters were not statistically different at the baseline: PANSS Total, PANSS Positive, PANSS Negative, PANSS General, age at the first hospitalization, NPS serum level, BMI (body mass index), and age of participants. Group comparisons were presented in Table 1B. The H statistic was not significant in terms of any parameter in Table 1B, indicating that all groups were from the same distribution.

Table 1. Initial (T1) parameters and pairwise comparisons (*t* test/Mann–Whitney test) for REH, CON and Non-clinical groups.

(A)										
Variable	**REH**		**CON**		**REH vs. CON**		**Non-Clinical**		**REH vs. Non-Clinical**	
	M	**SD**	**M**	**SD**	**t^{t}/U^{U}**	***p***	**M**	**SD**	**t^{t}/U^{U}**	***p***
d2-TN	304.63	36.99	330.65	36.99	1.79^{t}	0.083				
d2-Errors	144.06	23.51	137.71	23.51	-0.42^{t}	0.675				
d2-%Errors	47.71	8.71	43.23	8.71	-0.79^{t}	0.436				
d2-TN-E	160.56	38.83	192.94	38.83	1.45^{t}	0.158				
d-CP	110.69	29.77	134.06	41.17	130.00^{U}	0.843				
d-FR	15.25	29.77	15.94	41.17	87.00^{U}	0.081				
CTT-1	60.56	24.74	58.94	26.03	127.50^{U}	0.773				
CTT-2	126.06	39.58	123.12	55.48	120.50^{U}	0.589				
CTT-II	1.19	0.59	1.12	0.51	126.00^{U}	0.732				
BCIS-REF	20.81	3.53	22.94	5.26	114.00^{U}	0.439				
BCIS-CER	14.44	0.99	16.12	3.77	1.28^{t}	0.210				
BCIS-INDEX	6.38	2.50	6.82	4.07	0.38^{t}	0.707				
AIS-Total	26.44	9.12	29.06	6.98	0.93^{t}	0.359				
AIS (1–2 items)	6.69	2.47	7.00	2.53	121.50^{U}	0.614				
AIS (3–8 items)	19.75	7.25	22.06	5.15	1.06^{t}	0.298				
GSES-Total	28.88	7.25	31.59	6.27	1.15^{t}	0.258				
GSES-6 (items)	17.81	4.21	19.00	3.89	119.50^{U}	0.564				
PANSS Total	53.13	7.29	53.41	15.73	119.0^{U}	0.552				
Age of first hospitalization (years)	22.69	3.36	25.12	5.10	1.61^{t}	0.119				
DUP (years)	2.00	1.10	2.59	1.37	1.35^{t}	0.185				
Education (ISCED grades)	3.50	1.10	3.35	0.49	-0.05^{t}	0.619				
Antipsychotics in milligrams (equivalents of olanzapine)	21.28	6.88	19.32	4.97	121.5^{U}	0.614				
NPS (pg/mL)	48.46	16.32	39.67	7.14	82.5^{U}	0.061	42.97	16.55	64.0^{U}	0.360

Table 1. *Cont.*

(A)										
Variable	REH		CON		REH vs. CON		Non-Clinical		REH vs. Non-Clinical	
	M	SD	M	SD	t [t]/U [U]	*p*	M	SD	t [t]/U [U]	*p*
BMI (kg/m^{2})	29.84	4.05	27.39	2.81	−2.02 [t]	0.052	28.85	3.88	0.69 [t]	0.496
Age (years)	36.00	7.79	39.35	10.65	1.03 [t]	0.312	41.27	7.48	−1.92 [t]	0.065

(B)								
Variable	REH		CON		Non-Clinical		*H*-Test	
	Ranks Sum	Ranks Mean	Ranks Sum	Ranks Mean	Ranks Sum	Ranks Mean	*H*	*p*
NPS (pg/mL)	479.5	29.97	400.5	23.56	296.0	19.73	4.26	0.1189
BMI (kg/m^{2})	464.0	29.00	345.0	20.29	367.0	24.47	3.19	0.2032
Age (years)	310.0	19.38	437.5	25.74	428.5	28.57	3.56	0.1690

(**A**): REH—patient rehabilitation group, CON—patient control group, Non-clinical—healthy reference group, d2-TN—d2 total number, d2-E—d2 errors, d2-E%—d2 percentage of all errors, d2-TN-E—d2 total number minus all errors, d2-CP—concentration performance, d2-FR—d2 fluctuation rate, CTT—Color Trails Test, CTT-II—interference index, BCIS—Beck Cognitive Insight Scale (reflectiveness, certainty), AIS—Acceptance of Illness Scale, GSES—General Self-Efficacy Scale, PANSS Total—total result of Positive and Negative Syndrome Scale, DUP—duration of untreated psychosis, ISCED—International Standard Classification of Education, NPS—Neuropeptide S, BMI—body mass index, M—mean, SD—standard deviation, [t]—Student's *t*-test, [U]—Mann-Whitney U-test, *p*—*p*-value significance at $p < 0.05$. (**B**): REH—patient rehabilitation group, CON—patient control group, non-clinical—healthy reference group, NPS—Neuropeptide S, BMI—body mass index, *H*-test—Kruskal-Wallis *H*-test by ranks, *p*—*p*-value significance at $p < 0.05$.

Patients from the CON group had on average three previous psychiatric hospitalizations (M 2.77, SD 1.60), and the REH group-four (M 4.19, SD 1.17). Almost all the patients lived on a disability pension or other social benefits. A significant proportion of the participants smoked cigarettes: CON—76.5%, REH—56.3%, and Non-clinical—66.7%.

During the experiments, all patients continued their former antipsychotic treatment (daily dose olanzapine equivalents in milligrams: CON vs. REH: M 19.32 SD 4.97 vs. M 21.28 SD 6.88). The antipsychotic treatment pattern was not changed during experiment. All subjects were administered atypical antipsychotics (olanzapine, clozapine, quetiapine, risperidone, aripiprazole), and only some of them additionally received typicals (sulpiride, perazine, zuclopenthixol, flupenthixol, haloperidol). On average half of the study participants were subjected to monotherapy (only with atypical antipsychotics): REH group—9/16, CON group—8/17. Polytherapy was delivered with either 2 or more atypical antipsychotics (REH 4/16, CON 7/17) or a combination of atypical and typical antipsychotics (REH 3/16, CON 2/17). Chi-squared test for those three observations (atypical monotherapy, atypical polytherapy, and atypical/typical polytherapy) between REH and CON was insignificant ($\chi 2 = 1.91$, df = 2, $p = 0.385$). None of the patients had taken anticholinergic drugs.

2.3. Outcome Measures

The examinations were performed twice, at the beginning (T1) and after a period of 3 months (T2).

2.3.1. Neurocognitive Tests

d2 Sustained-Attention Test (d2)

The d2 test was used to measure a patients' cognitive performance, including attention, concentration endurance, execution speed, and ability to correct errors [37]. The test consists of 14 lines with 47 characters in each line. Participants have 20 s per line to cross out all lower-case d's with two apostrophes above or below the letter. Every 20 s, the subject moves on to the next line. There are various descriptive and complex indices of d2 results [38,39]:

TN—the total number of letters marked both correctly and incorrectly; the speed of processing score;

E—raw score of omission and commission errors; the attention carelessness and confusion score;
E%—percentage of all errors; the overall accuracy score;
TN-E—the total number of items processed minus all errors; the impact of attention on the combined scores of speed and accuracy as a perception ability;
CP—the concentration performance, the number of correctly processed items minus the commission errors;
FR—the fluctuation rate which is based on the difference in correct responses between the rows with the highest and lowest number of correct responses.

Color Trials Test (CTT)

The CTT is comprised of two different tasks [40]. First, the respondent must connect circles in an ascending numbered sequence (1–25; CTT-1). Then, the task is to connect numbers in an ascending sequence (1–25) while alternating between pink and yellow colors, ignoring the distracter color (CTT-2). CTT-1 and CTT-2 were developed to measure sustained and selective types of attention, visual spatial skills, and motor speed. CTT-2 is also dedicated to the cognitive assessment of Stroop-like effects based on mental flexibility–constantly reloaded tasks in the executive memory [41].

The Interference Index (CTT-II) is a difference between CTT-2 and CTT-1 time divided by CTT-1, what provides information about the increase in the relative time needed to perform a task with a higher degree of cognitive complexity.

Beck Cognitive Insight Scale (BCIS)

The BCIS is a complex 15-item self-report designed to estimate two aspects of cognitive insight in psychotic patients: the Self-Reflectiveness (9 items; BCIS-REF) and the Self-Certainty (6 items; BCIS-CER) [42]. By subtracting the Self-Certainty from the Self-Reflectiveness, the composite Reflectiveness–Certainty Index (BCIS-INDEX) score can be obtained, which is a balanced measure of cognitive insight.

Acceptance of Illness Scale (AIS)

The AIS consist of eight statements, each graded from 1 to 5 [43]. Its higher score is indicative of better disease acceptance. The AIS examines not only whether the patient "knows" that he or she has schizophrenia, but mostly the perception of a disease through its consequences.

According to the validation studies, two groups of questions can be distinguished from the scale: 1–2 and 3–8 [44]. Questions 1–2 deal with individual assessments and abstract issues, while questions 3–8 confront patients with real-life problems. The AIS result may therefore be heterogeneous, so the total AIS score and responses in groups 1–2 and 3–8 were analyzed separately.

General Self-Efficacy Scale (GSES)

GSES aims to assess adaptive potential challenging environmental demands by taking corrective action [45]. Because of the clear redundancy of all 10 questions, the scale was criticized as too homogenous and a short version of the GSES (GSE-6) was introduced with six items (2, 3, 5, 6, 7, 10, respectively) selected because of the highest coefficients of variation [46]. The GSE-6 was used in this study.

2.3.2. Other Measurements

PANSS

Clinical parameters were examined with the Positive and Negative Syndrome Scale (PANSS) [47]. This 30-item interview was conceived as an operationalized instrument that provides balanced representation of positive, negative, and general psychopathology in patients with schizophrenia. It consists of three subscales and a total score of psychotic severity.

Evoked Potentials

The auditory evoked potentials (AEPs) were acquired using a Cognitrace neuropsychiatry system. Twenty-four measurements consisted of the latencies to six alternating positive and negative peaks P50, N1, P2, N2, P3, and P4, and six amplitudes, respectively, in F-z and C-z locations.

Twenty-one cup electrodes (10–20 international system) with ear and ground electrodes were used: Fp-z, F-z, C-z, P-z, O-z, Fp1, Fp2, F3, F4, C3, C4, P3, P4, O1, O2, F7, F8, T3, T4, T5, T6, A1, A2, and GND. Participants stayed in a separate, dark room. The test was performed with the subject in a sitting position, with eyes closed, and wearing earphones through which the acoustic stimuli were delivered in accordance with the oddball paradigm (a series of tones with frequencies in the range from 1000 Hz to 2000 Hz of 70 dB for 100 ms in a random sequence). One test lasted 3 min and 20 s and contained 80% of frequent stimuli and 20% of rare (target) stimuli. The subject was required to respond to the target stimuli by pressing the button.

QEEG

A Quantitative Electroencephalography–Neurofeedback (QEEG) was performed to map and meta-analyze recordings. The QEEG involved measuring a number of frequency bands and indices in different locations (34 measurements in total): delta (0.5–4 Hz), theta (4–8 Hz), alpha (8–12 Hz), beta (>12 Hz), SMR (sensorimotor rhythm, 12–15 Hz), beta1 (15–18 Hz), beta2 (18 Hz), gamma (40 Hz and above), theta/beta-attention factor, theta/SMR-concentration factor, SMR/beta2-tension and stress factor, alpha/SMR- sensory and motor activity factor, alpha/beta-executive function index, and beta/alpha-thinking and action factor.

QEEG was performed twice, at the beginning of the experiment (T1) and after 3 months (T2) using the EEG Digi-Track ELMIKO apparatus (Elmico-Medical Company, Warsaw, Poland). The patients were tested with two electrodes, in the F-z and C-z regions and the Fast Fourier Transform (FFT) algorithm switched the raw EEG recording into QEEG power spectrum.

2.4. Rehabilitation Therapy

Our programme consisted of five main modules: social trainings, motivation/planning capacity, cognitive trainings, computer-assisted trainings (perception, attention, reasoning), and creativity module. It emphasizes not only teaching skills, but also improving metacognition and solving social problems. It was a largely balanced, psychosocial therapy programme, and the achievement of any particular skill was not an including or excluding criterion. Our rehabilitation program referred to some extent to the cognitive remediation therapy principles developed by Wykes et al., showing a predictive potential relating to the patient's ability to function in the community [48].

The primary aim of the intervention was to improve social competence of the patients. The programme was administered to groups and was not hierarchically or sequentially organized. It was aimed at changing the daily routine by means of additional social activities, building team competences, training social roles, increasing personal acceptance, and strengthening one's independence. Structured activities were held for up to 8-h blocks daily (except at weekends). The general plan of the day included group activities such as assertive training and role-playing techniques, psychotherapy, psychoeducation, cognitive training, art therapy, physiotherapy, sports, social events, cooking meals together, entertainment activities, and relaxation training. At least one session of group psychotherapy or psychoeducation was held every day.

2.5. Laboratory

The serum level of NPS was determined immunoenzymatically with the ELISA technique (Human NPS/Neuropeptide S ELISA Kit, EIAab Science Co., 6618 h catalog number, Biopark, Opties Valley, Wuhan, China). The NPS level was determined at 07:00 a.m. (pg/mL), using a non-contact method of blood sampling into a clot tube.

2.6. Statistical Analyses

The values of the investigated variables were presented as means and standard deviations. The sociological and demographic parameters were presented as numbers and percentages. The results were compared using Student's *t*-test for dependent samples, non-parametric Mann–Whitney U-test, Kruskal–Wallis *H*-test and Chi-squared test, as well as Pearson's r product-moment correlation coefficient. The Shapiro–Wilk test was used to check whether samples came from a normal distribution. Differences were considered statistically significant at $p < 0.05$. Analyses were performed using Statistica 13.3.

2.7. Ethical Issues

The study protocol was approved by the local Bioethics Committee-approval no. KE-0254/35/2016. All the patients invited to take part in the study gave their written informed consent.

3. Results

The baseline (T1) and 3-month (T2) neurocognitive results of rehabilitation therapy (REH) versus standard therapy (CON) programs were presented in Table 2.

Of the results of five neurocognitive tests, only two of the tools-d2 and BCIS-had significant changes in time between T1 and T2. 5 out of 6 d2 indices in the REH group improved significantly (TN, E, E%, TN-E, CP). However, in the case of the CON group, improvement was noted only in the TN-E index. The BCIS-REF and BCIS-INDEX scores improved in the REH group, but there were no significant changes in the CON group.

The results of the other three neurocognitive tests, CTT, AIS and GSES, did not change significantly over the three-month period neither in the REH group nor in the CON group. Also, the use of special, more measurement-specific variants of two tests (AIS 1–2/AIS 3–8 and GSES-6) did not change that.

In the REH group, the NPS serum level decreased significantly, in contrast to the CON group. The PANSS results turned out to be significantly different only for the Positive subscale in the REH group.

Table 2. T1 versus T2 neurocognitive tests, NPS and PANSS results.

Test	Subtest	Group	Baseline		Final		t/U	*p*
			M	SD	M	SD		
d2	TN	REH	304.63	36.99	361.31	36.02	−4.39 ᵗ	**0.000**
		CON	330.65	45.63	365.53	63.59	−1.84 ᵗ	0.075
	Errors	REH	144.06	23.51	77.75	18.47	8.87 ᵗ	**0.000**
		CON	137.71	55.53	107.53	33.31	1.92 ᵗ	0.064
	% Errors	REH	47.71	8.71	21.64	5.11	10.33 ᵗ	**0.000**
		CON	43.23	21.03	30.72	12.55	94.00 ᵁ	0.085
	TN-E	REH	160.56	38.83	283.56	38.26	−9.03 ᵗ	**0.000**
		CON	192.94	81.13	258.00	74.72	−2.43 ᵗ	**0.021**
	CP	REH	110.69	29.77	153.75	53.04	−2.83 ᵗ	**0.008**
		CON	134.06	41.17	134.82	40.10	−0.06 ᵗ	0.957
	FR	REH	15.25	9.66	14.00	6.81	126.00 ᵁ	0.955
		CON	15.94	9.43	15.65	10.74	135.00 ᵁ	0.757

Table 2. *Cont.*

Test	Subtest	Group	Baseline		Final		t/U	p
			M	SD	M	SD		
CTT	CTT-1	REH	60.56	24.74	55.56	19.63	110.50 U	0.522
		CON	58.94	26.03	56.08	20.02	141.50 U	0.931
	CTT-2	REH	126.06	39.58	114.81	33.73	101.50 U	0.327
		CON	123.12	55.48	113.28	45.48	136.50 U	0.796
	CTT-II	REH	1.19	0.59	1.14	0.43	124.00 U	0.895
		CON	1.12	0.51	1.10	0.57	0.10 t	0.918
BCIS	BCIS-REF	REH	20.81	3.53	24.44	3.76	−2.81 t	**0.009**
		CON	22.94	5.26	20.18	5.15	1.55 t	0.131
	BCIS-CER	REH	14.44	3.76	14.69	3.79	−0.19 t	0.853
		CON	16.12	3.77	16.53	3.22	−0.34 t	0.735
	BCIS-INDEX	REH	6.38	2.50	9.75	3.26	51.00 U	**0.004**
		CON	6.82	4.07	3.65	6.22	1.76 t	0.088
AIS	Total	REH	26.44	9.12	26.63	7.98	−0.06 t	0.951
		CON	29.06	6.98	30.59	7.04	−0.64 t	0.529
	AIS (1–2)	REH	6.69	2.47	6.31	2.91	120.50 U	0.792
		CON	7.00	2.53	7.47	2.07	133.50 U	0.718
	AIS (3–8)	REH	19.75	7.25	20.31	6.65	−0.23 t	0.821
		CON	22.06	5.15	23.12	5.57	−0.58 t	0.569
GSES	Total	REH	28.88	7.25	31.69	4.98	−1.28 t	0.211
		CON	31.59	6.27	32.00	6.38	−0.19 t	0.851
	GSES-6	REH	17.81	4.22	19.25	2.89	117.50 U	0.706
		CON	19.00	3.89	19.06	4.01	−0.04 t	0.966
NPS (pg/mL)		REH	48.46	16.32	36.01	3.45	34.00 U	**0.000**
		CON	39.67	7.14	38.96	6.76	134.00 U	0.731
PANSS	Total	REH	53.13	7.29	48.50	8.22	−1.68	0.103
		CON	53.41	15.73	57.88	7.40	1.06	0.297
	Positive	REH	9.75	1.73	8.25	1.39	−2.70	**0.011**
		CON	10.00	2.40	9.88	8.25	−0.12	0.906
	Negative	REH	15.44	3.46	14.00	3.39	−1.19	0.245
		CON	15.29	3.64	16.65	2.71	1.23	0.228
	General	REH	27.94	3.55	26.25	4.51	−1.18	0.2445
		CON	28.12	10.83	31.35	3.20	1.18	0.246

d2—d2 Sustained-Attention Test, TN—total number of letters marked, E—errors, E%—percentage of all errors, TN-E—total number of items processed minus errors, CP—concentration performance, FR—fluctuation rate, CTT—Color Trails Test, CTT-II—Interference Index, BCIS—Beck Cognitive Insight Scale, BCIS-REF—self-reflectiveness subscale, BCIS-CER—self-certainty subscale, AIS—Acceptance of Illness Scale, GSES—General Self-Efficacy Scale, NPS—neuropeptide S, PANSS—Positive and Negative Syndrome Scale, t—Student's *t*-test, U—Mann-Whitney U-test.

No significant differences were found in the REH and CON groups between T1 and T2 in terms of auditory evoked potentials (24 parameters in total). Similarly, there were no significant changes in the REH group in terms of QEEG (34 parameters in total). In the CON group, there were some sporadic differences in QEEG between T1 and T2 in indices mainly consisting of theta waveform (Fz theta/alpha, Fz theta/SMR, Fz alpha/theta).

A comparison of the main effects of rehabilitation therapy over a period of 3 months is presented in Table 3.

Table 3. Differences in the magnitude of change from pre- (T1) to post-therapy (T2) results in REH and CON groups.

Test	Subtest	REH (T2-T1)		CON (T2-T1)		In-between Comparisons	
		M	SD	M	SD	t/U	p
d2	TN	56.69	31.73	34.88	41.09	−1.70 t	0.100
	Errors	−66.31	24.22	−30.18	39.52	3.14 t	**0.004**
	% Errors	−26.08	10.09	−12.51	15.25	3.00 t	**0.005**
	TN-E	123.00	47.52	65.06	66.85	−2.85 t	**0.008**
	CP	43.06	43.72	0.77	43.02	−2.80 t	**0.009**
	FR	43.06	5.98	−0.29	6.98	0.42 t	0.678
CTT	CTT-1	−5.00	14.94	−2.86	13.71	0.42 t	0.671
	CTT-2	−11.25	27.81	−9.85	34.04	0.16 t	0.875
	CTT-II	−0.05	0.70	−0.02	0.73	0.14 t	0.893
BCIS	BCIS-REF	3.63	5.10	−2.77	6.82	−3.03 t	**0.005**
	BCIS-CER	0.25	4.77	0.41	3.81	125.00 U	0.719
	BCIS-INDEX	3.38	3.59	−3.18	7.15	56.00 U	**0.004**
AIS	Total	0.19	9.54	1.53	5.64	0.50 t	0.624
	AIS (1–2)	−0.38	3.34	0.47	2.32	0.85 t	0.403
	AIS (3–8)	0.56	9.04	1.06	4.44	0.20 t	0.841
GSES	Total	2.81	8.34	0.41	4.54	118.00 U	0.528
	GSES-6	1.44	5.05	0.06	1.44	116.50 U	0.494
NPS (pg/mL)		−12.46	15.97	−0.72	9.97	71.00 U	**0.020**
PANSS	Total	−4.63	3.40	4.47	10.93	23,50 U	**0.000**
	Positive	−1.50	1.26	−0.12	1.32	59,50 U	**0.006**
	Negative	−1.44	1.46	1.35	3.06	3.31 t	**0.002**
	General	−1.69	2.02	3.24	9.08	23,00 U	**0.000**

d2—d2 Sustained-Attention Test, TN—total number of letters marked, E—errors, E%—percentage of all errors, TN-E—total number of items processed minus errors, CP—concentration performance, FR –fluctuation rate, CTT—Color Trails Test, CTT-II—Interference Index, BCIS—Beck Cognitive Insight Scale, BCIS-REF—self-reflectiveness subscale, BCIS-CER—self-certainty subscale, AIS—Acceptance of Illness Scale, GSES—General Self-Efficacy Scale, NPS—neuropeptide S, PANSS—Positive and Negative Syndrome Scale, t—Student's *t*-test, U—Mann-Whitney U-test.

Only some neurocognitive results differentiated REH and CON. What is a common rule for those indices is that they were the same scales (d2, BCIS) that showed any cognitive improvement over the 3-month study period.

In the REH group, the decrease in serum NPS levels was greater than in the CON group. All PANSS scores (Total, Positive, Negative, General) improved more in REH group than CON group.

Supplementing the results of Table 3 with electrophysiological data, only one difference between REH and CON should be noted among all AEPs (out of 24 measurements) and QEEGs (out of 34 measurements):

- QEEG/F-z: Theta/SMR index-practically no theta shares vs. SMR in REH group and significant theta share in CON (respectively: 0.04, SD 0.54 vs. 0.49, SD 0.54; $p = 0.022$),
- AEP P2/C-z/amplitude: the P2 waveform was reduced in REH and increased in CON after 3-month period (respectively: −2.83, SD 5.71 vs. 1.55, SD 3.85; $p = 0.016$).

All of REH group results which changed significantly during 3-month trial (Table 3, T2-T1 differences) were correlated with the NPS serum scores (Table 4).

Table 4. The Pearson's r product–moment correlation coefficients: NPS T1, NPS T2, and NPS T2-T1 correlated with neurocognitive and physiological variables (T2-T1). Only strong correlations for absolute values of r > 0.5 ($p < 0.05$) were bolded. p-values in parentheses.

Variable (T2-T1 Difference)		NPS T1	NPS T2	NPS T2-T1
d2	Errors	−0.01 (0.469)	0.17 (0.787)	0.05 (0.424)
	%Errors	0.03 (0.650)	0.40 (0.322)	0.07 (0.802)
	TN-E	−0.21 (0.279)	**−0.68 (0.007)**	0.05 (0.563)
	CP	−0.35 (0.244)	−0.32 (0.043)	0.30 (0.445)
BCIS	BCIS-REF	−0.55 (0.117)	0.12 (0.738)	**0.62 (0.019)**
	BCIS-INDEX	0.01 (0.249)	0.38 (0.212)	0.09 (0.142)
PANSS	Total	0.45 (0.215)	−0.33 (0.383)	**−0.54 (0.040)**
	Positive	0.32 (0.430)	−0.34 (0.376)	−0.40 (0.315)
	Negative	−0.03 (0.824)	−0.15 (0.649)	0.00 (0.897)
	General	**0.54 (0.017)**	−0.20 (0.564)	**−0.60 (0.045)**
QEEG/F-z	Theta/SMR index	−0.44 (0.085)	−0.47 (0.461)	0.35 (0.114)
AEP/C-z	P2 amplitude	0.42 (0.280)	−0.07 (0.712)	−0.47 (0.234)

d2—d2 Sustained-Attention Test, E—errors, E%—percentage of all errors, TN-E—total number of items processed minus errors, CP—concentration performance, BCIS—Beck Cognitive Insight Scale, BCIS-REF—self-reflectiveness subscale, NPS—neuropeptide S, PANSS—Positive and Negative Syndrome Scale, QEEG—Quantitative Electroencephalography, AEP—Auditory evoked potentials.

Analyzing socio-epidemiological parameters, two of them correlated strongly and significantly with the NPS reduction (T2-T1):

- the increase in the number of **education** grades (r −0.67);
- the shorter duration of untreated psychosis (**DUP**) preceding the onset of schizophrenia (r −0.55).

4. Discussion

According to Andreasen et al., schizophrenia should be understood directly as a neurocognitive disorder [1]. Nevertheless, while obvious cognitive impairments have been repeatedly demonstrated in patients with schizophrenia, not all the necessary elements of a complete pathophysiological theory have been established yet [4]. There is no unequivocal neural and biochemical basis. Attempts to directly treat cognitive dysfunctions in schizophrenia have not brought satisfactory results [5]. There is currently no consensus on the internal systematics of cognitive disorders in schizophrenia, which deficits are primary or secondary, how to separate simple "data metabolism" from sophisticated metacognition, how to calculate emotional and personality influences on virtually all aspects of cognition, what is the hierarchy of dysfunction, etc. [49]. Most of neurocognitive hypotheses, for lack of better ones, refer directly or indirectly to the half-century model of Baddeley and Hitch's working memory [50]. In turn, some comprehensive models accept this "fuzzy logic" of reasoning and gather cognitive functions into several intentional processes, operating computationally and creating functional hierarchy [51]. In this context, research on cognitive dysfunction in schizophrenia still resembles classical 19th-century trial-and-error experiments. The results of our work provide some hints for those issues. Thus far, there have been no clinical studies with the primary goal of assessing the NPS serum level in relation to schizophrenia neurocognitive dysfunctions. The use of the structured rehabilitation therapy improved some, but not all, neurocognitive functions in schizophrenia. At the same time, a significant reduction in the serum NPS level was identified.

4.1. NPS and Neurocognitive Results

Only some neurocognitive tests responded positively to the rehabilitation therapy, what was at the same time related to significant NPS serum level reduction. Nearly all (five out of six) subtests of d2 were sensitive to 3-month therapy effects in REH group (except for FR; Table 2). Contrary to that, only one single response was noted in CON group. When compared head-to-head REH vs. CON results (Table 3), four out of six subtests of d2 in REH group specifically improved over CON group. Finally, the subtest valid mostly for tracking cognitive improvement and the relationship with NPS level was the TN-E complex score.

The TN-E is not just a "number of true responses", but rather the index of two balanced and integrated mental activities The first is a time-dependent, goal-oriented, and learning-while-performing activity. Consequently, it is similar to CTT or Trail Making Test (TMT)-like measurements [52,53]. The second is the potential to correct oneself, i.e., to avoid both omission and commission errors. As a result, the ability to manage contradictory patterns heavy weights on TN-E results. The final score does not depend on speed process alone but is the balanced measurement of final accuracy or problem solving in general. The TN-E is therefore not a measurement of trained activity, but it verifies the functioning strictly in metacognitive capacity [54,55]. It is important as metacognitive functions have not been tested sufficiently in schizophrenia so far, because of their measurement complexity [51,56].

Similarly, using two BCIS indices-Self-Reflectiveness and Reflectiveness-Certainty Index-a strong correlation of pro-cognitive effects with the NPS level was confirmed (Table 3). Like TN-E, the BCIS Index is a composite, internally confronted measure. This index verifies the ability to detect and correct misinterpretations diagnosed in patients using the Self-Certainty subscale. This time again, it is about the assessment of a complex mental process in which the final behavioral optimization is the result of a balance between the pursuit of assertive action in confrontation with the need to avoid psychotic experiences and anomalous beliefs. The Reflectiveness–Certainty Index structure is therefore appropriate for measuring metacognition.

The characteristics of the Self-Reflectiveness index from the BCIS are slightly different. It was also significantly and strongly correlated with the NPS level. Self-Reflectiveness is a collection of assessments that verify what the patient thinks other people think and feel about the patient's personal behavior. Therefore, it is a direct measurement of the ability to be empathetic, and more broadly, a measurement of the patient's social cognition resources [57]. While the *G12-lack of judgment and insight* from PANSS examines the insight only into the diagnosis and treatment itself, the BCIS provides a broader range of cognitive interpretations, including understanding of the patient's own situation and attitudes from the social environment, the ability to distinguish true-or-false experiences, and the level of assertiveness [58].

The essence of the positive correlation of the above-listed neurocognitive results and NPS would be a significant relationship that appear only using measurement tests specific for phenomena such as metacognition and social cognition. This also explains the "inactivity" of the remaining tests:

- CTT is a tool that verifies the ability to focus and maintain attention while performing one short task. This scheme is not changed by the slightly more task-related variant of the CTT-2. CTT does not require taking a position on any social context and is basically a dexterity test like many computer games. The CTT-2 variant in relation to the CTT-1 requires only a slightly greater "inhibition" of the competing instructions because there are only two instructions in total. This level of "inhibition" does not require complicated metacognition schemas to be used. Nevertheless, CTT or TMT tests are very sensitive in identifying cognitive disorders in schizophrenia [52,53], but these are not tools for verifying cognitive strategy building as in the case of problem-solving tests (e.g., Wisconsin Card Sorting Test, Tower of London);
- AIS is a tool for the comprehensive assessment patient's attitude to his/her disease, but the structure of the scale, including its excessive redundancy is monothematic and actually includes what in fact a single *G12-lack of judgment and insight* from PANSS can

offer [47]. The issue of the patient's lack of insight into suffering from schizophrenia is so fundamental that it defines this disease. Thus, a paradoxical methodological problem is that a patient who consistently disagrees with the diagnosis of schizophrenia would be instructed to freely reflect doubts on the AIS list of statements. Actually, it would be resolved at the level of defense mechanisms, and not of any cognitive flexibility processes. Of course, the AIS scale may be successfully used in the self-assessment of patients with psychosomatic diseases, where this type of paradox does not occur. Finally, it should be added that using the suggested methodological split into two groups of questions (1–2 and 3–8), it was also not possible to modify the results [44];

- GSES can determine in patients, especially those with psychosis, a "defensive" type of response resulting from a sense of their own disability. A patient with psychosis does not have sufficient cognitive capacity to relativize his/her psychotic position. Therefore, this would be a methodologically similar problem to that discussed in the case of applying AIS. In this situation, statements that sound almost identical and are repeated ten times, can only reinforce a defensive attitude. The scale was criticized because of this as being too homogenous and a short version of the GSES (GSE-6) was proposed with six items [46], however even by applying this modification we could not change the overall scale specificity that does not reach the metacognition spectrum.

The study managed to show a specific association of NPS with metacognition and social cognition tests. However, other neurocognitive tests were not effective when the challenge was to measure complex cognitive behavior (CTT for perceptual tracking and sequencing only, AIS and GSES operating below the threshold of defense mechanisms). Paradoxically, the cognitive impairment in schizophrenia is so generalized that using tests related to practically every cognitive domain we can differentiate the results of healthy and sick people [4,52,53]. However, due to this "excessive test sensitivity", it is problematic to carry out any specific measurement in schizophrenia, and more generally, to settle the model of integration of cognitive functions in schizophrenia [51]. That is why it was so important to establish in this study a significant relationship between the three neurocognition indices and the NPS level.

Finally, it should be emphasized that some socio-epidemiological parameters (education, duration of untreated psychosis) that accompanied the reduction of NPS and are commonly understood as co-factors of cognitive functioning in schizophrenia [1,4].

4.2. Clinical Results

A structured, 3-month rehabilitation therapy programme was implemented in the REH group, with partial improvement in clinical outcomes (Table 2: PANSS General, PANSS Total). The clinical results were even more favorable in the direct comparison of the REH and CON groups (Table 3). A significant correlation of NPS T1 and NPS T2–T1 was affiliated only to General and Total PANSS results (Table 4), but not to its more specific positive and negative factors. However, since the General subscale is a collection of a variety of symptoms, the result could not be tracked further based on the original PANSS model. For further analysis of PANSS symptomatology versus NPS serum level see Markiewicz-Gospodarek et al. (2022) [8].

The clinical effectiveness of the rehabilitation programme may have been due to the fact that it was not solely focused on cognitive training, but was a more complex, long-term psychosocial therapy. The meta-analysis of rehabilitation techniques shows that they have an impact on global functioning and improvement in psychopathology only if they implement integrated psychosocial rehabilitation [49]. Improvement of cognitive functions, even if it occurs, may be not a sufficient condition to obtain positive clinical effects.

4.3. Electrophysiology

It is assumed that the use of modern methods of electrophysiological diagnostics would benefit from biomarkers that will provide sensitive and reliable measurements of the neural events underlying cognitive dysfunctions in schizophrenia. However, so far, no unequivocal results have been obtained in this respect [59]. In our work, it was not possible to link cognitive variables and changes in the NPS level with the results of several dozen measurements using two basic methods of modern electrophysiological diagnostics (AEP, QEEG). This may be due to the structure of the study itself (long-term, 3-month), as well as the fact that the improvement of cognitive functions related specifically to metacognition or social cognition variables, and not to simple cognitive deficits.

4.4. Study Limitations

Research on cognitive functions in schizophrenia has been going on for over a century and is associated with a variety of concepts, tools, and limitations [2]. The neurocognitive approach assumes the connection of cognitive phenomena with neurophysiological substrates [1]. In works of this type, even such complex phenomena as insight, metacognition or social cognition are being examined [60,61]. This approach is of a research nature, and thus the results have their limitations, and entail changes in the methodology. This also applies to our work.

Relatively often used in schizophrenia research cognitive batteries such as MATRICS and BACS were not administered in our study as this would not be consistent with the main goals due to methodological limitations. We were focused on patients with a specific and dynamic clinical profile, while the results of MATRICS turned out to be only minimally related to clinical symptom type and schizophrenia severity [62], and in turn, BACS measurement has not been validated in relation to the longitudinal relationship of cognition with functional capacity, real-world functional outcome, and schizophrenia treatment [63].

The presented study confirmed the serum NPS level as a phenomenon accompanying the improvement of certain cognitive functions during treatment of patients with schizophrenia. This relationship, based on patients' clinical improvement, enables better treatment planning and prognosis. However, the study had some clear limitations: small groups, only men recruited, only the subtype episodic schizophrenia with stable or progressive development of negative symptoms and focus on rehabilitation effects. This does not allow us to draw unambiguous conclusions and means that the verification of all conclusions requires the extension of the study. Nevertheless, the results are pioneering the possible association of NPS (neuropeptides) with cognitive functions in schizophrenia and should be carefully considered as a chance to meet the diagnostic and therapeutic needs of patients.

5. Conclusions

(1) By using the long-term structured rehabilitation therapy in patients with schizophrenia, an improvement in selected cognitive functions was achieved, accompanied by a decrease in the level of neuropeptide S (NPS) in the serum;
(2) The primary effect was specific to the cognitive improvement described by specific test results:
    a. TN-E—combined score of the total responses minus omission and commission errors of d2 Sustained-Attention Test;
    b. Self-Reflectiveness score and Reflectiveness-Certainty Index of Beck Cognitive Insight Scale.
(3) Reduction of NPS, a neuropeptide associated with clinical disorganization in schizophrenia, has been associated with improved cognitive functioning in domains of metacognition and social cognition after 3-month rehabilitation therapy;
(4) The primary effect was related to the current improvement in the clinical condition (PANSS) and the course of schizophrenia (education, duration of untreated psychosis);
(5) The cognitive effects depending on the NPS level could not be associated with the results of QEEG and AEP measurements.

Author Contributions: Conceptualization, A.M.-G. and B.Ł.; methodology, A.M.-G., R.M. and B.Ł; formal analysis, R.M. and B.Ł.; investigation, A.M.-G., R.M., B.D., M.R. and B.Ł.; resources, A.M.-G.; R.M., B.D., M.R. and B.Ł; writing—original draft preparation, A.M.-G., R.M., B.D., M.R. and B.Ł.; writing—review and editing, A.M.-G., R.M., B.D., M.R. and B.Ł.; visualization, A.M.-G. and B.Ł.; supervision, R.M. and B.Ł. All authors have read and agreed to the published version of the manuscript.

Funding: This research was funded by the Medical University of Lublin (Poland) from Ministry of Science and Higher Education oh the Republic of Poland.

Institutional Review Board Statement: The study protocol was approved by the Medical University of Lublin Bioethics Committee—approval no. KE-0254/35/2016.

Informed Consent Statement: All the patients invited to take part in the study gave their written informed consent.

Data Availability Statement: Not applicable.

Conflicts of Interest: The authors declare no conflict of interest.

References

1. Andreasen, C.; Paradiso, S.; O'Leary, D.S. "Cognitive dysmetria" as an integrative theory of schizophrenia: A dysfunction in cortical-subcortical-cerebellar circuitry? *Schizophr. Bull.* **1998**, *24*, 203–218. [CrossRef] [PubMed]
2. Bleuler, E. *Dementia Praecox Oder Die GRUPPE der Schizophrenien*; Deuticke: Leipzig, Germany, 1911.
3. Karrer, T.M.; Bassett, D.S.; Derntl, B.; Gruber, O.; Aleman, A.; Jardri, R.; Laird, A.R.; Fox, P.T.; Eickhoff, S.B.; Grisel, O.; et al. Brain-based ranking of cognitive domains to predict schizophrenia. *Hum. Brain Mapp.* **2019**, *40*, 4487–4507 [CrossRef]
4. Green, M.F.; Nuechterlein, K.H. Should schizophrenia be treated as a neurocognitive disorder? *Schizophr. Bull.* **1999**, *25*, 309–319. [CrossRef] [PubMed]
5. Harvey, P.D.; Bowie, C.R. Cognitive enhancement in schizophrenia: Pharmacological and cognitive remediation approaches. *Psychiatr. Clin. N. Am.* **2012**, *35*, 683–698. [CrossRef] [PubMed]
6. LaCrosse, A.L.; Olive, M.F. Neuropeptide systems and schizophrenia. *CNS Neurol. Disord. Drug Targets* **2013**, *12*, 619–632. [CrossRef]
7. Markiewicz-Gospodarek, A.; Kuszta, P.; Baj, J.; Dobrowolska, B.; Markiewicz, R. Can Neuropeptide S be an indicator for assessing anxiety in psychiatric disorders? *Front. Public Health* **2022**, *10*, 872430. [CrossRef]
8. Markiewicz-Gospodarek, A.; Markiewicz, R.; Dobrowolska, B.; Maciejewski, R.; Łoza, B. Relationship of neuropeptide S with clinical and metabolic parameters of patients during rehabilitation therapy for schizophrenia. *Brain Sci.* **2022**, *12*, 768. [CrossRef]
9. Zhao, P.; Qian, X.; Nie, Y.; Sun, N.; Wang, Z.; Wu, J.; Wei, C.; Ma, R.; Wang, Z.; Chai, G.; et al. Neuropeptide S ameliorates cognitive impairment of APP/PS1 transgenic mice by promoting synaptic plasticity and reducing Aβ deposition. *Front. Behav. Neurosci.* **2019**, *13*, 138. [CrossRef]
10. Xu, Y.L.; Reinscheid, R.K.; Huitron-Resendiz, S.; Clark, S.D.; Wang, Z.; Lin, S.H.; Brucher, F.A.; Zeng, J.; Ly, N.K.; Henriksen, S.J.; et al. Neuropeptide S: A neuropeptide promoting arousal and anxiolytic-like effects. *Neuron* **2004**, *43*, 487–497. [CrossRef]
11. Tobinski, A.M.; Rappeneau, V. Role of the Neuropeptide S system in emotionality, stress responsiveness and addiction-like behaviors in rodents: Relevance to stress-related disorders. *Pharmaceuticals* **2021**, *14*, 780. [CrossRef]
12. Holanda, V.A.D.; Didonet, J.J.; Costa, M.B.B.; do Nascimento Rangel, A.H.; da Silva, E.D.; Gavioli, E.C. Neuropeptide S receptor as an innovative therapeutic target for Parkinson disease. *Pharmaceuticals* **2021**, *14*, 775. [CrossRef] [PubMed]
13. Clark, S.D.; Duangdao, D.M.; Schulz, S.; Zhang, L.; Liu, X.; Xu, Y.L.; Reinscheid, R.K. Anatomical characterization of the neuropeptide S system in the mouse brain by in situ hybridization and immunohistochemistry. *J. Comp. Neurol.* **2011**, *519*, 1867–1893. [CrossRef]
14. Adori, C.; Barde, S.; Bogdanovic, N.; Uhlén, M.; Reinscheid, R.R.; Kovacs, G.G.; Hökfelt, T. Neuropeptide S- and Neuropeptide S receptor-expressing neuron populations in the human pons. *Front. Neuroanat.* **2015**, *9*, 126. [CrossRef]
15. Zhu, H.; Mingler, M.K.; McBride, M.L.; Murphy, A.J.; Valenzuela, D.M.; Yancopoulos, G.D.; Williams, M.T.; Vorhees, C.V.; Rothenberg, M.E. Abnormal response to stress and impaired NPS-induced hyperlocomotion, anxiolytic effect and corticosterone increase in mice lacking NPSR1. *Psychoneuroendocrinology* **2010**, *35*, 1119–1132. [CrossRef]
16. Neugebauer, V.; Mazzitelli, M.; Cragg, B.; Ji, G.; Navratilova, E.; Porreca, F. Amygdala, neuropeptides, and chronic pain-related affective behaviors. *Neuropharmacology* **2020**, *170*, 108052. [CrossRef] [PubMed]
17. Kushikata, T.; Hirota, K.; Saito, J.; Takekawa, D. Roles of neuropeptide S in anesthesia, analgesia, and sleep. *Pharmaceuticals* **2021**, *14*, 483. [CrossRef] [PubMed]
18. Yang, F.; Peng, L.; Luo, J.; Yi, H.; Hu, X. Intra-amygdala microinfusion of neuropeptide S attenuates neuropathic pain and suppresses the response of spinal microglia and astrocytes after spinal nerve ligation in rats. *Peptides* **2016**, *82*, 26–34. [CrossRef] [PubMed]
19. Cannella, N.; Kallupi, M.; Ruggeri, B.; Ciccocioppo, R.; Ubaldi, M. The role of the neuropeptide S system in addiction: Focus on its interaction with the CRF and hypocretin/orexin neurotransmission. *Prog. Neurobiol.* **2013**, *100*, 48–59. [CrossRef]

20. Laas, K.; Reif, A.; Akkermann, K.; Kiive, E.; Domschke, K.; Lesch, K.P.; Veidebaum, T.; Harro, J. Neuropeptide S receptor gene variant and environment: Contribution to alcohol use disorders and alcohol consumption. *Addict. Biol.* **2014**, *20*, 605–616. [CrossRef]
21. Koob, G.F.; Greenwell, T.N. Neuropeptide S: A novel activating anxiolytic? *Neuron* **2004**, *43*, 441–442. [CrossRef]
22. Kolodziejczyk, M.H.; Fendt, M. Corticosterone treatment and incubation time after contextual fear conditioning synergistically induce fear memory generalization in neuropeptide S receptor-deficient mice. *Front. Neurosci.* **2020**, *14*, 128. [CrossRef] [PubMed]
23. Baykan, H.; Baykan, Ö.; Esen, E.C.; Kara, H.; Hişmioğullari, A.A.; Karlidere, T. Relationship between panic disorder and plasma neuropeptide-S level. *Arch. Clin. Psychiatry* **2018**, *45*, 79–81. [CrossRef]
24. Wegener, G.; Finger, B.C.; Elfving, B.; Keller, K.; Liebenberg, N.; Fischer, C.W.; Singewald, N.; Slattery, D.A.; Neumann, I.D.; Mathé, A.A. Neuropeptide S alters anxiety, but not depression-like behavior in Flinders Sensitive Line rats: A genetic animal model of depression. *Int. J. Neuropsychopharmacol.* **2012**, *15*, 375–387. [CrossRef] [PubMed]
25. Bruijnzeel, A.W. Neuropeptide systems and new treatments for nicotine addiction. *Psychopharmacology* **2017**, *234*, 1419–1437. [CrossRef] [PubMed]
26. Albanese, V.; Ruzza, C.; Marzola, E.; Bernardi, T.; Fabbri, M.; Fantinati, A.; Trapella, C.; Reinscheid, R.K.; Ferrari, F.; Sturaro, C.; et al. Structure-activity relationship studies on Oxazolo [3,4-a] pyrazine derivatives leading to the discovery of a novel neuropeptide S receptor antagonist with potent in vivo activity. *J. Med. Chem.* **2021**, *64*, 4089–4108. [CrossRef] [PubMed]
27. Lennertz, L.; Quednow, B.B.; Schuhmacher, A.; Petrovsky, N.; Frommann, I.; Schulze-Rauschenbach, S.; Landsberg, M.W.; Steinbrecher, A.; Höfels, S.; Pukrop, R.; et al. The functional coding variant Asn107Ile of the neuropeptide S receptor gene (NPSR1) is associated with schizophrenia and modulates verbal memory and the acoustic startle response. *Int. J. Neuropsychopharmacol.* **2012**, *15*, 1205–1215. [CrossRef]
28. Okamura, N.; Hashimoto, K.; Iyo, M.; Shimizu, E.; Dempfle, A.; Friedel, S.; Reinscheid, R.K. Gender-specific association of a functional coding polymorphism in the Neuropeptide S receptor gene with panic disorder but not with schizophrenia or attention-deficit/hyperactivity disorder. *Prog. Neuropsychopharmacol. Biol. Psychiatry* **2007**, *31*, 1444–1448. [CrossRef] [PubMed]
29. Okamura, N.; Reinscheid, R.K.; Ohgake, S.; Iyo, M.; Hashimoto, K. Neuropeptide S attenuates neuropathological, neurochemical, and behavioral changes induced by the NMDA receptor antagonist MK-801. *Neuropharmacology* **2010**, *58*, 166–172. [CrossRef]
30. Pałasz, A.; Rojczyk, E. Neuroleptics affect neuropeptide S and NPSR mRNA levels in the rat brain. *J. Mol. Neurosci.* **2015**, *57*, 352–357. [CrossRef]
31. Pałasz, A.; Rojczyk, E.; Golyszny, M.; Filipczyk, L.; Worthington, J.J.; Wiaderkiewicz, R. Long-term treatment with haloperidol affects neuropeptide S and NPSR mRNA levels in the rat brain. *Acta Neuropsychiatr.* **2016**, *28*, 110–116. [CrossRef]
32. Markiewicz, R.; Kozioł, M.; Olajossy, M.; Masiak, J. Can brain-derived neurotrophic factor (BDNF) be an indicator of effective rehabilitation interventions in schizophrenia? *Psychiatr. Pol.* **2018**, *52*, 819–834. [CrossRef]
33. Markiewicz, R.; Markiewicz-Gospodarek, A.; Dobrowolska, B.; Łoza, B. Improving clinical, cognitive, and psychosocial dysfunctions in patients with schizophrenia: A neurofeedback randomized control trial. *Neural Plast.* **2021**, *2021*, 4488664. [CrossRef] [PubMed]
34. Schulz, K.F.; Altman, D.G.; Moher, D.; for the CONSORT Group. CONSORT 2010 Statement: Updated guidelines for reporting parallel group randomised trials. *BMC Med.* **2010**, *8*, 18. [CrossRef] [PubMed]
35. Cohen, J. *Statistical Power Analysis for the Behavioral Sciences*, 2nd ed.; Lawrence Erlabaum Associates: Hilsdale, NJ, USA, 1988; ISBN 0-8058-083-5.
36. Walsh-Messinger, J.; Antonius, D.; Opler, M.; Aujero, N.; Goetz, D.M.; Goetz, R.; Malaspina, D. Factor structure of the positive and negative syndrome scale (PANSS) differs by sex. *Clin. Schizophr. Relat. Psychoses.* **2018**, *11*, 207–213. [CrossRef]
37. Bates, M.E.; Lemay, E.P. The d2 Test of attention: Construct validity and extensions in scoring techniques. *J. Int. Neuropsychol Soc.* **2004**, *10*, 392–400. [CrossRef] [PubMed]
38. Brickenkamp, R. *Test d2 Aufmerksamkeits-Belastungs Test*, 7th ed.; Verlag u Psychologie (Hogrefe): Gottingen, Germany, 1981.
39. Steinborn, M.B.; Langner, R.; Flehmig, H.C.; Huestegge, L. Methodology of performance scoring in the d2 sustained-attention test: Cumulative-reliability functions and practical guidelines. *Psychol. Assess.* **2017**, *30*, 339–357. [CrossRef] [PubMed]
40. D'Elia, L.; Satz, P.; Uchiyama, C.L.; White, T. *Color Trails Test. Professional Manual*; Psychological Assessment Resources: Odessa, FL, USA, 1996.
41. Dugbartey, A.T.; Townes, B.D.; Mahurin, R.K. Equivalence of the color trails test and trail making test in nonnative English-speakers. *Arch. Clin. Neuropsychol.* **2000**, *15*, 425–431. [CrossRef] [PubMed]
42. Beck, A.T.; Baruch, E.; Balter, J.M.; Steer, R.A.; Warman, D.M. A new instrument for measuring insight: The Beck cognitive insight scale. *Schizophr. Res.* **2004**, *68*, 319–329. [CrossRef]
43. Felton, B.J.; Revenson, T.A.; Hinrichsen, G.A. Stress and coping in the explanation of psychological adjustment among chronically ill adults. *Soc. Sci. Med.* **1984**, *18*, 889–898. [CrossRef]
44. Leong, W.C.; Azmi, N.A.; Wee, L.H.; Rajah, H.D.A.; Chan, C.M.H. Validation, and reliability of the Bahasa Malaysia language version of the Acceptance of Illness Scale among Malaysian patients with cancer. *PLoS ONE* **2021**, *16*, e0256216. [CrossRef]
45. Schwarzer, R.; Jerusalem, M. Generalized Self-Efficacy scale. In *Measures in Health Psychology: A User's Portfolio. Causal and Control Beliefs*; Weinman, J., Wright, S., Johnston, M., Eds.; NFER-NELSON: Windsor, UK, 1995; pp. 35–37.

46. Romppel, M.; Herrmann-Lingen, C.; Wachter, R.; Edelmann, F.; Düngen, H.D.; Pieske, B.; Grande, G. A short form of the General Self-Efficacy Scale (GSE-6): Development, psychometric properties and validity in an intercultural non-clinical sample and a sample of patients at risk for heart failure. *Psychosoc Med.* **2013**, *10*, Doc01. [CrossRef] [PubMed]
47. Kay, S.R.; Fiszbein, A.; Opler, L.A. The positive and negative syndrome scale (PANSS) for schizophrenia. *Schizophr. Bull.* **1987**, *13*, 261–276. [CrossRef] [PubMed]
48. Wykes, T.; Reeder, C.; Williams, C.; Corner, J.; Rice, C.; Everitt, B. Are the effects of cognitive remediation therapy (CRT) durable? Results from an exploratory trial in schizophrenia. *Schizophr. Res.* **2003**, *61*, 163–174. [CrossRef]
49. Tomás, P.; Fuentes, I.; Roder, V.; Ruiz, J.C. Cognitive rehabilitation programs in schizophrenia: Status and perspectives. *Int. J. Psychol. Psychol. Ther.* **2010**, *10*, 191–204.
50. Baddeley, A.D.; Graham, H. Working Memory. In *The Psychology of Learning and Motivation*; Bower, G.H., Ed.; Academic Press: New York, NY, USA, 1974; Volume 2, pp. 47–89; ISBN 978-0-12-543308-2. [CrossRef]
51. Gain, U. The cognitive function and the framework of the functional hierarchy. *Appl. Comput. Inform.* **2018**, *16*, 81–116. [CrossRef]
52. Laere, E.; Tee, S.F.; Tang, P.Y. Assessment of cognition in schizophrenia using trail making test: A meta-analysis. *Psychiatry Investig.* **2018**, *15*, 945–955. [CrossRef] [PubMed]
53. Tyburski, E.; Karabanowicz, E.; Mak, M.; Lebiecka, Z.; Samochowiec, A.; Pełka-Wysiecka, J.; Sagan, L.; Samochowiec, J. Color Trails Test: A new set of data on cognitive flexibility and processing speed in schizophrenia. *Front. Psychiatry* **2020**, *11*, 521. [CrossRef]
54. Green, M.F.; Horan, W.P.; Lee, J. Social cognition in schizophrenia. *Nat. Rev. Neurosci.* **2015**, *16*, 620–631. [CrossRef]
55. Lysaker, P.H.; Dimaggio, G.; Carcione, A.; Procacci, M.; Buck, K.D.; Davis, L.W.; Nicolò, G. Metacognition, and schizophrenia: The capacity for self-reflectivity as a predictor for prospective assessments of work performance over six months. *Schizophr. Res.* **2009**, *122*, 124–130. [CrossRef] [PubMed]
56. Lysaker, P.H.; Leonhardt, B.L.; Pijnenborg, M.; van Donkersgoed, R.; de Jong, S.; Dimaggio, G. Metacognition in schizophrenia spectrum disorders: Methods of assessment and associations with neurocognition, symptoms, cognitive style, and function. *Isr. J. Psychiatry Relat. Sci.* **2014**, *51*, 54–62. [PubMed]
57. Bonfils, K.A.; Haas, G.L.; Salyers, M.P. Emotion-specific performance across empathy tasks in schizophrenia: Influence of metacognitive capacity. *Schizophr. Res. Cogn.* **2019**, *19*, 100139. [CrossRef] [PubMed]
58. Favrod, J.; Zimmermann, G.; Raffard, S.; Pomini, V.; Khazaal, Y. The Beck Cognitive Insight Scale in outpatients with psychotic disorders: Further evidence from a French-speaking sample. *Can. J. Psychiatry.* **2008**, *53*, 783–787. [CrossRef] [PubMed]
59. Du, X.; Li, J.; Xiong, D.; Pan, Z.; Wu, F.; Ning, Y.; Chen, J.; Wu, K. Research on electroencephalogram specifics in patients with schizophrenia under cognitive load. *Sheng Wu Yi Xue Gong Cheng Xue Za Zhi* **2020**, *37*, 45–53. [CrossRef]
60. Burton, C.Z.; Harvey, P.D.; Patterson, T.L.; Twamley, E.W. Neurocognitive insight, and objective cognitive functioning in schizophrenia. *Schizophr. Res.* **2016**, *171*, 131–136. [CrossRef]
61. Lysaker, P.H.; Dimaggio, G.; Buck, K.D.; Carcione, A.; Nicolò, G. Metacognition within narratives of schizophrenia: Associations with multiple domains of neurocognition. *Schizophr. Res.* **2007**, *93*, 278–287. [CrossRef] [PubMed]
62. August, S.M.; Kiwanuka, J.N.; McMahon, R.P.; Gold, J.M. The MATRICS Consensus Cognitive Battery (MCCB): Clinical and cognitive correlates. *Schizophr. Res.* **2012**, *134*, 76–82. [CrossRef] [PubMed]
63. Keefe, R.S.; Poe, M.; Walker, T.M.; Harvey, P.D. The relationship of the Brief Assessment of Cognition in Schizophrenia (BACS) to functional capacity and real-world functional outcome. *J. Clin. Exp. Neuropsychol.* **2006**, *28*, 260–269. [CrossRef] [PubMed]

Journal of
Clinical Medicine

MDPI

Article

Emotional Processing Profile in Patients with First Episode Schizophrenia: The Influence of Neurocognition

Verónica Romero-Ferreiro [1,2,3,4], Lorena García-Fernández [2,5,6], Ana Isabel Aparicio [2,7,8], Isabel Martínez-Gras [3,9], Mónica Dompablo [2,3,10], Luis Sánchez-Pastor [3], David Rentero [2,3], Miguel Ángel Alvarez-Mon [11,12,13], Juan Manuel Espejo-Saavedra [3,14], Guillermo Lahera [2,11,13,15], Paloma Marí-Beffa [16], José Luis Santos [2,7,8] and Roberto Rodriguez-Jimenez [2,3,4,14,*]

1. Department of Psychology, Universidad Europea de Madrid, 28670 Madrid, Spain; veronica.romero@universidadeuropea.es
2. CIBERSAM (Biomedical Research Networking Centre in Mental Health), 28029 Madrid, Spain; lorena.garciaf@umh.es (L.G.-F.); aiaparicio@sescam.jccm.es (A.I.A.); monicadompablo@gmail.com (M.D.); davidrente7@hotmail.com (D.R.); guillermo.lahera@gmail.com (G.L.); joseluis.santosg@gmail.com (J.L.S.)
3. Instituto de Investigación Sanitaria Hospital 12 de Octubre (Imas12), 28041 Madrid, Spain; isabelmgras@gmail.com (I.M.-G.); lspastor@salud.madrid.org (L.S.-P.); juanmaespejosaavedra@gmail.com (J.M.E.-S.)
4. CogPsy Group, Universidad Complutense de Madrid (UCM), 28040 Madrid, Spain
5. Clinical Medicine Department, Universidad Miguel Hernández, 03550 Alicante, Spain
6. Psychiatry Department, Hospital Universitario de San Juan, 03550 Alicante, Spain
7. Psychiatry Department, Hospital Virgen de la Luz, 16002 Cuenca, Spain
8. Neurobiological Research Group, Institute of Technology, Universidad de Castilla-La Mancha, 16071 Cuenca, Spain
9. RETIC (Network of Addictive Conditions), Institute of Health Carlos III, 28029 Madrid, Spain
10. Cardenal Cisneros, Centro de Enseñanza Superior Adscrito a la Universidad Complutense de Madrid, 28040 Madrid, Spain
11. Department of Medicine and Medical Specialities, Faculty of Medicine and Health Sciences, University of Alcalá, 28801 Alcalá de Henares, Spain; maalvarezdemon@icloud.com
12. Department of Psychiatry and Mental Health, Hospital Universitario Infanta Leonor. 28031 Madrid, Spain
13. Ramón y Cajal Institute of Sanitary Research (IRYCIS), 28034 Madrid, Spain
14. Legal Medicine, Psychiatry and Pathology Department, Universidad Complutense de Madrid, 28040 Madrid, Spain
15. Department of Psychiatry, Príncipe de Asturias University Hospital, 28805 Alcalá de Henares, Spain
16. School of Psychology, University of Wales Bangor, Bangor LL57 2AS, UK; pbeffa@bangor.ac.uk

* Correspondence: roberto.rodriguez.jimenez@gmail.com; Tel.: +34-91-390-8536

Citation: Romero-Ferreiro, V.; García-Fernández, L.; Aparicio, A.I.; Martínez-Gras, I.; Dompablo, M.; Sánchez-Pastor, L.; Rentero, D.; Alvarez-Mon, M.Á.; Espejo-Saavedra, J.M.; Lahera, G.; et al. Emotional Processing Profile in Patients with First Episode Schizophrenia: The Influence of Neurocognition. *J. Clin. Med.* **2022**, *11*, 2044. https://doi.org/10.3390/jcm11072044

Academic Editors: Armida Mucci and Birgit Derntl

Received: 18 February 2022
Accepted: 4 April 2022
Published: 6 April 2022

Abstract: This study sought to investigate the influence of neurocognition on the emotional processing profiles of patients with first-episode schizophrenia, using the 4-branch Mayer-Salovey-Caruso Emotional Intelligence Test (MSCEIT) (Perceiving Emotions; Facilitating Emotions; Understanding Emotions and Managing Emotions). A sample of 78 patients with first-episode schizophrenia and a group of 90 non-psychiatric control subjects were included in this work. The initial results showed that patients had lower scores than controls for the "Understanding Emotions" and "Managing Emotions" MSCEIT branches. However, after controlling for neurocognition, the only deficits were found on the "Managing Emotions" branch of the MSCEIT. This branch can be considered as measuring a more sophisticated level of emotional processing, which may constitute a deficit in itself. In conclusion, patients with first-episode schizophrenia present deficits in social cognition at the highest level that seem to be independent from neurocognition. These findings support the inclusion of the "Managing Emotions" branch of the MSCEIT as part of the MCCB.

Keywords: schizophrenia; first episode; emotional processing; social cognition; MCCB; MSCEIT

1. Introduction

Social cognition includes theory of mind, social perception, social knowledge, attributional biases, and emotion processing [1]. Some of the most studied aspects of social cognition in schizophrenia are emotion processing and mentalizing. The study of emotion processing analyzes how people perceive and use emotions adaptively in different contexts. Mentalizing refers to the ability to infer the intentions, dispositions, emotions and beliefs of others [2]. People diagnosed with schizophrenia have consistently shown impairments in these aspects of social cognition [3,4], being linked to poor functioning across different stages of the disorder [5–8]. However, there has been a large debate in the literature about the extent of overlap in schizophrenia between social cognition and other more general aspects of non-social cognition with identifiable neural substrates, commonly referred to as neurocognition [9,10]. Neurocognition refers to cognitive domains that have traditionally been referred to as "cognitive" in the literature, such as speed of processing, working memory, attention, memory, or executive functions [7].There is some evidence supporting the notion that social cognition explains even more variance in community functioning (i.e., interpersonal relations, work functioning) than neurocognition [11], and that it may be a mediator between neurocognition and functional outcome in schizophrenia [1]. In fact, first-episode schizophrenia patients have been found to develop some compensatory strategies for both cognitive and emotional deficits [12,13].

Neurocognition has been extensively studied in schizophrenia [14,15]. The lack of a general consensus regarding the instruments to assess cognitive functioning in this population was one of the reasons that the U.S. National Institute of Mental Health (NIMH) promoted the creation of MATRICS—"Measurement and Treatment Research to Improve Cognition in Schizophrenia" [16]. One of the primary goals of this initiative was to reach a consensus and develop a cognitive battery for use in clinical trials and research. This initiative culminated with the creation of the MATRICS Consensus Cognitive Battery (MCCB) [9,10]. Several studies have been conducted using this battery with first-episode schizophrenia individuals (FESz) [17,18]. The MCCB comprises ten tasks assessing seven cognitive domains that are impaired in schizophrenia. Among them, only one task assesses social cognition (in particular, emotional processing): the Managing Emotions (branch 4) from the Mayer-Salovey-Caruso Emotional Intelligence Test (MSCEIT) [19]. The other three branches of the test (Perceiving Emotions, Facilitating Emotions and Understanding Emotions) were left out.

Several studies have applied the MCCB in FESz, and the results concerning emotional processing are sometimes conflicting. Specifically, some authors have found a relative preservation of these abilities in early-onset schizophrenia compared to controls [17,20], but others have found no differences between first-episode patients and controls [18,21–23]. Likewise, some authors found those impairments to be stable across phases of the disorder [24,25], while others found a decline in chronic patients [23], or an even better performance in chronic patients than in FESz [26]. Besides these inconsistent results, there are insufficient studies applying the full version of the MSCEIT to explore whether disturbances in other domains of emotional processing exist in patients with first-episode schizophrenia. The aims of the present study were to obtain a profile of emotional processing in a group of patients with first-episode schizophrenia assessed with the complete MSCEIT, compared with a healthy control group sample, and to study the possible modulatory role that neurocognition could have on social cognition. Specifically, the two hypotheses that were tested were that: (i) FESz patients would show a significant impairment in the four MSCEIT branches compared to controls; and (ii) that those impairments would be modulated by neurocognitive functioning to some extent.

2. Materials and Methods

2.1. Participants

This cross-sectional study was carried out between 1 March 2020, and 31 December 2021. The sample included 78 FESz outpatients who were consecutively recruited in the

First Episode Programs of the Universitary "12 de Octubre" Hospital (Madrid, Spain) and "Virgen de la Luz" Hospital (Cuenca, Spain). A total of 102 patients were initially considered, but 11 refused to participate, 3 were excluded due to poor language comprehension, and 10 for substance use. The inclusion criteria were: (1) diagnosis of schizophrenia or schizophreniform disorder according to DSM-5 criteria [27], using the Structured Clinical Interview for DSM-5 (SCID-5) [28]; (2) at least eight weeks of stabilization on their antipsychotic medication after discharge from the hospitalization unit; (3) age of 18 to 55 years; and (4) sufficient fluency in Spanish to allow them to complete the protocol. Exclusion criteria were: (1) substance abuse/dependence in the past eight weeks (excluding nicotine and caffeine) and using clinical interviews and urine analysis for this purpose; (2) neurological or somatic diseases that could interfere with the performance of the tasks; (3) traumatic head injury; and (4) premorbid IQ score estimated by the Word Accentuation Test (WAT) [29,30] below 70. The clinical sample was compared with 90 healthy control subjects. The inclusion criteria for this group were: (1) age of 18 to 55 years, and (2) sufficient fluency in Spanish to allow them to complete the protocol. Exclusion criteria were the same as for the schizophrenia patients, with the addition of: (5) no diagnosis of any mental disorder according to DSM-5 criteria, and (6) no psychotic disorder as antecedent in first-degree relatives. Controls were selected from cultural associations belonging to the same geographical area as the patient group. Both patients and controls were clinically assessed by experienced researchers who have used the scales for more than 5 years. The study was approved by the Clinical Research Ethics Committee of the Hospital 12 de Octubre, and all participants signed an informed consent form. The demographics and clinical characteristics of the patients and healthy controls are presented in Table 1.

Table 1. Mean (SD) of demographic and clinical characteristics of participants.

	FESz (n = 78)	Controls (n = 90)	Statistics
Age years	26.23 (7.3)	27.97 (7.0)	$t = 1.56$, $p = 0.12$
Sex, n (% male)	55 (70.5%)	43 (47.8%)	$\chi^2 = 8.89$, $p = 0.003$
Education years	12.0 (3.0)	14.2 (2.9)	$t = 4.87$, $p < 0.001$
PANSS—Positive	10.6 (4.5)		
PANSS—Negative	16.7 (8.0)		
PANSS—General Psychopathology	27.9 (8.7)		
CPZ [1]	403.9 (246.8)		
Duration of untreated psychosis (days)	168.9 (186.7)		

[1] Chlorpromazine equivalent dose (mg/day).

2.2. Instruments

Symptoms were assessed for descriptive purposes using the Positive and Negative Syndrome Scale (PANSS) [31]. Emotional processing was evaluated using the Mayer-Salovey-Caruso Emotional Intelligence Test (MSCEIT) which consists of 8 subscales assessing 4 components (branches) of emotion processing [19]. The first branch, Perceiving Emotions, has 2 subscales measuring emotion perception in faces and pictures (e.g., identifying the degree to which certain feelings are expressed by a color photograph of a human face). The second branch, Facilitating Emotions, is derived from 2 subscales examining how mood enhances thinking and reasoning, and which emotions are associated with which sensations (e.g., asking subjects to evaluate the usefulness of different emotions that would best assist a specific cognitive task and behavior). The third branch, Understanding Emotions, has 2 subscales that measure the ability to comprehend emotional information, including blends and changes between and among emotions (e.g., asking participants to select which 1 of 5 emotions best describes a situation). The fourth branch, Managing Emotions, has 2 subscales that examine the regulation of emotions in oneself and in relationships with others by presenting vignettes of various situations, along with ways to cope with the emotions depicted in these vignettes. For the current study, we examined the 4 MSCEIT branch scores corrected for age and gender. Finally, cognitive performance was evaluated using the MCCB which assesses seven cognitive domains: Speed of Processing,

Attention/Vigilance, Working Memory, Verbal Learning, Visual Learning, Reasoning and Problem Solving, and Social Cognition [9,10]. This battery allows the neurocognition score to be calculated by combining these different neurocognitive domains, excluding the social cognition domain. This study used the published and approved translation of the MCCB for Spain and the Spanish normative and standardized data correction [32]. With the objective of controlling the possible effect of neurocognition, the MCCB Neurocognition T-score, including all domains except social cognition, was also calculated for each participant. Age and gender correction for normative scoring were used, following the recommendations by the co-norming and standardization guidelines [9].

2.3. Statistical Analysis

Data were managed and analyzed with SPSS v.24. Raw data from each branch of MSCEIT were corrected according to age and gender. Similarly, raw scores from each test of MCCB were entered into the MCCB Computer Scoring Program to produce age- and gender-corrected T-scores. These data were submitted to a two (group: patients, controls) by four (MSCEIT branches) mixed model analysis, with random intercept for each subject and an identity covariance structure. The group x branch interaction was analyzed with an estimated marginal means post hoc analysis with the Bonferroni adjustment. As MSCEIT and MCCB scores were standardized according to age and gender, it was not felt necessary to include them as covariates in the analysis, even though differences between groups were found. However, years of education was included in the models, as there were differences between groups, and they were not controlled by standardized scores.

Finally, the same analysis was repeated including the MCCB Neurocognition T-score as a covariate, with the aim of studying the influence of neurocognition on emotional processing. Collinearity diagnostics were based on the variance inflation factor (VIF). Given that all VIF values were lower than 1.4, we can assume that there were no effects of collinearity.

3. Results

3.1. Descriptive Statistics

As can be seen in Table 1, there were no differences between patients and controls in terms of age $t(166)= 1.56$, $p = 0.12$. The distribution of gender differed across groups $\chi^2 = 8.89$, $p = 0.003$. Patients and controls also differed in years of education $t(159) = 4.87$, $p < 0.001$. Mean age- and gender-corrected T-scores for each MSCEIT branch and MCCB domains and neurocognition scores are presented in Table 2.

Table 2. Mean (standard deviations) of T-scores of the MSCEIT and MCCB domains (excluding social cognition) and Neurocognition. FESz = first episode of schizophrenia.

	FESz (*n* = 78)	Controls (*n* = 90)	*t* Test (*p* Value)
MSCEIT Perceiving Emotions	104.97 (14.3)	105.18 (14.4)	*t*(166) = 0.927 (0.927)
MSCEIT Facilitating Emotions	101.35 (14.3)	102.02 (14.9)	*t*(166) = 0.298 (0.766)
MSCEIT Understanding Emotions	90.32 (14.4)	98.8 (14.1)	*t*(166) = 3.85 (<0.001)
MSCEIT Managing Emotions	91.12 (14.1)	102.31 (15.7)	*t*(165) = 4.81 (<0.001)
MCCB Speed of Processing	35.6 (9.0)	51.9 (8.8)	*t*(165) = 11.75 (<0.001)
MCCB Attention/Vigilance	34.2 (8.8)	48.2 (9.5)	*t*(165) = 9.83 (<0.001)
MCCB Working Memory	38.1 (10.3)	49.3 (10.8)	*t*(165) = 6.85 (<0.001)
MCCB Verbal Learning	31.0 (13.9)	45.0 (11.8)	*t*(165) = 7.07 (<0.001)
MCCB Visual Learning	34.6 (15.2)	47.0 (10.8)	*t*(137) = 5.97 (<0.001)
MCCB Reasoning and Probl. Solving	40.8 (10.6)	52.6 (7.7)	*t*(139) = 8.16 (<0.001)
MCCB Neurocognition	30.54 (11.8)	48.27 (10.2)	*t*(153) = 10.30 (<0.001)

3.2. Mixed Model Analysis

3.2.1. Comparison between FESz and Controls in the Four Branches of the MSCEIT

There was a significant effect for the MSCEIT branch ($F(3, 476) = 26.51$, $p < 0.001$), and a significance for years of education ($F(1, 158) = 15.92$, $p < 0.001$). No significance of group was found ($F(1, 158) = 2.69$, $p = 0.103$). A significant interaction between the groups and the MSCEIT branch was found ($F(3, 476) = 7.85$, $p < 0.001$). Pairwise comparisons between groups showed that FESz patients had lower scores than the control group in Understanding Emotions ($p = 0.011$, mean diff = −5.97, 95%CI: −10.57; −1.37) and in Managing Emotions ($p < 0.001$, mean diff = −8.56, 95%CI: −13.17; −3.95). Neither Perceiving Emotions nor Facilitating Emotions showed differences between FESz and controls ($p = 0.409$ and $p = 0.449$, respectively).

3.2.2. Comparison between FESz and Controls in the Four Branches of the MSCEIT Controlling for Neurocognition Effects

After including the MCCB neurocognitive score as a covariate, the results were as follows: the main effect of MSCEIT branch ($F(3, 476) = 26.48$, $p < 0.001$), and years of education remained significant ($F(1, 157) = 7.50$, $p = 0.007$). Neurocognition revealed a significant effect on the model ($F(1, 157) = 5.32$, $p = 0.022$). Again, there was no main effect of group ($F(1, 157) = 0.007$, $p = 0.933$). Finally, the group by MSCEIT branch interaction was significant ($F(3, 494) = 8.74$, $p < 0.001$). Pairwise comparisons between groups showed that FESz patients had lower scores than the control group only in Managing Emotions (branch 4) ($p = 0.02$, mean diff = −6.00, 95%CI: −11.08; −0.93). There were no differences between patients and controls in Perceiving Emotions, Facilitating Emotions and Understanding Emotions ($p = 0.083$, $p = 0.095$ and $p = 0.182$, respectively).

4. Discussion

The main objective of this study was to investigate emotional processing of first-episode schizophrenia patients, considering the possible modulating effects of neurocognition.

Initially, results showed deficits in the schizophrenia patient group compared to controls in the branches measuring Understanding and Managing Emotions, which represent emotional abilities that require higher level cognitive processing. Importantly, when the MCCB neurocognition scores were included in the analysis, the effect changed, and the deficits were only observed in the Managing Emotions branch. This result implies that the poor capacity to understand emotional information showed by first-episode schizophrenia patients was accounted for, partially, by neurocognitive deficits. When the neurocognitive performance was controlled for, only the differences in the ability to regulate emotions with themselves and others remained significant. Our results show that emotional regulation entails a relatively independent deficit in first-episode schizophrenia, and is not linked to other aspects of general cognitive deficits. This result suggests that higher-order social cognition abilities might be controlled and regulated by a specific neural circuit. This finding also supports the inclusion of this single branch of the MSCEIT as part of the MCCB.

Literature comparing emotional processing between first-episode patients and controls with MSCEIT have mostly used the Managing Emotions branch as a sole measure of emotional processing, generally revealing deficits in the patients' group [22]. Some other authors, however, did not found this pattern, which could be explained by the differences in our experimental design. For example, some used relatively smaller sample sizes ($n = 31$ patients and $n = 67$ controls) [20];], or included patients with schizoaffective disorder, depressed type [17], making a close comparison difficult. As far as we know, only one study has compared patients and controls using the four branches of the MSCEIT. This study assessed a sample of three phases of psychotic illness: prodromal, first episode, and chronic schizophrenia, and a control group. They found deficits between patients (as a whole) and controls in the four branches, but none of them changed across the phases [24]. It is also important they did not study the potential effect of neurocognition. This may be the reason why their results do not correspond with those reported in the present study.

Finally, apart from understanding emotions, patients with first-episode schizophrenia in our study demonstrated preserved abilities regarding emotion perception (Perceiving Emotions) in line with previous research [33], and an appropriate evaluation of how different emotions guide behavior (Facilitating Emotions). These results need to be taken into account when designing cognitive remediation programs to improve social cognition in schizophrenia. Hypothetically, these programs should focus on (apart from, of course, neurocognition) the management of emotions, that is, in the "strategic" sector of emotional intelligence which entails high-level thought processing [34]. Patients with FESz could better benefit from broad social cognition training with a pragmatic, ecological, and action-based approach.

The main strengths of this study lay in the relatively large sample size, the use of the complete MSCEIT, and the use of MCCB to control the effect of neurocognition (and years of education) on the emotional processing scores. Despite this, there were some differences between the groups in terms of gender and years of education; however, their impact on our results was negligeable, as both MSCEIT and MCCB scores were corrected for age and gender. In fact, we performed an analysis including age and gender as covariates, but this had no impact on the results (data not shown). Additionally, given that some clinical manifestations of schizophrenia are earlier in men than women, and thus, available evidence suggest that their neurocognitive and social cognition abilities may differ, we reconducted the analyses using only the male participants of our total sample. The results were essentially the same as those exposed in this study, with variations according to the loss of statistical power. However, this should be considered a preliminary result. Future studies will be needed to address gender-specific differences in the social cognition of FESz patients. The results reported here using MSCEIT are important for evaluating the emotional processes in first-episode schizophrenia patients, but further studies should include other aspects of social cognition, such as social perception, theory of mind, or attributional bias [35].

5. Conclusions

This study shows that first-episode schizophrenia patients are selectively impaired in emotional processing when this requires high-level cognition, paired with other more general deficits in neurocognition. Current evidence supports the specific inclusion of the Managing Emotions branch when using MCCB, and the assessment of neurocognition in experimental and clinical settings.

Author Contributions: Conceptualization, R.R.-J., V.R.-F. and L.G.-F.; methodology, R.R.-J. and J.L.S.; statistical analysis, V.R.-F.; investigation, A.I.A., I.M.-G., M.D., L.S.-P., D.R., M.Á.A.-M. and J.M.E.-S.; resources, J.L.S., G.L. and P.M.-B.; data curation, V.R.-F.; writing—original draft preparation, V.R.-F., L.G.-F. and R.R.-J.; writing—review and editing, L.G.-F., G.L., P.M.-B. and R.R.-J. All authors have read and agreed to the published version of the manuscript.

Funding: This research was supported in part by the by the Instituto de Salud Carlos III (grants PI16/00359, PI19/00766; Fondo de Investigaciones Sanitarias/FEDER), by the European Development Regional Fund "A way to achieve Europe" (ERDF), by Madrid Regional Government (R&D activities in Biomedicine S2017/BMD-3740 (AGES-CM 2-CM)) and Structural Funds of the European Union.

Institutional Review Board Statement: The study was conducted in accordance with the Declaration of Helsinki and approved by the Comité de Ética e Investigación Clínica del Hospital Universitario 12 de Octubre (protocol code 16/329 and date of approval 25 February 2020).

Informed Consent Statement: Informed consent was obtained from all subjects involved in the study.

Data Availability Statement: The data from this study will be made publicly available following the completion of all publications and following the removal of all identifiers by request.

Conflicts of Interest: R. Rodriguez-Jimenez has been a consultant for, spoken in activities of, or received grants from: Instituto de Salud Carlos III, Fondo de Investigación Sanitaria (FIS), Centro de Investigación Biomédica en Red de Salud Mental (CIBERSAM), Madrid Regional Government (S2010/ BMD-2422 AGES; S2017/BMD-3740), JanssenCilag, Lundbeck, Otsuka, Pfizer, Ferrer, Juste, Takeda, Exeltis, Casen-Recordati, Angelini.

References

1. González-Ortega, I.; González-Pinto, A.; Alberich, S.; Echeburuá, E.; Bernardo, M.; Cabrera, B.; Amoretti, S.; Lobo, A.; Arango, C.; Corripio, I.; et al. Influence of social cognition as a mediator between cognitive reserve and psychosocial functioning in patients with first episode psychosis. *Psychol. Med.* **2019**, *50*, 2702–2710. [CrossRef] [PubMed]
2. Green, M.F.; Horan, W.P.; Lee, J. Nonsocial and social cognition in schizophrenia: Current evidence and future directions. *World Psychiatry* **2019**, *18*, 146–161. [CrossRef] [PubMed]
3. García-Fernández, L.; Cabot-Ivorra, N.; Romero-Ferreiro, V.; Pérez-Martín, J.; Rodriguez-Jimenez, R. Differences in theory of mind between early and chronic stages in schizophrenia. *J. Psychiatr. Res.* **2020**, *127*, 35–41. [CrossRef]
4. Hajdúk, M.; Harvey, P.D.; Penn, D.L.; Pinkham, A.E. Social cognitive impairments in individuals with schizophrenia vary in severity. *J. Psychiatr. Res.* **2018**, *104*, 65–71. [CrossRef] [PubMed]
5. Harvey, P.D.; Deckler, E.; Jarsksog, L.F.; Penn, D.L.; Pinkham, A.E. Predictors of social functioning in patients with higher and lower levels of reduced emotional experience: Social cognition, social competence, and symptom severity. *Schizophr. Res.* **2019**, *206*, 271–276. [CrossRef]
6. Javed, A.; Charles, A. The importance of social cognition in improving functional outcomes in schizophrenia. *Front. Psychiatry* **2018**, *9*, 157. [CrossRef]
7. Nuechterlein, K.H.; Barch, D.M.; Gold, J.M.; Goldberg, T.E.; Green, M.F.; Heaton, R.K. Identification of separable cognitive factors in schizophrenia. *Schizophr. Res.* **2004**, *72*, 29–39. [CrossRef]
8. Ospina, L.H.; Nitzburg, G.C.; Shanahan, M.; Perez-Rodriguez, M.M.; Larsen, E.; Latifoglu, A.; Burdick, K.E. Social cognition moderates the relationship between neurocognition and community functioning in bipolar disorder. *J. Affect. Disord.* **2018**, *235*, 7–14. [CrossRef]
9. Kern, R.S.; Nuechterlein, K.H.; Green, M.F.; Baade, L.E.; Fenton, W.S.; Gold, J.M.; Keefe, R.S.; Mesholam-Gately, R.; Mintz, J.; Seidman, L.J.; et al. The MATRICS Consensus Cognitive Battery, Part 2: Co-Norming and Standardization. *Am. J. Psychiatry* **2008**, *165*, 214–220. [CrossRef]
10. Nuechterlein, K.H.; Green, M.F.; Kern, R.S.; Baade, L.E.; Barch, D.M.; Cohen, J.D.; Essock, S.; Fenton, W.S.; Frese, F.J.; Gold, J.M.; et al. The MATRICS consensus cognitive battery, part 1: Test selection, reliability, and validity. *Am. J. Psychiatry* **2008**, *165*, 203–213. [CrossRef]
11. Fett, A.K.J.; Viechtbauer, W.; Dominguez, M.G.; Penn, D.L.; van Os, J.; Krabbendam, L. The relationship between neurocognition and social cognition with functional outcomes in schizophrenia: A meta-analysis. *Neurosci. Biobehav. Rev.* **2011**, *35*, 573–588. [CrossRef] [PubMed]
12. Ferri, F.; Salone, A.; Ebisch, S.J.; De Berardis, D.; Romani, G.L.; Ferro, F.M.; Gallese, V. Action verb understanding in first-episode schizophrenia: Is there evidence for a simulation deficit? *Neuropsychologia* **2012**, *50*, 988–996. [CrossRef] [PubMed]
13. Ferri, F.; Costantini, M.; Salone, A.; Ebisch, S.; De Berardis, D.; Mazzola, V.; Arciero, G.; Ferro, F.M.; Di Giannantonio, M.; Romani, G.L.; et al. Binding action and emotion in first-episode schizophrenia. *Psychopathology* **2014**, *47*, 394–407. [CrossRef] [PubMed]
14. Becker, M.L.; Ahmed, A.O.; Benning, S.D.; Barchard, K.A.; John, S.E.; Allen, D.N. Bifactor model of cognition in schizophrenia: Evidence for general and specific abilities. *J. Psychiatr. Res.* **2021**, *136*, 132–139. [CrossRef]
15. Davies, G.; Greenwood, K. A meta-analytic review of the relationship between neurocognition, metacognition and functional outcome in schizophrenia. *J. Ment. Health* **2020**, *29*, 496–505. [CrossRef]
16. Green, M.F.; Nuechterlein, K.H. The MATRICS initiative: Developing a consensus cognitive battery for clinical trials. *Schizophr. Res.* **2004**, *72*, 1–3. [CrossRef]
17. McCleery, A.; Ventura, J.; Kern, R.S.; Subotnik, K.L.; Gretchen-Doorly, D.; Green, M.F.; Hellemann, G.S.; Nuechterlein, K.H. Cognitive functioning in first-episode schizophrenia: MATRICS Consensus Cognitive Battery (MCCB) Profile of Impairment. *Schizophr. Res.* **2014**, *157*, 33–39. [CrossRef]
18. Rodriguez-Jimenez, R.; Santos, J.L.; Dompablo, M.; Santabárbara, J.; Aparicio, A.I.; Olmos, R.; Jiménez-López, E.; Sánchez-Morla, E.; Lobo, A.; Palomo, T.; et al. MCCB cognitive profile in Spanish first episode schizophrenia patients. *Schizophr. Res.* **2019**, *211*, 88–92. [CrossRef]
19. Mayer, J.D.; Salovey, P.; Caruso, D.R. *Mayer-Salovey-Caruso Emotional Intelligence Test*^{TM}; MHS Assessments: North Tonawanda, NY, USA, 2002; pp. 1–11.
20. Holmén, A.; Juuhl-Langseth, M.; Thormodsen, R.; Melle, I.; Rund, B.R. Neuropsychological profile in early-onset schizophrenia-spectrum disorders: Measured with the MATRICS battery. *Schizophr. Bull.* **2010**, *36*, 852–859. [CrossRef]
21. Vesterager, L.; Christensen, T.T.; Olsen, B.B.; Krarup, G.; Melau, M.; Forchhammer, H.B.; Nordentoft, M. Cognitive and clinical predictors of functional capacity in patients with first episode schizophrenia. *Schizophr. Res.* **2012**, *141*, 251–256. [CrossRef]

22. Zhang, H.; Wang, Y.; Hu, Y.; Zhu, Y.; Zhang, T.; Wang, J.; Ma, K.; Shi, C.; Yu, X.; Li, C. Meta-analysis of cognitive function in Chinese first-episode schizophrenia: MATRICS Consensus Cognitive Battery (MCCB) profile of impairment. *Gen. Psychiatry* **2019**, *32*, 100043. [CrossRef] [PubMed]
23. Wu, J.Q.; Chen, D.C.; Tan, Y.L.; Xiu, M.H.; De Yang, F.; Soares, J.C.; Zhang, X.Y. Cognitive impairments in first-episode drug-naive and chronic medicated schizophrenia: MATRICS consensus cognitive battery in a Chinese Han population. *Psychiatry Res.* **2016**, *238*, 196–202. [CrossRef] [PubMed]
24. Green, M.F.; Bearden, C.E.; Cannon, T.D.; Fiske, A.P.; Hellemann, G.S.; Horan, W.P.; Kee, K.; Kern, R.S.; Lee, J.; Sergi, M.J.; et al. Social Cognition in Schizophrenia, Part 1: Performance Across Phase of Illness. *Schizophr. Bull.* **2012**, *38*, 854–864. [CrossRef] [PubMed]
25. Thompson, A.; Papas, A.; Bartholomeusz, C.; Allott, K.; Amminger, G.P.; Nelson, B.; Wood, S.; Yung, A. Social cognition in clinical "at risk" for psychosis and first episode psychosis populations. *Schizophr. Res.* **2012**, *141*, 204–209. [CrossRef] [PubMed]
26. Chen, S.; Liu, Y.; Liu, D.; Zhang, G.; Wu, X. The difference of social cognitive and neurocognitive performance between patients with schizophrenia at different stages and influencing factors. *Schizophr. Res. Cogn.* **2021**, *24*, 100195. [CrossRef] [PubMed]
27. American Psychiatric Association. *Diagnostic and Statistical Manual of Mental Disorders (DSM-5®)*; American Psychiatric Pub.: Arlington, VA, USA, 2013.
28. First, M.; Williams, J.M.G.; Karg, R.; Spitzer, R. *Structured Clinical Interview for DSM-5 Disorders–Research Version (SCID-5-RV)*; American Psychiatric Association: Arlington, VA, USA, 2015.
29. Gomar, J.J.; Ortiz-Gil, J.; McKenna, P.J.; Salvador, R.; Sans-Sansa, B.; Sarró, S.; Guerrero, A.; Pomarol-Clotet, E. Validation of the Word Accentuation Test (TAP) as a means of estimating premorbid IQ in Spanish speakers. *Schizophr. Res.* **2011**, *128*, 175–176. [CrossRef] [PubMed]
30. Krueger, K.; Lam, C.; Wilson, R. The word accentuation test—Chicago. *J. Clin. Exp. Neuropsychol.* **2006**, *28*, 1201–1207. [CrossRef]
31. Kay, S.R.; Fiszbein, A.; Opfer, L.A. The positive and negative syndrome scale (PANSS) for schizophrenia. *Schizophr. Bull.* **1987**, *13*, 261–276. [CrossRef]
32. Rodriguez-Jimenez, R.; Bagney, A.; Garcia-Navarro, C.; Aparicio, A.I.; Lopez-Anton, R.; Moreno-Ortega, M.; Jimenez-Arriero, M.A.; Santos, J.L.; Lobo, A.; Kern, R.S.; et al. The MATRICS consensus Cognitive battery (MCCB): Co-norming and standardization in Spain. *Schizophr. Res.* **2012**, *134*, 279–284. [CrossRef]
33. Romero-Ferreiro, V.; Aguado, L.; Rodriguez-Torresano, J.; Palomo, T.; Rodriguez-Jimenez, R.; Pedreira-Massa, J.L. Facial affect recognition in early and late-stage schizophrenia patients. *Schizophr. Res.* **2016**, *172*, 177–183. [CrossRef]
34. Eack, S.M.; Greeno, C.G.; Pogue-Geile, M.F.; Newhill, C.E.; Hogarty, G.E.; Keshavan, M.S. Assessing social-cognitive deficits in schizophrenia with the mayer-salovey-caruso emotional intelligence test. *Schizophr. Bull.* **2010**, *36*, 370–380. [CrossRef] [PubMed]
35. Ludwig, K.A.; Pinkham, A.E.; Harvey, P.D.; Kelsven, S.; Penn, D.L. Social cognition psychometric evaluation (SCOPE) in people with early psychosis: A preliminary study. *Schizophr. Res.* **2017**, *190*, 136–143. [CrossRef] [PubMed]

Journal of
Clinical Medicine

MDPI

Article

Mismatch Negativity and P3a Impairment through Different Phases of Schizophrenia and Their Association with Real-Life Functioning

Giulia M. Giordano [1,*,†], Luigi Giuliani [1,†], Andrea Perrottelli [1], Paola Bucci [1], Giorgio Di Lorenzo [2], Alberto Siracusano [2], Francesco Brando [1], Pasquale Pezzella [1], Michele Fabrazzo [1], Mario Altamura [3], Antonello Bellomo [3], Giammarco Cascino [4], Anna Comparelli [5], Palmiero Monteleone [4], Maurizio Pompili [5], Silvana Galderisi [1], Mario Maj [1] and The Italian Network for Research on Psychoses ‡

1 Department of Psychiatry, University of Campania "Luigi Vanvitelli", 80138 Naples, Italy; luigi.giuliani.91@gmail.com (L.G.); andreaperrottelli@gmail.com (A.P.); paolabucci456@gmail.com (P.B.); brando.francesco@virgilio.it (F.B.); pezzella.pasquale3@gmail.com (P.P.); michele.fabrazzo@unicampania.it (M.F.); silvana.galderisi@gmail.com (S.G.); mario.maj@unicampania.it (M.M.)
2 Department of Systems Medicine, University of Rome Tor Vergata, 00133 Rome, Italy; di.lorenzo@med.uniroma2.it (G.D.L.); siracusano@med.uniroma2.it (A.S.)
3 Psychiatry Unit, Department of Clinical and Experimental Medicine, University of Foggia, 71122 Foggia, Italy; mario.altamura@unifg.it (M.A.); antonello.bellomo@unifg.it (A.B.)
4 Department of Medicine, Surgery and Dentistry "Scuola Medica Salernitana", Section of Neurosciences, University of Salerno, 84133 Salerno, Italy; gcascino@unisa.it (G.C.); pmonteleone@unisa.it (P.M.)
5 Department of Neurosciences, Mental Health and Sensory Organs, S. Andrea Hospital, University of Rome "La Sapienza", 00189 Rome, Italy; anna.comparelli@uniroma1.it (A.C.); maurizio.pompili@uniroma1.it (M.P.)
* Correspondence: giuliamgiordano@gmail.com; Tel.: +39-0815666512
† These authors contributed equally to the work.
‡ The members of the Italian Network for Research on Psychoses involved in the add-on EEG study are listed in the Acknowledgments.

Citation: Giordano, G.M.; Giuliani, L.; Perrottelli, A.; Bucci, P.; Di Lorenzo, G.; Siracusano, A.; Brando, F.; Pezzella, P.; Fabrazzo, M.; Altamura, M.; et al. Mismatch Negativity and P3a Impairment through Different Phases of Schizophrenia and Their Association with Real-Life Functioning. *J. Clin. Med.* **2021**, *10*, 5838. https://doi.org/10.3390/jcm10245838

Academic Editors: Armida Mucci and Birgit Derntl

Received: 23 November 2021
Accepted: 10 December 2021
Published: 13 December 2021

Abstract: Impairment in functioning since the onset of psychosis and further deterioration over time is a key aspect of subjects with schizophrenia (SCZ). Mismatch negativity (MMN) and P3a, indices of early attention processing that are often impaired in schizophrenia, might represent optimal electrophysiological candidate biomarkers of illness progression and poor outcome. However, contrasting findings are reported about the relationships between MMN-P3a and functioning. The study aimed to investigate in SCZ the influence of illness duration on MMN-P3a and the relationship of MMN-P3a with functioning. Pitch (p) and duration (d) MMN-P3a were investigated in 117 SCZ and 61 healthy controls (HCs). SCZ were divided into four illness duration groups: ≤ 5, 6 to 13, 14 to 18, and 19 to 32 years. p-MMN and d-MMN amplitude was reduced in SCZ compared to HCs, independently from illness duration, psychopathology, and neurocognitive deficits. p-MMN reduction was associated with lower "Work skills". The p-P3a amplitude was reduced in the SCZ group with longest illness duration compared to HCs. No relationship between P3a and functioning was found. Our results suggested that MMN amplitude reduction might represent a biomarker of poor functioning in SCZ.

Keywords: schizophrenia; ERP; mismatch negativity; MMN; P3a; illness duration; real-life functioning

1. Introduction

Schizophrenia is a severe mental illness with a high heterogeneity of risk factors, pathophysiology, psychopathology, and outcome [1–29].

People suffering from this disorder experience positive, disorganized, negative, depressive, extrapyramidal symptoms, cognitive impairment, as well as impairment in different areas of functioning [3,30–48]. In particular, positive symptoms usually begin with the onset of psychosis or are present in an attenuated form in the prodromal stages; they tend to recur in conjunction with the acute phases. Negative symptoms and cognitive deficits predate the onset of psychosis, might worsen when the first episode occurs, and are much more stable as compared to positive symptoms throughout the course of the illness [47–49].

Moreover, schizophrenia is often a chronic and relapsing disorder with incomplete symptomatic remission and variable levels of disability [50–59]. The impairment in various domains of real-life functioning, such as interpersonal relationships, everyday life skills, and work skills, represents to date the main target of care in subjects with schizophrenia since it poses a huge burden on patients, their families, and health-care systems [60–69]. It has been demonstrated that the impairment in real-life functioning is associated with different variables, some related to the illness, others to personal resources, and others to the context [66–69]. Among these variables, the duration of the illness and of untreated psychosis play a crucial role in determining a poor outcome [70–73].

The high heterogeneity in terms of pathophysiology, psychopathology, and how the illness progresses can usefully be addressed by a clinical staging approach of the illness. For this reason, the present research priorities include the identification of biomarkers of illness progression [3]. In fact, biomarkers, which are measurable indicators of biological conditions, could help to understand the pathophysiological mechanisms underpinning the poor outcome forms of the disorder, which are associated with chronic stages and high disability [74,75]. Therefore, the biomarkers can contribute to the early identification of subjects who might progress to a severe form of the illness in order to plan intensive interventions, which might control the progression of the disease and reduce the probability of poor functional outcome

Many electrophysiological indices have been used as potential biomarkers of schizophrenia. Indeed, electroencephalography (EEG) is a non-invasive, inexpensive method with a high temporal resolution that allows the identification of abnormalities of cortical brain functions and the study of the neurophysiological bases of different clinical and behavioral aspects [76–85]. Event-related potentials (ERPs) are very small brain voltages occurring in response to specific sensory, motor, or cognitive events. They have been used to investigate neurophysiological correlates of psychopathology, cognitive deficits, and functioning disturbances in subjects with schizophrenia [86–89]. In particular, the ERP components mismatch negativity (MMN) and P3 have been frequently explored in schizophrenia [90–94].

In the MMN-P3a auditory oddball paradigm, MMN is elicited by presenting a relatively rare deviant sound interspersed in a sequence of frequently occurring standard sounds [95], and its peak occurs generally 150–250 msec after the presentation of the stimulus, with the highest intensity recorded in temporal auditory and frontal areas [96–100]. In the auditory paradigm, the deviant stimulus might have a different duration (dMMN) or pitch (pMMN) with respect to the standard one [101]. MMN is an index of pre-attentive processing and sensory encoding and memory [90,102]. A reduction of MMN amplitude is frequently observed in schizophrenia [90,91,103,104]. According to a meta-analysis [92], the alterations in MMN amplitude are stable after the first years of illness throughout the life span. However, dMMN and pMMN amplitude are both reduced in subjects with chronic schizophrenia, while in the early stages of the disease, only a reduction of dMMN amplitude is present [103,104]. Therefore, the reduction of pMMN amplitude could represent an index of poor outcome and illness chronicity. Moreover, the MMN impairment has been reported also in other mental disorders, e.g., bipolar disorder, although to a lesser degree than in schizophrenia [89]. Kaur et al. showed that in subjects with first-episode psychosis, from both affective and schizophrenia spectrum, neurobiological disturbances could be already detected through reduced MMN amplitude [105]. These findings suggest that MMN alterations are linked to the psychosis dimension rather than to specific categorical diagnoses. However, MMN deficits are present during phases of clinical stability and are not associated with psychotic symptoms [106].

P3 is a positive peak that can be observed after 300 msec after the presentation of a deviant/rare stimulus during an oddball paradigm [107,108]. The P3a component is elicited by presenting rare non-target stimuli and can be observed even under passive conditions. As for the MMN, P3a might be elicited by deviant stimuli in terms of duration (dP3a) or pitch (pP3a). P3a is generated in frontal cerebral regions sustaining orientation of attention to novel stimuli. In fact, this ERP reflects early attention-mediated auditory processing, and consistent deficits of this index have been detected in subjects with schizophrenia [109–113] since the early stage of the disorder [90,114]. It has been demonstrated that P3 amplitude and latency are, respectively, decreased and delayed in patients with longer illness duration [110,111,115,116]. However, similar to MMN, the reduction in P3 amplitude is not specific of schizophrenia, as it can also be observed in other conditions, such as bipolar disorder and schizoaffective disorder [89,105,117].

Several studies investigated the relationship between MMN/P3a and poor outcome in subjects with schizophrenia. In particular, the impairment in MMN has been linked to cognitive and functional impairment in subjects with schizophrenia [88,90,91,118–120]. These relationships seem to be present since the early stages of the disorder [119,121–123]. On the other hand, fewer studies have examined the relationship between P3a and functioning, reporting often inconsistent results [88,90,124–126]. Hamilton et al. [90] investigated simultaneously the association of both MMN and P3a with functioning and assessed it using the Multidimensional Scale of Independent Functioning. Authors found that MMN but not P3a amplitude reduction was associated with the impairment in functioning of subjects with schizophrenia [90].

Although different studies investigating the relationship between ERPs and functional outcome reported associations of MMN and, to a lesser extent, of P3a with functioning measures, these results are not very robust due to some limitations. In fact, these works examined only a single or a few domain/s of functioning and did not take into account several factors that may influence real-life functioning (e.g., delusions, hallucinations, lack of insight, disorganized thinking, cognitive deficits, negative symptoms, or depression); furthermore, these studies generally included small samples of subjects with schizophrenia [88,91,118–120,126–128].

The current study aimed to investigate in clinically stable subjects with schizophrenia: (1) the impact of illness duration on MMN and P3a and (2) the relationships between MMN-P3a and real-life functioning. In order to overcome the above-reported limitations, we used the Specific Level of Functioning Scale (SLOF) for the assessment of real-life functioning. This instrument has good psychometric properties [129,130]. In contrast to other scales, it assesses multiple functional domains; providing separate scores for each domain; it can be rated on the basis of an interview with patient's key relative/caregiver, or staff members [129,131–133]; and it does not include elements concerning the psychopathology or cognitive dysfunctions but evaluates the patient's current functioning and observed behavior, focusing on person's abilities and resources [130].

2. Materials and Methods

2.1. Study Participants

The study has been conducted as part of the add-on EEG study of the Italian Network for Research on Psychoses (Galderisi et al., 2014). One hundred and forty-eight subjects with schizophrenia (SCZ) and 70 healthy controls (HCs) were enrolled for the study at five research sites in Naples, Foggia, Rome "Tor Vergata", Rome "Sapienza", and Salerno. Subjects with schizophrenia were outpatients in care at the five mentioned Italian university psychiatric clinics. Inclusion criteria for patients were: a diagnosis of schizophrenia based on the DSM-IV criteria and confirmed by the Structured Clinical Interview for DSM-IV—Patient version (SCID-I-P); age between 18 and 65 years; and no treatment modifications and/or hospitalization due to symptom exacerbation in the last three months. The HCs were recruited from the community at the same research sites. The inclusion criterion for HCs was the absence of a current or lifetime Axis I or II psychiatric diagnosis.

Exclusion criteria for SCZ and HCs were: (a) a history of head trauma with loss of consciousness; (b) a history of mental retardation (moderate to severe) or of neurological diseases; (c) a history of alcohol and/or substance abuse in the last six months; (d) current pregnancy or lactation; and (e) inability to provide an informed consent.

All participants signed a written informed consent after a clear and comprehensive description of the study procedures and goals.

The electrophysiological add-on study was approved by the Ethics Committee of the involved institutions. The study has been conducted in accordance with the ethical principles of the Declaration of Helsinki.

2.2. Assessments

All subjects were evaluated for socio-demographic variables, such as age, education and gender, using every available source of information.

The Positive and Negative Syndrome Scale (PANSS) was administered to patients to rate positive and disorganization symptoms [134]. All items are rated on a 7-point scale from 1 (absent) to 7 (extremely severe).

The Brief Negative Symptom Scale, a second-generation rating scale [135,136], was administered to patients to assess negative symptoms according to their current conceptualization. The scale has 13 items organized into six subscales (five negative symptom subscales, Anhedonia, A-sociality, Avolition, Blunted Affect, and Alogia, and a control subscale: Distress). All the items are rated on a 7-point (0–6) scale, thus ranging from absent (0) to moderate (3) to extremely severe (6) symptoms. A total score was computed by summing the 13 individual items; subscale scores were computed by summing the individual items within each subscale [135]. Two negative symptom domains were assessed: the Experiential domain, computed by summing the scores on the subscales Anhedonia, Avolition, and A-sociality, and the Expressive deficit, calculated by summing the scores on the subscales Blunted Affect and Alogia [135].

The Calgary Depression Scale for Schizophrenia (CDSS) was used to assess depressive symptoms in SCZ [137]; the St. Hans Rating Scale (SHRS) for Extrapyramidal Syndromes assessed extrapyramidal symptoms in SCZ [138].

Neurocognitive functions were evaluated with the Measurement and Treatment Research to Improve Cognition in Schizophrenia (MATRICS) Consensus Cognitive Battery (MCCB) [139,140]. Raw scores on the MCCB were standardized to T-scores, corrected for age and gender, and based on the Italian normative sample.

Real-life functioning was assessed using the SLOF, a scale that was endorsed by the panel of experts involved in the Validation of Everyday Real-World Outcomes (VALERO) initiative as a valid measure to evaluate real-life functioning [128,141]. The SLOF is a hybrid instrument that explores many aspects of functioning, and it is based on the key caregiver's judgment on behavior and functioning of patients. It consists of 43 items and includes the following domains: (1) physical functioning, (2) personal care skills, (3) interpersonal relationships, (4) social acceptability, (5) everyday life skills, and (6) work skills. Higher scores correspond to better functioning. In our study the SLOF was administered to the key caregiver, i.e., the person more frequently and closely in contact with the patient. For outpatients living in the community, it is possible to observe a ceiling effect for personal care skills and social acceptability; thus, according to Sabbag and colleagues [142], in our study we focused on three SLOF subscales: interpersonal relationships, everyday life skills, and work skills. The Italian version of the scale was validated as part of the Italian Network for Research on Psychoses project [129].

2.3. Recording Procedure

EEGs were recorded with two highly comparable EEG systems: EASYS2 (Brainscope, Prague, Czech Republic) and Galileo MIZAR-sirius (EBNeuro, Florence, Italy). In order to guarantee the same recording settings in all sites, a harmonization of the amplifier settings and recording procedures was performed. EEGs were recorded with a 29 unipolar leads cap electrode system (Fpz, Fz, Cz, Pz, Oz, F3, F4, C3, C4, FC5, FC6, P3, P4, O1, O2, Fp1, Fp2, F7, F8, T3, T4, T5, T6, AF3, AF4, PO7, PO8, Right Mastoid and Left Mastoid), placed following the 10–20 system (American Electroencephalographic Society Guidelines in Electroencephalography, 1994). All leads were referenced to earlobes (a resistor of 10 kOhm was interposed between the earlobe leads). A ground electrode was allocated on the forehead.

In order to check for artifacts, during the EEG recording, a horizontal electro-oculogram (hEOG) from the epicanthus of each eye and a vertical EOG (vEOG) from the leads beneath and above the right eye were also recorded. All impedances of the leads were kept below 5 kΩ. The EEG data were filtered with a band-pass of 0.15–70 Hz. The sampling rate was 512 Hz. Before each session, a calibration was carried out for all channels with a 50 μV sine wave.

MMN and P3a were recorded through a stereo headset during the presentation of 2400 tones (80 db SPL), of which 83.3% were standard tones (50 msec, 1000 Hz), 8.3% duration (d) deviant tones (100 msec, 1000 Hz), and 8.3% pitch (p) deviant tones (50 msec, 1200 Hz), with an interstimulus interval of 450 msec. During stimuli presentation subjects were asked to watch a silent animated cartoon, and after the paradigm ended, they were asked some questions regarding the video (test duration = 20 min).

For each recording, subjects were invited to relax and to minimize movements or muscle tension.

Participants were invited not to drink coffee or tea and abstain from smoking cigarettes in the 2 h before the recording session and not to take the psychotropic drugs during the morning. If the subject reported a non-restoring sleep during the night prior to the recording, EEG session was postponed.

2.4. EEG Data Analysis

The pre-processing analyses were performed by one expert from the coordinating center (Naples) using Brain Vision Analyzer software (Brain Products, Munich, Germany). In order to characterize MMN and P3a deflections, data were parsed into epochs of 1000-mc duration, which were time-locked to the onset of the cue and spanned from a 100-mc pre-stimulus period up to 900 msec post-stimulus. The recorded EEG was digitally filtered offline using a band-pass filter of 1–30 Hz. MMN and P3a waves were extracted in each subject by the averaging method on all the "deviant" trials separately for duration and pitch deviant trials in order to ameliorate the signal/noise ratio, ruling out baseline activity not related to the stimulus. Trials with drifts larger than ±75 μV in any scalp electrode were refused. If, following artifacts and noisy trials removal, less than 100 usable trials for either duration or deviant trials (50% of d- or p-deviant trials) remained, the subject was excluded from the analysis. Data were baseline-corrected using the 100-msec time window preceding stimuli. For MMN analysis, peaks resulting from the presentation of standard tones, duration deviant (dMMN), and pitch deviant (pMMN) were automatically marked using the "peak finder" function of Brain Analyzer, with the most negative point ranging from 90–250 msec. Then, we subtracted the standard tone waveform from the duration deviant and pitch deviant ones. For both subtraction waves (pMMN and dMMN), the amplitude was then measured. P3a peaks were automatically marked using the "peak finder" function of Brain Analyzer, with the most positive point ranging from 230–380 msec after pitch (pP3a) and duration deviant (dP3a) stimuli. According to previous literature, MMN peak was analyzed from Fz and P3a from Cz [119,143].

2.5. Statistical Analyses

SPSS Version 22.0 (IBM Corporation, 2014; Armonk, NY, USA) was used to perform all statistical analyses.

SCZ were divided into four groups using quartiles of the illness duration.

Pearson's χ^2 test was performed to evaluate differences on gender distribution between groups.

Analyses of variance (ANOVA) and covariance (ANCOVA) were used to test group differences on continuous variables. Bonferroni post-hoc comparisons were conducted following significant ANOVA F-tests.

Spearman's rank correlations were performed to test the relationships between MMN and P3a with real-life functioning domains. Furthermore, if correlations were statistically significant, we performed partial correlations to exclude the influence of possible confounding factors (positive, negative, disorganized, depressive, and extrapyramidal symptoms as well as cognitive impairment).

3. Results

3.1. Subject Characteristics

One hundred and forty-eight SCZ and 70 HCs were originally enrolled in the study. However, 23 SCZ and four HCs did not complete the paradigm for MMN-P3a recording. Furthermore, eight SCZ and five HCs were excluded for the presence of many artifacts in the ERP recordings. Thus, 117 SCZ and 61 HCs were included in the present analysis.

Data on relevant demographic and clinical characteristics of the study sample are provided in Table 1.

Table 1. Demographic and clinical characteristics of the study sample.

Demographic and Clinical Information	HC (n = 61)	SCZ (n = 117)	F/χ_2	p
Gender (M/F)	31/30	82/35	6.420	**0.01**
Age (years, mean ± SD)	33.8 ± 12.276	36.25 ±9.116	2.257	0.135
Education (years, mean ± SD)	13.95 ± 4.084	12.51 ± 2.999	7.139	**0.008**
Paternal Education (years, mean ± SD)	10.43 ± 4.612	9.97 ± 4.91	0.344	0.559
Maternal Education (years, mean ± SD)	9.818 ± 4.41	9.183 ± 4.0556	0.844	0.360
BNSS Total score (mean ± SD)		34.70 ± 16.381		
BNSS Expressive deficit domain (mean ± SD)		11.30 ± 7.31		
BNSS Experiential domain (mean ± SD)		21.10 ± 9.185		
PANSS Positive (mean ± SD)		8.32 ± 4.727		
PANSS Negative (mean ± SD)		15.65 ± 5.843		
PANSS Disorganization (mean ± SD)		8.64 ± 3.604		
CDSS Total score (mean ± SD)		3.23 ± 3.835		
SHRS global parkinsonism (mean ± SD)		0.86 ± 1.149		
SLOF Interpersonal relationships (mean ± SD)		23.09 ± 5.725		
SLOF Everyday life skills (mean ± SD)		46.85 ± 6.834		
SLOF Work Skills (mean ± SD)		20.72 ± 6.10		
MCCB Neurocognitive Composite Score (mean ± SD)		35.18 ± 10.902		
Duration of illness (mean ± SD)		12.98 ± 8.067		
Type of AP medication (%)		78.4% second-generation AP 11.2% first-generation AP 10.3% both AP		

AP, antipsychotic; BNSS, Brief Negative Symptom Scale; CDSS, Calgary Depression Scale for Schizophrenia; HCs, Healthy controls; MCCB, MATRICS Consensus Cognitive Battery; PANSS, Positive and Negative Syndrome Scale; SCZ, subjects with schizophrenia; SD, standard deviation; SHRS, The St. Hans Rating Scale for extrapyramidal syndromes; SLOF, The Specific Level of Functioning scale. p values in bold indicate statistical significance.

Gender distribution was significantly different between the two groups ($\chi^2 = 6.42$; $p = 0.01$) since, in the SCZ group, the number of male subjects was higher as compared to HCs. There was no significant difference in the mean age between the two sample groups (F = 2.257; $p = 0.135$). Furthermore, as expected, SCZ had significantly lower education as compared to controls (F = 7.139; $p = 0.008$). SCZ had a mild severity of both positive and disorganization symptoms (PANSS mean dimension score < 9 for both dimensions) and mild to moderate severity of the negative symptoms (BNSS total score of 34.70 ± 16.381). Finally, SCZ showed low scores of depression (CDSS total score < 4) and of parkinsonism (SHRS Parkinsonism score < 1) (Table 1).

Based on quartiles of illness duration, SCZ were divided into four groups: SCZ-A, ≤ years ($n = 23$); SCZ-B, 6 to 13 years ($n = 38$); SCZ-C, 14 to 18 years ($n = 27$), and SCZ-D > 18 years (19 to 32 years, $n = 29$). Table 2 shows demographic and clinical details of the four patients' groups. Subjects with the longest illness duration (SCZ-D) had a significantly higher positive symptom score than patients with the shortest illness duration (SCZ-A) ($p = 0.008$). Furthermore, SCZ-D group had a significantly higher global parkinsonism score (SHRS) and lower cognitive skills (MCCB) compared to the SCZ-A (respectively, $p = 0.008$; $p = 0.015$) and SCZ-B groups (respectively, $p = 0.003$; $p = 0.033$).

Table 2. Demographic and clinical characteristics of the four patients' groups, composed by subjects with different illness duration (SCZ-A, ID ≤ 5; SCZ-B, ID 6 to 13 years; SCZ-C, ID 14 to 18 years; SCZ-D, ID 19 to 32 years).

Demographic and Clinical Information	SCZ-A (23)	SCZ-B (38)	SCZ-C (27)	SCZ-D (29)	F/χ_2	p
Age (years, mean ± SD)	26.87 ± 6.75	33.1 ± 6.031	37.41 ± 4.925	46.62 ± 6.34	50.82	**<0.001** *
Gender (M/F)	19/4	22/16	19/8	22/7	4.877	0.181
Education (years, mean ± SD)	11.87 ± 2.68	12.76 ± 3.16	12.70 ± 3.074	12.52 ± 3.03	0.471	0.703
Paternal Education (years, mean ± SD)	9.65 ± 4.380	10.89 ± 4.9	10.42 ± 4.851	8.29 ± 5.238	1.51	0.217
Maternal Education (years, mean ± SD)	10.20 ± 3.75	9.368 ± 3.91	9.923 ± 4.3811	7.32 ± 3.761	2.604	0.056
BNSS Tot (mean ± SD)	30.13 ± 18.5	34.26 ± 15.3	36.58 ± 14.409	37.29 ± 17.7	0.951	0.419
Expressive deficit (mean ± SD)	10.57 ± 7.80	10.21 ± 6.99	11.92 ± 6.603	12.79 ± 7.99	0.803	0.495
Experiential domain (mean ± SD)	18.22 ± 10.8	21.74 ± 8.51	21.73 ± 7.754	22.04 ± 9.83	0.953	0.418
PANSS Positive (mean ± SD)	5.83 ± 2.552	8.24 ± 4.037	8.77 ± 4.616	10.07 ± 6.19	3.751	**0.013** **
PANSS Negative (mean ± SD)	14.74 ± 6.69	16.47 ± 5.72	14.54 ± 4.35	16.32 ± 6.49	0.872	0.458
PANSS Disorganization (mean ± SD)	7.35 ± 2.145	8.50 ± 3.790	9.04 ± 3.504	9.54 ± 4.194	1.72	0.167
CDSS Tot (mean ± SD)	2.78 ± 4.552	3.61 ± 3.803	2.96 ± 3.538	3.36 ± 3.654	0.273	0.845
SHRS global parkinsonism (mean ± SD)	0.52 ± 0.846	0.55 ± 0.86	0.89 ± 1.05	1.54 ± 1.503	5.35	**0.002** ***
SLOF Interpersonal relationships (mean ± SD)	23.43 ± 5.73	22.97 ± 6.21	3.30 ± 4.681	22.75 ± 6.22	0.076	0.973
SLOF Everyday life Skills (mean ± SD)	48.17 ± 6.7	47.34 ± 5.72	46.30 ± 6.638	45.64 ± 8.451	0.698	0.555
SLOF Work Skills (mean ± SD)	23.04 ± 5.62	21.32 ± 5.82	19.52 ± 5.905	19.14 ± 6.609	2.28	0.083
Neurocognitive Composite Score (mean ± SD)	38.57 ± 9.28	36.97 ± 11.5	35.93 ± 10.321	29.43 ± 10.29	3.99	**0.010** ****

BNSS, Brief Negative Symptom Scale; CDSS, The Calgary Depression Scale for Schizophrenia; HCs, Healthy controls; MCCB, MATRICS Consensus Cognitive Battery; PANSS, Positive and Negative Syndrome Scale; SCZ, subjects with schizophrenia; SD, standard deviation; SHRS, The St. Hans Rating Scale for extrapyramidal syndrome; SLOF, The Specific Level of Functioning scale. p values in bold indicate statistical significance. Post-hoc pairwise comparisons: * For age, each group differs from the others (all $p < 0.001$); ** SCZ-D had higher PANSS positive score compared to SCZ-A ($p = 0.008$); *** SCZ-D had higher SHRS global parkinsonism score compared to SCZ-A ($p = 0.008$) and SCZ-B ($p = 0.003$); **** SCZ-D had lower cognitive performance compared to SCZ-A ($p = 0.015$) and SCZ-B ($p = 0.033$).

3.2. Group Differences on ERPs

Group comparisons for the amplitude of MMN and P3a, elicited by duration (dMMN, dP3a) and pitch (pMMN, pP3a) deviants, were made between the five sample groups (HCs, SCZ-A, SCZ-B, SCZ-C, and SCZ-D), controlling for age and gender.

There was a significant group effect on dMMN (F = 8.3, $p < 0.001$) and pMMN (F = 7.5, $p < 0.001$) amplitudes. Post-hoc pairwise comparisons demonstrated that all groups of SCZ, compared to HCs, showed reduced dMMN (all $p < 0.001$) and pMMN amplitudes

(SCZ-A< HCs, $p = 0.01$; SCZ-B < HCs, $p = 0.03$; SCZ-C and SCZ-D< HCs, $p < 0.001$), while no statistically significant difference was observed between patients' groups.

In addition, there was a group effect on dP3a (F = 2.5, $p = 0.04$); however, this result did not survive the correction for multiple tests. Follow-up post-hoc pairwise comparisons demonstrated that this effect was driven by differences between SCZ-D and HCs (SCZ-D < HCs, $p = 0.003$), while no differences were found between patients' groups. In addition, we did not find any significant difference between the five groups for pP3a amplitude (F = 2.1, $p = 0.078$) (Figure 1, Table 3).

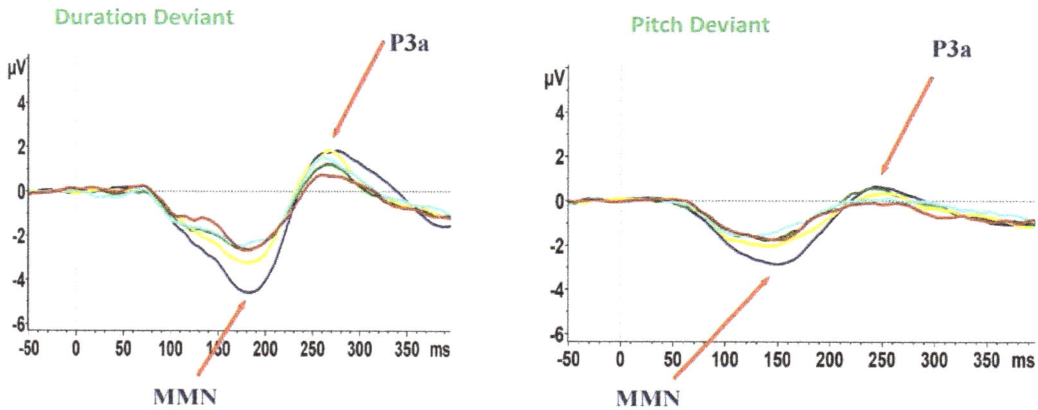

Figure 1. Mismatch negativity (MMN) and P3a waveforms recorded during the auditory paradigm in healthy controls and subjects with schizophrenia. HCs, healthy controls (blue line); SCZ, subjects with schizophrenia; ID, illness duration. SCZ-A, ID ≤ 5 (green line); SCZ-B, ID 6 to 13 years (yellow line); SCZ-C, ID 14 to 18 years (pale blue line); SCZ-D, ID 19 to 32 years (red line).

Table 3. Group differences for MMN and P3a. Age and gender as covariates.

MMN-P3a Amplitude	HCs ($n = 61$)	SCZ-A ($n = 23$)	SCZ-B ($n = 38$)	SCZ-C ($n = 27$)	SCZ-D ($n = 29$)	F	p
d-MMN	-5.51 ± 2.47	-3.456 ± 1.83	-3.87 ± 2.05	-3.55 ± 1.71	-3.208 ± 1.99	8.274	**<0.001** *
p-MMN	-3.50 ± 1.56	-2.43 ± 1.129	-2.70 ± 1.29	-2.11 ± 0.930	-2.35 ± -1.19	7.533	**<0.001** *
d-P3a	2.95 ± 1.95	2.02 ± 1.81	2.54 ± 1.79	2.13 ± 1.11	1.53 ± 1.21	2.5	0.04 **
p-P3a	1.52 ± 1.05	1.40 ± 1.26	1 ± 1.16	0.95 ± 0.87	0.70 ± 1.01	2.1	0.078

HCs, healthy controls; SCZ, subjects with schizophrenia; d-MMN, duration deviant MMN; p-MMN, pitch deviant MMN; d-P3a: duration deviant P3a; p-P3a, pitch deviant P3a. p values in bold indicate statistical significance (significant p-value threshold 0.002). Post-hoc pairwise comparisons: * All SCZ groups had reduced d-MMN (all $p < 0.001$) and p-MMN (SCZ-A< HCs, $p = 0.01$; SCZ-B < HCs, $p = 0.03$; SCZ-C and SCZ-D< HCs, $p < 0.001$) amplitude compared to HCs; ** SCZ-D had reduced d-P3a amplitude compared to HCs ($p = 0.003$).

Furthermore, since MMN and P3a amplitudes could be influenced by different factors, we also performed control analyses in order to reveal the possible effect of confounding factors on these results. In particular, we performed analysis of covariance in order to evaluate differences between the four groups of patients on MMN-P3a parameters, controlling for age, gender, positive symptoms, neurocognition, and global parkinsonism.

We did not find any statistically significant difference in the MMN and P3a amplitude ($p > 0.05$) among the four SCZ groups as well as when we controlled for the possible effects of the confounding variables.

3.3. Correlation Analyses

Correlation analyses revealed a negative relationship between pMMN amplitude and the "work skills" domain of the SLOF scale (r = −0.257; p = 0.005) (Figure 2). This correlation remained significant after controlling for positive, negative, and disorganized symptoms; depression; neurocognition; and global parkinsonism. No correlation was found between P3a and real-life functioning in SCZ.

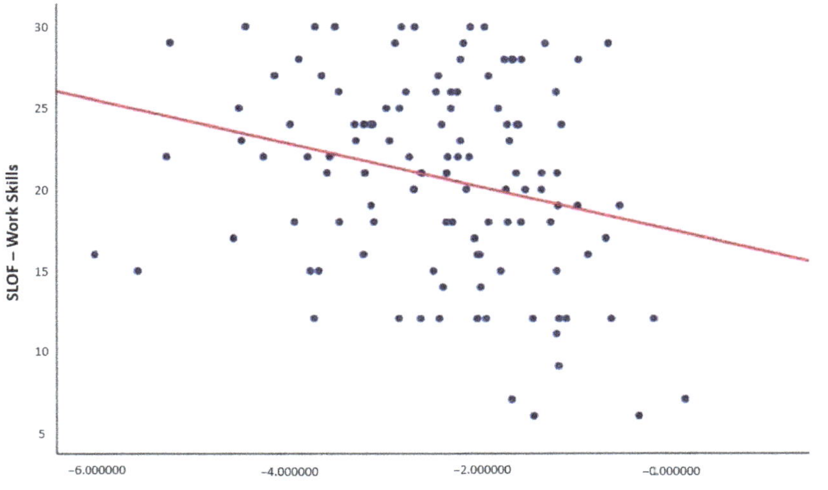

Figure 2. Correlation between p-MMN amplitude and the "work skills" domain of the SLOF scale. p-MMN, pitch deviant mismatch negativity. Negative correlation between p-MMN amplitude and the "work skills" domain of the SLOF scale (r = −0.257; p = 0.005) (significant p-value threshold 0.008). This correlation remained significant after controlling for positive, negative, and disorganized symptoms; depression; neurocognition; and global parkinsonism.

3.4. Additional Analyses

Additional control analyses were performed to test differences in MMN and P3a between between two subgroups of subjects with schizophrenia, divided on the basis of the "work skills" domain scores. We reported methods and results of this analysis within the Supplementary materials and Supplementary Tables S1–S3.

4. Discussion

The main results of our study included: (1) a reduction of MMN amplitude for pitch and duration deviant stimuli in all groups of subjects with schizophrenia as compared to healthy controls, independently from illness duration, age, gender, positive symptoms, neurocognition, and global parkinsonism; (2) subjects with a longer duration of illness had reduced dP3a amplitude as compared to healthy controls; and (3) in SCZs, pMMN was correlated with the "work skills" domain of the SLOF.

In line with previous findings, MMN amplitude was reduced in subjects with chronic schizophrenia compared to healthy controls, for both pitch and duration deviant stimuli [103,104]. Furthermore, as expected, our results showed that MMN was reduced independently from illness duration and other factors, such as age, gender, positive symptoms, neurocognition, and parkinsonism. Different studies reported that the impairment in MMN amplitude is present since the early stages of the illness as well as in subjects with chronic schizophrenia [90,91,103,104]. This MMN amplitude impairment is stable after the first years of illness, and it is not progressive throughout the life span [92]. Our results suggested that subjects with schizophrenia do present deficits in pre-attentive processing, as indexed by reduced MMN amplitude and that these deficits are independent from illness progression. Thus, deficit in MMN might represent a possible stable trait marker of schizophrenia, allowing early diagnosis and hopefully early intervention in subjects with schizophrenia.

With respect to P3a, we found that there was a weak group effect on dP3a amplitude; however, this result did not survive the correction for multiple tests. In particular, this effect was driven by the fact that patients with longer illness duration showed reduction in dP3a amplitude as compared to healthy controls, while no significant difference was found between patient's groups. Although we did not find any difference in pP3a and dP3a across different stages of the disease, our study showed a trend of P3a amplitude reduction in the group with the highest illness duration. These results are in line with previous studies which demonstrated that P3 amplitude is reduced in patients with longer illness duration [110,111,115,116]. Therefore, these findings suggest that P3, reflecting early attention-mediated auditory processing, might represent a marker of illness progression. However, whether P3a represent a marker of schizophrenia progression has to be further investigated, and more studies are needed to confirm this finding. Indeed, results of previous studies on the topic are controversial: some of these studies reported that P3a amplitude is reduced mainly in patients with longer illness duration, while some others found this alteration also in first-episode psychosis patients and at-risk subjects [90,110,111,113,114,116]. Moreover, some studies demonstrated that P3a amplitude is affected by antipsychotic administration [144], suggesting that the progressive P3a amplitude reduction across illness stages might depend on the use of antipsychotic drugs instead of the illness progression. Our results cannot add to this debate, as we could not compare drug-treated and untreated subjects.

As regard to the relationship of MMN and P3 with measures of functioning, according to a previous study [90], we found that only MMN and not P3a amplitude negatively correlated with real-life functioning in subjects with schizophrenia. In particular, we found an association between MMN amplitude reduction and impairment in the "work skills" domain of the SLOF. This finding of association between MMN and functioning was also supported by the additional analyses performed testing the differences between two subgroups of subjects with schizophrenia divided on the basis of the "work skills" domain scores.

Previous works reported in subjects with schizophrenia a relationship of MMN amplitude deficit with functional impairment and psychosocial and socio-occupational disability [88,90,91,118–120]. This association has been identified since the early stages of the disease [119,121–123]. On the contrary, scarce and inconsistent findings have been reported about the association between P3a amplitude and functioning [88,90,124–126].

As said before, MMN is an index of basic cognitive processes, which are usually impaired in subjects with schizophrenia [46–49]. Our results concerning the association between MMN and functioning might be interpreted in the light of the influence of deficits in cognitive processes on functioning in subjects with schizophrenia, a finding which has been extensively reported in literature [49,145,146]. This relationship is complex and mostly indirect, with many variables, such as social cognition, negative symptoms, and functional capacity, acting as mediators and moderators in the pathway from cognitive impairment to functioning [66–69,145,147]. Moreover, cognitive deficits are associated with everyday life skills, independent living, and occupational functioning [145]. This is in line with our results, which provide a deeper knowledge about the impact of basic cognitive processes alterations, as indexed by MMN amplitude reduction, on functioning in subjects with schizophrenia. In the light of these observations, further studies are encouraged in order to evaluate the pathways towards functioning impairment starting from pre-attentive processing deficits.

The strengths of our study stem from the fact that it overcomes different limitations of previous studies investigating associations between ERPs and functioning. As a matter of fact, previous studies on the topic examined only a single or fewer domain/s of functioning;

they did not take into account symptoms and cognitive deficits that may affect real-life functioning; they collected only information from patients that could be influenced by many factors (e.g., delusions, hallucinations, lack of insight, disorganized thinking, cognitive deficits, negative symptoms, or depression); and they had usually small samples [88, 91,118–120,126–128]. In order to overcome these limitations, we used a large sample of stabilized subjects with schizophrenia, and we assessed the functioning through the SLOF, which assesses multiple functional domains, and the scoring is based on patient's key relative/caregiver or staff members. Furthermore, this instrument does not include elements concerning psychopathology or cognitive impairment but evaluates the patient's current functioning and observed behavior, focusing on person's abilities and resources.

As a limit of the present study, the possible confounding effect of the pharmacological treatment should be taken into account, as we could not control for the dosage of the antipsychotic medications. However, subjects with schizophrenia with a longer illness duration (from 19 to 32 years) had a significantly higher global parkinsonism score (which might be regarded as an indirect measure of the use and dosage of antipsychotics) as compared to subjects with illness duration ≤ 5 or from six and 13 years. Therefore, in order to test the possible effect of confounding factors on group comparison for MMN-P3a, we used as covariates the global parkinsonism score alongside with other variables that were different across the SCZ subgroups (age, gender, positive symptoms, and neurocognition), with no change in the results. In addition, with regard to correlation analyses between MMN-P3a measures and functioning, we also performed partial correlations, controlling for variables that might affect the results, such as global parkinsonism; positive, negative, and disorganized symptoms; depression; and neurocognition, with no change in the results.

However, for a clear interpretation of our findings, further studies, including drug-naïve subjects at their first episode as well as subjects at high risk for psychosis, are needed to confirm that MMN reduction is an index of poor functional outcome.

In conclusion, our results demonstrated that deficits in pre-attentive processing, as indexed by MMN reduction, are key aspects of schizophrenia. In fact, these deficits have been reported already in the prodromal stage of the disorder, remain stable through the lifespan, and are associated with poor real-life functioning. Therefore, MMN amplitude reduction might represent a possible stable trait biomarker of schizophrenia, and thus, it might help clinicians in predicting the functional outcome and implementing early and effective treatment strategies for patients with these deficits.

Supplementary Materials: The following are available online at https://www.mdpi.com/article/10.3390/jcm10245838/s1, Additional control analyses, Methods and Results. Table S1: Demographic and clinical characteristics of the two patient subgroups; Table S2: Group differences for MMN and P3a amplitudes and Table S3: Group differences for MMN and P3a amplitudes (positive and disorganized symptoms and global parkinsonism as covariates).

Author Contributions: Conceptualization, G.M.G., L.G., A.P., P.B., G.D.L., A.S., F.B., P.P., M.F., M.A., A.B., G.C., A.C., P.M., M.P., S.G. and M.M.; methodology, G.M.G., L.G., A.P., P.B., G.D.L., A.S., F.B., P.P., M.F., M.A., A.B., G.C., A.C., P.M., M.P., S.G. and M.M.; project administration, G.M.G., P.B., S.G. and M.M.; supervision, S.G. and M.M.; writing—original draft, G.M.G., L.G., A.P., P.B., G.D.L., A.S., F.B., P.P., M.F., M.A., A.B., G.C., A.C., P.M., M.P., S.G. and M.M.; writing—review and editing, G.M.G., L.G., A.P., P.B., G.D.L., A.S., F.B., P.P., M.F., M.A., A.B., G.C., A.C., P.M., M.P., S.G. and M.M. All authors were responsible for the interpretation of the analyses, contributed to critically revising the content, and approved the final manuscript for submission to the Journal of Clinical Medicine. All authors have read and agreed to the published version of the manuscript.

Funding: The study was funded by the Italian Ministry of Education (grant number: 2010XP2XR4), the Italian Society of Psychopathology (SOPSI), the Italian Society of Biological Psychiatry (SIPB), Roche, Switzerland Lilly, United States AstraZeneca, United Kingdom Lundbeck foundation, Denmark and Bristol-Myers Squibb, United Kingdom. These entities had no role in the study design; in the collection, analysis and interpretation of data; in the writing of the report and in the decision to submit the paper for publication.

Institutional Review Board Statement: The study was conducted according to the guidelines of the Declaration of Helsinki and approved by the Ethics Committee of the Università degli Studi della Campania "Luigi Vanvitelli"—A.O.U. "Luigi Vanvitelli", A.O.R.N. "Ospedali dei Colli (protocol code 323 and approved on 2 August 2013).

Informed Consent Statement: Informed consent was obtained from all subjects involved in the study.

Data Availability Statement: All data supporting the findings of this study are available within the article and Supplementary materials.

Acknowledgments: Members of the Italian Network for Research on Psychoses participating in the add-on EEG study include: Edoardo Caporusso, Eleonora Merlotti, Giuseppe Piegari (University of Campania "Luigi Vanvitelli"); Fabio M.P. Tortorelli, Flavia A. Padalino (University of Foggia); Cinzia Niolu, Michele Ribolsi (University of Rome "Tor Vergata"); Valentina Corigliano, Roberto Brugnoli (University of Rome "La Sapienza"); Giulio Corrivetti, Giulia D'agostino (University of Salerno).

Conflicts of Interest: The authors declare no conflict of interest.

References

1. Andreasen, N.C. The diagnosis of schizophrenia. *Schizophr. Bull.* **1987**, *13*, 9–22. [CrossRef] [PubMed]
2. Lieberman, J.A.; Drake, R.E.; Sederer, L.I.; Belger, A.; Keefe, R.; Perkins, D.; Stroup, S. Science and recovery in schizophrenia. *Psychiatr. Serv.* **2008**, *59*, 487–496. [CrossRef]
3. Tandon, R.; Nasrallah, H.A.; Keshavan, M.S. Schizophrenia, "just the facts" 4. Clinical features and conceptualization. *Schizophr. Res.* **2009**, *110*, 1–23. [CrossRef]
4. Insel, T.R. Rethinking schizophrenia. *Nature* **2010**, *468*, 187–193. [CrossRef] [PubMed]
5. van Os, J.; Kenis, G.; Rutten, B.P. The environment and schizophrenia. *Nature* **2010**, *468*, 203–212. [CrossRef]
6. Fornito, A.; Zalesky, A.; Pantelis, C.; Bullmore, E.T. Schizophrenia, neuroimaging and connectomics. *Neuroimage* **2012**, *62*, 2296–2314. [CrossRef]
7. Bentall, R.P. Would a rose, by any other name, smell sweeter? *Psychol. Med.* **2013**, *43*, 1560–1562. [CrossRef]
8. Gaebel, W.; Zielasek, J. Schizophrenia in 2020: Trends in diagnosis and therapy. *Psychiatry Clin. Neurosci.* **2015**, *69*, 661–673. [CrossRef]
9. Guloksuz, S.; van Os, J. The slow death of the concept of schizophrenia and the painful birth of the psychosis spectrum. *Psychol. Med.* **2018**, *48*, 229–244. [CrossRef]
10. Reininghaus, U.; Bohnke, J.R.; Chavez-Baldini, U.; Gibbons, R.; Ivleva, E.; Clementz, B.A.; Pearlson, G.D.; Keshavan, M.S.; Sweeney, J.A.; Tamminga, C.A. Transdiagnostic dimensions of psychosis in the Bipolar-Schizophrenia Network on Intermediate Phenotypes (B-SNIP). *World Psychiatry* **2019**, *18*, 67–76. [CrossRef] [PubMed]
11. Guloksuz, S.; Pries, L.K.; Delespaul, P.; Kenis, G.; Luykx, J.J.; Lin, B.D.; Richards, A.L.; Akdede, B.; Binbay, T.; Altınyazar, V.; et al. Examining the independent and joint effects of molecular genetic liability and environmental exposures in schizophrenia: Results from the EUGEI study. *World Psychiatry* **2019**, *18*, 173–182. [CrossRef]
12. Grace, A.A.; Gomes, F.V. The Circuitry of Dopamine System Regulation and its Disruption in Schizophrenia: Insights into Treatment and Prevention. *Schizophr. Bull.* **2019**, *45*, 148–157. [CrossRef] [PubMed]
13. Kishimoto, T.; Hagi, K.; Nitta, M.; Kane, J.M.; Correll, C.U. Long-term effectiveness of oral second-generation antipsychotics in patients with schizophrenia and related disorders: A systematic review and meta-analysis of direct head-to-head comparisons. *World Psychiatry* **2019**, *18*, 208–224. [CrossRef] [PubMed]
14. Huhn, M.; Nikolakopoulou, A.; Schneider-Thoma, J.; Krause, M.; Samara, M.; Peter, N.; Arndt, T.; Bäckers, L.; Rothe, P.; Cipriani, A.; et al. Comparative efficacy and tolerability of 32 oral antipsychotics for the acute treatment of adults with multi-episode schizophrenia: A systematic review and network meta-analysis. *Lancet* **2019**, *394*, 939–951. [CrossRef]
15. Reed, G.M.; First, M.B.; Kogan, C.S.; Hyman, S.E.; Gureje, O.; Gaebel, W.; Maj, M.; Stein, D.J.; Maercker, A.; Tyrer, P.; et al. Innovations and changes in the ICD-11 classification of mental, behavioural and neurodevelopmental disorders. *World Psychiatry* **2019**, *18*, 3–19. [CrossRef]
16. Zandersen, M.; Parnas, J. Borderline personality disorder or a disorder within the schizophrenia spectrum? A psychopathological study. *World Psychiatry* **2019**, *18*, 109–110. [CrossRef] [PubMed]
17. McKenna, P.; Leucht, S.; Jauhar, S.; Laws, K.; Bighelli, I. The controversy about cognitive behavioural therapy for schizophrenia. *World Psychiatry* **2019**, *18*, 235–236. [CrossRef]
18. Bond, G.R.; Drake, R.E.; Becker, D.R. An update on Individual Placement and Support. *World Psychiatry* **2020**, *19*, 390–391. [CrossRef]
19. Taipale, H.; Tanskanen, A.; Mehtala, J.; Vattulainen, P.; Correll, C.U.; Tiihonen, J. 20-year follow-up study of physical morbidity and mortality in relationship to antipsychotic treatment in a nationwide cohort of 62,250 patients with schizophrenia (FIN20). *World Psychiatry* **2020**, *19*, 61–68. [CrossRef] [PubMed]

20. Richards, A.L.; Pardinas, A.F.; Frizzati, A.; Tansey, K.E.; Lynham, A.J.; Holmans, P.; Legge, S.E.; Savage, J.E.; Agartz, I.; Andreassen, O.A.; et al. The Relationship between Polygenic Risk Scores and Cognition in Schizophrenia. *Schizophr. Bull.* **2020**, *46*, 336–344. [CrossRef] [PubMed]
21. Correll, C.U.; Schooler, N.R. Negative Symptoms in Schizophrenia: A Review and Clinical Guide for Recognition, Assessment, and Treatment. *Neuropsychiatr. Dis. Treat.* **2020**, *16*, 519–534. [CrossRef] [PubMed]
22. Guloksuz, S.; Pries, L.K.; Ten Have, M.; de Graaf, R.; van Dorsselaer, S.; Klingenberg, B.; Bak, M.; Lin, B.D.; van Eijk, K.R.; Delespaul, P.; et al. Association of preceding psychosis risk states and non-psychotic mental disorders with incidence of clinical psychosis in the general population: A prospective study in the NEMESIS-2 cohort. *World Psychiatry* **2020**, *19*, 199–205. [CrossRef] [PubMed]
23. Singh, S.P.; Javed, A.; WPA Expert International Advisory Panel for Early Intervention in Psychosis. Early intervention in psychosis in low- and middle-income countries: A WPA initiative. *World Psychiatry* **2020**, *19*, 122. [CrossRef] [PubMed]
24. Gaebel, W.; Falkai, P.; Hasan, A. The revised German evidence- and consensus-based schizophrenia guideline. *World Psychiatry* **2020**, *19*, 117–119. [CrossRef] [PubMed]
25. Moritz, S.; Silverstein, S.M.; Dietrichkeit, M.; Gallinat, J. Neurocognitive deficits in schizophrenia are likely to be less severe and less related to the disorder than previously thought. *World Psychiatry* **2020**, *19*, 254–255. [CrossRef]
26. Smeland, O.B.; Frei, O.; Dale, A.M.; Andreassen, O.A. The polygenic architecture of schizophrenia—Rethinking pathogenesis and nosology. *Nat. Rev. Neurol.* **2020**, *16*, 366–379. [CrossRef] [PubMed]
27. Kotov, R.; Jonas, K.G.; Carpenter, W.T.; Dretsch, M.N.; Eaton, N.R.; Forbes, M.K.; Forbush, K.T.; Hobbs, K.; Reininghaus, U.; Slade, T.; et al. Validity and utility of Hierarchical Taxonomy of Psychopathology (HiTOP): I. Psychosis superspectrum. *World Psychiatry* **2020**, *19*, 151–172. [CrossRef]
28. McCutcheon, R.A.; Krystal, J.H.; Howes, O.D. Dopamine and glutamate in schizophrenia: Biology, symptoms and treatment. *World Psychiatry* **2020**, *19*, 15–33. [CrossRef]
29. McCutcheon, R.A.; Reis Marques, T.; Howes, O.D. Schizophrenia-An Overview. *JAMA Psychiatry* **2020**, *77*, 201–210. [CrossRef] [PubMed]
30. Grube, B.S.; Bilder, R.M.; Goldman, R.S. Meta-analysis of symptom factors in schizophrenia. *Schizophr. Res.* **1998**, *31*, 113–120. [CrossRef]
31. Kitamura, T.; Okazaki, Y.; Fujinawa, A.; Yoshino, M.; Kasahara, Y. Symptoms of psychoses. A factor-analytic study. *Br. J. Psychiatry* **1995**, *166*, 236–240. [CrossRef] [PubMed]
32. Van der Does, A.J.; Linszen, D.H.; Dingemans, P.M.; Nugter, M.A.; Scholte, W.F. A dimensional and categorical approach to the symptomatology of recent-onset schizophrenia. *J. Nerv. Ment. Dis.* **1993**, *181*, 744–749. [CrossRef] [PubMed]
33. Van Os, J.; Gilvarry, C.; Bale, R.; Van Horn, E.; Tattan, T.; White, I.; Murray, R. A comparison of the utility of dimensional and categorical representations of psychosis. UK700 Group. *Psychol. Med.* **1999**, *29*, 595–606. [CrossRef]
34. Nakaya, M.; Suwa, H.; Ohmori, K. Latent structures underlying schizophrenic symptoms: A five-dimensional model. *Schizophr. Res.* **1999**, *39*, 39–50. [CrossRef]
35. Lykouras, L.; Oulis, P.; Psarros, K.; Daskalopoulou, E.; Botsis, A.; Christodoulou, G.N.; Stefanis, C. Five-factor model of schizophrenic psychopathology: How valid is it? *Eur. Arch. Psychiatry Clin. Neurosci.* **2000**, *250*, 93–100. [CrossRef]
36. Scully, P.J.; Owens, J.M.; Kinsella, A.; Waddington, J.L. Dimensions of psychopathology in bipolar disorder versus other affective and non-affective psychoses among an epidemiologically complete population. *Bipolar Disord.* **2002**, *4* (Suppl. 1), 43–44. [CrossRef] [PubMed]
37. Drake, R.J.; Dunn, G.; Tarrier, N.; Haddock, G.; Haley, C.; Lewis, S. The evolution of symptoms in the early course of non-affective psychosis. *Schizophr. Res.* **2003**, *63*, 171–179. [CrossRef]
38. Loza, B.; Kucharska-Pietura, K.; Kopacz, G.; Debowska, G. Factor structure of paranoid schizophrenia: A prospective study. *Psychopathology* **2003**, *36*, 132–141. [CrossRef] [PubMed]
39. Alves, T.M.; Pereira, J.C.; Elkis, H. The psychopathological factors of refractory schizophrenia. *Braz. J. Psychiatry* **2005**, *27*, 108–112. [CrossRef]
40. Murray, V.; McKee, I.; Miller, P.M.; Young, D.; Muir, W.J.; Pelosi, A.J.; Blackwood, D.H. Dimensions and classes of psychosis in a population cohort: A four-class, four-dimension model of schizophrenia and affective psychoses. *Psychol. Med.* **2005**, *35*, 499–510. [CrossRef]
41. Klingberg, S.; Wittorf, A.; Wiedemann, G. Disorganization and cognitive impairment in schizophrenia: Independent symptom dimensions? *Eur. Arch. Psychiatry Clin. Neurosci.* **2006**, *256*, 532–540. [CrossRef] [PubMed]
42. Tirupati, S.N.; Padmavati, R.; Thara, R.; McCreadie, R.G. Psychopathology in never-treated schizophrenia. *Compr. Psychiatry* **2006**, *47*, 1–6. [CrossRef] [PubMed]
43. Villalta-Gil, V.; Vilaplana, M.; Ochoa, S.; Dolz, M.; Usall, J.; Haro, J.M.; Almenara, J.; González, J.L.; Lagares, C.; NEDES Group. Four symptom dimensions in outpatients with schizophrenia. *Compr. Psychiatry* **2006**, *47*, 384–388. [CrossRef]
44. Boks, M.P.; Leask, S.; Vermunt, J.K.; Kahn, R.S. The structure of psychosis revisited: The role of mood symptoms. *Schizophr. Res.* **2007**, *93*, 178–185. [CrossRef] [PubMed]
45. Levine, S.Z.; Rabinowitz, J. Revisiting the 5 dimensions of the Positive and Negative Syndrome Scale. *J Clin. Psychopharmacol.* **2007**, *27*, 431–436. [CrossRef] [PubMed]

46. Barch, D.M. Nonsocial and social cognitive function in psychosis: Interrelationships, specificity and innovative approaches. *World Psychiatry* **2019**, *18*, 117–118. [CrossRef] [PubMed]
47. Green, M.F.; Horan, W.P.; Lee, J. Nonsocial and social cognition in schizophrenia: Current evidence and future directions. *World Psychiatry* **2019**, *18*, 146–161. [CrossRef] [PubMed]
48. Melle, I. Cognition in schizophrenia: A marker of underlying neurodevelopmental problems? *World Psychiatry* **2019**, *18*, 164–165. [CrossRef]
49. Grant, P.M.; Best, M.W.; Beck, A.T. The meaning of group differences in cognitive test performance. *World Psychiatry* **2019**, *18*, 163–164. [CrossRef]
50. Andreasen, N.C.; Carpenter, W.T., Jr.; Kane, J.M.; Lasser, R.A.; Marder, S.R.; Weinberger, D.R. Remission in schizophrenia: Proposed criteria and rationale for consensus. *Am. J. Psychiatry* **2005**, *162*, 441–449. [CrossRef]
51. Bebbington, P.E.; Craig, T.; Garety, P.; Fowler, D.; Dunn, G.; Colbert, S.; Fornells-Ambrojo, M.; Kuipers, E. Remission and relapse in psychosis: Operational definitions based on case-note data. *Psychol. Med.* **2006**, *36*, 1551–1562. [CrossRef]
52. Haro, J.M.; Novick, D.; Suarez, D.; Alonso, J.; Lepine, J.P.; Ratcliffe, M.; SOHO Study Group. Remission and relapse in the outpatient care of schizophrenia: Three-year results from the Schizophrenia Outpatient Health Outcomes study. *J. Clin. Psychopharmacol.* **2006**, *26*, 571–578. [CrossRef] [PubMed]
53. Vita, A.; Barlati, S. Recovery from schizophrenia: Is it possible? *Curr. Opin. Psychiatry* **2018**, *31*, 246–255. [CrossRef] [PubMed]
54. Jaaskelainen, E.; Juola, P.; Hirvonen, N.; McGrath, J.J.; Saha, S.; Isohanni, M.; Veijola, J.; Miettunen, J. A systematic review and meta-analysis of recovery in schizophrenia. *Schizophr. Bull.* **2013**, *39*, 1296–1306. [CrossRef] [PubMed]
55. Liberman, R.P.; Kopelowicz, A. Recovery from schizophrenia: A concept in search of research. *Psychiatr. Serv.* **2005**, *56*, 735–742. [CrossRef] [PubMed]
56. Davidson, M. Cognitive impairment as a diagnostic criterion and treatment target in schizophrenia. *World Psychiatry* **2019**, *18*, 171–172. [CrossRef]
57. Harvey, P.D.; Bellack, A.S. Toward a terminology for functional recovery in schizophrenia: Is functional remission a viable concept? *Schizophr. Bull.* **2009**, *35*, 300–306. [CrossRef]
58. Harvey, P.D.; Strassnig, M.T. Cognition and disability in schizophrenia: Cognition-related skills deficits and decision-making challenges add to morbidity. *World Psychiatry* **2019**, *18*, 165–167. [CrossRef]
59. Shrivastava, A.; Johnston, M.; Shah, N.; Bureau, Y. Redefining outcome measures in schizophrenia: Integrating social and clinical parameters. *Curr. Opin. Psychiatry* **2010**, *23*, 120–126. [CrossRef] [PubMed]
60. Leifker, F.R.; Bowie, C.R.; Harvey, P.D. Determinants of everyday outcomes in schizophrenia: The influences of cognitive impairment, functional capacity, and symptoms. *Schizophr. Res.* **2009**, *115*, 82–87. [CrossRef] [PubMed]
61. Fleischhacker, W.W.; Arango, C.; Arteel, P.; Barnes, T.R.; Carpenter, W.; Duckworth, K.; Galderisi, S.; Halpern, L.; Knapp, M.; Marder, S.R.; et al. Schizophrenia—time to commit to policy change. *Schizophr. Bull.* **2014**, *40* (Suppl. 3), S165–S194. [CrossRef]
62. Green, M.F.; Hellemann, G.; Horan, W.P.; Lee, J.; Wynn, J.K. From perception to functional outcome in schizophrenia: Modeling the role of ability and motivation. *Arch. Gen. Psychiatry* **2012**, *69*, 1216–1224. [CrossRef]
63. Ventura, J.; Subotnik, K.L.; Gitlin, M.J.; Gretchen-Doorly, D.; Ered, A.; Villa, K.F.; Hellemann, G.S.; Nuechterlein, K.H. Negative symptoms and functioning during the first year after a recent onset of schizophrenia and 8 years later. *Schizophr. Res.* **2015**, *161*, 407–413. [CrossRef] [PubMed]
64. Strauss, J.S.; Carpenter, W.T., Jr. The prognosis of schizophrenia: Rationale for a multidimensional concept. *Schizophr. Bull.* **1978**, *4*, 56–67. [CrossRef]
65. Strassnig, M.T.; Raykov, T.; O'Gorman, C.; Bowie, C.R.; Sabbag, S.; Durand, D.; Patterson, T.L.; Pinkham, A.; Penn, D.L.; Harvey, P.D. Determinants of different aspects of everyday outcome in schizophrenia: The roles of negative symptoms, cognition, and functional capacity. *Schizophr. Res.* **2015**, *165*, 76–82. [CrossRef]
66. Galderisi, S.; Rossi, A.; Rocca, P.; Bertolino, A.; Mucci, A.; Bucci, P.; Rucci, P.; Gibertoni, D.; Aguglia, E.; Amore, M.; et al. The influence of illness-related variables, personal resources and context-related factors on real-life functioning of people with schizophrenia. *World Psychiatry* **2014**, *13*, 275–287. [CrossRef] [PubMed]
67. Galderisi, S.; Rucci, P.; Kirkpatrick, B.; Mucci, A.; Gibertoni, D.; Rocca, P.; Rossi, A.; Bertolino, A.; Strauss, G.P.; Aguglia, E.; et al. Interplay Among Psychopathologic Variables, Personal Resources, Context-Related Factors, and Real-life Functioning in Individuals with Schizophrenia: A Network Analysis. *JAMA Psychiatry* **2018**, *75*, 396–404. [CrossRef]
68. Galderisi, S.; Rucci, P.; Mucci, A.; Rossi, A.; Rocca, P.; Bertolino, A.; Aguglia, E.; Amore, M.; Bellomo, A.; Bozzatello, P.; et al. The interplay among psychopathology, personal resources, context-related factors and real-life functioning in schizophrenia: Stability in relationships after 4 years and differences in network structure between recovered and non-recovered patients. *World Psychiatry* **2020**, *19*, 81–91. [CrossRef] [PubMed]
69. Mucci, A.; Galderisi, S.; Gibertoni, D.; Rossi, A.; Rocca, P.; Bertolino, A.; Aguglia, E.; Amore, M.; Bellomo, A.; Biondi, M.; et al. Factors Associated with Real-Life Functioning in Persons with Schizophrenia in a 4-Year Follow-up Study of the Italian Network for Research on Psychoses. *JAMA Psychiatry* **2021**, *78*, 550–559. [CrossRef] [PubMed]
70. Galderisi, S.; Mucci, A.; Bitter, I.; Libiger, J.; Bucci, P.; Fleischhacker, W.W.; Kahn, R.S.; Eufest Study Group. Persistent negative symptoms in first episode patients with schizophrenia: Results from the European First Episode Schizophrenia Trial. *Eur. Neuropsychopharmacol.* **2013**, *23*, 196–204. [CrossRef] [PubMed]

71. Lieberman, J.A.; Perkins, D.; Belger, A.; Chakos, M.; Jarskog, F.; Boteva, K.; Gilmore, J. The early stages of schizophrenia: Speculations on pathogenesis, pathophysiology, and therapeutic approaches. *Biol. Psychiatry* **2001**, *50*, 884–897. [CrossRef]
72. Lieberman, J.A.; Small, S.A.; Girgis, R.R. Early Detection and Preventive Intervention in Schizophrenia: From Fantasy to Reality. *Am. J. Psychiatry* **2019**, *176*, 794–810. [CrossRef]
73. Altamura, A.C.; Serati, M.; Buoli, M. Is duration of illness really influencing outcome in major psychoses? *Nord. J. Psychiatry* **2015**, *69*, 403–417. [CrossRef] [PubMed]
74. Pratt, J.; Hall, J. Biomarkers in Neuropsychiatry: A Prospect for the Twenty-First Century? *Curr. Top. Behav. Neurosci.* **2018**, *40*, 3–10. [CrossRef] [PubMed]
75. Biomarkers Definitions Working Group. Biomarkers and surrogate endpoints: Preferred definitions and conceptual framework. *Clin. Pharmacol. Ther.* **2001**, *69*, 89–95. [CrossRef] [PubMed]
76. Galderisi, S.; Mucci, A.; Volpe, U.; Boutros, N. Evidence-based medicine and electrophysiology in schizophrenia. *Clin. EEG Neurosci.* **2009**, *40*, 62–77. [CrossRef]
77. Koukkou, M.; Koenig, T.; Bänninger, A.; Rieger, K.; Diaz Hernandez, L.; Higuchi, Y.; Sumiyoshi, T.; Vignapiano, A.; Giordano, G.M.; Amodio, A.; et al. Neurobiology of schizophrenia: Electrophysiological indices. In *Advances in Psychiatry*; Javed, A., Fountoulakis, N.K., Eds.; Springer International Publishing: Cham, Switzerland, 2019; pp. 433–459.
78. Bullmore, E.T.; Frangou, S.; Murray, R.M. The dysplastic net hypothesis: An integration of developmental and dysconnectivity theories of schizophrenia. *Schizophr. Res.* **1997**, *28*, 143–156. [CrossRef]
79. Friston, K.J.; Frith, C.D. Schizophrenia: A disconnection syndrome? *Clin. Neurosci.* **1995**, *3*, 89–97.
80. Di Lorenzo, G.; Daverio, A.; Ferrentino, F.; Santarnecchi, E.; Ciabattini, F.; Monaco, L.; Lisi, G.; Barone, Y.; Di Lorenzo, C.; Niolu, C.; et al. Altered resting-state EEG source functional connectivity in schizophrenia: The effect of illness duration. *Front. Hum. Neurosci.* **2015**, *9*, 234. [CrossRef]
81. Li, F.; Wang, J.; Jiang, Y.; Si, Y.; Peng, W.; Song, L.; Jiang, Y.; Zhang, Y.; Dong, W.; Yao, D.; et al. Top-Down Disconnectivity in Schizophrenia During P300 Tasks. *Front. Comput. Neurosci.* **2018**, *12*, 33. [CrossRef] [PubMed]
82. Schmitt, A.; Hasan, A.; Gruber, O.; Falkai, P. Schizophrenia as a disorder of disconnectivity. *Eur. Arch. Psychiatry Clin. Neurosci.* **2011**, *261* (Suppl. 2), S150–S154. [CrossRef]
83. Giordano, G.M.; Brando, F.; Perrottelli, A.; Di Lorenzo, G.; Siracusano, A.; Giuliani, L.; Pezzella, P.; Altamura, M.; Bellomo, A.; Cascino, G.; et al. Tracing links between early auditory information processing and negative symptoms in schizophrenia: An ERP study. *Front. Psychiatry* **2021**, in press.
84. Giordano, G.M.; Koenig, T.; Mucci, A.; Vignapiano, A.; Amodio, A.; Di Lorenzo, G.; Siracusano, A.; Bellomo, A.; Altamura, M.; Monteleone, P.; et al. Neurophysiological correlates of Avolition-apathy in schizophrenia: A resting-EEG microstates study. *Neuroimage Clin.* **2018**, *20*, 627–636. [CrossRef] [PubMed]
85. Vignapiano, A.; Koenig, T.; Mucci, A.; Giordano, G.M.; Amodio, A.; Altamura, M.; Bellomo, A.; Brugnoli, R.; Corrivetti, G.; Di Lorenzo, G.; et al. Disorganization and cognitive impairment in schizophrenia: New insights from electrophysiological findings. *Int. J. Psychophysiol.* **2019**, *145*, 99–108. [CrossRef]
86. Pfefferbaum, A.; Roth, W.T.; Ford, J.M. Event-related potentials in the study of psychiatric disorders. *Arch. Gen. Psychiatry* **1995**, *52*, 559–563. [CrossRef] [PubMed]
87. Sur, S.; Sinha, V.K. Event-related potential: An overview. *Ind. Psychiatry J.* **2009**, *18*, 70–73. [CrossRef]
88. Hermens, D.F.; Ward, P.B.; Hodge, M.A.; Kaur, M.; Naismith, S.L.; Hickie, I.B. Impaired MMN/P3a complex in first-episode psychosis: Cognitive and psychosocial associations. *Prog. Neuropsychopharmacol. Biol. Psychiatry* **2010**, *34*, 822–829. [CrossRef] [PubMed]
89. Kaur, M.; Lagopoulos, J.; Lee, R.S.; Ward, P.B.; Naismith, S.L.; Hickie, I.B.; Hermens, D.F. Longitudinal associations between mismatch negativity and disability in early schizophrenia- and affective-spectrum disorders. *Prog. Neuropsychopharmacol. Biol. Psychiatry* **2013**, *46*, 161–169. [CrossRef] [PubMed]
90. Hamilton, H.K.; Perez, V.B.; Ford, J.M.; Roach, B.J.; Jaeger, J.; Mathalon, D.H. Mismatch Negativity but Not P300 Is Associated with Functional Disability in Schizophrenia. *Schizophr. Bull.* **2018**, *44*, 492–504. [CrossRef] [PubMed]
91. Umbricht, D.; Krljes, S. Mismatch negativity in schizophrenia: A meta-analysis. *Schizophr. Res.* **2005**, *76*, 1–23. [CrossRef] [PubMed]
92. Erickson, M.A.; Ruffle, A.; Gold, J.M. A Meta-Analysis of Mismatch Negativity in Schizophrenia: From Clinical Risk to Disease Specificity and Progression. *Biol. Psychiatry* **2016**, *79*, 980–987. [CrossRef]
93. Urban, A.; Kremlacek, J.; Libiger, J. Mismatch negativity in patients with schizophrenia. *Acta Med.* **2007**, *50*, 23–28. [CrossRef]
94. Turetsky, B.I.; Bilker, W.B.; Siegel, S.J.; Kohler, C.G.; Gur, R.E. Profile of auditory information-processing deficits in schizophrenia. *Psychiatry Res.* **2009**, *165*, 27–37. [CrossRef] [PubMed]
95. Nagai, T.; Tada, M.; Kirihara, K.; Yahata, N.; Hashimoto, R.; Araki, T.; Kasai, K. Auditory mismatch negativity and P3a in response to duration and frequency changes in the early stages of psychosis. *Schizophr. Res.* **2013**, *150*, 547–554. [CrossRef]
96. McCarley, R.W.; Faux, S.F.; Shenton, M.E.; Nestor, P.G.; Adams, J. Event-related potentials in schizophrenia: Their biological and clinical correlates and a new model of schizophrenic pathophysiology. *Schizophr. Res.* **1991**, *4*, 209–231. [CrossRef]
97. Naatanen, R.; Paavilainen, P.; Rinne, T.; Alho, K. The mismatch negativity (MMN) in basic research of central auditory processing: A review. *Clin. Neurophysiol.* **2007**, *118*, 2544–2590. [CrossRef] [PubMed]

98. Oknina, L.B.; Wild-Wall, N.; Oades, R.D.; Juran, S.A.; Ropcke, B.; Pfueller, U.; Weisbrod, M.; Chan, E.; Chen, E.Y. Frontal and temporal sources of mismatch negativity in healthy controls, patients at onset of schizophrenia in adolescence and others at 15 years after onset. *Schizophr. Res.* **2005**, *76*, 25–41. [CrossRef] [PubMed]
99. Garrido, M.I.; Kilner, J.M.; Stephan, K.E.; Friston, K.J. The mismatch negativity: A review of underlying mechanisms. *Clin. Neurophysiol.* **2009**, *120*, 453–463. [CrossRef] [PubMed]
100. Earls, H.A.; Curran, T.; Mittal, V. Deficits in Early Stages of Face Processing in Schizophrenia: A Systematic Review of the P100 Component. *Schizophr. Bull.* **2016**, *42*, 519–527. [CrossRef]
101. Naatanen, R. The mismatch negativity: A powerful tool for cognitive neuroscience. *Ear Hear.* **1995**, *16*, 6–18. [CrossRef]
102. Fitzgerald, K.; Todd, J. Making Sense of Mismatch Negativity. *Front. Psychiatry* **2020**, *11*, 468. [CrossRef] [PubMed]
103. Haigh, S.M.; Coffman, B.A.; Salisbury, D.F. Mismatch Negativity in First-Episode Schizophrenia: A Meta-Analysis. *Clin. EEG Neurosci.* **2017**, *48*, 3–10. [CrossRef] [PubMed]
104. Perrottelli, A.; Giordano, G.M.; Brando, F.; Giuliani, L.; Mucci, A. EEG-Based Measures in At-Risk Mental State and Early Stages of Schizophrenia: A Systematic Review. *Front. Psychiatry* **2021**, *12*, 653642. [CrossRef]
105. Kaur, M.; Battisti, R.A.; Ward, P.B.; Ahmed, A.; Hickie, I.B.; Hermens, D.F. MMN/P3a deficits in first episode psychosis: Comparing schizophrenia-spectrum and affective-spectrum subgroups. *Schizophr. Res.* **2011**, *130*, 203–209. [CrossRef] [PubMed]
106. Hirt, V.; Schubring, D.; Schalinski, I.; Rockstroh, B. Mismatch negativity and cognitive performance in the course of schizophrenia. *Int. J. Psychophysiol.* **2019**, *145*, 30–39. [CrossRef]
107. Polich, J. Updating P300: An integrative theory of P3a and P3b. *Clin. Neurophysiol.* **2007**, *118*, 2128–2148. [CrossRef] [PubMed]
108. Huang, W.J.; Chen, W.W.; Zhang, X. The neurophysiology of P 300–an integrated review. *Eur. Rev. Med. Pharmacol. Sci.* **2015**, *19*, 1480–1488. [PubMed]
109. Ford, J.M. Schizophrenia: The broken P300 and beyond. *Psychophysiology* **1999**, *36*, 667–682. [CrossRef]
110. Mathalon, D.H.; Ford, J.M.; Rosenbloom, M.; Pfefferbaum, A. P300 reduction and prolongation with illness duration in schizophrenia. *Biol. Psychiatry* **2000**, *47*, 413–427. [CrossRef]
111. Jeon, Y.W.; Polich, J. Meta-analysis of P300 and schizophrenia: Patients, paradigms, and practical implications. *Psychophysiology* **2003**, *40*, 684–701. [CrossRef]
112. Bramon, E.; Rabe-Hesketh, S.; Sham, P.; Murray, R.M.; Frangou, S. Meta-analysis of the P300 and P50 waveforms in schizophrenia. *Schizophr. Res.* **2004**, *70*, 315–329. [CrossRef]
113. Raghavan, D.V.; Shanmugiah, A.; Bharathi, P.; Jeyaprakash, R. P300 and neuropsychological measurements in patients with schizophrenia and their healthy biological siblings. *Indian J. Psychiatry* **2016**, *58*, 454–458. [CrossRef]
114. Lepock, J.R.; Mizrahi, R.; Korostil, M.; Bagby, R.M.; Pang, E.W.; Kiang, M. Event-Related Potentials in the Clinical High-Risk (CHR) State for Psychosis: A Systematic Review. *Clin. EEG Neurosci.* **2018**, *49*, 215–225. [CrossRef]
115. Mori, Y.; Kurosu, S.; Hiroyama, Y.; Niwa, S. Prolongation of P300 latency is associated with the duration of illness in male schizophrenia patients. *Psychiatry Clin. Neurosci.* **2007**, *61*, 471–478. [CrossRef]
116. Oribe, N.; Hirano, Y.; Kanba, S.; Del Re, E.; Seidman, L.; Mesholam-Gately, R.; Goldstein, J.M.; Shenton, M.; Spencer, K.M.; McCarley, R.W.; et al. Progressive reduction of visual P300 amplitude in patients with first-episode schizophrenia: An ERP study. *Schizophr. Bull.* **2015**, *41*, 460–470. [CrossRef] [PubMed]
117. Bestelmeyer, P.E. The visual P3a in schizophrenia and bipolar disorder: Effects of target and distractor stimuli on the P300. *Psychiatry Res.* **2012**, *197*, 140–144. [CrossRef] [PubMed]
118. Naatanen, R.; Shiga, T.; Asano, S.; Yabe, H. Mismatch negativity (MMN) deficiency: A break-through biomarker in predicting psychosis onset. *Int. J. Psychophysiol.* **2015**, *95*, 338–344. [CrossRef]
119. Tada, M.; Kirihara, K.; Mizutani, S.; Uka, T.; Kunii, N.; Koshiyama, D.; Fujioka, M.; Usui, K.; Nagai, T.; Araki, T.; et al. Mismatch negativity (MMN) as a tool for translational investigations into early psychosis: A review. *Int. J. Psychophysiol.* **2019**, *145*, 5–14. [CrossRef] [PubMed]
120. Hochberger, W.C.; Thomas, M.L.; Joshi, Y.B.; Molina, J.; Treichler, E.B.H.; Nungaray, J.; Cardoso, L.; Sprock, J.; Swerdlow, N.; Light, G.A. Oscillatory biomarkers of early auditory information processing predict cognitive gains following targeted cognitive training in schizophrenia patients. *Schizophr. Res.* **2020**, *215*, 97–104. [CrossRef] [PubMed]
121. Koshiyama, D.; Kirihara, K.; Tada, M.; Nagai, T.; Fujioka, M.; Koike, S.; Suga, M.; Araki, T.; Kasai, K. Association between mismatch negativity and global functioning is specific to duration deviance in early stages of psychosis. *Schizophr. Res.* **2018**, *195*, 378–384. [CrossRef]
122. Thomas, M.L.; Green, M.F.; Hellemann, G.; Sugar, C.A.; Tarasenko, M.; Calkins, M.E.; Greenwood, T.A.; Gur, R.E.; Gur, R.C.; Lazzeroni, L.C.; et al. Modeling Deficits from Early Auditory Information Processing to Psychosocial Functioning in Schizophrenia. *JAMA Psychiatry* **2017**, *74*, 37–46. [CrossRef] [PubMed]
123. Salisbury, D.F.; Shafer, A.R.; Murphy, T.K.; Haigh, S.M.; Coffman, B.A. Pitch and Duration Mismatch Negativity and Heschl's Gyrus Volume in First-Episode Schizophrenia-Spectrum Individuals. *Clin. EEG Neurosci.* **2020**, *51*, 359–364. [CrossRef] [PubMed]
124. Light, G.A.; Swerdlow, N.R.; Thomas, M.L.; Calkins, M.E.; Green, M.F.; Greenwood, T.A.; Gur, R.E.; Gur, R.C.; Lazzeroni, L.C.; Nuechterlein, K.H.; et al. Validation of mismatch negativity and P3a for use in multi-site studies of schizophrenia: Characterization of demographic, clinical, cognitive, and functional correlates in COGS-2. *Schizophr. Res.* **2015**, *163*, 63–72. [CrossRef] [PubMed]

125. Monaghan, C.K.; Brickman, S.; Huynh, P.; Ongur, D.; Hall, M.H. A longitudinal study of event related potentials and correlations with psychosocial functioning and clinical features in first episode psychosis patients. *Int. J. Psychophysiol.* **2019**, *145*, 48–56. [CrossRef]
126. Koshiyama, D.; Thomas, M.L.; Miyakoshi, M.; Joshi, Y.B.; Molina, J.L.; Tanaka-Koshiyama, K.; Sprock, J.; Braff, D.L.; Swerdlow, N.R.; Light, G.A. Hierarchical Pathways from Sensory Processing to Cognitive, Clinical, and Functional Impairments in Schizophrenia. *Schizophr. Bull.* **2021**, *47*, 373–385. [CrossRef]
127. Bowie, C.R.; Twamley, E.W.; Anderson, H.; Halpern, B.; Patterson, T.L.; Harvey, P.D. Self-assessment of functional status in schizophrenia. *J. Psychiatr. Res.* **2007**, *41*, 1012–1018. [CrossRef] [PubMed]
128. Leifker, F.R.; Patterson, T.L.; Heaton, R.K.; Harvey, P.D. Validating measures of real-world outcome: The results of the VALERO expert survey and RAND panel. *Schizophr. Bull.* **2011**, *37*, 334–343. [CrossRef] [PubMed]
129. Mucci, A.; Rucci, P.; Rocca, P.; Bucci, P.; Gibertoni, D.; Merlotti, E.; Galderisi, S.; Maj, M.; Italian Network for Research on Psychoses. The Specific Level of Functioning Scale: Construct validity, internal consistency and factor structure in a large Italian sample of people with schizophrenia living in the community. *Schizophr. Res.* **2014**, *159*, 144–150. [CrossRef]
130. Montemagni, C.; Rocca, P.; Mucci, A.; Galderisi, S.; Maj, M. Italian version of the "Specific Level of Functioning". *J. Psychopathol.* **2015**, *21*, 287–296.
131. Apiquian, R.; Elena Ulloa, R.; Herrera-Estrella, M.; Moreno-Gomez, A.; Erosa, S.; Contreras, V.; Nicolini, H. Validity of the Spanish version of the Personal and Social Performance scale in schizophrenia. *Schizophr. Res.* **2009**, *112*, 181–186. [CrossRef] [PubMed]
132. Nicholl, D.; Nasrallah, H.; Nuamah, I.; Akhras, K.; Gagnon, D.D.; Gopal, S. Personal and social functioning in schizophrenia: Defining a clinically meaningful measure of maintenance in relapse prevention. *Curr. Med. Res. Opin.* **2010**, *26*, 1471–1484. [CrossRef] [PubMed]
133. Lindenmayer, J.P.; McGurk, S.R.; Khan, A.; Kaushik, S.; Thanju, A.; Hoffman, L.; Valdez, G.; Wance, D.; Herrmann, E. Improving social cognition in schizophrenia: A pilot intervention combining computerized social cognition training with cognitive remediation. *Schizophr. Bull.* **2013**, *39*, 507–517. [CrossRef]
134. Kay, S.R.; Fiszbein, A.; Opler, L.A. The positive and negative syndrome scale (PANSS) for schizophrenia. *Schizophr. Bull.* **1987**, *13*, 261–276. [CrossRef] [PubMed]
135. Kirkpatrick, B.; Strauss, G.P.; Nguyen, L.; Fischer, B.A.; Daniel, D.G.; Cienfuegos, A.; Marder, S.R. The brief negative symptom scale: Psychometric properties. *Schizophr. Bull.* **2011**, *37*, 300–305. [CrossRef]
136. Mucci, A.; Galderisi, S.; Merlotti, E.; Rossi, A.; Rocca, P.; Bucci, P.; Piegari, G.; Chieffi, M.; Vignapiano, A.; Maj, M.; et al. The Brief Negative Symptom Scale (BNSS): Independent validation in a large sample of Italian patients with schizophrenia. *Eur. Psychiatry* **2015**, *30*, 641–647. [CrossRef] [PubMed]
137. Addington, J.; Shah, H.; Liu, L.; Addington, D. Reliability and validity of the Calgary Depression Scale for Schizophrenia (CDSS) in youth at clinical high risk for psychosis. *Schizophr. Res.* **2014**, *153*, 64–67. [CrossRef] [PubMed]
138. Gerlach, J.; Korsgaard, S.; Clemmesen, P.; Lauersen, A.M.; Magelund, G.; Noring, U.; Povlsen, U.J.; Bech, P.; Casey, D.E. The St. Hans Rating Scale for extrapyramidal syndromes: Reliability and validity. *Acta Psychiatr. Scand.* **1993**, *87*, 244–252. [CrossRef] [PubMed]
139. Nuechterlein, K.H.; Green, M.F.; Kern, R.S.; Baade, L.E.; Barch, D.M.; Cohen, J.D.; Essock, S.; Fenton, W.S.; Frese, F.J., 3rd; Gold, J.M.; et al. The MATRICS Consensus Cognitive Battery, part 1: Test selection, reliability, and validity. *Am. J. Psychiatry* **2008**, *165*, 203–213. [CrossRef] [PubMed]
140. Kern, R.S.; Nuechterlein, K.H.; Green, M.F.; Baade, L.E.; Fenton, W.S.; Gold, J.M.; Keefe, R.S.; Mesholam-Gately, R.; Mintz, J.; Seidman, L.J.; et al. The MATRICS Consensus Cognitive Battery, part 2: Co-norming and standardization. *Am. J. Psychiatry* **2008**, *165*, 214–220. [CrossRef] [PubMed]
141. Harvey, P.D.; Raykov, T.; Twamley, E.W.; Vella, L.; Heaton, R.K.; Patterson, T.L. Validating the measurement of real-world functional outcomes: Phase I results of the VALERO study. *Am. J. Psychiatry* **2011**, *168*, 1195–1201. [CrossRef]
142. Sabbag, S.; Twamley, E.M.; Vella, L.; Heaton, R.K.; Patterson, T.L.; Harvey, P.D. Assessing everyday functioning in schizophrenia: Not all informants seem equally informative. *Schizophr. Res.* **2011**, *131*, 250–255. [CrossRef] [PubMed]
143. Perlman, G.; Foti, D.; Jackson, F.; Kotov, R.; Constantino, E.; Hajcak, G. Clinical significance of auditory target P300 subcomponents in psychosis: Differential diagnosis, symptom profiles, and course. *Schizophr. Res.* **2015**, *165*, 145–151. [CrossRef]
144. Mondragon-Maya, A.; Solis-Vivanco, R.; Leon-Ortiz, P.; Rodriguez-Agudelo, Y.; Yanez-Tellez, G.; Bernal-Hernandez, J.; Cadenhead, K.S.; de la Fuente-Sandoval, C. Reduced P3a amplitudes in antipsychotic naive first-episode psychosis patients and individuals at clinical high-risk for psychosis. *J. Psychiatr. Res.* **2013**, *47*, 755–761. [CrossRef] [PubMed]
145. Kharawala, S.; Hastedt, C.; Podhorna, J.; Shukla, H.; Kappelhoff, B.; Harvey, P.D. The relationship between cognition and functioning in schizophrenia: A semi-systematic review. *Schizophr. Res. Cogn.* **2022**, *27*, 100217. [CrossRef] [PubMed]
146. Falkai, P.; Schmitt, A. The need to develop personalized interventions to improve cognition in schizophrenia. *World Psychiatry* **2019**, *18*, 170. [CrossRef] [PubMed]
147. Reichenberg, A.; Velthorst, E.; Davidson, M. Cognitive impairment and psychosis in schizophrenia: Independent or linked conditions? *World Psychiatry* **2019**, *18*, 162–163. [CrossRef]

Journal of *Clinical Medicine*

MDPI

Article

Investigating the Relationship between White Matter Connectivity and Motivational Circuits in Subjects with Deficit Schizophrenia: A Diffusion Tensor Imaging (DTI) Study

Giulia M. Giordano [1,*,†], Pasquale Pezzella [1,†], Mario Quarantelli [2], Paola Bucci [1], Anna Prinster [2], Andrea Soricelli [3,4], Andrea Perrottelli [1], Luigi Giuliani [1], Michele Fabrazzo [1] and Silvana Galderisi [1]

1 Department of Psychiatry, University of Campania "Luigi Vanvitelli", 80138 Naples, Italy; pezzella.pasquale3@gmail.com (P.P.); paolabucci456@gmail.com (P.B.); andreaperrottelli@gmail.com (A.P.); luigi.giuliani.91@gmail.com (L.G.); michele.fabrazzo@unicampania.it (M.F.); silvana.galderisi@gmail.com (S.G.)

2 Biostructure and Bioimaging Institute, National Research Council, 80134 Naples, Italy; quarante@unina.it (M.Q.); anna.prinster@ibb.cnr.it (A.P.)

3 Department of Integrated Imaging, IRCCS SDN, 80143 Naples, Italy; andrea.soricelli@uniparthenope.it

4 Department of Motor Sciences and Healthiness, University of Naples Parthenope, 80133 Naples, Italy

* Correspondence: giuliamgiordano@gmail.com; Tel.: +39-0815666512; Fax: +39-0815666523

† These authors contributed equally to this work.

Abstract: Deficit schizophrenia is a subtype of schizophrenia presenting primary and enduring negative symptoms (NS). Although one of the most updated hypotheses indicates a relationship between NS and impaired motivation, only a few studies have investigated abnormalities of motivational circuits in subjects with deficit schizophrenia (DS). Our aim was to investigate structural connectivity within motivational circuits in DS. We analyzed diffusion tensor imaging (DTI) data from 46 subjects with schizophrenia (SCZ) and 35 healthy controls (HCs). SCZ were classified as DS (n = 9) and non-deficit (NDS) (n = 37) using the Schedule for Deficit Syndrome. The connectivity index (CI) and the Fractional Anisotropy (FA) of the connections between selected brain areas involved in motivational circuits were examined. DS, as compared with NDS and HCs, showed increased CI between the right amygdala and dorsal anterior insular cortex and increased FA of the pathway connecting the left nucleus accumbens with the posterior insular cortex. Our results support previous evidence of distinct neurobiological alterations underlying different clinical subtypes of schizophrenia. DS, as compared with NDS and HCs, may present an altered pruning process (consistent with the hyperconnectivity) in cerebral regions involved in updating the stimulus value to guide goal-directed behavior.

Keywords: motivation circuits; negative symptoms; RDoC; positive valence system; salience system; schizophrenia; deficit syndrome

Citation: Giordano, G.M.; Pezzella, P.; Quarantelli, M.; Bucci, P.; Prinster, A.; Soricelli, A.; Perrottelli, A.; Giuliani, L.; Fabrazzo, M.; Galderisi, S. Investigating the Relationship between White Matter Connectivity and Motivational Circuits in Subjects with Deficit Schizophrenia: A Diffusion Tensor Imaging (DTI) Study. *J. Clin. Med.* **2022**, *11*, 61. https://doi.org/10.3390/jcm11010061

Academic Editors: Armida Mucci and Birgit Derntl

Received: 26 November 2021
Accepted: 22 December 2021
Published: 23 December 2021

1. Introduction

Negative symptoms represent a core aspect of schizophrenia, with a negative impact on the functioning of people suffering from this disorder. To date, they remain an unmet therapeutic need, since no effective treatment is available for these symptoms, particularly when they are primary to the disorder [1–14].

According to the current conceptualization provided by the Consensus Conference of the National Institute of Mental Health—Measurement and Treatment Research to Improve Cognition in Schizophrenia (NIMH-MATRICS), the negative symptom construct includes five individual symptoms, namely avolition, anhedonia, asociality, blunted affect and alogia [15]. These symptoms cluster into two domains, the Experiential domain (which includes avolition, anhedonia and asociality) and the Expressive Deficit domain (which includes blunted affect and alogia) [4,13–20].

Negative symptoms might be the primary manifestation of schizophrenia (primary negative symptoms) or the consequence of different factors (secondary negative symptoms), i.e., psychopathological factors (moderate positive symptoms, clinically significant depression), syndrome-unrelated factors (social isolation, environmental hypostimulation) or medication side effects (extrapyramidal symptoms and sedation), and might be transient or persistent over time. Primary and persistent negative symptoms characterize a subtype of schizophrenia, named deficit schizophrenia, which is associated with a greater impairment of general cognitive functions and poorer treatment response and outcome, in comparison with non-deficit schizophrenia [21–30].

One of the most updated neurobiological hypotheses underlying negative symptoms indicates a relationship between the Experiential domain and an impairment in different aspects of motivation [4,27,31–42]. Indeed, subjects with schizophrenia show impairments in several aspects of motivation, except for the pleasure experience [31,32,34–36]. Notably, patients show greater difficulty in reward-related learning and adaptive integration of value information with action selection [43,44], which could be linked to an alteration of the connectivity between brain areas involved in the dopaminergic circuits. On the other hand, the Expressive Deficit domain is less understood and probably is related to deficits in neurocognitive and social cognition abilities—often observed in subjects with schizophrenia, particularly in subjects with a high genetic risk for schizophrenia [5,7,45–51]—and to neurological soft signs, suggesting that Expressive Deficit symptoms, akin to cognitive deficits, are probably driven by a diffuse neurodevelopmental disconnectivity [4,52,53].

Two possible mechanisms and circuits might be implicated in the pathophysiology of motivational deficits in subjects with schizophrenia: an impairment in the "motivational value system or reward circuit" (NIMH Research Domain Criteria "positive valence system") and/or an impairment in the "motivational salience circuit". The brain areas belonging to the motivational value system are the ventral tegmental area (VTA) and the ventro-medial substantia nigra pars compacta (VMSNpc), which project to the nucleus accumbens shell (sNAcc), the dorsal striatum (DStr), the medial orbito-frontal cortex (mOFC) and the ventro-medial prefrontal cortex (VMPFC) [4,33,39]. Abnormalities in these areas and/or in their connections may result in an impairment in anticipatory pleasure, action evaluation and encoding of the value of stimuli, action outcome contingency learning (the ability to know the causal consequences of an action) and instrumental learning (the integration of value with action selection) [4].

The motivational salience system includes the VTA and the dorso-lateral substantia nigra pars compacta (DLSNpc) with projections to the accumbens core (cNAcc), which, in turn, projects to the DSr, the dorso-lateral prefrontal cortex (DLPFC), the ventro-lateral prefrontal cortex (VLPFC) and the anterior cingulate cortex (ACC) [33]. Abnormalities in these areas and/or in their connections might lead to an impairment in general and energetic aspects of motivation, vigor in motivated behavior, cognitive activation and the ability to orient oneself towards salient stimuli [4,33,54–57]. The identification of biobehavioral data associated with specific psychopathological features might refine hypotheses on negative symptoms [58], clarify the relationships with cognitive impairment and pave the way towards innovative treatment options for some of these symptoms [59].

Although several brain regions are part of these two interconnected circuits (motivational value and salience systems), the nucleus accumbens (NAcc) and the VTA represent key central regions within these circuits [60,61]. Other brain structures interconnected with these circuits are the amygdala (Amy) and hippocampus [62,63].

As far as we know, only rarely have these pathophysiological models of negative symptoms been applied to the deficit schizophrenia construct [4,37,64]. In particular, one study [64] reported the presence in subjects with deficit schizophrenia of structural brain abnormalities in several brain areas, such as the insula, anterior cingulate cortex, medial prefrontal cortex and putamen, which are involved in motivation and goal-directed behavior. In a functional magnetic resonance imaging study during a reward anticipation task, Mucci and colleagues [37] reported that subjects with deficit schizophrenia showed a significant reduction in dorsal caudate activity, compared with both healthy controls and subjects with non-deficit schizophrenia.

Diffusion tensor imaging (DTI) studies have highlighted the presence of "disconnectivity" within and between cortical and subcortical areas in subjects with schizophrenia and in those with psychotic disorders [37,39,40,65–73]. This disconnectivity might lead to abnormalities in those pathways that underlie cognitive abilities and motivated behavior [65,74].

In subjects with deficit schizophrenia, white matter (WM) abnormalities in the superior longitudinal fasciculus [75], left uncinate fasciculus [76,77], right inferior longitudinal fasciculus, right arcuate fasciculus [77], postcentral area, left forceps minor [78], right posterior thalamic radiation [79] and posterior corpus callosum [80] have been reported.

However, these studies did not investigate abnormalities of motivational circuits in subjects with deficit schizophrenia, since this was not the primary objective of these studies. Furthermore, some of the above-mentioned studies [77,79,80] did not use the Schedule for the Deficit Syndrome (SDS), which represents the gold standard to assess deficit schizophrenia, but they instead used a proxy from the Positive and Negative Syndrome Scale (PANSS) [81]. However, it has been demonstrated that the proxy for categorizing patients in subjects with deficit and non-deficit schizophrenia has some problems in terms of face validity and temporal stability [14]. In addition, the PANSS includes some aspects that are not conceptualized as negative symptoms and evaluates symptoms belonging to the Experiential domain only at a behavioral level.

Therefore, in light of the above observations, our study aimed to fill the gap in the previous literature, investigating, in subjects with deficit schizophrenia (assessed with a state-of-the-art instrument), the presence of abnormalities within motivational circuits. To this aim, using a bilateral probabilistic approach on DTI data, the present study examined differences between subjects with deficit schizophrenia, subjects with non-deficit schizophrenia and healthy controls in WM connections between major brain regions involved in motivational pathways. We hypothesized that subjects with deficit schizophrenia would show abnormalities in WM connections between brain areas involved in motivational circuits, compared to subjects with non-deficit schizophrenia and healthy controls.

2. Materials and Methods

2.1. Subjects

Fifty-two subjects with schizophrenia (SCZ) were enrolled at the Department of Psychiatry of the University of Campania "Luigi Vanvitelli", in the period between September 2010 and July 2012. All subjects were right-handed.

The inclusion criteria were as follows:

- diagnosis of schizophrenia based on the criteria of the DSM-IV, confirmed by the Mini International Neuropsychiatric Interview Plus (MINI-Plus);
- age between 18 and 65 years;
- negative history of intellectual disability, head trauma with unconsciousness, alcohol or substance abuse within the previous six months (except for cigarette smoking);
- no treatment modifications and/or hospitalization due to symptom exacerbation in the last three months;
- treatment with second-generation antipsychotics [82].

Thirty-five right-handed healthy controls (HCs) were included. The subjects were enrolled from the community through the distribution of informative leaflets. Exclusion criteria for HCs were:

- presence of current or lifetime Axis I or II psychiatric diagnosis; history of psychiatric hospitalization;
- history of head trauma with unconsciousness;
- history of substance abuse or dependence (except for cigarette smoking) and use of drugs that affect the central nervous system.

The study was approved by the University Ethics Committee. All participants signed a written informed consent form after a detailed description of the study procedures and goals.

The study was performed in accordance with the ethical principles of the Declaration of Helsinki.

A subsample of thirty-five SCZ and seventeen HCs was included in a previous publication [40].

2.2. Assessment Instruments

Socio-demographic variables such as age, paternal and maternal education and gender were evaluated for all subjects. A semi-structured interview, the Schedule for the Deficit Syndrome [83], was used to categorize patients as subjects with deficit schizophrenia (DS) and subjects with non-deficit schizophrenia (NDS). In particular, deficit schizophrenia was diagnosed when subjects had at least two out of six primary negative symptoms (curbing of interests, diminished sense of purpose, diminished social drive, restricted affect, diminished emotional range and poverty of speech) for at least 12 months, including periods of clinical stability. Positive symptoms, depression and disorganization were assessed using the Positive and Negative Syndrome Scale [81].

The daily antipsychotic dose was converted to chlorpromazine equivalents, according to Gardner et al. [84].

2.3. MRI Acquisition and Parameters

We recorded all MRI with a 3 T scanner (Achieva, Philips Medical Systems, Best, The Netherlands), and we acquired DTI data using an EPI sequence (repetition time/echo time (TR/TE) 9300/102 ms, voxel $2 \times 2 \times 2$ mm^3, 32 directions uniformly distributed in 3-dimensional (3D) space 25, B-factors 0 and 1000 s/mm^2, 50 axials slices covering the whole brain). In addition, we obtained a 3D T1-weighted brain volume (Turbo-Field-Echo sequence, TR/TE 7.7/3.5 ms, voxel $1 \times 1 \times 1$ mm^3, 181 sagittal slices covering the whole brain) to improve the spatial normalization of the data to the MNI space (see below). During the MRI acquisition, subjects were lying on their back with their heads lightly fixed by straps and foam pads to minimize head movement.

2.4. Region of Interest

We choose a set of ROIs relevant to the reward system for tractographic analysis, following the approach proposed by Bracht et al. [85], integrated by a set of insular ROIs. We defined the following ROIs bilaterally as seeds: NAcc (5 mm radius sphere, MNI coordinates of the center $\pm$ 8, 11, -9) [86], Amy (as defined in the WFUPick-Atlas) [87], VTA (4 mm radius sphere, MNI coordinates of the center ± 5, -20, -10) [88]. Then, we defined the following as target ROIs: mOFC, lateral orbito-frontal cortex (lOFC), DLPFC, along with ventral-anterior (vaIC), dorsal-anterior (daIC) and posterior (pIC) insular cortex.

- Left and right DLPFC were defined combining on each side the Brodmann areas 9 and 46 [89], as defined in the WFUPick-Atlas.
- Orbito-frontal cortices were preliminarily obtained by combining the Brodmann areas 10 and 11, as defined in the WFUPick-Atlas, and were then divided on each side of the brain in their medial (mOFC) and lateral (lOFC) parts using the sagittal planes placed 20 mm off-center as separators [90].
- For each side, vaIC, daIC and pIC ROIs were obtained by dividing the entire available ROIs of insular cortex in the Harvard-Oxford Cortical Structural Atlas [91], based on its connectivity [92]. DTI pre-processing and probabilistic tractography were performed using the software modules provided in the FMRIB Software Library (FSL, http://fsl.fmrib.ox.ac.uk/fsl, accessed on 15 July 2017).

2.5. Probabilistic Tractography

We preliminarily corrected all DTI datasets for head movements using the eddy_correct routine implemented in FSL [93], thereby correcting accordingly diffusion sensitizing gradient directions [94]. A brain mask was obtained from the B0 images using the Brain Extraction Tool routine [95], and a diffusion tensor model was fitted at each voxel using FSL's algorithm for Bayesian Estimation of Diffusion Parameters Obtained using Sampling Techniques (BEDPOSTX). From the parameters of affine co-registration (translation along and rotation around the 3 axes), the mean movement over the brain mask was calculated for each of the 32 DTI volumes, as compared with the previous one. To avoid the effects of motion, which strongly influences apparent diffusion parameters, we excluded from the analysis datasets that exceeded at any time point 3 mm of head movement, and used mean head movement as a covariate in the second-level analysis (see below).

Then, we normalized the deskulled B0 volumes to the MNI space using the corresponding T1-weighted volumes as a proxy, using the 152 subject T1 template provided by SPM, and the FMRIB's Linear Image Registration Tool [96]. The resulting normalization matrices were inverted and applied to the ROIs (defined in the MNI space), to apply them to each patient's study. We assessed visually the quality of the normalization by verifying the match between normalized B0 volumes and the EPI template provided with SPM.

Then, we carried out probabilistic tractography using ProbTrackx [97], modeling 5000 iterations within each voxel of the seed ROI, with a curvature threshold (cosine of the minimum allowable angle between 2 steps) of 0.2, a step length of 0.5 and a maximum number of 2000 steps. For each seed–target couple, we used the percentage of the total pathways starting from the seed that reached the target as a measure of the connectivity strength between the 2 ROIs (Connectivity Index, CI). In addition, we calculated the cumulated fractional anisotropy (FA) over each pathway in order to provide a measure of its structural integrity. Given the lack of consensus on this statistical issue, we did not use a threshold for either CI or FA calculations [98].

For each seed, only connections to homolateral target ROIs were examined.

2.6. Statistical Analysis

SPSS (Version 25.0, SPSS Inc, Chicago, IL, USA) was used to perform statistical analyses. A general linear model was fitted separately for each measure to assess differences between groups, including in the model as covariates age, gender and mean head movement (root mean square realignment estimates, RMS), as derived from the eddy_correct procedure. Bonferroni post-hoc comparisons between the three sample groups (HCs, DS and NDS) were performed when a significant main effect of the group emerged.

Results were considered significant for $p < 0.05$, corrected according to Bonferroni for the number of connections assessed. In particular, as only homolateral connections were examined, a total of 36 seed–target couples were tested (3 seeds $\times$ 6 targets $\times$ 2 hemispheres), so that $p < 0.0014$ was used as a statistical threshold.

3. Results

3.1. Subject Characteristics

We included only 46 patients and 35 HCs in the group-level analysis, as the MRI scans of six patients were discarded due to excessive motion artifacts during visual inspection. Please refer to Table S1 for the demographic and clinical characteristics of the whole sample of SCZ, as compared to HCs.

According to the SDS criteria, the whole sample of SCZ was divided into DS ($n = 9$) and NDS ($n = 37$) patients. Table 1 summarizes the demographic and clinical characteristics of the three groups of the study sample (DS, NDS and HCs). There was no significant difference in the mean age ($p = 0.149$), gender ($p = 0.268$) or paternal ($p = 0.057$) and maternal ($p = 0.265$) education between DS, NDS and HCs. There was a small difference between the three groups in terms of RMS ($p = 0.049$). NDS, as compared to DS, had higher scores on PANSS Depression ($p = 0.003$). There was no statistically significant difference between DS and NDS on the SDS scores, although DS, as compared to NDS, had higher SDS total and subdomain scores.

Table 1. Demographic characteristics, RMS and illness-related variables of the study sample (HCs, NDS and DS).

	HCs (n = 35)	NDS (n = 37)	DS (n = 9)	F	p
Age (years)	32.94 ± 8.80	36.57 ± 7.50	33.00 ± 8.53	1.952	0.149
Gender (M/F)	17/18	25/12	5/4	1.340	0.268
Paternal education (years)	11.31 ± 5.85	8.41 ± 4.64	9.00 ± 4.09	2.965	0.057
Maternal education (years)	10.34 ± 5.67	8.49 ± 4.69	8.33 ± 4.47	1.352	0.265
RMS	0.34 ± 0.10	0.41 ± 0.10	0.40 ± 0.11	3.131	**0.049** *
Total SDS	-	7.82 ± 5.60	11.00 ± 6.70	1.740	0.195
SDS Experiential domain	-	4.76 ± 3.45	6.29 ± 3.20	1.161	0.288
SDS Expressive Deficit domain	-	3.06 ± 2.47	4.71 ± 3.59	2.196	0.147
PANSS Positive	-	8.09 ± 4.28	6.00 ± 2.45	1.541	0.222
PANSS Disorganization	-	7.33 ± 3.68	7.43 ± 4.28	0.004	0.952
PANSS Depression	-	2.49 ± 0.85	1.43 ± 0.50	10.224	**0.003**
Chlorpromazine equivalent doses	-	402.01 ± 190.05	263.37 ± 92.34	3.003	0.092

DS: patients with deficit schizophrenia; HCs: healthy controls; NDS: patients with non-deficit schizophrenia; PANSS: Positive and Negative Syndrome Scale; RMS: root-mean-square of the movement during the examination; SDS: Schedule for Deficit Syndrome. p values in boldface indicate statistical significance. * Bonferroni's post-hoc bivariate test: DS—HCs, p = 0.44; NDS—HCs, p = 0.057.

3.2. Group Comparison on the Connectivity Index and Fractional Anisotropy between Couples of ROIs

The results of the comparison on the CI and FA between SCZ and HCs are reported in Tables S2 and S3. In particular, SCZ, as compared to HCs, had a reduced CI between rAmy and homolateral DLPFC; however, this result did not survive correction for multiple tests (p = 0.004) (Table S2, Figures S1 and S2).

When we compared the three sample groups (DS, NDS and HCs), we observed a statistically significant difference in CI in the rAmy-daIC pathway (p = 0.001). Post hoc pairwise comparisons demonstrated that DS, as compared to NDS (p = 0.001) and HCs (p = 0.001), showed an increase in CI in the rAmy-daIC pathway, while no statistically significant difference was found between NDS and HCs (Table 2, Figures 1 and 2).

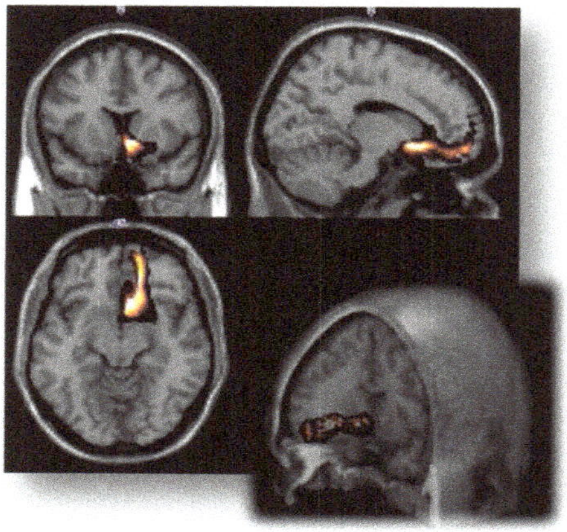

Figure 1. Three-dimensional representation of the average distribution of the connection patterns between the right amygdala and the ipsilateral dorsal anterior insular cortex.

Table 2. Group differences between DS, NDS and HCs in CI.

Brain Pathways	NDS (n = 37)	DS (n = 9)	HCs (n = 35)	F	p
		CI			
lNAcc to daIC	10.52 ± 14.31	6.02 ± 6.64	9.36 ± 10.88	0.831	0.440
lNAcc to DLPFC	41.35 ± 54.84	15.23 ± 19.29	49.31 ± 101.35	0.654	0.523
lNAcc to lOFC	119.56 ± 209.92	105.95 ± 116.48	120.02 ± 156.09	0.114	0.892
lNAcc to mOFC	2192.74 ± 1283.04	1975.77 ± 859.34	2903.13 ± 1783.21	2.023	0.139
lNAcc to pIC	552.43 ±591.62	1132.7 ± 850.63	463.43 ± 408.79	4.823	0.011
lNAcc to vaIC	646.07 ± 509.67	1246.7 ± 1052.93	920.0 ± 881.79	2.453	0.093
lAmy to daIC	66.28 ± 66.38	29.66 ± 24.57	69.33 ± 69.13	1.532	0.223
lAmy to DLPFC	40.26 ± 35.93	23.7 ± 17.01	53.3 ± 46.16	1.795	0.173
lAmy to lOFC	160.01 ± 175.11	74.5 ±31.49	14,328 ± 160.88	1.922	0.153
lAmy to mOFC	832.51 ±547.32	598.92 ±337.07	1012.18 ± 647.54	1.662	0.197
lAmy to pIC	2231.79 ± 1861.32	3076.22 ± 1806.24	1748.80 ± 1274.76	3.323	0.041
lAmy to vaIC	2418.53 ± 1169.48	2452.89 ± 916.74	2908.10 ± 1094.67	1.424	0.247
lVTA to daIC	57.8 ± 89.75	12.48 ± 13.78	33.06 ± 41.98	1.428	0.246
lVTA to DLPFC	125.04 ± 157.90	76.05 ± 100.19	129.57 ± 85.92	1.101	0.338
lVTA to lOFC	90.15 ± 79.93	36.76 ± 32.64	126.96 ± 140.15	2.560	0.084
lVTA to mOFC	66.57 ± 67.51	80.52 ± 153.03	102.19 ± 131.15	1.027	0.363
lVTA to pIC	76.27 ± 91.95	59.45 ± 68.97	46.88 ± 58.16	1.251	0.292
lVTA to vaIC	17.21 ± 27.71	8.95 ± 3.49	16.54 ± 17.90	0.763	0.470
rNAcc to daIC	11.09 ± 44.34	12.36 ± 14.58	7.99 ± 16.06	0.088	0.916
rNAcc to DLPFC	18.54 ± 26.02	17.21 ± 23.43	31.69 ± 59.31	0.874	0.421
rNAcc to lOFC	449.74 ± 512.68	552.32 ± 553.16	583.00 ± 575.02	0.099	0.906
rNAcc to mOFC	1352 ± 943.98	1660.94 ± 1159.38	2216.77 ± 1315.54	3.717	0.029
rNAcc to pIC	129.18 ± 244.89	89.27 ± 110.05	80.98 ± 92.41	0.119	0.888
rNAcc to vaIC	732.42 ± 961.42	1369.91 ± 1410.50	718.38 ± 700.50	2.082	0.132
rAmy to daIC	8.39 ± 11.46	25.53 ± 21.64	7.82 ± 9.24	8.190	**0.001**
rAmy to DLPFC	20.1 ±24.27	18.14 ± 9.89	38.16 ± 32.92	4.356	0.016
rAmy to lOFC	95.41 ± 101.87	59.48 ± 39.84	129.18 ± 107.97	1.436	0.244
rAmy to mOFC	1246.66 ± 1069.13	937.87 ± 852.42	1075.12 ± 992.10	0.389	0.679
rAmy to pIC	77.06 ± 144.08	118.83 ± 138.32	70.62 ± 80.30	0.985	0.378
rAmy to vaIC	736.59 ± 824.11	818.15 ± 756.58	631.73 ± 508.82	0.502	0.607
rVTA to daIC	23.3 ± 40.78	17.45 ± 28.28	35.64 ± 59.95	0.683	0.508
rVTA to DLPFC	122.45 ± 94.52	77.53 ± 68.19	148.46 ± 124.59	2.100	0.130
rVTA to lOFC	149.33 ± 169.72	64.63 ± 82.54	134.87 ± 151.53	1.262	0.289
rVTA to mOFC	67.24 ± 93.39	26.85 ± 29.73	52.22 ± 91.28	0.656	0.522
rVTA to pIC	14.77 ± 17.26	30.91 ± 69.09	14.17 ± 18.00	1.283	0.283
rVTA to vaIC	10.68 ± 11.90	13.23 ± 17.42	17.54 ± 18.96	0.543	0.583

Amy: amygdala; CI: connectivity index; daIC: dorsal-anterior insular cortex; DLPFC: dorso-lateral prefrontal cortex; HCs: healthy controls; l: left; lOFC: lateral orbito-frontal cortex; mOFC: medial orbito-frontal cortex; Nacc: nucleus accumbens; pIC: posterior insular cortex; r: right; SCZ: subjects with schizophrenia; vaIC: ventral-anterior insular cortex; VTA: ventral tegmental area. $p < 0.0014$ was used as statistical threshold; p values in boldface indicate statistical significance corrected for multiple tests; Bonferroni's post-hoc bivariate test: CI rAmy to daIC: DS—NDS, $p = 0.001$; DS—HCs, $p = 0.001$.

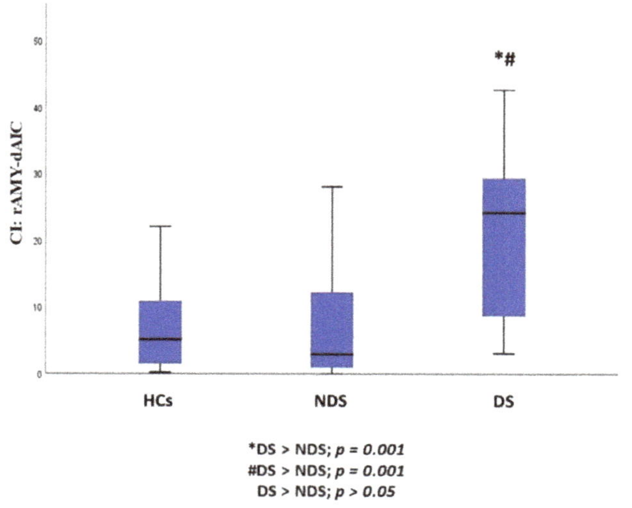

Figure 2. Group differences between DS, NDS and HCs in the CI of the rAmy-daIC pathway. HCs: healthy controls; DS: subjects with deficit schizophrenia; NDS: subjects with non-deficit schizophrenia CI: connectivity index; rAmy: right amygdala; daIC: dorsal-anterior insular cortex.

Furthermore, a statistically significant difference between DS, NDS and HCs was observed in FA of the lNAcc-pIC pathway (p = 0.001). Post hoc pairwise comparisons demonstrated an increase in FA of the lNAcc-pIC pathway in DS compared to both NDS (p = 0.001) and HCs (p < 0.001), while no differences were found between NDS and HCs (Table 3, Figure 3).

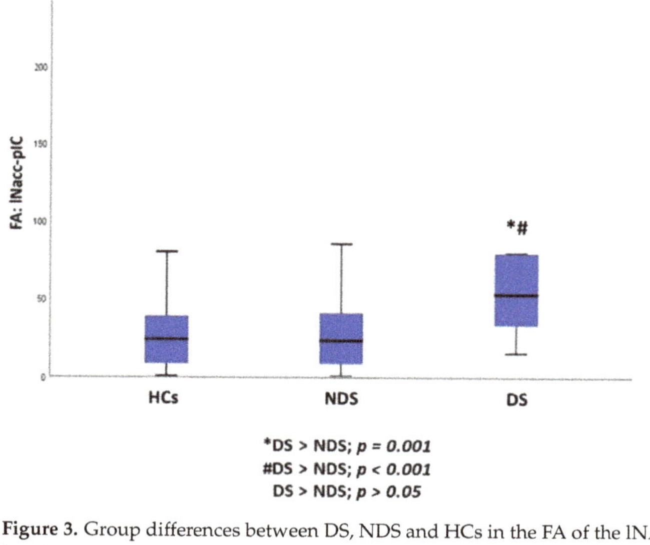

Figure 3. Group differences between DS, NDS and HCs in the FA of the lNAcc-pIC pathway. HCs: healthy controls; DS: subjects with deficit schizophrenia; NDS: subjects with non-deficit schizophrenia FA: fractional anisotropy; lNAcc: left nucleus accumbens; pIC: posterior insular cortex.

Table 3. Group differences between DS, NDS and HCs in FA.

Brain Pathways	NDS ($n = 37$)	DS ($n = 9$)	HCs ($n = 35$)	F	p
		FA			
lNAcc to daIC	1.54 ± 1.27	1.26 ± 0.81	1.60 ± 1.20	0.273	0.762
lNAcc to DLPFC	3.35 ± 3.76	1.69 ± 1.25	3.27 ± 3.55	0.967	0.385
lNAcc to lOFC	7.14 ± 10.8	6.45 ± 4.54	7.32 ± 7.66	0.081	0.923
lNAcc to mOFC	49.93 ± 29.7	61.72 ± 41.81	63.01 ± 46.42	0.857	0.429
lNAcc to pIC	31.77 ± 27.32	76.48 ± 68.31	28.20 ± 22.57	7.760	**0.001**
lNAcc to vaIC	27.45 ± 22.09	52.3 ± 39.84	29.48 ± 20.19	4.202	0.019
lAmy to daIC	6.85 ± 5.22	4.01 ± 1.93	6.78 ± 5.80	1.645	0.200
lAmy to DLPFC	1047.97 ± 167.3	1099.55 ± 207	1030.49 ± 232.41	0.347	0.708
lAmy to lOFC	0.99 ± 1.36	0.57 ± 0.32	0.86 ± 0.91	0.792	0.457
lAmy to mOFC	12.80 ± 17.30	5.14 ± 5.73	6.74 ± 9.25	0.935	0.397
lAmy to pIC	51.63 ± 36.29	74.7 ± 31.73	45.06 ± 27.15	3.351	0.040
lAmy to vaIC	43.46 ± 17.84	43.71 ± 14.56	51.67 ± 22.79	2.098	0.130
lVTA to daIC	5.00 ± 5.80	2.11 ± 0.71	4.12 ± 3.99	1.079	0.345
lVTA to DLPFC	8.29 ± 8.86	5.84 ± 5.69	8.36 ± 4.55	0.848	0.432
lVTA to lOFC	8.53 ± 6.07	5.16 ± 4.09	10.04 ± 8.15	1.982	0.145
lVTA to mOFC	6.11 ± 4.86	5.24 ± 5.8	8.04 ± 6.98	1.967	0.147
lVTA to pIC	5.99 ± 5.42	4.66 ± 3.48	3.76 ± 3.35	2.324	0.105
lVTA to vaIC	1.96 ± 1.45	1.62 ± 0.5	2.01 ± 1.12	0.389	0.679
rNAcc to daIC	1.58 ± 3.42	2.13 ± 1.72	1.14 ± 0.94	0.540	0.585
rNAcc to DLPFC	2.20 ± 2.93	1.67 ± 1.47	2.82 ± 4.03	0.454	0.637
rNAcc to lOFC	20.76 ± 21.26	24.71 ± 25.40	24.17 ± 20.67	0.019	0.981
rNAcc to mOFC	55.36 ± 42.34	65.68 ± 44.25	81.19 ± 54.45	1.465	0.238
rNAcc to pIC	9.65 ± 14.76	7.84 ± 8.17	7.32 ± 6.61	0.065	0.937
rNAcc to vaIC	33.99 ± 34.61	50.40 ± 39.62	26.54 ± 19.49	2.392	0.098
rAmy to daIC	2.00 ± 1.75	3.99 ± 2.16	1.85 ± 1.24	6.792	0.002
rAmy to DLPFC	17.86 ± 10.45	13.17 ± 10.71	15.21 ± 11.37	0.788	0.459
rAmy to lOFC	1.43 ± 1.53	0.65 ± 0.48	1.72 ± 2.99	1.692	0.191
rAmy to mOFC	8.49 ± 8.26	7.91 ± 7.39	9.39 ± 9.86	0.114	0.892
rAmy to pIC	8.07 ± 11.83	9.18 ± 6.32	7.21 ± 5.35	0.366	0.695
rAmy to vaIC	17.07 ± 11.95	20.13 ± 14.73	13.61 ± 7.93	1.740	0.183
rVTA to daIC	3.75 ± 7.44	2.73 ± 2.9	3.97 ± 4.86	0.214	0.808
rVTA to DLPFC	8.49 ± 5.63	5.57 ± 4.14	8.44 ± 5.63	1.222	0.300
rVTA to lOFC	12.23 ± 11.34	6.27 ± 7.3	9.24 ± 8.24	1.782	0.175
rVTA to mOFC	6.81 ± 5.86	3.36 ± 3.49	5.17 ± 8.93	0.750	0.476
rVTA to pIC	1.88 ± 1.54	2.99 ± 4.41	1.76 ± 1.26	1.437	0.244
rVTA to vaIC	1.66 ± 1.13	1.95 ± 1.64	2.10 ± 1.38	0.357	0.701

Amy: amygdala; daIC: dorsal-anterior insular cortex; DLPFC: dorso-lateral prefrontal cortex; FA: fractional anisotropy; HCs: healthy controls; l: left; lOFC: lateral orbito-frontal cortex; mOFC: medial orbito-frontal cortex; Nacc: nucleus accumbens; pIC: posterior insular cortex; r: right; SCZ: subjects with schizophrenia; vaIC: ventral-anterior insular cortex; VTA: ventral tegmental area. $p < 0.0014$ was used as statistical threshold; p values in boldface indicate statistical significance corrected for multiple tests; Bonferroni's post-hoc bivariate test: FA lNAcc to pIC: DS—NDS, $p = 0.001$; DS—HCs, $p < 0.001$.

Finally, the three groups differed at a trend level in the CI and FA of different pathways (Table 2). However, these results did not survive correction for multiple tests.

4. Discussion

In this study, we carried out a probabilistic DTI analysis to explore abnormalities in structural connectivity within motivational circuits in subjects with schizophrenia, differentiating patients with DS and NDS.

We found that all subjects with schizophrenia had a reduced CI between rAmy and homolateral DLPFC; however, this result did not survive correction for multiple tests. The altered connectivity within this circuit suggests that subjects with schizophrenia have an impairment in the integration of motivational and cognitive information for goal-directed behavior [4,39]. It is possible that the heterogeneity within the syndrome might obscure findings concerning connectivity indices within the motivational circuit.

Considering the three sample groups (DS, NDS and HCs), we found that, DS, as compared to NDS and HCs, showed 1) a significant increase in CI in the rAmy-daIC pathway and 2) a significant increase in FA of the lNAcc-pIC pathway.

According to our findings, only subjects with DS showed abnormalities in the neural pathways involving mainly the Amy, the IC and the NAcc.

Firstly, DS, in comparison to NDS and HCs, showed an increase in CI between the rAmy and the daIC. Although at a trend level, the FA of the same pathway was also increased in DS, as compared to NDS and HCs. Therefore, DS showed abnormal connectivity strength (indicated by an increased CI) and disturbed fiber integrity (indicated by an increased FA) between the amygdala and dorsal-anterior insular cortex, probably suggesting an altered pruning process [99]. Pathways connecting the amygdala and insular cortex play a critical role in modulating and mediating connections between the two motivational systems [4] and are involved in upgrading and recalling the value information to support goal-directed behavior [100,101]. In particular, the amygdala, which seems to act in close collaboration with the OFC [102–105] and the ventral and medial areas of the prefrontal cortex and ventral striatum [106,107], plays a key role in reward processing and in stimulus–reward associations [108–112]. It is involved in the stimulus–response association and in orienting attention towards salient stimuli, which suggests its usefulness in evaluating the environmental context [62].

As regards the daIC, several studies have suggested that this brain region plays a key role in salience processing [113] and also modulates cognitive flexibility and autonomic activation in response to environmental changes with a general recruitment of attention, executive and working memory resources [114].

Furthermore, in our work, we observed abnormalities in fiber integrity, as suggested by the increase in FA for pathways connecting the lNAcc with pIC in DS, not present in NDS and in HCs. NAcc plays a critical role in transferring information from the IC to the "associative" medial DSr and the "sensorimotor" lateral one, connected to the cortical executive circuit, to influence motivated behavior.

In addition, previous findings indicated that the NAcc-IC pathway is strongly interconnected with the social decision-making network [115], thus playing a critical role in social behaviors—for instance, social cognition, which is often impaired in subjects with schizophrenia [49,116–118]. The IC is a site of multisensory integration [119–121] that provides an important cortical input to the NAcc, involved in reward [122,123]. Abnormalities in pathways connecting the lNAcc with pIC in DS observed in our study might be interpreted in light of the presence in DS of a greater impairment of social cognition, in comparison with NDS and HCs [21–30].

Overall, our results could be interpreted in light of previous observations in animal studies. For instance, as has been demonstrated in rodents, the connections of IC with the basolateral amygdala (BLA) and NAcc within the motivational pathways are involved in the dynamic adjustment of behavior with respect to changes in outcome valuation, depending on the current motivational state (e.g., reduced motivation to look for a drink when not thirsty), an important aspect of motivation to engage in goal-directed behavior. BLA and IC give rise to a circuit in which BLA encodes and upgrades changes in outcome value, while IC, due to its connections with the NAcc, plays a key role in retrieving the encoded changes in outcome values to direct choices between motivated actions [100,101]. Therefore, our findings seem to highlight that a dysfunction within the motivational salience circuit and impaired connections between brain regions (Amy and IC) that serve as an interface between the two motivational circuits are fundamental aspects of DS. The structural hyperconnectivity found in these subjects might be interpreted as an altered pruning process in cerebral regions devoted to updating the value that a stimulus has for a subject to support goal-directed behavior [4,39,40,99].

Our study has several strengths. Indeed, previous studies that investigated WM alterations in DS did not search for abnormalities of motivational circuits, since this was not the primary objective of these studies [4,39,40,75–80]. Furthermore, in our study, the assessment of deficit schizophrenia was made using the SDS, which is regarded as the gold-standard instrument in this field. In some of the previously mentioned studies [77,79,80], deficit schizophrenia was assessed using a proxy derived from the PANSS. The latter method for categorizing patients as DS and NDS has some problems in terms of face validity and temporal stability [14].

Structural connectivity analysis, which is used in this study, is not affected by poor general intellectual abilities or memory impairment, often present in subjects with schizophrenia, as subjects do not have to perform a task.

Our findings should be also interpreted in light of some limitations. First, the sample size is relatively small, which limits the possibility of generalizing the results. The small number of DS included in the analysis could prevent the detection of significant results. Further studies with larger samples, including a higher number of DS, are needed. In addition, the use of the SDS has prevented the evaluation of the severity of negative symptoms and testing of its association with structural connectivity parameters. Indeed, the SDS was developed to categorize subjects with schizophrenia as DS and NDS, and it is not appropriate to use the scale to evaluate symptom severity. Moreover, the use of the SDS might explain why, in our study, DS did not differ from NDS in terms of negative symptom severity, since other factors are considered to differentiate DS and NDS—for instance, the distinction between primary vs. secondary negative symptoms and transient vs. enduring negative symptoms. Future studies, using both SDS and an instrument for the evaluation of negative symptom severity, are needed to test the association between the impairment in motivational circuits in DS and negative symptom severity, as well as the possible differential associations with the two negative symptom domains.

Finally, DS and NDS differed in terms of depression scores, which we could not use as a covariate in the main analysis since we did not evaluate depression in the group of healthy controls. However, we should take into account that DS, which had lower depression scores than NDS, differed in terms of structural connectivity parameters from HCs and NDS, while no difference was found between NDS and HCs. Finally, the scores of depression were very low in both patient groups, as DS had a minimal level of depression and NDS a mild level of depression, far below the threshold of clinical significance.

In conclusion, our results lend support to the hypothesis of the presence of alterations in the motivational circuits as possible pathophysiological mechanisms of negative symptoms in subjects with schizophrenia. In addition, our data support previous evidence of distinct neurobiological alterations underlying the different clinical subtypes of schizophrenia. In particular, subjects with deficit schizophrenia, as compared to those with non-deficit schizophrenia and to healthy controls, probably present an altered pruning process (consistent with the hyperconnectivity) in cerebral regions devoted to updating the value that a stimulus has for a subject in order to support goal-directed behavior.

Supplementary Materials: The following are available online at https://www.mdpi.com/article/10.3390/jcm11010061/s1, Table S1. Demographic characteristics, RMS and illness related variables; Table S2. Group differences between SCZ and HCs in CI; Table S3. Group differences between SCZ and HCs in FA. Figure S1. 3D representation of the average distribution of the connection patterns between the right amygdala and the ipsilateral dorso-lateral prefrontal cortex; Figure S2. Group differences between SCZ and HCs in the CI of the pathway connecting right amygdala and the ipsilateral dorsolateral prefrontal cortex.

Author Contributions: Conceptualization, G.M.G., P.P., M.Q., P.B., A.P. (Anna Prinster) A.S., A.P. (Andrea Perrottelli), L.G., M.F. and S.G.; Methodology, G.M.G., P.P., M.Q., P.B., A.P. (Anna Prinster), A.S., A.P. (Andrea Perrottelli), L.G., M.F. and S.G.; Project administration, G.M.G., P.B. and S.G.; Supervision, P.B. and S.G.; Writing—original draft, G.M.G., P.P., M.Q., P.B., A.P. (Anna Prinster), A.S., A.P. (Andrea Perrottelli), L.G., M.F. and S.G.; Writing—review and editing, G.M.G., P.P., M.Q., P.B., A.P. (Anna Prinster), A.S., A.P. (Andrea Perrottelli), L.G., M.F. and S.G. All authors were responsible for the interpretation of the analyses, contributed to critically revising the content and approved the final manuscript for submission to the *Journal of Clinical Medicine*. All authors have read and agreed to the published version of the manuscript.

Funding: The author(s) declare that Compagnia di San Paolo, Turin, Italy, partially funded this study within the project 'Reward system and primary negative symptoms in schizophrenia' (Grant No.: 2008.24011).

Institutional Review Board Statement: The study was performed in accordance with the ethical principles of the Declaration of Helsinki and approved by the Ethics Committee of the Seconda Università degli Studi di Napoli—A.O.U. "Seconda Università degli Studi di Napoli", A.O.R.N. "Ospedali dei Colli" (protocol code 126, 1 July 2010).

Informed Consent Statement: All participants gave written informed consent after a detailed description of the study procedures and goals.

Data Availability Statement: All data supporting the findings of this study are available within the article and Supplementary Materials.

Conflicts of Interest: The authors declare no conflict of interest.

References

1. Kraepelin, E. *Dementia Praecox and Paraphrenia*; Chicago Medical Book: Chicago, IL, USA, 1919.
2. Bleuler, E. *Dementia Praecox or the Group of Schizophrenias*; International Universities Press: New York, NY, USA, 1950.
3. Foussias, G.; Agid, O.; Fervaha, G.; Remington, G. Negative symptoms of schizophrenia: Clinical features, relevance to real world functioning and specificity versus other CNS disorders. *Eur. Neuropsychopharmacol.* **2014**, *24*, 693–709. [CrossRef]
4. Galderisi, S.; Mucci, A.; Buchanan, R.W.; Arango, C. Negative symptoms of schizophrenia: New developments and unanswered research questions. *Lancet Psychiatry* **2018**, *5*, 664–677. [CrossRef]
5. Sahakian, B.; Savulich, G. Innovative methods for improving cognition, motivation and wellbeing in schizophrenia. *World Psychiatry* **2019**, *18*, 168–170. [CrossRef]
6. Falkai, P.; Schmitt, A. The need to develop personalized interventions to improve cognition in schizophrenia. *World Psychiatry* **2019**, *18*, 170. [CrossRef]
7. Harvey, P.D.; Strassnig, M.T. Cognition and disability in schizophrenia: Cognition-related skills deficits and decision-making challenges add to morbidity. *World Psychiatry* **2019**, *18*, 165–167. [CrossRef]
8. Keefe, R.S. Why are there no approved treatments for cognitive impairment in schizophrenia? *World Psychiatry* **2019**, *18*, 167–168. [CrossRef] [PubMed]
9. Reichenberg, A.; Velthorst, E.; Davidson, M. Cognitive impairment and psychosis in schizophrenia: Independent or linked conditions? *World Psychiatry* **2019**, *18*, 162–163. [CrossRef] [PubMed]
10. Correll, C.U.; Schooler, N.R. Negative Symptoms in Schizophrenia: A Review and Clinical Guide for Recognition, Assessment, and Treatment. *Neuropsychiatr. Dis. Treat.* **2020**, *16*, 519–534. [CrossRef] [PubMed]
11. Galderisi, S.; Rucci, P.; Mucci, A.; Rossi, A.; Rocca, P.; Bertolino, A.; Aguglia, E.; Amore, M.; Bellomo, A.; Bozzatello, P.; et al. The interplay among psychopathology, personal resources, context-related factors and real-life functioning in schizophrenia: Stability in relationships after 4 years and differences in network structure between recovered and non-recovered patients. *World Psychiatry* **2020**, *19*, 81–91. [CrossRef]
12. Heckers, S.; Kendler, K.S. The evolution of Kraepelin's nosological principles. *World Psychiatry* **2020**, *19*, 381–388. [CrossRef]
13. Galderisi, S.; Kaiser, S.; Bitter, I.; Nordentoft, M.; Mucci, A.; Sabé, M.; Giordano, G.M.; Nielsen, M.; Glenthøj, L.B.; Pezzella, P.; et al. EPA guidance on treatment of negative symptoms in schizophrenia. *Eur. Psychiatry* **2021**, *64*, e21. [CrossRef]
14. Galderisi, S.; Mucci, A.; Dollfus, S.; Nordentoft, M.; Falkai, P.; Kaiser, S.; Giordano, G.M.; Vandevelde, A.; Nielsen, M.; Glenthøj, L.B.; et al. EPA guidance on assessment of negative symptoms in schizophrenia. *Eur. Psychiatry* **2021**, *64*, 1–91. [CrossRef]

15. Kirkpatrick, B.; Fenton, W.S.; Carpenter, W.T.; Marder, S.R. The NIMH-MATRICS Consensus Statement on Negative Symptoms. *Schizophr. Bull.* **2006**, *32*, 214–219. [CrossRef]
16. Marder, S.R.; Galderisi, S. The current conceptualization of negative symptoms in schizophrenia. *World Psychiatry* **2017**, *16*, 14–24. [CrossRef]
17. Reed, G.M.; First, M.B.; Kogan, C.S.; Hyman, S.E.; Gureje, O.; Gaebel, W.; Maj, M.; Stein, D.; Maercker, A.; Tyrer, P.; et al. Innovations and changes in the ICD-11 classification of mental, behavioural and neurodevelopmental disorders. *World Psychiatry* **2019**, *18*, 3–19. [CrossRef] [PubMed]
18. Gaebel, W.; Falkai, P.; Hasan, A. The revised German evidence- and consensus-based schizophrenia guideline. *World Psychiatry* **2020**, *19*, 117–119. [CrossRef]
19. Giordano, G.M.; Koenig, T.; Mucci, A.; Vignapiano, A.; Amodio, A.; di Lorenzo, G.; Siracusano, A.; Bellomo, A.; Altamura, M.; Monteleone, P.; et al. Neurophysiological correlates of Avolition-apathy in schizophrenia: A resting-EEG microstates study. *NeuroImage Clin.* **2018**, *20*, 627–636. [CrossRef] [PubMed]
20. Giordano, G.M.; Brando, F.; Perrottelli, A.; Di Lorenzo, G.; Siracusano, A.; Giuliani, L.; Pezzella, P.; Altamura, M.; Bellomo, A.; Cascino, G.; et al. Tracing links between early auditory information processing and negative symptoms in schizophrenia: An ERP study. *Front. Psychiatry*, 2021; *in press*.
21. Galderisi, S.; Maj, M.; Mucci, A.; Cassano, G.B.; Invernizzi, G.; Rossi, A.; Vita, A.; Dell'Osso, L.; Daneluzzo, E.; Pini, S. Historical, Psychopathological, Neurological, and Neuropsychological Aspects of Deficit Schizophrenia: A Multicenter Study. *Am. J. Psychiatry* **2002**, *159*, 983–990. [CrossRef]
22. Buchanan, R.W. Persistent Negative Symptoms in Schizophrenia: An Overview. *Schizophr. Bull.* **2007**, *33*, 1013–1022. [CrossRef]
23. Kirkpatrick, B.; Galderisi, S. Deficit schizophrenia: An update. *World Psychiatry* **2008**, *7*, 143–147. [CrossRef]
24. Galderisi, S.; Maj, M. Deficit schizophrenia: An overview of clinical, biological and treatment aspects. *Eur. Psychiatry* **2009**, *24*, 493–500. [CrossRef]
25. Kirkpatrick, B. Progress in the Study of Negative Symptoms. *Schizophr. Bull.* **2014**, *40*, S101–S106. [CrossRef] [PubMed]
26. Kirkpatrick, B. Recognizing Primary vs. Secondary Negative Symptoms and Apathy vs. Expression Domains. *J. Clin. Psychiatry* **2014**, *75*, e09. [CrossRef]
27. Galderisi, S.; Merlotti, E.; Mucci, A. Neurobiological background of negative symptoms. *Eur. Arch. Psychiatry Clin. Neurosci.* **2015**, *265*, 543–558. [CrossRef] [PubMed]
28. Mucci, A.; Merlotti, E.; Üçok, A.; Aleman, A.; Galderisi, S. Primary and persistent negative symptoms: Concepts, assessments and neurobiological bases. *Schizophr. Res.* **2016**, *186*, 19–28. [CrossRef] [PubMed]
29. Bucci, P.; Galderisi, S. Categorizing and assessing negative symptoms. *Curr. Opin. Psychiatry* **2017**, *30*, 201–208. [CrossRef]
30. Kirkpatrick, B.; Mucci, A.; Galderisi, S. Primary, Enduring Negative Symptoms: An Update on Research. *Schizophr. Bull.* **2017**, *43*, 730–736. [CrossRef]
31. Barch, D.M.; Dowd, E.C. Goal Representations and Motivational Drive in Schizophrenia: The Role of Prefrontal-Striatal Interactions. *Schizophr. Bull.* **2010**, *36*, 919–934. [CrossRef]
32. Foussias, G.; Remington, G. Negative Symptoms in Schizophrenia: Avolition and Occam's Razor. *Schizophr. Bull.* **2008**, *36*, 359–369. [CrossRef]
33. Bromberg-Martin, E.S.; Matsumoto, M.; Hikosaka, O. Dopamine in Motivational Control: Rewarding, Aversive, and Alerting. *Neuron* **2010**, *68*, 815–834. [CrossRef]
34. Simpson, E.H.; Waltz, J.A.; Kellendonk, C.; Balsam, P.D. Schizophrenia in Translation: Dissecting Motivation in Schizophrenia and Rodents. *Schizophr. Bull.* **2012**, *38*, 1111–1117. [CrossRef] [PubMed]
35. Strauss, G.P.; Horan, W.P.; Kirkpatrick, B.; Fischer, B.A.; Keller, W.R.; Miski, P.; Buchanan, R.W.; Green, M.F.; Carpenter, W.T. Deconstructing negative symptoms of schizophrenia: Avolition–apathy and diminished expression clusters predict clinical presentation and functional outcome. *J. Psychiatr. Res.* **2013**, *47*, 783–790. [CrossRef] [PubMed]
36. Morris, R.; Quail, S.; Griffiths, K.R.; Green, M.; Balleine, B.W. Corticostriatal Control of Goal-Directed Action Is Impaired in Schizophrenia. *Biol. Psychiatry* **2015**, *77*, 187–195. [CrossRef] [PubMed]
37. Mucci, A.; Dima, D.; Soricelli, A.; Volpe, U.; Bucci, P.; Frangou, S.; Prinster, A.; Salvatore, M.; Galderisi, S.; Maj, M. Is avolition in schizophrenia associated with a deficit of dorsal caudate activity? A functional magnetic resonance imaging study during reward anticipation and feedback. *Psychol. Med.* **2015**, *45*, 1765–1778. [CrossRef] [PubMed]
38. Salamone, J.D.; Yohn, S.E.; Lopez-Cruz, L.; Miguel, N.S.; Correa, M. Activational and effort-related aspects of motivation: Neural mechanisms and implications for psychopathology. *Brain* **2016**, *139*, 1325–1347. [CrossRef]
39. Giordano, G.M.; Stanziano, M.; Papa, M.; Mucci, A.; Prinster, A.; Soricelli, A.; Galderisi, S. Functional connectivity of the ventral tegmental area and avolition in subjects with schizophrenia: A resting state functional MRI study. *Eur. Neuropsychopharmacol.* **2018**, *28*, 589–602. [CrossRef]
40. Amodio, A.; Quarantelli, M.; Mucci, A.; Prinster, A.; Soricelli, A.; Vignapiano, A.; Giordano, G.M.; Merlotti, E.; Nicita, A.; Galderisi, S. Avolition-Apathy and White Matter Connectivity in Schizophrenia: Reduced Fractional Anisotropy between Amygdala and Insular Cortex. *Clin. EEG Neurosci.* **2017**, *49*, 55–65. [CrossRef]
41. Sanislow, C.A. RDoC at 10: Changing the discourse for psychopathology. *World Psychiatry* **2020**, *19*, 311–312. [CrossRef]
42. Menon, V. Brain networks and cognitive impairment in psychiatric disorders. *World Psychiatry* **2020**, *19*, 309–310. [CrossRef]

43. Barch, D.M.; Pagliaccio, D.; Luking, K. Mechanisms Underlying Motivational Deficits in Psychopathology: Similarities and Differences in Depression and Schizophrenia. *Curr Top. Behav. Neurosci.* **2016**, *27*, 411–449. [CrossRef]
44. Striatal dopamine, reward, and decision making in schizophrenia. *Dialog. Clin. Neurosci.* **2016**, *18*, 77–89. [CrossRef]
45. Green, M.F.; Horan, W.P.; Barch, D.M.; Gold, J.M. Effort-Based Decision Making: A Novel Approach for Assessing Motivation in Schizophrenia. *Schizophr. Bull.* **2015**, *41*, 1035–1044. [CrossRef]
46. Mucci, A.; Galderisi, S.; Green, M.F.; Nuechterlein, K.; Rucci, P.; Gibertoni, D.; Rossi, A.; Rocca, P.; Bertolino, A.; Bucci, P.; et al. Familial aggregation of MATRICS Consensus Cognitive Battery scores in a large sample of outpatients with schizophrenia and their unaffected relatives. *Psychol. Med.* **2017**, *48*, 1359–1366. [CrossRef] [PubMed]
47. Davidson, M. Cognitive impairment as a diagnostic criterion and treatment target in schizophrenia. *World Psychiatry* **2019**, *18*, 171–172. [CrossRef] [PubMed]
48. Grant, P.M.; Best, M.W.; Beck, A.T. The meaning of group differences in cognitive test performance. *World Psychiatry* **2019**, *18*, 163–164. [CrossRef]
49. Green, M.F.; Horan, W.P.; Lee, J. Nonsocial and social cognition in schizophrenia: Current evidence and future directions. *World Psychiatry* **2019**, *18*, 146–161. [CrossRef]
50. Besteher, B.; Brambilla, P.; Nenadić, I. Twin studies of brain structure and cognition in schizophrenia. *Neurosci. Biobehav. Rev.* **2019**, *109*, 103–113. [CrossRef]
51. Moritz, S.; Silverstein, S.M.; Dietrichkeit, M.; Gallinat, J. Neurocognitive deficits in schizophrenia are likely to be less severe and less related to the disorder than previously thought. *World Psychiatry* **2020**, *19*, 254–255. [CrossRef]
52. Caputo, F.; Giordano, G.M.; Mucci, A.; Galderisi, S. Aetiopathological mechanisms of negative symptoms in schizophrenia. *Die Psychiatr.* **2016**, *13*, 121–129. [CrossRef]
53. Melle, I. Cognition in schizophrenia: A marker of underlying neurodevelopmental problems? *World Psychiatry* **2019**, *18*, 164–165. [CrossRef] [PubMed]
54. Miller, E.M.; Shankar, M.U.; Knutson, B.; McClure, S.M. Dissociating Motivation from Reward in Human Striatal Activity. *J. Cogn. Neurosci.* **2014**, *26*, 1075–1084. [CrossRef] [PubMed]
55. Bissonette, G.B.; Roesch, M.R. Development and function of the midbrain dopamine system: What we know and what we need to. *Genes Brain Behav.* **2015**, *15*, 62–73. [CrossRef]
56. Bissonette, G.B.; Roesch, M.R. Neurophysiology of Reward-Guided Behavior: Correlates Related to Predictions, Value, Motivation, Errors, Attention, and Action. *Curr. Top. Behav. Neurosci.* **2016**, *27*, 199–230. [CrossRef]
57. O'Doherty, J.P. Multiple Systems for the Motivational Control of Behavior and Associated Neural Substrates in Humans. *Curr. Top. Behav. Neurosci.* **2016**, *27*, 291–312. [CrossRef] [PubMed]
58. Cohen, A.; Schwartz, E.; Le, T.P.; Fedechko, T.; Kirkpatrick, B.; Strauss, G.P. Using biobehavioral technologies to effectively advance research on negative symptoms. *World Psychiatry* **2019**, *18*, 103–104. [CrossRef] [PubMed]
59. Bowie, C.R. Cognitive remediation for severe mental illness: State of the field and future directions. *World Psychiatry* **2019**, *18*, 274–275. [CrossRef]
60. Stefani, M.R. Rule Learning and Reward Contingency Are Associated with Dissociable Patterns of Dopamine Activation in the Rat Prefrontal Cortex, Nucleus Accumbens, and Dorsal Striatum. *J. Neurosci.* **2006**, *26*, 8810–8818. [CrossRef] [PubMed]
61. Hikosaka, O.; Bromberg-Martin, E.; Hong, S.; Matsumoto, M. New insights on the subcortical representation of reward. *Curr. Opin. Neurobiol.* **2008**, *18*, 203–208. [CrossRef] [PubMed]
62. Haber, S.N.; Knutson, B. The Reward Circuit: Linking Primate Anatomy and Human Imaging. *Neuropsychopharmacology* **2009**, *35*, 4–26. [CrossRef] [PubMed]
63. Sesack, S.R.; Grace, A.A. Cortico-Basal Ganglia Reward Network: Microcircuitry. *Neuropsychopharmacology* **2010**, *35*, 27–47. [CrossRef] [PubMed]
64. Cascella, N.G.; Fieldstone, S.C.; Rao, V.A.; Pearlson, G.D.; Sawa, A.; Schretlen, D.J. Gray-matter abnormalities in deficit schizophrenia. *Schizophr. Res.* **2010**, *120*, 63–70. [CrossRef]
65. Friston, K.J.; Frith, C.D. Schizophrenia: A disconnection syndrome? *Clin. Neurosci.* **1995**, *3*, 89–97. [PubMed]
66. Buchsbaum, M.S.; Tang, C.Y.; Peled, S.; Gudbjartsson, H.; Lu, D.; Hazlett, E.A.; Downhill, J.; Haznedar, M.; Fallon, J.H.; Atlas, S.W. MRI white matter diffusion anisotropy and PET metabolic rate in schizophrenia. *NeuroReport* **1998**, *9*, 425–430. [CrossRef]
67. Lim, K.O.; Hedehus, M.; Moseley, M.; de Crespigny, A.; Sullivan, E.V.; Pfefferbaum, A. Compromised White Matter Tract Integrity in Schizophrenia Inferred from Diffusion Tensor Imaging. *Arch. Gen. Psychiatry* **1999**, *56*, 367–374. [CrossRef] [PubMed]
68. Ardekani, B.A.; Nierenberg, J.; Hoptman, M.J.; Javitt, D.C.; Lim, K.O. MRI study of white matter diffusion anisotropy in schizophrenia. *NeuroReport* **2003**, *14*, 2025–2029. [CrossRef]
69. Hoptman, M.J.; D'Angelo, D.; Catalano, D.; Mauro, C.J.; Shehzad, Z.E.; Kelly, A.M.C.; Castellanos, F.X.; Javitt, D.C.; Milham, M.P. Amygdalofrontal Functional Disconnectivity and Aggression in Schizophrenia. *Schizophr. Bull.* **2009**, *36*, 1020–1028. [CrossRef]
70. Pettersson-Yeo, W.; Allen, P.; Benetti, S.; McGuire, P.; Mechelli, A. Dysconnectivity in schizophrenia: Where are we now? *Neurosci. Biobehav. Rev.* **2011**, *35*, 1110–1124. [CrossRef]
71. Kelly, S.; Jahanshad, N.; Zalesky, A.; Kochunov, P.; Agartz, I.; Alloza, C.; Andreassen, O.A.; Arango, C.; Banaj, N.; Bouix, S.; et al. Widespread white matter microstructural differences in schizophrenia across 4322 individuals: Results from the ENIGMA Schizophrenia DTI Working Group. *Mol. Psychiatry* **2017**, *23*, 1261–1269. [CrossRef]

72. Reininghaus, U.; Böhnke, J.R.; Chavez-Baldini, U.; Gibbons, R.; Ivleva, E.; Clementz, B.A.; Pearlson, G.D.; Keshavan, M.S.; Sweeney, J.A.; Tamminga, C.A. Transdiagnostic dimensions of psychosis in the Bipolar-Schizophrenia Network on Intermediate Phenotypes (B-SNIP). *World Psychiatry* **2019**, *18*, 67–76. [CrossRef] [PubMed]
73. Nath, M.; Wong, T.P.; Srivastava, L.K. Neurodevelopmental insights into circuit dysconnectivity in schizophrenia. *Prog. Neuro-Psychopharmacol. Biol. Psychiatry* **2020**, *104*, 110047. [CrossRef]
74. Bullmore, E.; Frangou, S.; Murray, R. The dysplastic net hypothesis: An integration of developmental and dysconnectivity theories of schizophrenia. *Schizophr. Res.* **1997**, *28*, 143–156. [CrossRef]
75. Rowland, L.M.; Spieker, E.A.; Francis, A.; Barker, P.B.; Carpenter, W.T.; Buchanan, R.W. White Matter Alterations in Deficit Schizophrenia. *Neuropsychopharmacology* **2008**, *34*, 1514–1522. [CrossRef] [PubMed]
76. Kitis, O.; Ozalay, O.; Zengin, E.B.; Haznedaroglu, D.; Eker, M.C.; Yalvac, D.; Oguz, K.; Coburn, K.; Gonul, A.S. Reduced left uncinate fasciculus fractional anisotropy in deficit schizophrenia but not in non-deficit schizophrenia. *Psychiatry Clin. Neurosci.* **2012**, *66*, 34–43. [CrossRef] [PubMed]
77. Voineskos, A.N.; Foussias, G.; Lerch, J.; Felsky, D.; Remington, G.; Rajji, T.K.; Lobaugh, N.; Pollock, B.G.; Mulsant, B.H. Neuroimaging Evidence for the Deficit Subtype of Schizophrenia. *JAMA Psychiatry* **2013**, *70*, 472–480. [CrossRef] [PubMed]
78. Spalletta, G.; de Rossi, P.; Piras, F.; Iorio, M.; Dacquino, C.; Scanu, F.; Girardi, P.; Caltagirone, C.; Kirkpatrick, B.; Chiapponi, C. Brain white matter microstructure in deficit and non-deficit subtypes of schizophrenia. *Psychiatry Res. Neuroimaging* **2015**, *231*, 252–261. [CrossRef]
79. Tan, A.S.; Chew, Q.H.; Sim, K. Cerebral white matter changes in deficit and non-deficit subtypes of schizophrenia. *J. Neural Transm.* **2020**, *127*, 1073–1079. [CrossRef]
80. Podwalski, P.; Tyburski, E.; Szczygieł, K.; Waszczuk, K.; Rek-Owodziń, K.; Mak, M.; Plichta, P.; Bielecki, M.; Rudkowski, K.; Kucharska-Mazur, J.; et al. White Matter Integrity of the Corpus Callosum and Psychopathological Dimensions in Deficit and Non-Deficit Schizophrenia Patients. *J. Clin. Med.* **2021**, *10*, 2225. [CrossRef]
81. Kay, S.R.; Fiszbein, A.; Opler, L.A. The Positive and Negative Syndrome Scale (PANSS) for Schizophrenia. *Schizophr. Bull.* **1987**, *13*, 261–276. [CrossRef]
82. Fabrazzo, M.; Prisco, V.; Sampogna, G.; Perris, F.; Catapano, F.; Monteleone, A.M.; Maj, M. Clozapine versus other antipsychotics during the first 18 weeks of treatment: A retrospective study on risk factor increase of blood dyscrasias. *Psychiatry Res.* **2017**, *256*, 275–282. [CrossRef]
83. Kirkpatrick, B.; Buchanan, R.W.; McKenny, P.D.; Alphs, L.D.; Carpenter, W.T. The schedule for the deficit syndrome: An instrument for research in schizophrenia. *Psychiatry Res.* **1989**, *30*, 119–123. [CrossRef]
84. Gardner, D.M.; Murphy, A.L.; O'Donnell, H.; Centorrino, F.; Baldessarini, R.J. International Consensus Study of Antipsychotic Dosing. *Am. J. Psychiatry* **2010**, *167*, 686–693. [CrossRef] [PubMed]
85. Bracht, T.; Horn, H.; Strik, W.; Federspiel, A.; Razavi, N.; Stegmayer, K.; Wiest, R.; Dierks, T.; Müller, T.J.; Walther, S. White matter pathway organization of the reward system is related to positive and negative symptoms in schizophrenia. *Schizophr. Res.* **2014**, *153*, 136–142. [CrossRef] [PubMed]
86. Pizzagalli, D.A.; Holmes, A.; Dillon, D.G.; Goetz, E.L.; Birk, J.; Bogdan, R.; Dougherty, D.D.; Iosifescu, D.V.; Rauch, S.L.; Fava, M. Reduced Caudate and Nucleus Accumbens Response to Rewards in Unmedicated Individuals with Major Depressive Disorder. *Am. J. Psychiatry* **2009**, *166*, 702–710. [CrossRef] [PubMed]
87. Maldjian, J.A.; Laurienti, P.J.; Kraft, R.A.; Burdette, J.H. An automated method for neuroanatomic and cytoarchitectonic atlas-based interrogation of fMRI data sets. *NeuroImage* **2003**, *19*, 1233–1239. [CrossRef]
88. Blood, A.J.; Iosifescu, D.V.; Makris, N.; Perlis, R.H.; Kennedy, D.N.; Dougherty, D.D.; Kim, B.W.; Lee, M.J.; Wu, S.; Lee, S.H.; et al. Microstructural Abnormalities in Subcortical Reward Circuitry of Subjects with Major Depressive Disorder. *PLoS ONE* **2010**, *5*, e13945. [CrossRef]
89. Nieuwenhuys, R.; Voogd, J.; van Huizen, C. *The Human Central Nervous System*, 4th ed.; Springer: Berlin, Germany, 2008.
90. Kringelbach, M.L. The human orbitofrontal cortex: Linking reward to hedonic experience. *Nat. Rev. Neurosci.* **2005**, *6*, 691–702. [CrossRef]
91. Makris, N.; Goldstein, J.M.; Kennedy, D.; Hodge, S.M.; Caviness, V.S.; Faraone, S.; Tsuang, M.T.; Seidman, L.J. Decreased volume of left and total anterior insular lobule in schizophrenia. *Schizophr. Res.* **2006**, *83*, 155–171. [CrossRef]
92. Deen, B.; Pitskel, N.B.; Pelphrey, K.A. Three Systems of Insular Functional Connectivity Identified with Cluster Analysis. *Cereb. Cortex* **2010**, *21*, 1498–1506. [CrossRef]
93. Smith, S.M.; Jenkinson, M.; Woolrich, M.W.; Beckmann, C.F.; Behrens, T.E.; Johansen-Berg, H.; Bannister, P.R.; de Luca, M.; Drobnjak, I.; Flitney, D.E.; et al. Advances in functional and structural MR image analysis and implementation as FSL. *NeuroImage* **2004**, *23*, S208–S219. [CrossRef]
94. Leemans, A.; Jones, D.K. TheB-matrix must be rotated when correcting for subject motion in DTI data. *Magn. Reson. Med.* **2009**, *61*, 1336–1349. [CrossRef]
95. Smith, S.M. Fast robust automated brain extraction. *Hum. Brain Mapp.* **2002**, *17*, 143–155. [CrossRef] [PubMed]
96. Smith, S.; Zhanga, Y.; Jenkinson, M.; Chenab, J.; Matthews, P.M.; Federico, A.; de Stefano, N. Accurate, Robust, and Automated Longitudinal and Cross-Sectional Brain Change Analysis. *NeuroImage* **2002**, *17*, 479–489. [CrossRef]
97. Behrens, T.; Johansen-Berg, H.; Jbabdi, S.; Rushworth, M.; Woolrich, M. Probabilistic diffusion tractography with multiple fibre orientations: What can we gain? *NeuroImage* **2007**, *34*, 144–155. [CrossRef] [PubMed]

98. Morris, D.M.; Embleton, K.V.; Parker, G.J. Probabilistic fibre tracking: Differentiation of connections from chance events. *NeuroImage* **2008**, *42*, 1329–1339. [CrossRef] [PubMed]
99. Keshavan, M.; Lizano, P.; Prasad, K. The synaptic pruning hypothesis of schizophrenia: Promises and challenges. *World Psychiatry* **2020**, *19*, 110–111. [CrossRef]
100. Parkes, S.; Balleine, B.W. Incentive Memory: Evidence the Basolateral Amygdala Encodes and the Insular Cortex Retrieves Outcome Values to Guide Choice between Goal-Directed Actions. *J. Neurosci.* **2013**, *33*, 8753–8763. [CrossRef]
101. Parkes, S.; Bradfield, L.; Balleine, B.W. Interaction of Insular Cortex and Ventral Striatum Mediates the Effect of Incentive Memory on Choice between Goal-Directed Actions. *J. Neurosci.* **2015**, *35*, 6464–6471. [CrossRef] [PubMed]
102. Pickens, C.; Saddoris, M.P.; Setlow, B.; Gallagher, M.; Holland, P.C.; Schoenbaum, G. Different Roles for Orbitofrontal Cortex and Basolateral Amygdala in a Reinforcer Devaluation Task. *J. Neurosci.* **2003**, *23*, 11078–11084. [CrossRef]
103. Izquierdo, A.; Suda, R.K.; Murray, E. Bilateral Orbital Prefrontal Cortex Lesions in Rhesus Monkeys Disrupt Choices Guided by Both Reward Value and Reward Contingency. *J. Neurosci.* **2004**, *24*, 7540–7548. [CrossRef]
104. Ostlund, S.B.; Balleine, B. Orbitofrontal Cortex Mediates Outcome Encoding in Pavlovian but Not Instrumental Conditioning. *J. Neurosci.* **2007**, *27*, 4819–4825. [CrossRef] [PubMed]
105. Burke, K.A.; Franz, T.M.; Miller, D.N.; Schoenbaum, G. The role of the orbitofrontal cortex in the pursuit of happiness and more specific rewards. *Nature* **2008**, *454*, 340–344. [CrossRef] [PubMed]
106. Takahashi, Y.K.; Roesch, M.R.; Stalnaker, T.A.; Haney, R.Z.; Calu, D.; Taylor, A.R.; Burke, K.A.; Schoenbaum, G. The Orbitofrontal Cortex and Ventral Tegmental Area Are Necessary for Learning from Unexpected Outcomes. *Neuron* **2009**, *62*, 269–280. [CrossRef] [PubMed]
107. Kahnt, T.; Heinzle, J.; Park, S.; Haynes, J.-D. The neural code of reward anticipation in human orbitofrontal cortex. *Proc. Natl. Acad. Sci. USA* **2010**, *107*, 6010–6015. [CrossRef]
108. Everitt, B.; Cador, M.; Robbins, T. Interactions between the amygdala and ventral striatum in stimulus-reward associations: Studies using a second-order schedule of sexual reinforcement. *Neuroscience* **1989**, *30*, 63–75. [CrossRef]
109. Everitt, B.J.; Parkinson, J.A.; Olmstead, M.C.; Arroyo, M.; Robledo, P.; Robbins, T. Associative Processes in Addiction and Reward the Role of Amygdala-Ventral Striatal Subsystems. *Ann. N. Y. Acad. Sci.* **1999**, *877*, 412–438. [CrossRef]
110. Baxter, M.G.; Murray, E. The amygdala and reward. *Nat. Rev. Neurosci.* **2002**, *3*, 563–573. [CrossRef]
111. Murray, E.A. The amygdala, reward and emotion. *Trends Cogn. Sci.* **2007**, *11*, 489–497. [CrossRef]
112. Ramirez, D.R.; Savage, L.M. Differential involvement of the basolateral amygdala, orbitofrontal cortex, and nucleus accumbens core in the acquisition and use of reward expectancies. *Behav. Neurosci.* **2007**, *121*, 896–906. [CrossRef]
113. Harsay, H.A.; Spaan, M.; Wijnen, J.G.; Ridderinkhof, K.R. Error Awareness and Salience Processing in the Oddball Task: Shared Neural Mechanisms. *Front. Hum. Neurosci.* **2012**, *6*, 246. [CrossRef]
114. Liang, X.; He, Y.; Salmeron, B.J.; Gu, H.; Stein, E.A.; Yang, Y. Interactions between the Salience and Default-Mode Networks Are Disrupted in Cocaine Addiction. *J. Neurosci.* **2015**, *35*, 8081–8090. [CrossRef] [PubMed]
115. Rogers-Carter, M.; Christianson, J.P. An insular view of the social decision-making network. *Neurosci. Biobehav. Rev.* **2019**, *103*, 119–132. [CrossRef] [PubMed]
116. Rogers-Carter, M.M.; Djerdjaj, A.; Gribbons, K.B.; Varela, J.A.; Christianson, J.P. Insular Cortex Projections to Nucleus Accumbens Core Mediate Social Approach to Stressed Juvenile Rats. *J. Neurosci.* **2019**, *39*, 8717–8729. [CrossRef] [PubMed]
117. Barch, D.M. Nonsocial and social cognitive function in psychosis: Interrelationships, specificity and innovative approaches. *World Psychiatry* **2019**, *18*, 117–118. [CrossRef]
118. Kotov, R.; Jonas, K.G.; Carpenter, W.T.; Dretsch, M.N.; Eaton, N.R.; Forbes, M.K.; Forbush, K.T.; Hobbs, K.; Reininghaus, U.; Slade, T.; et al. Validity and utility of Hierarchical Taxonomy of Psychopathology (HiTOP): I. Psychosis superspectrum. *World Psychiatry* **2020**, *19*, 151–172. [CrossRef]
119. Rodgers, K.M.; Benison, A.M.; Klein, A.; Barth, D.S. Auditory, Somatosensory, and Multisensory Insular Cortex in the Rat. *Cereb. Cortex* **2008**, *18*, 2941–2951. [CrossRef]
120. Gogolla, N.; Takesian, A.E.; Feng, G.; Fagiolini, M.; Hensch, T.K. Sensory Integration in Mouse Insular Cortex Reflects GABA Circuit Maturation. *Neuron* **2014**, *83*, 894–905. [CrossRef]
121. Gogolla, N. The insular cortex. *Curr. Biol.* **2017**, *27*, R580–R586. [CrossRef]
122. Wright, C.; Groenewegen, H. Patterns of overlap and segregation between insular cortical, intermediodorsal thalamic and basal amygdaloid afferents in the nucleus accumbens of the rat. *Neuroscience* **1996**, *73*, 359–373. [CrossRef]
123. Wise, R.A. Brain Reward Circuitry: Insights from Unsensed Incentives. *Neuron* **2002**, *36*, 229–240. [CrossRef]

Journal of
Clinical Medicine

MDPI

Article

Effect of Antipsychotic Treatment on Neutrophil-to-Lymphocyte Ratio during Hospitalization for Acute Psychosis in the Course of Schizophrenia—A Cross-Sectional Retrospective Study

Bartosz Dawidowski [1], Grzegorz Grelecki [1], Adam Biłgorajski [1], Piotr Podwalski [1,*], Błażej Misiak [2] and Jerzy Samochowiec [1]

1 Department of Psychiatry, Pomeranian Medical University, 71-460 Szczecin, Poland; aravial.mg@gmail.com (B.D.); grzegorz271195@wp.pl (G.G.); bilgorajski@gmail.com (A.B.); samoj@pum.edu.pl (J.S.)
2 Department of Psychiatry, Division of Consultation Psychiatry and Neuroscience, Wroclaw Medical University, 50-367 Wroclaw, Poland; blazej.misiak@umed.wroc.pl
* Correspondence: piotr.podwalski@pum.edu.pl; Tel.: +48-91-3511307

Abstract: Background: Studies have shown that there are deviations in the results of peripheral blood counts, which lead to increased values of the neutrophils-to-lymphocytes ratio (NLR) in schizophrenia. Antipsychotic drugs have proven to lower the levels of pro-inflammatory cytokines and a growing number of studies indicate a similar effect on NLR values. Methods: We identified inpatients with schizophrenia and collected data of NLR at the beginning (NLR_1) and end (NLR_2) of hospitalization, the status of antipsychotic medication on admission and potential confounding factors. In the statistical analysis, we applied a linear mixed model. Results: After the inclusion and exclusion process the records of 40 patients (n_p = 40) and 71 hospitalizations (n_h = 71) were analyzed. We found that in the group of antipsychotics-naive patients, the NLR_1 were significantly higher than the NLR_2 values. Such a difference did not occur in the case of non-antipsychotics-naïve patients. Age and the diagnosis of hypothyroidism influenced the value of change in NLR from the beginning to the end of hospitalization in a given patient (ΔNLR). Conclusions: The study confirmed the lowering effect of antipsychotics on NLR values in psychosis. The NLR may potentially be a tool for assessing response to treatment with antipsychotics.

Keywords: neutrophil-to-lymphocyte ratio; antipsychotics; schizophrenia; hypothyroidism; inflammatory markers

Citation: Dawidowski, B.; Grelecki, G.; Biłgorajski, A.; Podwalski, P.; Misiak, B.; Samochowiec, J. Effect of Antipsychotic Treatment on Neutrophil-to-Lymphocyte Ratio during Hospitalization for Acute Psychosis in the Course of Schizophrenia—A Cross-Sectional Retrospective Study. *J. Clin. Med.* **2022**, *11*, 232. https://doi.org/10.3390/jcm11010232

Academic Editors: Armida Mucci and Nuri B. Farber

Received: 22 November 2021
Accepted: 30 December 2021
Published: 31 December 2021

1. Introduction

Schizophrenia is a chronic mental illness characterized by positive symptoms (e.g., delusions, hallucinations), negative symptoms (e.g., anhedonia, avolition), and cognitive impairment (e.g., impairment of abstract thinking or executive functions) accompanied by degenerative changes in the nervous tissue of the central nervous system (CNS) [1]. Disturbances in neurotransmission (e.g., dopaminergic or glutamatergic pathways) and nervous tissue metabolism (e.g., in the kynurenine pathway, glucose metabolism, antioxidants metabolism) are also important for the symptomatology of schizophrenia and its etiopathogenesis [2–5]. Several different hypotheses have been proposed to explain the causes of these disorders, however, growing evidence suggests that immune dysfunction, neuroinflammation, and the associated oxidative stress, additionally modulated by dysregulation of the hypothalamic-pituitary-adrenal axis (HPA axis), may play a key role in the etiopathogenesis of schizophrenia [6,7].

Cytokines are immune system signaling proteins produced by a wide variety of cells, including lymphocytes, macrophages, and granulocytes, which are growth and proliferation factors for various leukocyte fractions [8]. Disturbances in the cytokine network in schizophrenia, both in the blood and in the cerebrospinal fluid, with a distinct imbalance between pro-inflammatory and anti-inflammatory cytokines, are well documented [9–11]. They are mainly expressed in elevated peripheral levels of pro-inflammatory cytokines, such as interleukin-1β (IL-1β), interleukin-6 (IL-6), or tumor necrosis factor (TNF-α) [9,11]. These cytokines, apart from causing excessive activation of astrocytes and microglia, probably also influence hematopoiesis and differentiation of cells of the immune system, not directly related to the pathophysiology of schizophrenia. [7,12,13]. Moreover, after treatment of acute psychosis with antipsychotics, the peripheral levels of pro-inflammatory cytokines decrease, suggesting that these drugs may reduce the severity of inflammation and potentially also affect hematopoiesis and mobilization of immune system cells into the blood [14].

The neutrophils to lymphocytes ratio (NLR) is a simple and easily accessible marker of systemic inflammation obtained by blood count of peripheral blood, whose normal values for healthy people are estimated to be 0.78–3.53, or 0.88–4.0, depending on the population studied [15,16]. NLR is largely independent of age and gender in the healthy adult population, which is a significant advantage over other similar indicators such as monocyte to lymphocyte ratio (MLR) or platelet to lymphocyte ratio (PLR) [17]. However, its values may be elevated, among others, in the metabolic syndrome [18], as a result of smoking [19], in arterial hypertension [20], or hypothyroidism [21], which occur more often in patients with schizophrenia than in the general population [22–24].

The meta-analysis by Mazza et al. showed that patients in the state of non-affective psychosis had significantly higher NLR values compared to the healthy controls [25]. In turn, the meta-analysis by Karageorgiou et al. showed that the NLR value in patients with schizophrenia was increased both in the first episode of psychosis and in later episodes [13]. In the same meta-analysis, the value of NLR was positively correlated with the intensity of psychotic symptoms [13], as indicated also by the recent study by Zhou et al. [26,27]. Moreover, the study by Özdin et al. demonstrates that also in the state of remission in schizophrenia, the NLR values are higher than in the control group but lower than during relapse [28]. Furthermore, NLR appears to be elevated in patients with schizophrenia regardless of the presence of metabolic syndrome, laboratory markers such as glycemia, triglyceridemia, or cholesterolemia, and smoking status [17,28]. Additionally, patients medicated with antipsychotics have lower NLR values than drug-naïve patients [26,28].

In this study, we hypothesized that the effect of antipsychotic medication is revealed not only by decreased NLR values in patients who received said treatment before admission but also by decreased NLR values at the end of hospitalization compared to the beginning of hospitalization. In addition, we also proposed that it could be possible to predict the NLR value at the end of hospitalization, when the patient is in complete or partial remission, based on the NLR value on admission. To confirm these hypotheses, we adopted the following aims of the study: (1) determining whether a difference between the NLR values at the beginning and the end of hospitalization due to the psychotic episode existed and whether the status of antipsychotic medication during the month before hospitalization, determined based on the patient's declaration on admission included in the medical records, influenced said difference; (2) determining the influence of other potential cofounding factors on such difference; (3) determining whether the NLR value at the beginning of hospitalization may be used to predict an NLR change to its end, which could contribute to the future use of the indicator as a marker of remission or response to treatment in schizophrenia, and (4) how likely, cofounding factors frequently present in the population of schizophrenia patients may affect the NLR's change during hospitalization.

2. Materials and Methods

2.1. Patients and Study Design

Our study was retrospective. We obtained the data from the archives of the medical records of the Department of Psychiatry of the Pomeranian Medical University in Szczecin. The inclusion criteria for patients were as follows: (1) diagnosed with schizophrenia according to the International Classification of Diseases (ICD-10); (2) physical and psychiatric examination performed by an experienced psychiatrist; (3) hospitalization from 1 January 2015 until 31 July 2020.

Selection bias, which can be defined as systematic differences between baseline characteristics of the groups that are compared, is one of the main weaknesses of observational and retrospective studies, in which the selection of a research sample significantly different from the general population may affect the results obtained [29]. One method of reducing the risk of selection bias is to use randomization [30]. For this reason, in our study, we included only a part of randomly chosen that met the inclusion criteria in the study sample patients (300 files, approximately 50% of all files), and then we excluded hospitalizations from this sample based on the exclusion criteria.

The following exclusion criteria were applied to individual hospitalizations of patients in this group, which were as follows: (1) age < 18 and >65 years; (2) use of psychoactive substances other than alcohol within 1 month prior to admission; (3) present on admission or diagnosed during hospitalization: infectious diseases, autoimmune diseases (other than Hashimoto's thyroiditis), cardiovascular diseases (other than hypertension), cancer, parasitic diseases, gastrological diseases, diabetes, history of major surgery or head injuries; (4) medication with glucocorticosteroids, their analogs, antibiotics, or cytostatics; (5) BMI > 30; (6) termination of hospitalization by discharge on-demand or discharge without partial or complete remission of symptoms; (7) no peripheral blood counts available at the beginning or end of hospitalization; (8) first blood count performed >5 days after admission, and (9) no data on the variables included in the statistical analysis.

Based on routinely collected medical records, we were not able to explicitly exclude patients who met the criteria of the metabolic syndrome due to the lack of triglyceride and high-density lipoprotein (HDL) concentration tests performed in all patients, as well as the lack of waist circumference measurements. Nevertheless, the exclusion of patients with a BMI > 30 and patients diagnosed with diabetes at least partially reduced the risk of including patients meeting the criteria of the metabolic syndrome in the research sample.

In the case of most patients, we were also unable to determine how many of them were in the first psychotic episode (FEP), therefore we could not stratify the research sample into FEP and chronic patients.

Due to the fact that we did not collect data on earlier hospitalizations (before 1 January 2015) of patients included in the research sample, we did not make comparisons between patients hospitalized many times during the study period and those who were hospitalized once. A patient who was hospitalized once in the analyzed period could even be hospitalized earlier or later many times. For this reason, the information on multiple hospitalizations in the analyzed period is not informative.

Due to the frequent occurrence of hypertension and hypothyroidism in the studied population of patients, we decided not to exclude patients diagnosed with them from the study. We included the potential impact of these diseases on the NLR values in the statistical analysis. On the other hand, we decided to exclude patients with cardiovascular disease and diabetes due to the fact that the number of patients with these diagnoses in the research sample was too small to be included in the statistical analysis.

For all hospitalizations included in the study, information from the physical documentation was coded into the electronic database with the participation of 6 independent persons, which included: the number of neutrophils and lymphocytes in the peripheral blood counts performed at the beginning and at the end of a given hospitalization (based on which the corresponding NLR values were calculated), gender, the status of antipsychotics medication within 1 month prior to hospitalization (A_{med}—antipsychotics medication status, antipsychotics-naïve—AN, non-antipsychotics-naïve—Non-AN), smoking status, diagnosis of hypertension, diagnosis of hypothyroidism, age, BMI, the time between the first and last complete peripheral blood count (the duration of therapy measured in days) and the time from admission to the first peripheral blood count (t_{lag}, measured in days). In addition, data on antipsychotics used during hospitalization were also collected for descriptive purposes. The change in NLR from the first to the last peripheral blood count (ΔNLR) was then calculated based on the NLR values of the first peripheral blood count (NLR_1) and the NLR of the last peripheral blood count (NLR_2).

The staff responsible for performing the laboratory tests was not aware of the study or the clinical status of the patients, and all the peripheral blood counts included in the study were ordered and performed as part of routine therapeutic activities. All laboratory analyzes were performed in one, the same commercial laboratory with a permanent contract with the Department of Psychiatry of the Pomeranian Medical University and using the same analyzer. Thus, the occurrence of a batch effect seems unlikely. Due to its retrospective nature, the study did not require the consent of the Bioethics Committee of the Pomeranian Medical University in Szczecin.

2.2. Statistical Analysis

The main objectives of the analysis were: (1) determining whether there was a statistically significant difference between NLR_1 and NLR_2 and whether the status of A_{med} moderated this difference; (2) determining the influence of other potential confounding factors on the occurrence of such a difference (3) determining whether the NLR_1 value allows ΔNLR prediction; (4) evaluation of the influence of potential confounding factors on ΔNLR.

Descriptive statistics included standard deviation (SD), median, and mean for continuous variables, as well as frequencies and percentage of all included hospitalizations for categorical variables. For gender, the frequency and percentage were also calculated for all patients included in the study. Due to the fact that not all observations were independent of each other (there were multiple hospitalizations for the same patient), we used a linear mixed model (LMM) for statistical analysis.

LMM is a family of linear models, one of the main applications of which is the analysis of data with repeatable and interdependent measurements (in our study, these are hospitalizations) within the same object (in our study, it is a patient), disregarding the assumption of the independence of observations that applies to classical linear regression models [31]. The use of LMM in the analysis of our data allows one to prevent the impact of multiple hospitalizations of the same patients on the quality of the results obtained. Moreover, LMMs can also be used to include corrections for the possible occurrence of a batch effect, although this was not the immediate goal of our analysis.

To determine the differences between NLR_1 and NLR_2, the data were transformed so that the NLR values, regardless of whether the measurement was performed at the beginning or at the end of hospitalization, were represented by the same dependent variable (NLR_x). On the other hand, the timing of blood count was represented by the categorical grouping variable (2 levels: NLR_1 and NLR_2) as a fixed effect that interacted with the Amed categorical variable to control for the effect of pre-hospitalization antipsychotic medication. In addition, the individual patient ID (ID_p) with the nested hospitalization ID (ID_h) in it was included in the model as a random effect, so that the dependence of data from different hospitalizations of the same patient did not affect the results, and at the same time to take into account the relationship between the values of NLR_1 and NLR_2 in the same hospitalization.

To determine the predictability of ΔNLR with the use of the NLR_1, a model in which the dependent variable was ΔNLR was fitted. ID_p were entered into the model as a random effect, to account for the relationship of data from different hospitalizations of the same patients. NLR_1 was introduced as the main fixed effect in the model.

In both models, categorical variables were introduced as additional fixed effects, i.e., gender, A_{med}, smoking status, diagnosis of arterial hypertension, diagnosis of hypothyroidism, and continuous variables such as age, BMI, duration of therapy, and t_{lag}.

In the case of both models, all of the above-mentioned predictors were initially taken into account, and then those that did not significantly improve the goodness of fit of the model were eliminated stepwise from the model. The goodness of fit of the model was assessed based on the Akaike Information Criterion (AIC), treating the predictor as irrelevant if its removal from the model did not increase AIC by >2. The predictors whose elimination from the model caused the smallest increase in AIC were eliminated in the first place. If the difference in AIC values between the models was less than 2, the model with a smaller number of predictors was selected. In the case of the NLR_x model, before the predictor elimination, its effect after adjusting for interaction with the grouping variable was also tested to determine its different potential effects on the values of NLR_1 or NLR_2 and AN or non-AN patients. Thus, the final models only included predictors that improved their goodness of fit. Such a model-fitting algorithm makes it possible to reduce the risk of overfitting the model, as well as to obtain results that do not reflect real dependencies.

During the stepwise elimination of predictors and the assessment of goodness of fit, restricted maximal likelihood (REML) was not used to obtain the correct AIC values. Instead, the maximum likelihood (ML) was used. In further stages of the analysis, REML was used to more accurately assess the values of the coefficients and confidence intervals (CIs).

Then, the possible interactions between the predictors that were included in the final model for ΔNLR were considered, using a similar methodology initially introducing all of them and interactions between them into the model and looking for the model best suited to the data based on AIC. When the difference in AIC values between the models was less than 2, the model with fewer predictors and interactions was selected.

The linearity of the predictors was checked by visual assessment of the plot of the predictions versus residual plots. The homogeneity of variance was checked by analysis of variance (ANOVA) of the linear model with the squared absolute residual values as the dependent variable and IDp (in the ΔNLR model) or ID_p with nested ID_h (in the NLR_x model) as predictors. The independence of the residuals was checked by visual assessment of the residuals versus predictors plots. In turn, the normality of the residual distribution was checked by visual assessment of the Quartile-Quartile plot (Q-Q plot).

In the case of the model for NLR_x, the distribution of residuals significantly differed from the normal distribution, therefore a logarithmic transformation of the dependent variable was performed, which further improved the goodness of fit of this model to the data.

Post-hoc tests were performed using the Kenward–Roger method to evaluate the differences between the groups in the model for $\log(NLR_x)$.

We used 95% confidence intervals (95% CI) to assess the statistical significance of the predictors. Additionally, although the methodological correctness of the *p*-value application for linear models with mixed effect is still not unequivocal, we calculated them using the Satterthwaite *t*-tests.

W used the conditional $_{pseudo}R^2$ ($_{pseudo}R^2{}_c$) calculated by the Nakagawa method, which determines the proportion of variance explained by the entire model taking into account the fixed and random effects, as well as the marginal $_{pseudo}R^2$ ($_{pseudo}R^2{}_m$), which determines the proportion of variance explained by the fixed effects of the model.

All *p* values used in the analysis were two-tailed. The significance level was $\alpha = 0.05$. All stages of the statistical analysis were performed in R studio version 4.0.3 using the lmer, lmerTest, car, and MuMln packages.

3. Results

3.1. Patients Characteristics

Inclusion criteria for the study were met by 578 patients with a total of 849 hospitalizations. From this group, 300 patients were randomly selected, with a total of 482 hospitalizations during the study period. After excluding hospitalizations in accordance with the established criteria, the analysis included data on 40 patients ($n_p = 40$) and 71 hospitalizations ($n_h = 71$). The study inclusion and exclusion processes are shown in Figure 1. Descriptive statistics of the research group are presented in Table 1 for continuous variables and categorical variables in Table 2. Among the hospitalizations that were ultimately included in the research sample, in $n_h = 12$ (16.9%), pharmacotherapy with only one antipsychotic was administered, and in n_h = 59 (83%), pharmacotherapy with more than one drug from this group was administered. During the time period included in the study, 16 patients (n_p = 16, 40%) were hospitalized more than once. The exact counts for each comorbidity can be found in Table S1.

Table 1. Descriptive statistics for continuous variables were included in the study.

Predictor	Median	Mean	SD
Age (years)	35.953	39.510	11.500
BMI	24.802	24.398	3.233
t_{lag} (days)	2.000	2.746	1.779
Duration of therapy (days)	33.000	40.694	20.767
NLR_1	1.369	1.614	0.974
NLR_2	1.274	1.421	0.666
ΔNLR	−0.090	−0.193	0.767

SD—standard deviation, BMI—Body-Mass Index, t_{lag}—time from admission to the first blood count, NLR_1—neutrophil to lymphocyte ratio value from the first peripheral blood count, NLR_2—neutrophil to lymphocyte ratio value from the last peripheral blood count, ΔNLR—change in the value of the neutrophil to lymphocyte from the first to the last peripheral blood count.

Table 2. The frequencies of the categorical variables included in the study and the number of hospitalizations during which the patient was taking the given antipsychotic drug.

Variable	All Hospitalizations (n_h = 71)	All Patients (n_p = 40)
Male	–	21 (52.5%)
Non-antipsychotics naïve	58 (81.7%)	34 (85.0%)
Smoking	39 (54.9%)	21 (52.5%)
Hypertension	12 (16.9%)	4 (10%)
Hypothyroidism	12 (14.1%)	6 (15%)
Amisulpiride	9 (12.7%)	8 (20%)
Aripiprazole	16 (22.5%)	14 (35%)
Chloroprotixen	3 (4.2%)	3 (7.5%)
Flupentixol	4 (5.6%)	3 (7.5%)
Haloperidol	2 (2.8%)	2 (5%)
Clozapine	30 (42.3%)	13 (32.5%)
Quetiapine	7 (9.9%)	6 (15%)
Levomepromazine	7 (9.9%)	6 (15%)
Olanzapine	28 (39.4%)	22 (55%)
Perazine	6 (8.5%)	4 (10%)
Promazine	27 (38%)	18 (45%)
Risperidone	12 (16.9%)	11 (27%)
Sulpiride	8 (11.3%)	6 (15%)
Zuclopentixol	13 (18.3%)	5 (12.5%)
Valproate	30 (42.3%)	18 (45%)
Lamotrigine	12 (17.0%)	9 (22.5%)
Lorazepam	22 (31.0%)	12 (30%)
Clonazepam	6 (8.5%)	4 (10%)
Diazepam	2 (2.8%)	1 (2.5%)
Estazolam	7 (9.9%)	4 (10%)
Lithium	2 (2.8%)	1 (2.5%)
Trazodone	1 (1.4%)	1 (2.5%)
Sertraline	2 (2.8%)	1 (2.5%)
Fluoxetine	2 (2.8%)	1 (2.5%)
Zolpidem	3 (4.2%)	1 (2.5%)
Escitalopram	1 (1.4%)	1 (2.5%)
Pregabalin	2 (2.8%)	1 (2.5%)

The percentage in the whole group is given in parentheses. n_p—number of patients, n_h—number of hospitalizations. The column for all patients includes the occurrence of a given factor if it appeared in any of the hospitalizations of a given patient.

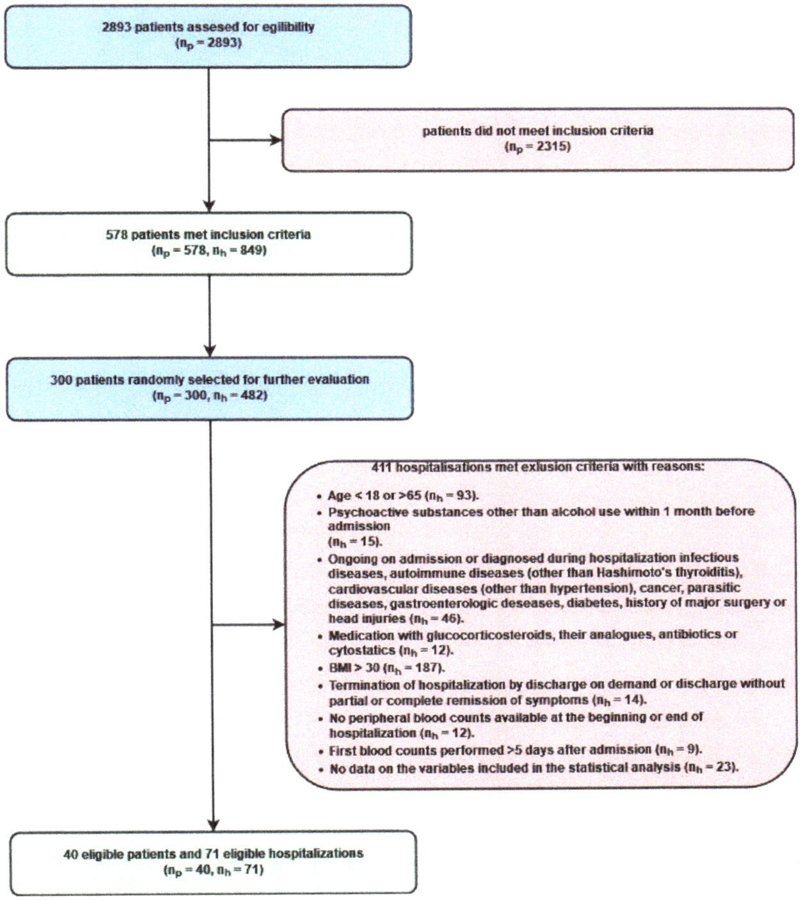

Figure 1. The process of inclusion and exclusion from the study. n_p = number of patients, n_h = number of hospitalizations.

3.2. The Difference between the Values of NLR_1 and NLR_2

In the final model, the only fixed effect which remained was the interaction between the grouping variable and A_{med}. Stepwise elimination of the remaining predictors and their interactions with the grouping variable showed that they did not improve the goodness of fit of the model. The results of this model are summarized in Table 3 and Figure 2 for fixed effects and Table 4 for random effects. The fixed effects of the model explained a small proportion of the variance ($_{pseudo}R^2{}_c$ = 0.020) as opposed to the random effects ($_{pseudo}R^2{}_m$ = 0.683). The low $_{pseudo}R^2{}_c$ value may be due to the fact that, despite the statistically significant difference between the mean values of NLR_1 and NLR_2 in the group of AN patients, only in 5 hospitalizations (n_h = 5) the value of the difference between NLR_1 and NLR_2 was higher than the differences between the means (Figure S3). The model had insignificantly better goodness of fit than the original model with AIC = 141.275. The model predictors were linear, variance was homogeneous (ID_p: $F(39, 86) = 0.433$, $p = 0.998$; ID_h: $F(16, 86) = 0.413$, $p = 0.976$), residuals were independent and normally distributed.

Table 3. Summary of the fixed effects of the final model for log(NLR_x). NLR_1—neutrophil to lymphocyte ratio value from the first peripheral blood count, non-AN—non-antipsychotics-naïve, AN—antipsychotics-naïve. 95% CI—95% confidence interval. Statistically significant *p*-values are **bolded**.

Fixed Effect	β	t	*p*	95% CI
Intercept	0.309	3.960	**<0.001**	0.156–0.462
NLR_1 i non-AN	0.040	0.764	0.447	−0.063–0.144
NLR_1 i AN	0.253	2.100	**0.039**	0.015–0.489
NLR_2 i AN	−0.019	−0.159	0.874	−0.258–0.216

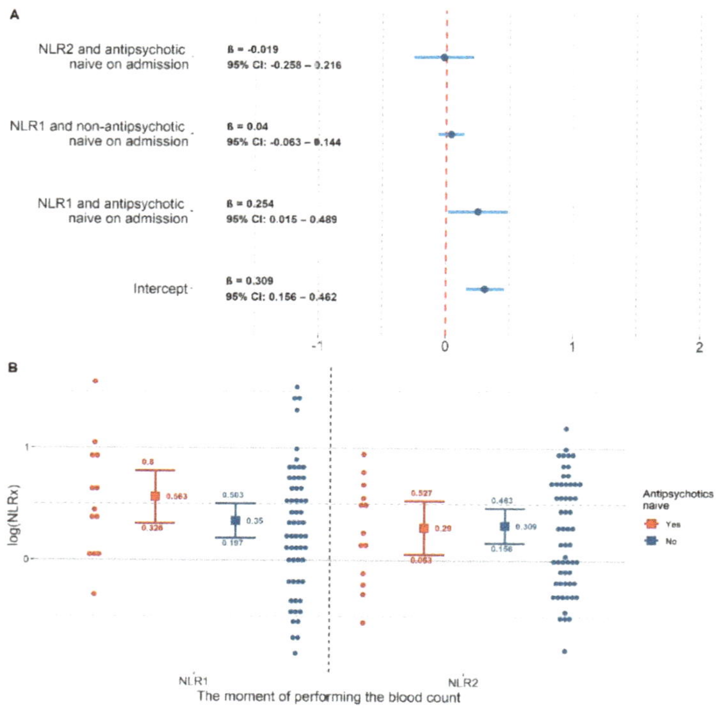

Figure 2. Final model for log(NLR_x) (**A**) Coefficients plot of the final model for log(NLR_x). NLR_1—neutrophil to lymphocyte ratio value from the first peripheral blood count. NLR_2—neutrophil to lymphocyte ratio value from the last peripheral blood count. (**B**) Visualization of the final model for log(NLR_x). The squares represent the predicted mean values for each group. 95% confidence intervals were also marked. The colors represent the status of taking antipsychotic drugs during the 1 month prior to admission. Points are individual cases where a shift has been applied for overlapping points.

Table 4. Summary of the random effects of the final model for log(NLR_x).

Random Effect	SD	σ^2	95% CI
ID_p:ID_h	0.100	0.010	0.000–0.216
ID_p	0.399	0.159	0.294–0.519
Residuals	0.284	0.081	0.240–0.332

ID_p—patient ID. ID_h—hospitalization ID. SD—standard deviation, σ^2—variance, 95% CI—95% confidence interval.

The results of the original model with all predictors are summarized in Table S2 and Figure S1 for fixed effects, and Table S3 for random effects. This model had insignificantly lesser goodness of fit to the data than the final model (AIC = 142.709, REML = 165.7). It also explained the greater proportion of NLR_x variance ($_{pseudo}R^2{}_c = 0.184$, $_{pseudo}R^2{}_m = 0.729$), which was probably due to overfitting the model.

Post-hoc tests showed that AN patients had a significantly higher $\log(NLR_1)$ than $\log(NLR_2)$ ($\beta = 0.273$, t = 2.447, $p = 0.017$, 95% CI: 0.050–0.496) and a significantly higher $\log(NLR_1)$ than $\log(NLR_2)$ of non-AN patients ($\beta = 0.254$, t = 2.065, $p = 0.042$, 95% CI: 0.010–0.498). The difference between the $\log(NLR_1)$ of non-AN patients and the $\log(NLR_1)$ of AN patients were non-significant, but statistical trend was shown to higher $\log(NLR_1)$ values in the latter group ($\beta = 0.213$, t = 1.736, $p = 0.086$, 95% CI: −0.031–0.458). There were no statistically significant differences between $\log(NLR_1)$ in non-AN patients and $\log(NLR_2)$ in AN patients ($\beta = 0.060$, t = 0.485, $p = 0.086$, 95% CI: −0.185–0.304), between $\log(NLR_1)$ and $\log(NLR_2)$ in AN patients ($\beta = 0.040$, t = 0.765, $p = 0.447$, 95% CI: −0.065–0.146), and also between $\log(NLR_2)$ of non-AN patients and $\log(NLR_2)$ of AN patients ($\beta = -0.019$, t = −0.157, $p = 0.876$, 95% CI: −0.263–0.225). A summary of the post-hoc test results is provided in Table 5 and Figure 3.

Table 5. Summary of post-hoc tests of differences between groups using the Kenward–Roger method in the model for $\log(NLR_x)$.

Comparison	β	df	t	*p*	95% CI
NLR_1 and AN vs. NLR_1 and non-AN	0.213	87.465	1.736	*0.086*	−0.031–0.458
NLR_1 and AN vs. NLR_2 and AN	0.273	69.000	2.447	**0.017**	0.050–0.496
NLR_1 and AN vs. NLR_2 and non-AN	0.254	87.465	2.065	**0.042**	0.010–0.498
NLR_1 and non-AN vs. NLR_2 and AN	0.060	87.465	0.485	0.629	−0.185–0.304
NLR_1 and non-AN vs. NLR_2 and non-AN	0.040	69.000	0.764	0.447	−0.065–0.146
NLR_2 and AN vs. NLR_2 and non-AN	−0.019	87.465	−0.157	0.876	−0.263–0.225

NLR_1—neutrophil to lymphocyte ratio value from the first peripheral blood count, NLR_2—neutrophil to lymphocyte ratio value from the last peripheral blood count, non-AN—non-antipsychotics-naïve, AN—antipsychotics-naïve, 95% CI—95% confidence interval. Statistically significant *p*-values are **bolded**. Statistical trends *p* values are shown in *italics*.

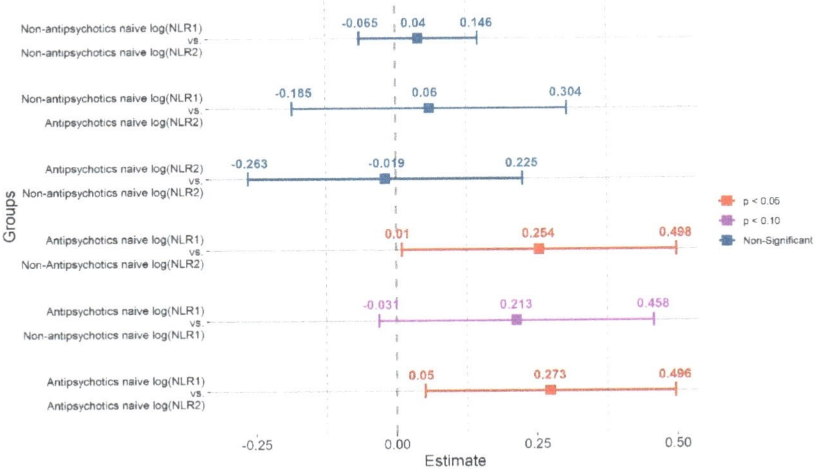

Figure 3. Summary of post-hoc test results for the final model for log (NLR_x). NLR_1—neutrophil to lymphocyte ratio value from the first peripheral blood count. NLR_2—neutrophil to lymphocyte ratio value from the last peripheral blood count. 95% confidence intervals and marginal means have been marked. Red indicates a statistically significant result, violet indicates a statistical trend, and blue indicates statistically insignificant *p* values.

3.3. The Difference between the Values of NLR_1 and NLR_2

The results of the primary model ($model_P$), including all predictors, are summarized in Table S4 and Figure S2. This model had significantly lesser goodness of fit for the data than the final model ($model_F$) (AIC = 109,979, REML = 131.3). It also explained the smaller proportion of the variance ΔNLR ($_{pseudo}R^2{}_c = 0.750$, $_{pseudo}R^2{}_m = 0.619$).

In the final model ($model_F$), there were only statistically significant fixed effects shown in Table 6, i.e., age (β = 0.013, t = 2.143, p = 0.042, 95% CI: 0.002–0.024), diagnosis of hypothyroidism (β = 0.523, t = 2.695, p = 0.012, 95% CI: 0.147–0.897) and NLR_1 (β = −0.643, t = −9.960, p <0.001, 95% CI: −0.768––0.499). ID_p was also taken into account as a random effect (SD_{ID} = 0.303, $SD_{residuals}$ = 0.388). The goodness of fit was not improved by the following predictors: gender, smoking status, hypertension diagnosis, duration of therapy, BMI, A_{med}, and t_{lag}. These predictors were not included in the $model_F$ and it can be assumed that ΔNLR was largely independent of them. The model predictors were linear, variance homogeneous (F(39, 31) = 0.242, p = 1.000), the residuals were independent and had a normal distribution. This model fit the data well and had AIC = 101.68 without the use of REML. Using REML (REML = 107), the model had the values of $_{pseudo}R^2{}_c = 0.772$ and $_{pseudo}R^2{}_m = 0.634$. The visualization of the model and the graph of its fixed effects coefficients are presented in Figure 4.

Table 6. Summary of the fixed effects of the final model for ΔNLR ($model_F$).

Fixed Effect	β	t	p	95% CI
Intercept	0.281	1.056	0.301	−0.229–0.790
Age	0.013	2.143	**0.042**	0.002–0.024
Hypothyroidism	0.523	2.695	**0.012**	0.147–0.897
NLR_1	−0.644	−9.960	**<0.001**	−0.768––0.768

NLR_1—neutrophil to lymphocyte ratio value from the first peripheral blood count. 95% CI—95% confidence interval. Statistically significant p-values are **bolded**.

We then repeated this procedure for a model including age, diagnosis of hypothyroidism, and NLR_1, and possible interactions between them. The model with interaction ($model_I$) obtained this way was slightly but significantly better fitted to the data (AIC = 98.629). The model calculated using REML (REML = 105.4), in addition to the random effect of the patient's ID (SD_{ID} = 0.298, $SD_{residuals}$ = 0.379), contained the following fixed effects shown in Table 7: age (β = 0.013, t = 2.230, p = 0.035, 95% CI: 0.002–0.024), NLR_1 in patients without a diagnosis of hypothyroidism (β = −0.656, t = −10.328, p <0.001, 95% CI: −0.780––0.515) and NLR_1 in patients diagnosed with hypothyroidism (β = −0.343, t = −3.136, p = 0.003, 95% CI: −0.551––0.134). With the introduction of the interaction between NLR_1 and the diagnosis of hypothyroidism, the variables of hypothyroidism and NLR_1 no longer improved the goodness of the fit of the model to the data. Interactions between age and NLR_1 as well as age and hypothyroidism diagnosis also did not improve the goodness of fit of the model. In the case of the interaction model, all LMM assumptions were still met. The model also explained a slightly higher proportion of the ΔNLR variance with the values of $_{pseudo}R^2{}_c = 0.783$ and $_{pseudo}R^2{}_m = 0.650$. The visualization of the model and the graph of its fixed effects coefficients are presented in Figure 5.

Table S5 presents a comparison of the goodness of fit statistics of the original, final, and interaction models.

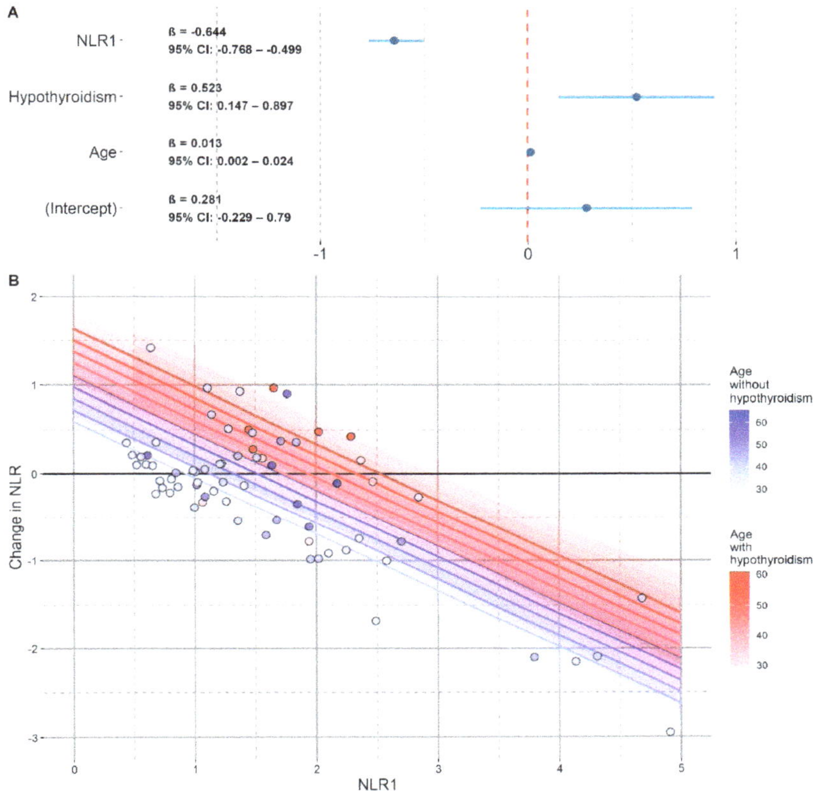

Figure 4. Final model for ΔNLR (model$_F$). (**A**) Coefficients plot of the final model for ΔNLR (model$_F$). NLR$_1$—neutrophil to lymphocyte ratio value from the first peripheral blood count. (**B**) Visualization of model$_F$. The horizontal axis represents the value of NLR$_1$. The vertical axis represents the change in NLR from peripheral blood counts performed at the beginning of hospitalization to the pre-discharge examination. Patients diagnosed with hypothyroidism were marked on the blue scale, and patients diagnosed with hypothyroidism on the red scale. The darker the shade, the higher the age of the patient. Similarly, different colors of the lines represent predictions for patients without a diagnosis of hypothyroidism (blue scale) and with a diagnosis of hypothyroidism (red scale) and at different ages (the darker the shade, the higher the age). The 95% confidence intervals were marked in a similar manner.

Table 7. Summary of the fixed effects of the model for ΔNLR with interaction (model$_I$).

Fixed Effect	β	t	*p*	95% CI
Intercept	0.284	1.090	0.285	−0.216–0.786
Age	0.013	2.230	**0.035**	0.002–0.024
NLR$_1$ with hypothyroidism	−0.343	−3.136	**0.003**	−0.551–−0.134
NLR$_1$ without hypothyroidism	−0.656	−10.328	**<0.001**	−0.780–−0.515

NLR$_1$—neutrophil to lymphocyte ratio value from the first peripheral blood count. 95% CI—95% confidence interval. Statistically significant *p*-values are **bolded**.

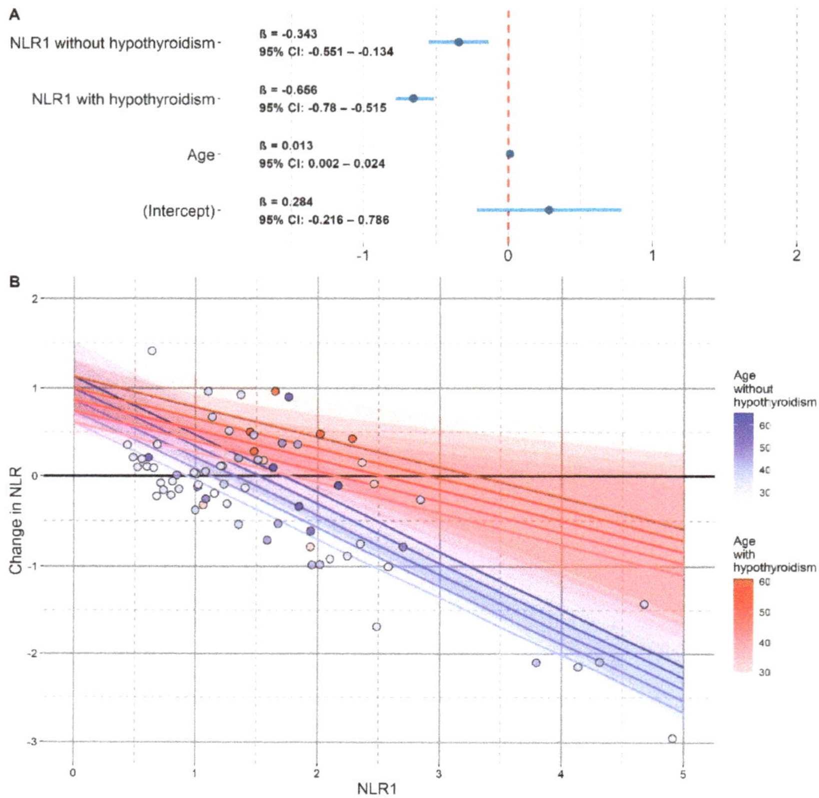

Figure 5. Model for ΔNLR with interaction ($model_I$). (**A**) Coefficients plot of model for ΔNLR with interaction ($model_I$). NLR_1—neutrophil to lymphocyte ratio value from the first peripheral blood count. (**B**) Visualization of $model_I$. The horizontal axis represents the value of NLR_1. The vertical axis represents the change in NLR from peripheral blood counts performed at the beginning of hospitalization to the pre-discharge examination. Patients diagnosed with hypothyroidism were marked on the blue scale, and patients diagnosed with hypothyroidism on the red scale. The darker the shade, the higher the age of the patient. Similarly, different colors of the lines represent predictions for patients without a diagnosis of hypothyroidism (blue scale) and with a diagnosis of hypothyroidism (red scale) and at different ages (the darker the shade, the higher the age). The 95% confidence intervals were marked in a similar manner.

4. Discussion

In this retrospective study, we analyzed the effect of antipsychotics on the NLR value in patients hospitalized due to exacerbation of schizophrenia. The NLR values from the first blood count after admission to the hospital (NLR_1) in patients who were antipsychotic-naïve before admission (AN) were statistically significantly higher than the NLR values from the last blood count (NLR_2) and the analogous values in patients who were non-antipsychotic-naïve (non-AN). Although the difference between NLR_1 values in non-AN and AN patients was not statistically significant, we showed a trend towards elevated NLR_1 values in AN patients versus non-AN patients. The difference between NLR_2 values in non-AN patients and AN patients was not statistically significant. The obtained results suggest that antipsychotics reduce the NLR values to a similar level both during and before hospitalization, even though both groups of patients were admitted due to an exacerbation. The reported differences were also independent of BMI, duration of therapy, hypertension, hypothyroidism, smoking, gender, time from admission to the first blood count (t_{lag}), and age, although the small sizes of the groups made it impossible to take into account the influence of the interaction of the third or a greater degree.

We have also shown that knowing the NLR_1 value we can predict with high probability the change in the NLR value until the measurement of NLR_2 when the patient achieves partial or complete remission (ΔNLR). Moreover, we have shown that ΔNLR is independent of BMI, duration of therapy, hypertension diagnosis, smoking status, gender, antipsychotics naivety status on admission (A_{med}), and t_{lag}. Our study suggests that ΔNLR during hospitalization increases with age, i.e., the possible decrease in NLR value is smaller, and the possible increase is greater in older patients. Additionally, to our knowledge, we were the first to consider the possible influence of hypothyroidism on ΔNLR during hospitalization due to an episode of psychosis in patients diagnosed with schizophrenia. In schizophrenic patients with coexisting hypothyroidism, ΔNLR values were higher than in patients without diagnosed hypothyroidism, thus in such patients, the NLR decreased to a lesser degree or increased more during hospitalization. To put it another way, hypothyroidism interacted with NLR_1 to reduce the effect of high NLR_1 values on ΔNLR.

We replicated the results of the meta-analysis by Mazza et al. on the statistical trend to higher values of NLR_1 in AN patients compared to non-AN patients [25]. Zhou et al. showed significant differences in NLR_1 values between these groups of patients, taking into account the larger AN sample (however, smaller than in the meta-analysis by Mazza et al.) and the larger non-AN sample [25,26]. Likewise, the meta-analysis by Karageorgiou et al., including the largest sample of AN patients, showed significantly higherNLR_1 values in AN patients compared to non-AN patients [13]. Similarly, based on a much smaller research sample than ours, the study by Kovacs et al. demonstrated statistically significant differences [27]. Therefore, it is possible that the lack of a significant statistical difference in NLR_1 values between AN and non-AN patients in our study may result from the smaller size of the research sample, inclusion and exclusion criteria used, or logarithmic transformation of the dependent variable. The significant difference shown in our study between the values of NLR_1 and NLR_2 in AN patients with the simultaneous lack of significant differences between these values in non-AN patients further supports this interpretation and is consistent with the results obtained by Bustan et al. on a smaller sample [32].

The independence of the differences between NLR_1 and NLR_2 in both AN and non-AN patients on the BMI value seems to be consistent with the results of the studies by Kovacs et al., Semiz et al., and Bustan et al., which showed no influence of this factor on the differences in NLR_1 values between patients and the healthy control group [27,32,33]. Similarly, in line with our results, the meta-analysis by Karageorgiou et al. and the study by Kovacs et al. showed that smoking had no significant effect on the NLR_1 values. [13,27]. Our suggested lack of gender influence is also consistent with the results of meta-analyses and individual studies [13,25,27,28]. Although it has been reported that elevated NLR values may be associated with an increased risk of developing arterial hypertension, in our study, in both the ΔNLR and the differences between NLR_1 and NLR_2, we did not find any effect of hypertension on these values in the population of patients diagnosed with schizophrenia [20]. In our study, these confounding factors did not have a significant impact on the ΔNLR values, which further supports the observation that the NLR values are largely independent of them, regardless of antipsychotic medication and clinical condition.

The independence of ΔNLR and the values of NLR_1 and NLR_2 both in the AN and non-AN groups from the duration of the therapy may indirectly indicate that the NLR values correlate with the clinical state because the patients included in the study were in partial or complete remission at the time of the NLR_2 measurement. Although the meta-analysis of Karageorgiou et al. did not show a correlation of NLR values with the intensity of symptoms in schizophrenia, later studies that used other methods of assessing the clinical condition of patients, such as those of Zhou et al. and Kovacs et al. seem to strongly indicate this kind of dependency [13,26,27].

The lack of influence of t_{lag} on ΔNLR values and the differences between NLR_1 and NLR_2 may indirectly indicate that the effect of antipsychotic treatment on NLR values becomes significantly evident after more than 5 days, which was the upper limit of t_{lag} necessary to account for hospitalization in the study. However, it should be noted that we have not analyzed the results in terms of the exact moment of starting antipsychotic treatment.

Age turned out not to significantly affect the differences between NLR_1 and NLR_2 in both AN and non-AN patients, which is consistent with the results of meta-analyses by Mazza et al. and Karageorgiou et al. [13,25], however, it significantly affected ΔNLR. Zhou et al. demonstrated significant collinearity between age and NLR_1, and although in our study we did not detect significant interactions between NLR_1 and age, this could be due to a smaller research sample and the inability to account for third-degree interactions [26]. The discrepancy between the impact of age on the difference between NLR_1 and NLR_2, and the effect of age on ΔNLR may result from a different statistical methodology of fitting the models for both variables. It is also worth noting that we did not take into account the influence of time from the onset of the disease, which, although, as indicated by Zhou et al. does not seem to have a significant effect on the NLR_1 values, it could interact with the patient's age at the time of hospitalization [26]. It is also possible that, while age does not contribute to the difference in mean NLR values between groups, it does contribute to a specific ΔNLR value in individual patients.

Hypothyroidism is a common condition associated with a deficiency of thyroid hormones [34]. It is assumed that in European countries hypothyroidism has autoimmunological underpinnings in the vast majority of cases [35]. This disease is more common in patients with schizophrenia than in the general population [22]. In addition, antipsychotics may contribute to the occurrence of hypothyroidism, possibly both by negatively affecting the activity of the hypothalamic-pituitary-thyroid axis, disturbing iodine metabolism, and inducing the formation of autoantibodies [36]. For these reasons, the influence of hypothyroidism on NLR values, as demonstrated by the Önalan and Dönder study, may be particularly important for its use in clinical practice [21]. In our study, the diagnosis of hypothyroidism did not significantly alter the differences in NLR_1 and NLR_2 values in the AN and non-AN groups, but it had a significant impact on ΔNLR. As in the case of age, it may be related to a different methodology for fitting both models to the data or a relatively small proportion of patients diagnosed with hypothyroidism in our research sample. However, the ΔNLR results seem to indicate that although hypothyroidism may not be substantial to the differences between NLR_1 and NLR_2 in the general population of patients, it may heavily affect the outcome of antipsychotics in the subpopulation of patients with this comorbidity. Future studies should take into account the fact that in patients with hypothyroidism, the NLR values may not only not decrease, but also, as in the case of most of our patients, increase during hospitalization. Such studies should also control their results in terms of the levels of thyrotropin, thyroid hormones, and anti-thyroid antibodies in the blood due to possible interference of subclinical forms of hypothyroidism.

Medicating with antipsychotics within 1 month prior to admission (A_{med}), despite statistically significant influence on differences between NLR_1 and NLR_2 values, was non-significant in the case of ΔNLR. It may be related to the use of NLR_1 values as a predictor in the model for ΔNLR. The statistical trend shown by us in the differences between the NLR_1 values between AN and non-AN patients indicates that these values are likely to be dependent on A_{med}. The lower ${}_{pseudo}R^2{}_c$ value for the $\log(NLR_x)$ model compared to the ΔNLR model may also be related to the fact that despite the statistically significant difference between the mean values of NLR_1 and NLR_2 in the AN group, only in a small part of hospitalizations ($n_h = 5$) the difference between NLR_1 and NLR_2 was higher than the difference between the averages (Figure S3). As shown by the model for ΔNLR, the NLR value decreased during hospitalization more significantly in patients with a higher baseline NLR value (NLR_1), which, however, does not exclude the influence of pharmacotherapy with antipsychotics on the NLR value, among other things, because these drugs can only lower the NLR value to a certain baseline level. For this reason, NLR_1 values alone would be a much better predictor of NLR_2 values, which is further supported by a much higher proportion of explained ΔNLR variance in models incorporating NLR_1 as a predictor compared to the model for NLR_x. This could explain both the lack of significance of A_{med} in the case of the model for ΔNLR and indicate the greater potential usefulness of using ΔNLR as a marker of response to pharmacotherapy with antipsychotics than the usefulness of NLR values alone.

There is ample evidence from meta-analyses of alterations in the cytokine system in patients with schizophrenia [9–11] and the effect of antipsychotic drugs on their levels peripherally [14]. The levels of some cytokines peripherally also correlate with the intensity of schizophrenia symptoms [37,38]. One of the key pro-inflammatory cytokines whose blood levels are elevated in both psychotic and remitted patients, compared to the healthy controls as well as lowered by antipsychotic drugs, is interleukin-6 (IL-6) [9]. Likewise, the levels of interferon-γ (IFN-γ) in the peripheral blood are elevated both in the first and subsequent episodes of psychosis, but unchanged or even lower compared to the healthy controls during remission [9,37]. Similarly, IFN-γ levels are lowered by antipsychotic drugs [14,39]. Not as apparent but similar effects of antipsychotic drugs may also apply to other cytokines such as interleukin-1β (IL-1β), interleukin-4 (IL-4), or tumor necrosis factor α (TNF-α) [9,11]. One of the important common features of IL-1β, IL-6, IFN-γ and TNF-α is their effect on hematopoiesis, in particular stimulation of the differentiation, maturation, and proliferation of cells of the myeloid lineage, which includes neutrophils, and not lymphoid lineage [40]. It is, therefore, possible that elevated levels of these cytokines in schizophrenic patients may increase the number of neutrophils in the blood, but do not significantly affect the number of lymphocytes. Such activity could be associated with increased NLR values in the period of and would be consistent with the reports on the increased number of neutrophils in the blood in patients diagnosed with schizophrenia, while the number of lymphocytes in the blood of this group of patients was within the normal range [41]. At the same time, the decreasing levels of these cytokines, especially IFN-γ, due to the action of antipsychotic drugs, could reduce the NLR presented by the results of our study. However, the confirmation of such a cause-and-effect sequence requires further future research.

Our study has certain limitations. First of all, it was a retrospective study, which made it impossible to fully control the results obtained by us in terms of the patients' clinical condition. We did not use data obtained through more quantifiable methods of its assessment, such as scales, inventories, or structured interviews. All the premises relating to this were indirect. Moreover, we did not have data on the age of onset of the disease and its course before hospitalizations included in the study. We also did not control the results obtained by us in terms of the use of specific forms of pharmacotherapy or other methods of treatment. We also did not take into account the levels of thyroid hormones, thyrotropin, and anti-thyroid antibodies, which would allow us to capture the impact of subclinical hypothyroidism. Likewise, we did not collect data on other markers of inflammation, such as blood C-reactive protein or cytokine levels, which made it impossible to assess the independence of NLR as a marker of treatment response. The same problem applies to the lack of complete diagnosis of metabolic syndrome in patients included in the research sample. The meta-analysis by Mazza et al. suggested that NLR may be a better marker for FEP patients [25]. Unfortunately, because we did not perform the stratification of chronic and FEP patients, we were unable to address this thesis. Finally, we based our study on a relatively small research sample, which limits the possibility of making more certain conclusions about the variability of NLR values during hospitalization due to exacerbation of schizophrenia. A small research sample also made it impossible to thoroughly investigate possible interactions between cofounders during statistical analysis, which could potentially prevent the capture of the influence of individual cofounders on NLR values. Although the mean values of NLR_1 and NLR_2 in the group of AN patients were statistically significantly different, in the case of the majority of specific hospitalizations, the differences between the values of NLR_1 and NLR_2 were not greater than the difference between the mean values of

NLR_1 and NLR_2 in this group. However, the statistical significance of the results obtained by us, combined with the lower risk of selection bias due to randomization, does not seem to indicate that the statistical power was too low to perform the analyzes.

5. Conclusions

In conclusion, in our retrospective study, we showed that NLR values have been significantly different at the beginning and the end of hospitalization in patients who had not taken antipsychotic drugs within one month before admission to the hospital due to exacerbation of schizophrenia. We also showed no significant differences between such NLR values in patients who had been treated with antipsychotics before admission and a statistical trend for differences between the NLR values on admission between patients treated with antipsychotics on admission and antipsychotics-naïve patients. Eventually, we also indicated the predictive potential of NLR at admission versus discharge NLR after partial or complete remission. Such an approach could discount the effects of previous antipsychotic medication but would require consideration of age and the diagnosis of hypothyroidism. The assessment of the change in NLR with the use of antipsychotics could potentially be used to assess the response to pharmacotherapy in patients with schizophrenia.

Supplementary Materials: The following supporting information can be downloaded at: https://www.mdpi.com/article/10.3390/jcm11010232/s1, Figure S1: Coefficients plot of primary model for log(NLR_x); Figure S2: Coefficients plot of primary model for ΔNLR ($model_P$); Figure S3: Changes in NLR values during hospitalization in the group of antipsychotic-naive patients; Table S1: Incidence of comorbidities among hospitalizations before excluding patients from the research sample and after randomly selecting 300 patient files; Table S2: Summary of the fixed effects of the primary model for NLR_x; Table S3: Summary of primary model random effects for log(NLR_x); Table S4: Summary of the fixed effects of the primary model for ΔNLR ($model_P$); Table S5: Comparison of the goodness of fit statistics of the primary ($model_P$), final ($model_F$) and with interaction ($model_I$) models for ΔNLR.

Author Contributions: Conceptualization, B.D.; methodology, B.D.; software, B.D.; validation, B.D.; formal analysis, B.D.; investigation, B.D., G.G. and A.B.; resources, P.P. and J.S.; data curation, P.P. and J.S.; writing—original draft preparation, B.D., G.G. and A.B.; writing—review and editing, B.D., P.P., J.S. and B.M.; visualization, B.D.; supervision, P.P. and J.S.; project administration, B.D.; funding acquisition, J.S. All authors have read and agreed to the published version of the manuscript.

Funding: The project is financed from the program of the Minister of Science and Higher Education under the name "Regional Initiative of Excellence" in 2019–2022 project number 002/RID/2018/2019 amount of financing 12,000,000.

Institutional Review Board Statement: Not applicable.

Informed Consent Statement: Not applicable.

Data Availability Statement: All data included in the statistical analysis are available on request via the corresponding author.

Conflicts of Interest: The authors declare no conflict of interest.

References

1. Heilbronner, U.; Samara, M.; Leucht, S.; Falkai, P.; Schulze, T.G. The Longitudinal Course of Schizophrenia Across the Lifespan: Clinical, Cognitive, and Neurobiological Aspects. *Harv. Rev. Psychiatry* **2016**, *24*, 118–128. [CrossRef]
2. Weinstein, J.J.; Chohan, M.O.; Slifstein, M.; Kegeles, L.S.; Moore, H.; Abi-Dargham, A. Pathway-Specific Dopamine Abnormalities in Schizophrenia. *Biol. Psychiatry* **2017**, *81*, 31–42. [CrossRef]
3. Schwartz, T.L.; Sachdeva, S.; Stahl, S.M. Glutamate Neurocircuitry: Theoretical Underpinnings in: Schizophrenia. *Front. Pharmacol.* **2012**, *3*, 1–11. [CrossRef] [PubMed]
4. Plitman, E.; Iwata, Y.; Caravaggio, F.; Nakajima, S.; Chung, J.K.; Gerretsen, P.; Kim, J.; Takeuchi, H.; Chakravarty, M.M.; Remington, G.; et al. Kynurenic Acid in Schizophrenia: A Systematic Review and Meta-Analysis. *Schizophr. Bull.* **2017**, *43*, 764–777. [CrossRef]
5. Bryll, A.; Skrzypek, J.; Krzyściak, W.; Szelagowska, M.; Śmierciak, N.; Kozicz, T.; Popiela, T. Oxidative-Antioxidant Imbalance and Impaired Glucose Metabolism in Schizophrenia. *Biomolecules* **2020**, *10*, 384. [CrossRef]

6. Pillinger, T.; D'Ambrosio, E.; McCutcheon, R.; Howes, O.D. Is Psychosis a Multisystem Disorder? A Meta-Review of Central Nervous System, Immune, Cardiometabolic, and Endocrine Alterations in First-Episode Psychosis and Perspective on Potential Models. *Mol. Psychiatry* **2019**, *24*, 776–794. [CrossRef] [PubMed]
7. Najjar, S.; Pearlman, D.M.; Alper, K.; Najjar, A.; Devinsky, O. Neuroinflammation and Psychiatric Illness. *J. Neuroinflamm.* **2013**, *10*, 816. [CrossRef] [PubMed]
8. Akdis, M.; Aab, A.; Altunbulakli, C.; Azkur, K.; Costa, R.A.; Crameri, R.; Duan, S.; Eiwegger, T.; Eljaszewicz, A.; Ferstl, R.; et al. Interleukins (from IL-1 to IL-38), Interferons, Transforming Growth Factor β, and TNF-α: Receptors, Functions, and Roles in Diseases. *J. Allergy Clin. Immunol.* **2016**, *138*, 984–1010. [CrossRef]
9. Goldsmith, D.R.; Rapaport, M.H.; Miller, B.J. A Meta-Analysis of Blood Cytokine Network Alterations in Psychiatric Patients: Comparisons between Schizophrenia, Bipolar Disorder and Depression. *Mol. Psychiatry* **2016**, *21*, 1696–1709. [CrossRef]
10. Orlovska-waast, S.; Köhler-forsberg, O.; Wiben, S.; Merete, B.; Kondziella, D.; Krogh, J.; Eriksen, M. Cerebrospinal Fl Uid Markers of in Fl Ammation and Infections in Schizophrenia and Affective Disorders: A Systematic Review and Meta-Analysis. *Mol. Psychiatry* **2019**, 869–887. [CrossRef]
11. Çakici, N.; Sutterland, A.L.; Penninx, B.W.; Dalm, V.A.; de Haan, L.; van Beveren, N.J. Altered Peripheral Blood Compounds in Drug-Naïve First-Episode Patients with Either Schizophrenia or Major Depressive Disorder: A Meta-Analysis. *Brain Behav. Immun.* **2020**, *88*, 547–558. [CrossRef]
12. Marques, T.R.; Ashok, A.H.; Pillinger, T.; Veronese, M.; Turkheimer, F.E.; Dazzan, P.; Sommer, I.E.C.; Howes, O.D. Neuroinflammation in Schizophrenia: Meta-Analysis of in Vivo Microglial Imaging Studies. *Psychol. Med.* **2019**, *49*, 2186–2196. [CrossRef] [PubMed]
13. Karageorgiou, V.; Milas, G.P.; Michopoulos, I. Neutrophil-to-Lymphocyte Ratio in Schizophrenia: A Systematic Review and Meta-Analysis. *Schizophr. Res.* **2019**, *206*, 4–12. [CrossRef]
14. Marcinowicz, P.; Więdłocha, M.; Zborowska, N.; Dębowska, W.; Podwalski, P.; Misiak, B.; Tyburski, E.; Szulc, A. A Meta-Analysis of the Influence of Antipsychotics on Cytokines Levels in First Episode Psychosis. *J. Clin. Med.* **2021**, *10*, 2488. [CrossRef]
15. Forget, P.; Khalifa, C.; Defour, J.P.; Latinne, D.; van Pel, M.C. What Is the Normal Value of the Neutrophil-to-Lymphocyte Ratio? *BMC Res. Notes* **2017**, *10*, 12. [CrossRef]
16. Luo, H.; He, L.; Zhang, G.; Yu, J.; Chen, Y.; Yin, H.; Goyal, H.; Zhang, G.-M.; Xiao, Y.; Gu, C.; et al. Normal Reference Intervals of Neutrophil-To-Lymphocyte Ratio, Platelet-To-Lymphocyte Ratio, Lymphocyte-To-Monocyte Ratio, and Systemic Immune Inflammation Index in Healthy Adults: A Large Multi-Center Study from Western China. *Clin. Lab.* **2019**, *65*, 255–265. [CrossRef] [PubMed]
17. Yüksel, R.N.; Ertek, I.E.; Dikmen, A.U.; Göka, E. High Neutrophil-Lymphocyte Ratio in Schizophrenia Independent of Infectious and Metabolic Parameters. *Nord. J. Psychiatry* **2018**, *72*, 336–340. [CrossRef] [PubMed]
18. Mirhafez, S.R.; Pasdar, A.; Avan, A.; Esmaily, H.; Moezzi, A.; Mohebati, M.; Meshkat, Z.; Mehrad-Majd, H.; Eslami, S.; Rahimi, H.R.; et al. Cytokine and Growth Factor Profiling in Patients with the Metabolic Syndrome. *Br. J. Nutr.* **2015**, *113*, 1911–1919. [CrossRef]
19. Grieshober, L.; Graw, S.; Barnett, M.J.; Thornquist, M.D.; Goodman, G.E.; Chen, C.; Koestler, D.C.; Marsit, C.J.; Doherty, J.A. Methylation-Derived Neutrophil-to-Lymphocyte Ratio and Lung Cancer Risk in Heavy Smokers. *Cancer Prev. Res.* **2018**, *11*, 727–734. [CrossRef]
20. Liu, X.; Zhang, Q.; Wu, H.; Du, H.; Liu, L.; Shi, H.; Wang, C.; Xia, Y.; Guo, X.; Li, C.; et al. Blood Neutrophil to Lymphocyte Ratio as a Predictor of Hypertension. *Am. J. Hypertens.* **2015**, *28*, 1339–1346. [CrossRef]
21. Önalan, E.; Dönder, E. Neutrophil and Platelet to Lymphocyte Ratio in Patients with Hypothyroid Hashimoto's Thyroiditis. *Acta Biomed.* **2020**, *91*, 310–314. [CrossRef] [PubMed]
22. Sharif, K.; Tiosano, S.; Watad, A.; Comaneshter, D.; Cohen, A.D.; Shoenfeld, Y.; Amital, H. The Link between Schizophrenia and Hypothyroidism: A Population-Based Study. *Immunol. Res.* **2018**, *66*, 663–667. [CrossRef]
23. Dieset, I.; Andreassen, O.A.; Haukvik, U.K. Somatic Comorbidity in Schizophrenia: Some Possible Biological Mechanisms Across the Life Span. *Schizophr. Bull.* **2016**, *42*, 1316–1319. [CrossRef]
24. Robabeh, S.; Somayeh, S.; Masoomeh, S.F.; Melikad, J.S. Comparison of the Metabolic Syndrome Risk Factors in Antipsychotic Naïve and Chronic Schizophrenia Patients. *Arch. Psychiatry Psychother.* **2021**, *23*, 44–54. [CrossRef]
25. Mazza, M.G.; Lucchi, S.; Rossetti, A.; Clerici, M. Neutrophil-Lymphocyte Ratio, Monocyte-Lymphocyte Ratio and Platelet-Lymphocyte Ratio in Non-Affective Psychosis: A Meta-Analysis and Systematic Review. *World J. Biol. Psychiatry* **2020**, *21*, 326–338. [CrossRef]
26. Zhou, X.; Wang, X.; Li, R.; Yan, J.; Xiao, Y.; Li, W.; Shen, H. Neutrophil-to-Lymphocyte Ratio Is Independently Associated With Severe Psychopathology in Schizophrenia and Is Changed by Antipsychotic Administration: A Large-Scale Cross-Sectional Retrospective Study. *Front. Psychiatry* **2020**, *11*, 581061. [CrossRef] [PubMed]
27. Kovács, M.Á.; Tényi, T.; Kugyelka, R.; Prenek, L.; Hau, L.; Magyar, É.E.; Herold, R.; Balogh, P.; Simon, D. Elevated Osteopontin and Interferon Gamma Serum Levels and Increased Neutrophil-to-Lymphocyte Ratio Are Associated With the Severity of Symptoms in Schizophrenia. *Front. Psychiatry* **2020**, *10*, 996. [CrossRef]
28. Özdin, S.; Böke, Ö. Neutrophil/Lymphocyte, Platelet/Lymphocyte and Monocyte/Lymphocyte Ratios in Different Stages of Schizophrenia. *Psychiatry Res.* **2019**, *271*, 131–135. [CrossRef]

29. Mansournia, M.A.; Higgins, J.P.T.; Sterne, J.A.C.; Hernán, M.A. Biases in Randomized Trials. *Epidemiology* **2017**, *28*, 54–59. [CrossRef] [PubMed]
30. Odgaard-Jensen, J.; Vist, G.E.; Timmer, A.; Kunz, R.; Akl, E.A.; Schünemann, H.; Briel, M.; Nordmann, A.J.; Pregno, S.; Oxman, A.D. Randomisation to Protect against Selection Bias in Healthcare Trials. *Cochrane Database Syst. Rev.* **2011**, *2011*, 1–31. [CrossRef]
31. Paterson, S.; Lello, J. Mixed Models: Getting the Best Use of Parasitological Data. *Trends Parasitol.* **2003**, *19*, 370–375. [CrossRef]
32. Bustan, Y.; Drapisz, A.; ben Dor, D.H.; Avrahami, M.; Schwartz-Lifshitz, M.; Weizman, A.; Barzilay, R. Elevated Neutrophil to Lymphocyte Ratio in Non-Affective Psychotic Adolescent Inpatients: Evidence for Early Association between Inflammation and Psychosis. *Psychiatry Res.* **2018**, *262*, 149–153. [CrossRef]
33. Semiz, M.; Yildirim, O.; Canan, F.; Demir, S.; Hasbek, E.; Tuman, T.C.; Kayka, N.; Tosun, M. Elevated Neutrophil/Lymphocyte Ratio in Patients with Schizophrenia. *Psychiatr. Danub.* **2014**, *26*, 220–225.
34. Chaker, L.; Bianco, A.C.; Jonklaas, J.; Peeters, R.P. Hypothyroidism. *Lancet* **2017**, *390*, 1550–1562. [CrossRef]
35. McLeod, D.S.A.; Cooper, D.S. The Incidence and Prevalence of Thyroid Autoimmunity. *Endocrine* **2012**, *42*, 252–265. [CrossRef]
36. Bou Khalil, R.; Richa, S. Thyroid Adverse Effects of Psychotropic Drugs. *Clin. Neuropharmacol.* **2011**, *34*, 248–255. [CrossRef]
37. Miller, B.; Peter, B.; Seabolt, W.; Mellor, A.; Kirkpatrick, B. Meta-Analysis of Cytokine Alterations in Schizophrenia: Clinical Status and Antipsychotic Effects. *Biol. Psychiatry* **2011**, *70*, 663–671. [CrossRef]
38. Momtazmanesh, S.; Zare-Shahabadi, A.; Rezaei, N. Cytokine Alterations in Schizophrenia: An Updated Review. *Front. Psychiatry* **2019**, *10*, 892. [CrossRef] [PubMed]
39. Romeo, B.; Brunet-Lecomte, M.; Martelli, C.; Benyamina, A. Kinetics of Cytokine Levels during Antipsychotic Treatment in Schizophrenia: A Meta-Analysis. *Int. J. Neuropsychopharmacol.* **2018**, *21*, 828–836. [CrossRef]
40. Jahandideh, B.; Derakhshani, M.; Abbaszadeh, H.; Akbar Movassaghpour, A.; Mehdizadeh, A.; Talebi, M.; Yousefi, M. The Pro-Inflammatory Cytokines Effects on Mobilization, Self-Renewal and Differentiation of Hematopoietic Stem Cells. *Hum. Immunol.* **2020**, *81*, 206–217. [CrossRef] [PubMed]
41. Wysokiński, A.; Margulska, A. Comparison of White Blood Cells Parameters in Patients with Acute Schizophrenia, Unipolar Depression and Bipolar Disorder. *Arch. Psychiatry Psychother.* **2017**, *19*, 16–26. [CrossRef]

MDPI
St. Alban-Anlage 66
4052 Basel
Switzerland
www.mdpi.com

Journal of Clinical Medicine Editorial Office
E-mail: jcm@mdpi.com
www.mdpi.com/journal/jcm

www.ingramcontent.com/pod-product-compliance
Lightning Source LLC
Chambersburg PA
CBHW061501210926
51850CB00008B/1788
9783036598161